Rationality and the Environment

Rationality and the Environment

Decision-making in Environmental Politics and Assessment

Bo Elling

publishing for a sustainable future

London • Sterling, VA

First published by Earthscan in the UK and USA in 2008

ISBN-13: 978-1-84407-524-9

Typeset by MapSet Ltd, Gateshead, UK
Printed and bound in the UK by Cromwell Press, Trowbridge
Cover design by Yvonne Booth

For a full list of publications please contact:
Earthscan
8–12 Camden High Street
London, NW1 0JH, UK
Tel: +44 (0)20 7387 8558
Fax: +44 (0)20 7387 8998
Email: earthinfo@earthscan.co.uk
Web: www.earthscan.co.uk

22883 Quicksilver Drive, Sterling, VA 20166-2012, USA

Earthscan publishes in association with the International Institute for Environment and
Development

A catalogue record for this book is available from the British Library

Library of Congress Cataloging-in-Publication Data

Elling, Bo.
  Rationality and the environment : decision-making in environmental politics and
assessment / Bo Elling.
     p. cm.
  Includes bibliographical references.
  ISBN 978-1-84407-524-9 (hardback)
 1. Environmental policy. 2. Environmental policy–Citizen participation. 3. Political
science–Decision making. 4. Decision making–Moral and ethical aspects. I. Title.
  GE170.E46 2008
  363.7'0561–dc22

                                                                      2007041582

The paper used for this book is FSC-certified and
totally chlorine-free. FSC (the Forest Stewardship
Council) is an international network to promote
responsible management of the world's forests.

Mixed Sources
Product group from well-managed
forests and other controlled sources
www.fsc.org Cert no. TT-COC-2082
© 1996 Forest Stewardship Council
FSC

Prologue

Feeling and knowledge can be opposed.

But feeling at the price of knowledge is powerlessness.

Knowledge without feeling is sterile.

Power used to enforce is destructive. Power as a result of agreement is constructive.

He who has confidence has power. He who trusts others does not need it.

Without confidence and trust science becomes power.

This book deals with planning that shows people confidence and gives them power.

Contents

Preface

This book aims to contribute to the development of a theoretical basis for the specific formation of environmental policy, for environmental decision-making and in particular for environmental assessment. The view in the book is that without a theory enabling a critical analysis of society as a whole, we will not be able to give solid and coherent answers to core issues in environmental regulation and management.

The book links critical social theory with the issue of the environment on three main themes. The first is modernization. How can we understand the process of modernization and why do modern societies continue to reproduce their failures and mistakes, leading to environmental problems and disasters? The second theme is rationality. What is a modern rationality and why has modern rationality become instrumental in environmental matters? The third theme is public involvement and participation. I make the case in this book that only by involving the public can we bring the ethical and aesthetic aspects of rationality into the process of modernization. What does that mean and why is this called for, in particular, in environmental matters?

In my view, since the work of Max Weber, it is the German philosopher and sociologist Jürgen Habermas who has dealt most seriously with the concept of modernization and the theoretical identification of modern society. That is why he plays a major role in the book. His concepts of modernity have been inspiring, applicable and fruitful for the analysis in this book. Their presentation here is highly comprehensive but I hope that I have limited myself to what is relevant. However, I would like to add one thing: in my view, we are at the tentative beginning of a modern society and not at its end. This is in contrast to most modern and, of course, postmodern social theory, but, with this point of view as my starting point, it will become clear why I tie a political form of regulation so closely to the structure of society itself.

As a specific regulatory form, environmental assessment is based upon dialogue, evaluation and co-decision. These are quite fundamental elements of modern society and are constantly being developed. Though the impact of capitalist modernity on all aspects of social life is only just beginning to have an effect, a number of pressing problems have arisen that demand dialogue, evaluation and participation. Many areas need to be addressed, and the project might seem overwhelming as perspectives expand regionally and globally. It will therefore be very important to try and create clarity and understanding in relation to the basic phenomena.

As the work progressed, it became clear that the book would also come to have an aspect of the theory of history attached to it. I have therefore made an effort to be diligent with quotations and to allow them to be part of the text in such a way that both the reading and the understanding of my text are facilitated.

Writing the book has been a long process. At the end of 1998, having finished my 'field work' and empirical studies in environmental impact assessment (EIA) and strategic environmental assessment (SEA) practice and reported my findings, I started to draw up the theoretical framework for the interpretation of the findings and their submission to a wider audience and discussion. That work led me to follow an increasingly thorough path. I ended up examining the most fundamental philosophical and sociological matters of the entire environmental question, how they are addressed in theory and how they could be addressed in wider political strategies and decisions. Thus, it is my hope that my analysis and views will inspire a wider audience within environmental science, policy and politics as well as within sociology and political science, with a view towards developing a theory of modern society.

The first manuscript in Danish was completed and published in 2003 and since then I have been working on an English edition and to refine and clarify my analysis and views. Parallel to the latter part of the work I have more specifically carried on to develop environmental assessment, and have published on SEA in land use planning,[1] SEA at the policy level[2] and public participation in EIA and SEA.[3] That work as well as writing this book has resulted from international cooperation and networking in the development of theoretical understanding as well as practical application.

Therefore, I would like to start the acknowledgements by thanking my many colleagues and fellow scholars in the European and international network for environmental assessment and planning, for their collaboration, discussions and participation. They have contributed to my view of environmental assessment as a tool for regulation and planning and to sharpening the views that I present in the book. Some of them are mentioned by name in the book. Also, when connected to criticism, this is put forward in profound recognition of their importance for the development of the subject and with the greatest respect for their views and contributions.

I would also like to thanks the following institutions that have contributed to this collaboration and networking: The European Commission, DG XI, B2, Brussels; The Ministry of the Environment, The Department for Spatial Planning, Copenhagen; NordPLAN/NordRegio, Stockholm; Academia Danimarca, Rome; and The Nordic Council of Ministers, Copenhagen.

I am extremely grateful to the following individuals: Gregers Algreen Ussing, Ib Jørgen Larsen, Palle Koch[+], Gert Johansen, Henrik Wulff, Will T. H. Thissen, Chris Wood, Norman Lee[+], Barry Sadler, Niels West, Lars Emmelin and Rasmus Sønderriis.

Finally my family have been there for me and have helped me to come through the other side. All my love and thanks to Eva, Eskil and Sigurd.

Bo Elling
Roskilde University
December 2007

Notes

1   'Strategic environmental assessment in land-use planning in Denmark', in Jones et al (2005).
2   'SEA of Bills and other Governmental Proposals in Denmark', in Sadler (2005).
3   'Public participation', in Sadler et al (2007).

List of Acronyms and Abbreviations

EFTA	European Free Trade Association
EIA	environmental impact assessment
EU	European Union
FAO	Food and Agriculture Organization (of the UN)
IUCN	World Conservation Union (formerly known as International Union for the Conservation of Nature and Natural Resources)
NEPA	National Environmental Policy Act (US)
NGO	non-governmental organizations
OECD	Organisation for Economic Co-operation and Development
SEA	strategic environmental assessment
TLV	threshold limit value
UN-ECE	United Nations Economic Commission for Europe
UNEP	United Nations Environment Programme
UNESCO	United Nations Educational, Scientific and Cultural Organization
WWF	Worldwide Fund for Nature

Chapter 1

Introduction

The problematic

Between 1995 and 1998 I produced two research projects that aimed to clarify the possibility of using environmental assessments during the process of political decision-making. One project[1] was to carry out a strategic environmental assessment when a spatial development plan was to be revised at county level. The new or revised regional planning guidelines were to be assessed for their environmental impact, and this assessment could be used as a basis for its implementation. The other project[2] was about the initiation of a strategic environmental assessment in connection with the preparation of a bill by the ministry for its presentation to the Danish Parliament and its final adoption. For both these projects my task was to participate as a concept developer and counsellor to the implementing authorities. Despite my proposals and input, the ultimate responsibility for the production of the environmental assessments remained at the county and ministerial levels.

My tasks in relation to the project on strategic environmental assessment in county planning were also to collect, analyse and evaluate the experiences gained from similar international projects. Based on these results, and on the experience from this project, I had to then produce a model of how environmental assessments could be integrated into the regional plan making process. When this model was ready, and the environmental assessment implemented, and the regional plan adopted by the county council, the project was further enlarged to incorporate interviews with all the people concerned – that is, the county planning officers, interested citizens, organizations and politicians. The aim was to collect both the experience gained in the total research period and the different perspectives of the participants with the aim of formulating proposals for improvements to the model, as the previous results of the original environmental assessment seemed unsatisfactory.

In the project concerning the use of environmental assessments in legislation, my task was to report on and evaluate the whole scheme up to the final proposals in parliament. The project was later enlarged to encompass the study of a number of ministries and their implementation of environmental assessments, a qualitative evaluation of a number of chosen examples of how the quality of the environmental assessments presented to parliament influenced the debate.

The understanding of environmental assessment that I have tried to put into practice in these two projects can be described briefly as follows:

An environmental assessment is a political process based upon accessible technical and scientific knowledge. Moreover, an important amount of knowledge and insight is to be found among the general public, in the form of values and priorities. An environmental assessment cannot, therefore, meaningfully be realized without the participation of the public in a more precisely defined form. The purpose of environmental assessment is not to weigh probable effects against each other to enable the decision-makers to arrive at a decision, but rather to bring about an open dialogue among the implementers, the affected groups and ultimate decision-makers about the propositions and results of these assessments.

This aim was formulated in such a way as to give the politico-democratic elements in the process considerable weight in the decision-making process. If an environmental assessment is *not* the process that leads to knowledge about *the* best solution, but is a process that presents *different* scenarios of the impact on the environment, including the premise for assessment, basic values, and so on, of those evaluations, and in so doing draws a picture of the conflicts and contradictions that exist in the protection and exploitation of the environment, then it becomes a political process in itself. A number of the more fundamental problems on which both projects were based were the following:

How can such an action be implemented in the existing political decision-making process – can it exist parallel to, or rather as a prototype for, the proper political decision-making process? Is there not a risk that the proper political decision-making process is drawn into the assessment process and hence renders itself superfluous? Alternatively, does the assessment process itself get involved in real political decision-making to the extent that the assessment becomes unclear or even redundant? In other words, is it possible for the two processes, environmental assessment and the political decision-making process, to exist alongside each other – the former with a number of technical evaluations based on special interests with a politically determined content, and the latter as a political process of decision-making using the former as the knowledge base? And, if so, will the total process eventually result in better protection of the environment than if there was no such process?

The proposed form of understanding is, in reality, not so different from what is already happening in a planning process or in the work of preparing a bill in the ministry. A combination of technical and scientific knowledge with political intentions is, after all, what results in political decisions. The small, but fundamental difference is the fact that in the proposed form of understanding, the knowledge interests of *all* the participants are incorporated into the process, and not just those who are engaged in controlling the process. Clearly this requires that the different premises, priorities and so on, used as the basis of assessment and the presentation of findings, are made visible and accessible to everybody: the planners, politicians and the public alike. Thus the decision is acknowledged as a political priority on the basis of the assessment presented, instead of being interpreted as an example of 'the technically most efficient' or 'the only correct scientific solution'. It is therefore recognized as being a political and not a technocratic solution.

Taking into account these problems, the results of the projects in question were very encouraging, as an integration of environmental assessments had turned out to be fully possible and meaningful within the framework described. Yet, at the same time, they could also be described as being disappointing, as there was very limited understanding by the planners and politicians of the differences between assessment and political decision. Pushed to the limit, neither the planners nor the politicians were capable of distinguishing between a process of assessment of the environmental impact and a political process of decision-making.

An extensive description of the content and results of the projects can be found in the published research reports,[3] and in shorter scientific publications.[4] Those interested in a more detailed description are referred to this material. In the following I will restrict myself to presenting the major, crucial results.

In the integration of environmental assessment into regional land-use planning, the regional planners tried, without much success, to feed the process with information from other planners and technicians, though they forgot or failed to involve the public. However, during the inquiry into the views of the public, county planning officers and politicians revealed many relevant public viewpoints, values, priorities and so on. Furthermore, although not plainly formulated, this inquiry clearly indicated that the planners' attempt to balance or weigh up different environmental issues was not wanted by the politicians, as they could not see how they could make use of this information. Instead, they would prefer to receive material – on environmental or public conflicts – about the various priorities.

Concerning the environmental assessment of the legislation, the ministry's reaction revealed a number of strategic dilemmas relating to the knowledge on environmental impact and other interests in the preparation of the Bill. I define these separately as *the system*, *the planning* and *the political dilemma*. 'System' refers to the internal workings of the ministry, 'planning' to other long-term planning interests that have to be taken into account, and finally 'the political dilemma' to the many different ministerial political considerations and interests.

The strategic dilemmas exposed two important considerations:

1　The political character of environmental assessment, as opposed to its technical and scientific content, should be revealed and not concealed, as is the case in actual practice.
2　The necessity of enlarging environmental assessment so that not only the techno-scientific content, but also both the ethical and aesthetical insights and appreciation may be included.

Further examination of the ministries' *practices* in development of environmental assessments showed a very low level of communication between colleagues in the various ministries, and little noticeable communication between the ministries themselves. The work of ministries is characterized by customary work patterns and existing or random knowledge about environmental conditions. The possibilities for the inclusion of other disciplines are not developed.

However, the evaluation of the *quality* of the selected examples showed that information about environmental impact did *not* render the related debate among politicians superfluous. On the contrary, it was found to improve considerations insofar as, rather than relying on platitudes, a more serious level of considerations could be adopted, in the case of a good, or at least honest, environmental assessment.

Combined with the findings from the application of environmental assessment on projects – the so-called EIA-process – these general conclusions highlighted the problems of environmental assessment by showing that their real aim had not been achieved. The data on the environmental impact reach the decision-makers only to a limited extent. This limitation concerns not only the quantitative dimension and the technical-scientific insight, but also the fact that aesthetic and ethical problems are not included, although they play a constantly growing role in relation to environmental issues. Furthermore, the inclusion of the public in assessments, which is the basic aim of environmental assessment, has only succeeded to a very limited extent. In short, this planning procedure has coalesced into a familiar pattern, which is the very thing the technique was supposed to break out of.

The situation might also be described by saying that the existing practice reflects a power struggle between production, distribution and the implementation of knowledge in environmental politics, and that the winners in this struggle have until now been the planners or administrators. They are the ones who do not provide the pertinent knowledge and furthermore do not pass on the knowledge they do possess to the political decision-makers.

The existing practice also reflects a widespread illusion in the governmental administration about environmental solutions, as something that can be techno-scientifically controlled, instead of conceiving environmental issues as something that should be increasingly included in a dialogue with the public. It can rightly be postulated that no noticeable effort is being made to overcome such an illusion.

It is, of course, important to realize that a power struggle over the production, distribution and implementation of knowledge will always – and should – take place in a democracy. But it is equally important to understand that if the administration always turns out to be the winner in this struggle, techno-instrumental aspects will cause a stagnation of progress. It would probably not be too much to say that this does not lead us towards a more environmentally favourable process of development. The situation is in no way unique for Denmark: variations on the same pattern can be found all over the Western world.

It might seem paradoxical to maintain that environmental assessment as a tool is applied to a growing number of cases, for example in relation to several different types of projects and to the so-called strategic environmental assessment. This tool is still considered to be one of the most important contributions to renewal and enhancement of environmental politics since its inception in the beginning of the 1970s. It is considered a key tool for the environmental politics for the future.

Developments within the European Union (EU) confirm this. It is obvious that environmental assessment should play the leading role in the environmental politics of the future; with the adoption of the directive about assessment of the effects of certain plans and programmes on the environment from 2001,[5] and the 1997 extended directive about environmental assessment of projects.[6]

This development is furthermore confirmed by the adoption of the so-called Aarhus Convention of 1998, where the processes of environmental assessment are used in all decisions and the planning of environmental policies in the participating countries.[7]

There are indications that the *politicians*, even after several years of work with EIA and strategic environmental assessment, still feel a strong need for knowledge and information about environmental conditions and consequences to keep up with the situation. A situation where environmental problems are less tangible but are of increasing importance, as they are complicated insofar as they have increasingly become more involved with society's other problems – for example, ethical aspects can often become of greater importance than what can be technically and scientifically measured. But the situational deadlock, as I will characterize it, also indicates that these same politicians do not fully understand the inherent possibilities and potential of using environmental assessment as a tool to solve these problems.

In the Danish conference on the implementation of the Aarhus Convention in 1999,[8] I had the honour of delivering the initial lecture. I took advantage of the opportunity to underline the following:

> *If politicians and not least administrators and planners fail to understand that the Convention should be used to give the public a de facto influence on the decisions taken, and thus change the intended decision-making process at all levels, then the aims of the Convention will have been negated. The process will have become manipulative and create the impression of influence rather than actually being a more democratic decision-making process.*
>
> Elling, 1999b, pp9, 18

The same warning must be given about environmental assessments. What is the use of them if the public has the clear impression that everything has been settled or decided beforehand? What purpose does it serve when the planners and administrators conspicuously consider this tool to be a means to solving their problems by giving *themselves* more information, but taking no account of the *societal* needs revealed by the use and development of the tool? How does it help that the politicians feel strongly about the increasing need for information if they are not aware that all the existing possibilities are actually being ignored? There can be no doubt that those three groups must learn to *communicate with each other*, besides communicating internally. The decision-making processes must be opened up to become more visible, and space must be given for participation. Three questions arise:

• Can such communication lead to more rational decisions about the environment?
• Can openness and participation counter the abuse of power?
• Can communication and information influence a situation with more complicated environmental problems and growing risks?

These are some of the more burning questions characterizing the modern debate in the social sciences. They are my points of departure for an analysis of the reasons for the obvious standstill in environmental politics. I hope to be able to create understanding and knowledge of the social necessity of a democratization of the environmental decision-making process. Not only to democratize, although this might be the key, but also to develop an in-depth understanding of what makes it necessary to change and renew the process of environmental planning and regulation, and to include public participation as a determining factor.

The German sociologist and philosopher Jürgen Habermas has given some answers to the first question concerning communication and rational decision-making. He calls the resulting rationality 'communicative rationality'. By this he understands something radically different from what we normally understand by rationality, which he calls 'instrumental rationality' – something with a final aim that is determined in advance and controlled by definite interests.

We have grown accustomed to understanding a rational decision as being one that builds on something sensible and planned, a rationale that everybody ought to be able to accept. For many decades, it has been a social-democratic way of reasoning. Political economists have also been diligent producers of economic rationales, which are widely exploited by politicians. Today it is to a large extent the natural scientists who contribute to this kind of construction of rationales when they indicate what is most environmentally defendable in a given situation. However, it is becoming more and more apparent that such rationales do not exist.

When, on the other hand, Habermas speaks about the existence of a communicative rationality, he understands by this a rationality that can only be produced by communication and comprises much more than the instrumental. I am therefore going to follow that path in this book.

The French sociologist Michel Foucault considers openness, information and participation to be a necessary, but not a sufficient, precondition for hindering the abuse of power by the administration. He finds it dangerous to *institutionalize* free access to public records and participation, as this poses a considerable risk for an increase in the abuse of power by rulers. Foucault points out that openness and transparency need to be created, by encouraging the parties involved in creating their own rules of play in specific situations. In contrast to this, Habermas talks about discursive rules. In the following, I will discuss why I follow Habermas' rather than Foucault's path.

In questions about complicated environmental problems and risks, a fundamental point for any environmental assessment must be the belief that knowledge can transform a situation, and that the knowledge about risks allows one to avoid them – though the public is not exposed to risks and dangers to the same extent. The risk theoreticians Ulrich Beck and Antony Giddens have postulated that risks would be apportioned differently if the public was informed and involved in decision-making. They consider risks to be produced in a specific society, which they call *reflexive modernity*.

In reflexive modernity, science is not only a factor of development, but also a factor of development *risk*. Monopolies of knowledge have broken down, but this has also led to a lack of predictability. Political cultures have not only been developed and spread, but have also broken down any consensus on future progress. Unlike earlier times, where specialization and monopoly were a condition for developments in both science and politics, reflexive modernization implies a generalization of both science and politics and an extension of the boundaries for both. For both Beck and Giddens, this situation implies that the public's participation must lead to *changes*, instead of a differentiation from above, the only purpose of which was to *defend the status quo against collapse* or to *shift responsibility elsewhere*.

I fully agree with them about this. However, I find it astonishing that Beck can describe reflexive modernity as a society that creates environmental problems while, at the same time, the tool used in environmental politics, anticipated with most expectations, is itself based on a reflexive process concerning the environmental problems attached to activities, which can be described as being so profound in societal terms. Moreover, other sociologists designate current society as modernity[9] and work with concepts such as reflexivity and risks to characterize this modernity, without establishing a clear connection between these phenomena.

In the following discourse, I therefore take a closer look at Beck's thesis, and also to a certain extent that of Giddens, in relation to *reflexive* modernity. If society, at the current time when environmental problems and solutions are becoming critical, concurrently develops a specific reflexive form that contributes to the continuity of environmental problems, then this must create contradictions either on the real level or on the formal or theoretical level. First, this will be fundamental in determining the functionality of the tool for environmental assessment, and second it will be decisive in pinpointing real problems.

I have therefore decided to start from the very bottom – or, one might say, from the top – with modernity as a central concept concerning society. What is understood by modernity as a concept of society? Can the characteristics of modernity contribute to an understanding of the reasons why environmental problems are created, or inversely to our understanding of the problems? Does modernity influence possibilities for action in relation to such environmental problems? And if so, how? Can knowledge about these questions bring us closer to an adequate understanding of the necessity to democratize the process of decision-making, and thus create a worthwhile renewal of the planning process?

Method of analysis

When the experience gained from environmental assessments at strategic and project levels reveals that the tool is not being used to its full potential or in the way intended, and that a solution must be that the process for making environmental assessments should be made transparent and open for discussion, there is ambiguity.

This ambiguity arises because it has to be recognized that an environmental assessment, beyond what is scientific and technical, is an illustration of the values and interests of the public in regard to their environment. An environmental assessment is therefore also a *political* manifestation, which *must* have an impact on the final decision. Only in this way can it be said to be independent of the established interests and power structures.

A more detailed analysis of why such a democratization and clarification of the public's values and interests are linked to the environmental question must therefore be sought in an analysis of the character of such environmental problems: what impact they have on the public, and how they influence the institutions and power structures of society. In other words, we need to clarify the character of environmental problems, and how they are institutionalized into the public and political structure. This will highlight the importance of the environmental problems, not only in relation to the environment, but in relation to the political process as well.

On the contrary, the social conditions for the political decision-making process must also be analysed; specifically whether, and eventually how, the decision-making process for environmental assessment can be established in a way that takes into consideration the public's room for action and choice, as mentioned above.

An analysis of environmental problems and their institutionalization in the public and political structure is set out in Chapter 2. A proper historical analysis of this, a so-called real analysis, would exceed the brief of this book. Instead, the focus will be centred on the character of the environmental question and its institutionalization in society from the perspectives of the social sciences, primarily sociology. This not only makes the analysis more feasible. Following this course, the analysis of the social institutionalization can also advantageously choose to adopt the general sociological forms of understanding as a point of departure. This entails matching the environmental problems with the modern problematic, central to general sociological thinking.

The modern problematic is concerned with what can be considered the truth and how true knowledge can be obtained in the modern era. The relationship to environmental politics is thus not only a question of how we create a true knowledge of environmental problems and their effects on both nature and culture, but also about *which* truth, or which form of truth is attainable, and so, to a larger extent, it concerns the situation or the intended goal when society intervenes and tries to regulate the environmental effect.

The point of departure in terms of the forms of understanding has thus been chosen for reasons of practicality. The ongoing link of this understanding to the modern problematic has already been incorporated in sociological theory or sociological analysis of environmental problems and their societal institutionaliza-tion. For the same reason, the point of departure for the analysis of the character of environmental problematic will be brief, only giving a short account of the changes that have taken place over the last 20–30 years, ontologically, substan-tially and in the course of action.

However, the relation of the environmental question to the modern problem-atic must be given a full analysis for several reasons. First of all, as already pointed out, this is central to the sociological forms of understanding and therefore central to the analysis itself. Second, the content of the modern problematic must be clarified. What is the problem in the modern problematic, and how does it arise in the current sociological conception of the environmental question? Finally, it is necessary to clarify why I choose to keep the further analysis of the social condi-tions in the political decision-making process within a modern form of understanding. In other words, it is necessary to state why the analysis is taking a modern form of understanding society, rather than a postmodern form. Inevitably, the latter has been on the scientific agenda through almost all the period during which such analyses have taken place.

The central points in Chapter 2 will therefore concentrate on sociological reflection as regards:

1   Societal institutionalization of the environmental question and the political apparatus related to it.
2   The connection of the environmental question to the modern problematic.
3   A discussion of why I do not consider a transcending of the modern to be a practical route rather than an approach based on reason.

Thus, the discussion in Chapter 2 has to substantiate why neither considerations of ecology [the term 'ecology' is used here and throughout the text to mean conservation using the concepts of ecology] as a societal aim nor postmodern alternatives for normative reasoning can be recommended. Why they both lead to absolutism and the suppression of *socially* reflected environmental discourses.

The discourse for a modern view needs to be followed by a real analysis of society as a concept of modernity. What do such concepts and characteristics imply in the understanding of society as such and what does this clarify as to the question of why social practices lead to environmental problems. Furthermore, a clarification is needed as to how the characteristics of modernity influence our possibilities for action.

In Chapter 3, the meaning of modernity is made explicit in the form of a categorical determination of this. Thus the analysis of Chapter 2 is taken further, but now in a more abstract categorical context, where the societal concept itself is taken up for discussion. The central authors of the forms of understanding mentioned in Chapter 2 will thus be part of this extended analysis. This concerns principally Habermas, Beck and Giddens.

In Chapter 3 it will be made clear that the former understanding of rationality has failed in the environmental discourse and needs to be characterized as instrumental yet outside an overall societal consideration. If a concept of modernity is to be used we need to justify that such a point of departure can lead to another concept of rationality other than the instrumental. For this reason, Habermas' assertion, mentioned in Chapter 2, about such a concept of rationality will be discussed by way of a presentation of his theory of communicative action.

The aim of this is moreover to clarify the process of modernization itself. What is the driving force behind societal modernization, and in what way can its civilizing effects be pinpointed? We will see that the concept of modernization in Habermas' view is not only something systemic, as for example was the theory of the sociologist Max Weber, but that its fundamental substance must be traced back to the lifeworld. This distinction between system and lifeworld will therefore be a determining analytical factor in this book, not only for the analysis of the concept of rationality, but also with regard to the question of the inclusion of the public in the decision-making process.

In Habermas' view, the civilizing effects of the process of modernization also imply liberation from traditions, norms and cultures via the release of reflexivity. As such, a liberation carries the risk that new practices might lead to mistakes and might have the ability to change to ways that turn out to be problematic; the concept of reflexivity will be the third key point after the concept of rationality and the concept of modernization.

This question of reflexivity and modernization is taken up by Ulrich Beck in his analysis of the risk society. He sees a specific epoch in societal modernization, reflexive modernity, as the background for the environmental problematic of modernity. Also Anthony Giddens' understanding of the connection between modernity and environmental problems is linked to a reflexive modernity that he also terms high or late modernity. This is the reason why the concept of reflexivity that stems from Habermas is compared to the concept of reflexivity presented by Beck and Giddens.

In this confrontation, the different conceptions of reflexivity appear to imply very different forms of knowledge relating to reflexivity. Therefore the critique of Beck and Giddens will be directed towards an elucidation of these differences as regards the concepts of knowledge and their consequences. Thus the debate on the concept of reflexivity and the related forms of knowledge linked to the further analysis of environmental politics is brought into focus.

Finally, as a part of the clarification of the concept of reflexivity, some of Marx's central concepts of modernization, namely the concepts of formal and real subsumption will be brought into the debate. This connection will be broadened to include a comparison of the increasing reflexivity within society with the expanding sphere of modernization. This is important because an isolated consideration of a more generalized reflexivity can lead to a misunderstanding of the concept of reflexivity with a reduction of instrumentality. Thus a continued modernization of the modern, as proposed by Beck among others, can be excluded as an alternative, as it can be shown to reinforce the tendency towards an ecological crisis.

What now remains is to analyse the trend in sociology and social science, which assert that a 'modern' process of modernization and a social reception of the environmental discourse will find a solution to the ecological crisis by making the process of modernization itself ecologically sound. This will be taken up in Chapter 4.

A wide range of views relating to this trend, albeit all having an aspect of ecological modernization, makes it necessary for me to argue why I specifically choose to focus on the forms of understanding as represented by Arthur Mol and Maarten Hajer. Both base their perception of the environmental discourse on Beck's and Giddens' theories, and for that reason I will use this selection and the critique of the latter two, along with the concepts developed to this end, to characterize and criticize ecological modernization as a theory.

However, Moll and Hajer make a wider use of the concept of reflexivity than do Beck and Giddens, as they see no less than three forms of reflexivity, namely as systemic or cultural processes (Mol) and reflexive institutional arrangements (Hajer) in addition to Beck's and Giddens' individualistic approach to reflexivity. Despite the fact that I consider these approaches to the concept of reflexivity theoretically non-contributive, partly because they repeat Beck's and Giddens' misconceptions and partly because of the use of a 'rational choice' of the understanding of reflexivity, I will nevertheless take up the theories. Thus, by way of an interpretation of Habermas' concept of reflexivity and his distinction between system and lifeworld, I wish to deduce three forms of reflexivity, which I will use in a reconstructive interpretation of environmental assessment. This follows up the critique of Mol and Hajer, and will be done partly on a theoretical basis, partly by way of a deduction of the three possible reflexive forms as elements of an environmental assessment, and finally, in the last chapter, by way of a formulation of a model for a democratized and de-instrumental environmental assessment which I will characterize as communicative reflection.

The fact that, since the 1980s, the new European agenda for environmental politics has, in a very direct manner, reflected the critique of various forms of understanding of ecological modernization, allows one to focus on the context of environmental politics, of which environmental assessment is a part. Using the concepts that have been analysed in the preceding chapters and in the critique of Hajer and Mol, I will show that although these forms of understanding might, indeed, manage in a quite stringent fashion to include environmental assessment as an adequate tool for the new agenda on environmental politics, nevertheless, the agenda cannot claim to produce elements of de-instrumentalization. On the contrary, while it may be characterized as modernization where the environmental question is implicitly involved, it only forms a part of the existing political, economic and technological instrumentalism.

A recurring question that will be addressed in Chapter 5 concerns an interpretation of this new agenda of environmental politics, and the insights and concepts resulting from the analysis:

1   To understand and interpret environmental assessment as a part of this agenda or as a part of its realization and changes in relation to this.
2   To show an interpretation of environmental assessment that does not repeat or reproduce the political instrumentalism of the agenda, but which indicates a departure from this.

In light of what has been said up to now, the first interpretation shows that the problematic, as it has been drawn up in the introduction on the basis of specific experiences, is not accidental but can be understood precisely as a consequence of a practised instrumentalism.

The last interpretation shows that, following the existing political agenda and the existing formal demands – among other things valid directives – it is possible to realize environmental assessment in such a way that the desired democratization of the process and a de-instrumentalization of its basis of knowledge can take place.

Notes

1   The project was financed by The Nordic Council of Ministers and the Ministry of the Environment with a view to developing an inter-Nordic model for environmental assessments at the planning level that could become part of the European (EU and EFTA) discussion about the creation of an EU directive for strategic environmental assessment, cf. the directive adopted later as described in note 5. Concerning publication see notes 3 and 4 below.
2   The project was financed by the European Commission, DG XI, B2, and the Danish Ministry of the Environment with the scope of developing a European model for strategic environmental assessment at the policy level (bills and governmental proposals to be presented in the national parliaments), and also to test the possibilities for this in a precise context. That Denmark was selected for this experiment was due, among other things, to the fact that Denmark was the only member state that had obligatory rules for the application of environmental assessments at the policy level and in full publicity. Compare note 2 preceding and note 5. Concerning publications see notes 3 and 4 below.
3   Elling and Nielsen, 1996, 1997, 1998; Elling, 1998, 1999, 2000. See also Elling, 2005.
4   Elling, 1997, 2000.
5   Directive from the European Parliament and the Council on the assessment of the effects of certain plans and programmes on the environment, Directive 2001/42/EC. Similar efforts to broaden the application of environmental assessment in the strategic environmental assessment take place in the rest of the Western world. Furthermore, most countries work on the inclusion of environmental assessment of policies.

6   Directive 97/11/EC enlarges the number and categories of different projects to be subject to mandatory environmental impact assessment following Annex I, and formulates increased claims as to the content of the process.

7   The official title is *The Convention on Access to Information, Public Participation in Decision-making and Access to Justice in Environmental Matters*, adopted in Aarhus 25 June 1998. The convention was ratified by 40 European and Central Asian countries and, by 1 January 2003, 23 countries had ratified the convention.

8   See *The Environmental Rights of the Citizens*. Conference held by The National Agency of Environmental Protection concerning The Aarhus Convention, September 8 1999, *Miljønyt* (Environmental News) no. 38, 1999.

9   See, for example, Bourdieu and Wacquant, 1996; Luhmann, 1993.

Chapter 2

The Environment as a Goal

A revolution in the environmental field has taken place during the last 25 years. It is true that a revolution is usually something that happens violently, suddenly and is highly visible. Indeed, all revolutions are manifested by changes of dramatic proportions, which have fundamentally altered a field or structure and left their mark on the areas involved. There has simply been a revolution in the environmental field over the last quarter of the century from being a question about fighting for the recognition of a problem that society ought to do something about, to the environmental question becoming a dominating societal discourse. Just the fact that today we talk about *the environment* speaks for itself. All of us know what it is. We value it and know that we must take care of it. Even if we do not do anything, we know, in the last resort, that we ought to take care of it.

When the first real environmental laws saw the light of day, which in most Western countries was two or three decades ago, the environment could allegorically be described as a drain. It was something *outside* what ordinary people thought about. It was just there; it did not really have a name. When the environmental movements put the issue on the agenda and asked for action, it was against all usual conceptions. It signified a fight that only a few understood, very few regarded with sympathy and even fewer would join. The fight was confined to a few fanatical activists. It might be for a good cause, but in the opinion of the great majority of the population, most of the environmental movement's assertions about damages to the environment and their claim for the need for intervention were wildly exaggerated or expressed daydreams and naïve ideas about a 'clean' world. Progress costs money, and people were not usually ready to pay the price or did not even think about it at all.

It was not that the authorities were immovable. A number of international pollution scandals had already given a signal,[1] and the first environmental laws might be better compared to a kind of fire-fighting rather than fire protection. When the damage had been done, the possibility should exist to quickly take action. The regulatory framework for this should exist and a number of tools be made available. The first environmental laws thus had a defensive character, and the goals were restoration and cleaning up, as well as what was possible under the circumstances and within the framework of a reasonable budget. To control pollution was something that cost money, and the price had to be reasonable in relation to the return.

Since then, the revolutionary changes can be encapsulated in the form of three major questions.

First, the conception of what is an environmental problem has changed – this is *the ontological question*. During the first period of environmental politics, environmental problems were directly identifiable –for example, a badly smelling lake or polluted waterways with dead fish. The problems were closely or directly linked to disruptions of nature, which manifested themselves in sudden and unwanted changes of various ecosystems. Thus, in considering problems created by, for example, alterations of the landscape, visual changes and changes of the cultural heritage, a change has taken place. Problems related to culture are more and more often seen as environmental problems, and, in this way, a broadening has taken place of our concept of the environment, and what we consider environmental influences.

Second, the character and proportions of environmental problems change – this is *the substantial question*. Problems that, in the first place, were solely or mainly linked to the immediately observable effects, are now increasingly linked to their ultimate effects. Concerns have shifted – for example from immediate poisoning to disturbances in DNA, and from air pollution to climatic problems. The substantial question expresses, primarily, that the extent of pollution grows in relation to the accumulating effects of environmental interference that takes place, thus giving rise to yet other problems. But it can also be related to the use of new substances or new practices leading to environmental changes – for example, genetic engineering. In the latter case, the ontological question can determine whether or not a change should be considered a potential influence on the environment, even if no immediate effects on the environment are apparent.

Third, we see a change in relation to the question of what initiates environmental politics – this is *the action-related question*. The original national environmental legislation was, to a large extent, caused by pressure from the so-called environmental movements. They wanted the state to intervene and introduce legislation against conditions that led to demonstrable environmental damage. From the beginning, it was clearly understood that environmental measures were linked to additional costs both for the authorities and the commercial enterprises that were subjected to actions or restrictions. Consequently, national environmental legislation was passed following the so-called PPP, the Polluter Pays Principle. This principle did not prevent the simultaneous granting of state subsidies for environmental measures. Such legislation can be seen as a confirmation that environmental measures are generally perceived as being a cost. But at the same time, this also shows a change in attitude insofar as the fight against environmental pollution is now considered worthwhile. This is increasingly the motivation of both commercial enterprises and public authorities in questions about the initiation of environmental considerations and measures. Symbolically this is expressed by the PPP being increasingly interpreted as

'Pollution Prevention Pays' rather than 'the polluter pays principle'. Yet, this does not imply that the environmental struggle or the popular pressure to obtain environmental/political measures has disappeared. The crucial point is that environmental political initiatives and considerations can now be motivated by economic expectations and not merely by considerations for the environment itself. It is *profitable* to do something for the environment – in time and taking a long-term view. Environmental concerns can, in other words, be motivated from inside an organization and do not need to be the result of pressure or a claim from outside.

The situation has thus moved considerably forward. The environment is not only a part of an agenda but *determines* it, in an immediate way, in many important areas. A plan or political action, national or international, that does not include *sustainable development* as its goal, is hard to find. Every international policy favours such a development, although there may be doubt about what is actually implied. Furthermore, almost all political actions comprise formalized claims about environmental considerations. Rather than being considered long-term ideals, the issues revolving around green policies are taken as something quite serious and concrete that need to be part of all actions whether big or small. The concept of *ecology* is not a word that needs searching for in a dictionary, but is on everybody's lips. An organic consumer is not an abstract phantom, but a real person shopping from the supermarket's special shelves for organic products. Organic agriculture is not a dream for a few idealists who want to put back the development of the world to the 1950s, but is something that can benefit from financial support from the Ministry of Agriculture. Every self-respecting enterprise has not only an ethical profile, but also an environmental profile that is actively applied in marketing.

In short, the environmental efforts and goals have been *institutionalized* in all fields, public as well as private, from the international to the domestic, from what is concrete to what is superior and far-sighted.

Does this shift mean that the environmental movements, or merely environmental causes, have been victorious? Have the environmental questions become the crank that drives the purpose and content of decisions?

Of course not, we know immediately that this is not the case. Because, at the same time as this revolutionary shift has happened, we also understand that environmental problems have never appeared more widespread and serious. We need only consider one problem – that is, climate change – to grasp the extent of such an assertion. The damage to the environment has now taken on such proportions that they contribute to changes that are quite fundamental to life on Earth – the climate.

Another example could be that nowadays some people describe our society as a risk society. This means that we live with the risk of being injured or being exposed to adverse influences. The primary nature of our society is that it implies risks. What, according to its concept, should be a protection of each individual implies, at the same time, the direct opposite, namely the exposure of individuals to risk.

As a final example, we could mention the paradox that while the ecological movement gets stronger and stronger among consumers and producers, there is talk about a fundamental *ecological crisis* in our society.[2]

What, on one hand, seems to be the guiding light for decision-making – sustainable development – on the other hand takes the form of a social crisis. Ideologies are dead, and what immediately appears to take their place as a guideline, both for institutions and individuals, turns out to be incapable of resolution. The question about what should guide our actions remains unanswered. Never before has the complexity of society been so extensive and volatile that every decision must be based on values, while at the same time values have become a discussion about, for example, whether Denmark should use the Crown or the Euro.[3] The necessity for action has increased along with the difficulty for modern development in achieving this. Reasoned decisions used until now have collapsed. What, until just a few years ago, could function as the basis for rational action does not exist anymore, or may only result in a counterclaim. What was earlier considered a big advance for humanity – for example, the development of new chemical substances – is now often perceived as a catastrophe. Where subject-oriented knowledge used to justify decision-making, there is now a vacuum of political powerlessness, or rather, the victory of the market.

What has happened is that what was earlier considered objective certainty has lost meaning. The noble task of getting to the truth, which the sciences have sought to achieve since the dawn of the modern epoch more than 200 years ago, can no longer be applied. What is true and false can no longer be defined by scientific questions, and this appears to be the very core of our philosophy of life. By the same token, moral imperatives have become relative and vague.

This problematic as to whether things are true or false is usually referred to as the modern problematic, or the problematic of modernity. The acceptance of the environmental question has in this way triggered this problematic, making it a general question rather than a scientific one.

It is therefore also characteristic of the latest sociological reflection over the environmental problematic that it is linked to the modern problematic.[4]

Before taking a closer look at the connection between the modern problematic and the environmental question, especially as to how this can be determined, I would like to quote the sociologist Bronislaw Szerszynski. In his introduction to a quite remarkable article entitled 'On knowing what to do: Environmentalism and the modern problematic', he states the following:

> *Once, it seems, we knew what to do. Until the early modern period, knowing who we were, and in what practice we were engaged, told us all we needed to know about what we ought to do. That was the nature of moral experience then. There was no distinction, as today, between a world of facts and a world of values – the word 'moral' simply meant 'customary', and to know what a creature or object was also to know its 'telos', its good. The world was finite, ordered and suffused with meaning and purpose. Our – humanity's – place and role in the world was central and secure.*

Then came modernity – rapid social, economic and cultural change both brought about and sustained by this epochal shift. The stable customary character of social relationships was eroded by a rapidly expanding capitalism. Religious authority was fragmented and pitted against itself by schism and sectarianism. Science displaced theology as the highest form of knowledge, and replaced the organic medieval cosmos with an infinite universe of matter in motion. The self-contained medieval world was thus shattered, and we were burdened with the necessity of creating our own meaning and our own projects in an infinite world, which no longer told us anything about how we should live, all significance and purpose now being confined to the human mind.

But then came ecology. The shift towards systemic thought in the natural sciences problematized the view of ourselves as being somehow outside of nature – as being able to possess it, to use it and control it. A growing technical and political awareness of the environmental costs of modern life undermined our Promethean confidence in progress and science. Cultural changes produced a heightened awareness of our profound alienation from nature, and its spiritual cost. In more and more spheres of human existence – politics, consumption, culture, and so on – there is occurring a displacement of the idea of the human subject as sovereign, and as subject to no normative claims that are not derived from what we want. In its place is emerging a recognition that all human projects have to take account of natural limits, and of the intrinsic value of non-human nature. Once again, the world does indeed tell us what to do. Once again, an objective ethic has become possible – indeed imperative, since survival itself is contingent on our full embracing of it.

Szerszynski, 1996, pp104–105

He admits that this is quite a biased way of presenting an extremely complex story. Indeed, it is only meant as an introduction to other points such as the claim that today's return to nature is but the latest feature or link in a long series of attempts, in a world deprived of meaning and purpose, to find arguments for actions and evaluations that are based on something other than pure human self-assertion.

That this latter point is also doomed to be overruled by the new is testified by the above references to climate changes, the ecological *crisis* and risk society, notwithstanding the dominating societal discourse about a sustainable development. This is basically built upon an assumption of control of the ecological system, although in different variations it is also provided with goals from the economic and social system.

The world, evoked by the discourse about sustainable development, is in many respects similar to the world before modern times, with the existence of meaning and purpose and with a population living in harmony with it. It forms a contrast to the whole of development in modern times. This refers to the epoch beginning at the end of the 1700s at the start of what we call the Enlightenment, characterized by constant cultural, social and economic changes propelled by an even more active capitalism. This is a situation in which people gain a new idea of themselves as individuals, but in which their harmony with the surrounding world is diluted and meaning and purpose no longer exist as before. Also, religious authorities have lost their importance in society, and the only hope people are offered in place of all this is modern science and the belief in its capacity to create progress and improved living standards.

In recent years, it is exactly this hope that has lost its force. The attempt of science to control nature and exploit it to create a drive forward has turned out to be difficult.

Human beings cease to place themselves in the centre and to give themselves priority over all other creatures on earth. On the contrary, nature is attributed its own value and meaning, and humans ought to learn from it instead of trying to conquer it. We have to adjust to it.

It is not the first time in the modern period of the Western world that, in times when the economic imperatives of capitalism generally prevail, attempts have been made to make nature the ethical principle and the point of orientation. Indeed, when the modern period was beginning to unfold, Rousseau pleaded for maintaining nature as a measure for a healthy life, in contrast to the emerging civilization. And in the following century, romanticism was widely encouraging the dream of a return to a world where nature was the leading and guiding factor.

Nevertheless, the search for a basis in nature, as it is seen in modern times, does not imply a total abandonment of science as a source of insight and understanding. It is, indeed, the system theory *within* the natural sciences that points to *ecology* as the necessary source for an insight into the world capable of fixing the border lines for nature, thus providing modern man with an objectively ethical imperative. That this return to nature as an ethical principle in the form of ecology is not an unequivocal breach with modernity but is seen in the splitting up of modern ecology into a modernistic (and neomodernistic) tendency, as expressed, for example, in the theories about sustainable development, and a romantic tendency, expressed by the so-called depth-ecology (Szerszynski, 1996, pp112, 120). That the latter does not manage to escape the modern problematic will be shown below. At present it is enough to see this as an indication of the central position of the modern problematic in the contemporary philosophical and sociological discussion of the environmental problematic.

This 'in-between land' and ambiguity, as described above by contrasting sustainable development and ecological crisis, is exactly what Hegel formulated as 'the dialectic of enlightenment' and what Horkheimer and Adorno discussed in their famous work of precisely that title.[5] It expresses the fact that progress simultaneously implies alienation, or seen from the perspective of the individual: that the price for the newly conquered self-consciousness is an increasing objectification, both of the outer nature as well as of one's own, 'inner' nature (Nørager, 1985, p21).

This is what leads to today's situation in which anti-modernistic currents, perceiving ecology to be an alternative to the modern mode of development of society, at the same time are lead to talk about an ecological crisis (Giddens, 1994a, p11).

But why is the environmental question today linked so closely to the modern problematic? And why is the modern problematic so central to contemporary sociological thinking?

I will start by giving a short and provisional answer to the latter question and let this open the way for a more profound reply to the former. However, both these problems will be present throughout the book and developed further concurrently with the presentation.

In *The Theory of Communicative Action* Habermas has emphasized that the basic theme for all modern philosophy is a theory of reason.[6] By this he understands that everybody, irrespective of differences in conception, takes this question up for consideration. And, he continues to emphasize, precisely why sociology sticks to this problematic when it develops towards becoming a science in the modern period. By so doing, it stands in contrast to political as well as economic science, both of which in their development to modern sciences have dropped the problematic of reasoning that considers society an entity. Political science is instead based on a societal subsystem – politics – where the question about legitimacy becomes the central issue. Economics, since it quit its position as a political economy during the latter part of the 19th century, also refers to a societal subsystem, economy, where problems of rationality are reduced to sub-questions such as economic equilibriums and rational economic choices (TCA 1, pp3–4). Sociology takes up what political science and economics have pushed aside, namely the changes in social integration brought about during the modern period by the creation of the present system of national states and by the differentiation of an economic system regulated by the market. 'Sociology became the science of crisis par excellence; it concerned itself above all with the anomic aspects of the dissolution of traditional social systems and the development of modern ones' (TCA 1, p4). This distinction is also the reason why I talk about the treatment of the environmental question from a sociological rather than a social science perspective.

Habermas shows that all central sociologists in the modern period, using Max Weber and Talcott Parsons as examples, have a common consensus about three basic questions. In the metatheoretical question concerning the choice of frame of action they concentrate upon those aspects of action that can be rationalized – that is, can carry social development further towards an increased modernization. In the methodological question, they take up the issue of understanding the societal phenomena, which aims to ensure objectivity and the relation between meaning and validity, which can then lead to a theory of meaning. And, finally, in the empirical question, the issue of whether modernization of a society can be defined as an ongoing rationalization (TCA 1, pxlii).

Thus, according to Habermas, we can give a short answer to the question of why the modern problematic is so central in contemporary sociological thinking, since he asserts that the question of rationalization is raised simultaneously at all three levels. The empirical level in the contemporary debate engages centrally in this problematic, since the question of *how* the ongoing modernization – exemplified by globalization, IT revolution, enormous changes and displacements in the occupational and population structures – can be seen as a societal rationalization, a central theme for sociology today. While, during the 1960s and 1970s, sociology was either in awe of the on-rushing turn to positivism, or otherwise was focusing on how crisis-infested capitalism could lead to a new non-capitalistic society, it could once again during the 1980s occupy the position around which it was historically created – that is, analysing the social process of modernization. Yet, as will be shown in the following chapters, this return has not been a revival of, for example, Weber's analyses of rationalization or the 1930s' critique of the process of modernization. The vigorous critique of capitalism in the intermediate period has left its mark, first and foremost because of its non-existence.

This short answer can then be developed further in aiming to answer the question: why is the environmental question today so closely linked to the modern problematic? Despite the connection of modern sociological concerns on environmental matters with the modern problematic, this does not imply it is adopted in the *debate* about environmental politics. In fact, this does not happen, even if it might seem to be self-evident and necessary. The current debate about environmental politics largely takes the aim of giving answers rather than posing questions of why. But from the perspective of the development of modernity – the modernization process – it must be considered fundamental that environmental goals are defined within the framework of the societal process of development. Thus, the problem becomes profound by its lack of a determining framework

To this end I want to indicate four factors that can illustrate the problem raised:

1   The institutionalization of the environmental question in the public debate.
2   The institutionalization of the environmental question in politics.
3   The environmental question's actualization/accentuation of the value problematic of the modern.
4   The environmental question's transcendence of the modern.

The institutionalization of the environmental question in public debate

As already mentioned, it was the environmental movement that from the end of the Sixties and for about a decade thereafter brought the environmental question into the public debate, making the subject of the environment something that should be taken seriously, instead of considering it as something that can be used by everybody as they wish. During this period, the environmental movement considered the public environmental debate a battlefield that only they could define. They set the agenda or, in other words, they controlled the environmental discourse.

But as the problems related to the protection of the environment are gradually recognized by different interests and different 'solutions' manifest themselves in the public debate, the environmental movement loses its monopoly. From then on they have had to fight to get heard on equal terms with a wide range of other voices. A series of different discourses concerning the environment are now competing to get heard in the public debate and to define knowledge about the environment. An indication of this is the presentation of *ecology* as an environmental discourse, which implies that the environmental movement ceased to place the environmental question as a counterdiscourse to existing social practice.

As early as in the middle of the 1980s, the sociologist Ulrich Beck had stated that the established expert knowledge about the environment, and the use of this knowledge, must be confronted with alternative expertise and alternative forms of knowledge, and also that the established public institutions must be demolished or challenged. According to Beck, the established social institutions and expert cultures had already taken over the environmental discourse, including the definition of knowledge. Therefore, he saw a need for a counterculture – or what he called subpolitics (Beck, 1992, p183). This point of view also indicated that, by counterculture of knowledge, Beck understood something other than what the environmental movement represents. But the fact that in the middle of the 1980s, he asked for alternatives can in any event be interpreted as an indication of the extent to which established society was controlling both the definition of knowledge and the public discourse about environmental questions, and/or that environmental movements have lost their dominant position.

Another German sociologist, Klaus Eder, thought that, de facto, a reconstruction of the environmental public was taking place, and that this was leading to a change of the public sphere in general (Eder, 1996, pp205–206). In this way, environmental movements lost their monopoly of the ecological discourse, and instead created what he called an 'ecological masterframe', with new cognitive, normative and aesthetical frameworks for the public. This new masterframe not only served as a guide for environmental questions, but also established an ideology that complemented the two existing major ideologies, liberalism and socialism. Thus the environmental question was institutionalized in modern society, leaving in its wake a context that could not be controlled by any single party or movement. The environmental question had become part of modern society and was thereby exposing itself to the dynamism of the modern discourse that made the environmental question the object of processes of rationalization or disillusion (Eder, 1996, p205). But, at the same time, this question had started a process that had brought back *collective rationality* to the theory and practice of modern societies (Eder, 1996, p205).

This is, in effect, enough to indicate the core issue of the environmental question for the modern problematic. The new ecological ideology holds two dimensions, the *ethical* and the *identity*-based – Eder also calls them sub-frames – both of which are central to the modern problematic.

The *ethical* dimension in modern ecological ideology concerns the importance of ethical demands and ethical theories for the relation between modern political institutions and environmental questions. One example is the formation of the environment as a *collective good*, as seen in the ideas about sustainable development.

When the ethical dimension in the legitimization of political institutions is no longer totally dominated by the two ideologies of liberalism and socialism, then the environment as a collective good becomes an issue in terms of the question of allocation. Criteria must be found for a fair distribution of this *good*. This also concerns the allocation of restrictions that are thought to help reduce the damage to the environment.

Traditionally, the state has been the executor or creator of this equilibrium, but environmental questions, or decisions that influence the environment in general, are not only controlled by state institutions, but by a series of players, and, in the execution of its functions, the State itself is equally a 'consumer of the environment'. Therefore, the defence for this collective good becomes a political question, and the defence is left to those who define this *good*. The result is that this defence – or at least a part of it – has to be organized outside of the state and economic sphere. This is a determining factor for the understanding of the concept of non-governmental organizations (NGOs) and part of the explanation as to why both the State and the economic interests wish to be players in the decision-making process on environmental questions. This problematic will be discussed from several perspectives in the following chapters.

The *identity*-based dimension of the new ecological ideology concerns the continuing individualization in modern society as well as the symbolic figures that mark this. Where, for instance, the great ideologies' visions of freedom from the alienation of work or material equality, until now, managed to mould such figures of identification, this is no longer the case. The ecological ideology revitalizes the ideas of earlier figures linked to religious currents or creates the base for new self-knowledge and identity in a (new) modern society.[7]

Eder maintains that the emergence of both dimensions is explained by the fact that what is decisive is the way in which environmental questions and ideas are presented, and not the state of the environment in itself (Eder, 1996, p209). Without forming information and perspective, called 'packaging', nothing is gained, whether it be the legitimacy of political institutions, the mobilization for the environment, or the creation of rational attitudes. Compare, for example, the concept of sustainable development.

This is why Eder calls the ecological discourse of the 1980s and 1990s a historically and ideologically specific discourse – 'a reflexively organised symbolic packaging of environmental issues that is detached from the lifeworld'.[8] Certainly, this discourse has been institutionalized in the structure of modern society, but, simultaneously, it has neutralized competing 'packages' such as deep ecology and conservative ideologies of preservation. By so doing, it has made itself a dominating discourse, capable of including the environmental question in the public debate to such an extent that it has redefined what is considered rational in this debate.

Where, during the 1960s and 1970s, the environmental questions were problems directly transformed from the lifeworld, from the middle of the 1980s, we saw an institutionalization of environmental questions taking place by the establishment of an ecological masterframe, to which everybody could refer. This formed the basis for further development of the public space as a genuine modern condition or place that secure a cognitive, moral and aesthetic rationality in the culture of modernity (Eder, 1996, p216).

The institutionalization of the environmental question in the political apparatus

The institutionalization of the environmental question in the public debate is also materially manifested in the political apparatus, partly as a consequence of the institutionalization itself. On the other hand, such a material manifestation can also be characterized as part of the precondition for institutionalization. During the period in question, from whatever angle of perspective it is considered, an enormous expansion of the political machinery has taken place, which is now surveying modern environmental management and influencing the frames of reference for the political process. Thus we see not only an institutionalization of the environmental question taking place in the public debate, but also in the political mechanism.

An extension of the political apparatus that deals with environmental regulation is a necessity, because the political system accepts environmental questions and the related imperatives for action, whether they happen by free will or not. They range from the enforcement of directives and orders to gentle persuasion of a guiding and animating kind as well as to more explorative and discursive matters. Parts of these are regulated by the international relations in the environmental field, which have become increasingly involved, particularly within the EU. To this is added the whole effort concerning education and research, directed not only towards individual or narrowly defined environmental questions, but increasingly involving all new 'rationales' that are being created through the institutionalization of the environmental question within an ecological masterframe. As an example of this can be mentioned the former processing of purely empirical knowledge about nature with the goal of subordinating nature to progress, which has been replaced by efforts that also comprise insights into nature, based on aesthetic and moral perspectives. The environmental question is integrated in, and thereby enlarges a long series of other questions that need to be made in order to establish knowledge and make use of it.

The development, in its entirety, considered in connection with the above, has been characterized as an ecological modernization.[9] The characterization suggests a direct relation between environmental regulation and the process of modernization – that is, it is *not* seen as just another field of modernization/rationalization, but rather as a problematic that is providing the headlines for the process of modernization.

Such an understanding of the recent and actual developments in the environmental field is central to the present book. In Chapter 4, I therefore analyse a number of theories on ecological modernization in greater detail and also evaluate the practical implications of this point of view for the process of modernization. The analysis is based on the problems of ecology as a societal goal: (i) the analytical focus, in the next section of this chapter, on the way the theory comprehends the process of modernization; (ii) the analytical subject in Chapter 3.

Regarding the question of institutionalization of the environmental question in the political apparatus, it is enough to emphasize that concurrent with the construction of the political apparatus that handles modern environmental management this, itself, becomes the object of the rationalization process in modern society. Thus, the environmental effort, and its effectiveness, is influenced equally by those processes of rationalization – in fact it becomes directly dependent on them. So the goal of the environmental effort is not only the protection or amelioration of the influence on the environment as such, but is also conditioned by the above-mentioned efforts to rationalize. Thus these processes become fundamental factors for the sociological analysis of the environmental question.

The environmental question's accentuation of the value problematic of the modern

The moment the environmental question was institutionalized in the public debate and in the political mechanism, the processes of rationalization in modern society become dependent on a rational attitude to questions concerning ethics and values – that is: Why does this ecosystem have to be protected? What is its value compared to other ecosystems or in relation to society? What sort of priorities should animals have over humans, or vice versa? Indeed, is it possible to make priorities in this way? Is it defensive to expose species to the danger of extinction (just) because we have a certain societal goal? What is beautiful and what is ugly? Do we have to take this into consideration?

It is characteristic, however, that such questions are rarely posed.

Both economists and ecologists have tried to evade the questions, although each has approached them in their separate ways.

Economists have tried to make the question of the environment a matter of economics and have developed concepts by using the environment as a dustbin or, inversely, in protecting the environment against such use have served the market forces. But it has become evident that it is impossible to reduce the environment to an economic model, to make it a commodity. Yet not entirely, as it is possible to trade in pollution permits for specifically definable types of pollution. In effect, market conditions often play a decisive role in environmental regulations – that is, when the aim is to avoid distorting a market through a specific regulation. But in the last resort, none of this can encompass the environment in its totality, nor all the environmental relationships or questions. The reason for this is that environmental factors, individually, are unique and undergo permanent changes of contents that cannot be ruled by 'formulas', but also because moral questions remain unresolved when economic priorities are given.

Inversely we have seen how ecologists refer to nature itself as something that can give *society* meaning and aim, and can deliver the criteria for answers to questions of both a scientific and moral character. Ecology can guide us. Ecology can give us the answer to the question about how we can defend our actions and evaluations in a world devoid of meaning.

But we have also seen that this does not hold. It turns out to be a falsehood like all other previous proposals on how to build a bridge between language and the real world; a separation, as the following will clarify, precisely resulting from the modern perception of the world. Even non-modernistic environmental strategies are trapped in this problematic, because they continuously pose the question of *how* we can know *what* we have to do.

At this juncture, Szerszynski's account becomes most interesting for the present work. He asserts that the reason that this is the case is, to a large extent, due to the role the scientific mode of thinking plays in the environmental question, and even more fundamentally, to the fact that modern ethics is based on a model of the relationship between language and truth, embedded in a scientific discourse. Thus, only if it is presumed that language is the quintessence of science, can the modern ethical problematic arise (Szerszynski, 1996, p106).

In the modern view scientific truth is universal. It is specific statements (accounts, representations) of the surrounding world that pose universal validity irrespective of social context and culture. In pre-modern time, in antiquity and in the Middle Ages, there was no clear separation between the world of thoughts or words and the material world. Words and other objects had their natural sympathies and connections in a timeless order.[10] The surrounding world was treated as a text that should be interpreted rather than viewed as an object outside the language. Language had conjunctive status.

This is the conjunction that breaks down in modern times and so helps give birth to what is called *the modern problematic*: how can such a conjunction, or better such a true relation, be *created*?

The modern problematic – scientifically and ethically

In the following I will describe how the modern problematic arises with the development of the modern. The aim is specifically to clarify the modern conception of scientific and ethical truth. The latter concerns how to attain moral truth in a society where religion and tradition no longer have an attributive role in explaining what the right moral action is.[11]

The question is, therefore, what is understood by true knowledge, scientifically and ethically, and how it is possible to distinguish between science and ethics. This differentiation will later form a part of the account of what is understood by the modern as society – here called modernity, cf. Chapter 3. More specifically, this analysis of the history of theory intends to answer the question of how the environmental question is actualized or, as I also describe it, accentuates the modern value problematic. Or, expressed more simply, why is a specifically modern phenomenon such as the environmental question contributing to questions about central values in a culture that has the very aim of being value-free, whether generally or universally?

This formulation also highlights the fact that a characteristic of modern society is its lack of preparation to take care of problems that imply values and especially differentiation of values.

The modern problematic arose gradually between the 12th and 16th centuries, when language was assigned a disjunctive status insofar as the descriptive language was distinguished from the extra-discursive reality to which it refers. Thus the notion of the Middle Ages that harmony between language and the surrounding world was prescribed in advance was replaced by the concept that, by the use of a 'neutral' and 'objective' scientific discourse, thought and language *might be brought* into harmony. Language was thus considered a human construct rather than being part of a given reality (the world), and this view led to a scientific problem of representation, namely: what measures can guarantee the relation between the studied objects and the proposed statements about these objects (Woolgar, 1988, p31)?

All epistemological discussion presupposes the existence of a separation between language and extra-discursive reality. The disagreements are about how to create a connection – how true knowledge can be created.

All preceding thought that created modern science found that the determining guarantee for truth in relation to an extra-discursive reality was that a formalization and purification of language took place. To Hobbes[12] knowledge was dependent on clear words, purged of ambiguity. Bacon[13] distinguished between rhetoric and logic, where a precisely created, universal language for scientific use is seen as distinct from the rhetoric in normal language, ethics and in poetry. Locke[14] found that all use of language must be liberated from ambiguity (Szerszynski, 1996, p108).

In recent times such purification and formalization of language – as a solution to the modern problematic – is called *modernism*.

The modern ethical thinking that emerged is closely entangled with modern scientific discourse.

From the end of the 18th century, morality has been understood to have its own cultural or discursive space, in relation to the differentiation of science, ethics and the arts, which are considered to be governed by their own internal and independent laws.

Furthermore, ethical language becomes *disjunctive*, like the descriptive languages, by the introduction of a separation between *context* and *meaning*, between *description* and *allegation*. In classical times, morality was bound up with social context. But in modern times, morality is seen as being separated from the historical conditions in a specific society, a specific role or a specific situation. It becomes a matter of course to distinguish between facts and values, between the human language and moral realities. Nature, which now becomes the world of facts, no longer gives humanity any indications as to its role in the world (Blumenberg, 1983, pp137–143, referred to in Szerszynski, 1996, p109).

Ethics, now liberated from religion and the traditional bonds of earlier societies, is therefore considered to be a form of universal knowledge governed by its own internal rules and capable of expressing itself rationally and in the abstract.

The principal question for modern ethics is therefore: *how can the human subject as an autonomous observer of reality – or at least of part of reality – obtain moral knowledge?*

The question is parallel to the principal question for the modern sciences, as, in the sciences, it becomes the task of the philosophy of morality (that is, ethics) to create a universal, neutral and abstract moral language that precisely indicates the moral characteristics in every situation.[15]

Such a relation between human language and moral reality can be created principally in two different ways, in a modern – especially modernistic – discourse: *origin and autonomy* (Crook, 1991, pp174–181):

- As to *origin*: moral knowledge is derived from an extra-discursive reality or a primary, *indubitable* knowledge as, for example, Descartes' *cogito*. Or it arises in an epochal breach that can distil 'true' knowledge from suspicious familiarity to something false – that is, as the separation of medieval superstition and modern science.
- As to *autonomy*: different forms of moral knowledge are presented as descending from their own internal laws, separated from external influence and material interests or historical coincidences.

In this way, modern ethicists have tried to build a bridge between language and reality and produce moral norms for action. In all cases, the attempts are motivated by the perception of an extra-discursive reality – for example, *Utilitarianism* – abstract concepts about human happiness, across different human contexts; *Kantianism* – the sovereign individual's rational action, confronted with external authorities and habits, in a simple concordance with universal laws; *Rights theory* – humanity as something transcendentally given more than something culturally determined; *Intuitionism* – objective relations not related to nature, where the knowledge results in self-evident moral truths that do not have to, and cannot, be justified further; *Emotionalism* – presumed non-discursive preferences and attitudes (Szerszynski, 1996, p110).

However, these forms of original or autonomous justification for ethical values, independently of culture and debate/discourse, are problematic. For instance, human happiness cannot be considered a concept that can give us criteria for decisive choices. Happiness is not a stable extra-discursive reality used as an argument for and emphasis of moral standpoints. The same can be said about attitudes and values when they are ascribed to individuals as personal attributes.

So a vacuum is created between, on the one hand, modernity's disjunctive perception of language as something that can represent an extra-discursive reality and, on the other, the situation whereby different attempts to find original or autonomous reasons for ethical values outside of culture and debate collapse. Thus ethics becomes a purely human project, since the 'true'character of the world is no longer capable of telling us what to do.

If, however, we could identify an autonomous and purified ethical language, guided by its own internal laws and based on an extra-discursive reality, then language and reality could be brought into harmony. Two fundamental reasons prevent this from happening. First, the perception of a world behind the language, to which language refers, is a result of our modern conception and is therefore not available when we are talking about giving the reasons for language as such. Second, the ideal of a formalized language, abstracted from the social and cultural reality, is impossible to attain (Szerszynski, 1996, p111).

Ecology as the solution

Here ecology enters the scene and offers another solution. Instead of trying to purify and formalize the discourse to assure its agreement with moral realities, ethics give credence to our engagement with the world. Instead of accepting a separation between facts and values, as a consequence of our modern disjunctive perception of language, ecology insists that *nature* tells us what to do. In this way, ethics is no longer a mere human project, but a confirmation of the laws that are written into nature itself.

However, ecology is *not* capable of surpassing the modern problematic, no matter how hard it tries and how much merit can be ascribed to it by its recognition of human limitations, and by its rejection of more or less mystical assumption that we do not fit into the scheme of things because of our destructive nature. This can be demonstrated whether ecology presents itself in a modernistic manner (modernism/neomodernism) or adopts romantic forms (expressionism and traditionalism).

A determining reason for this is the fact that ecological thinking is mostly based on precisely this unattainable modernistic ideal about truth in total harmony with an extra-discursive reality. This kind of dependence is not only something from which ecological thinking is suffering; it can be traced back to the environmental movement as such, to its very substance and starting point. The way it gained sympathy was to base its statements on scientific insights and moral criteria that had a touch of neutrality or incontestability. Furthermore, it often argued that environmental destruction was irrational, or inversely that environmental destruction indicated that society was not sufficiently rational.

An example of this is the work of Barry Commoner who, in the wider circles of the environmental movement, especially those parts that had a scientific approach, both in the US and in Western Europe, was an ideal model with enormous influence. His four ecological laws: 'Everything is connected to everything else', 'Everything must go somewhere', 'Nature knows best' and 'There is no such thing as a free lunch' (Commoner, 1972, pp33–48), are famous for their simplicity. In Commoner's view, the universal laws of nature can be unveiled by rational science that, accordingly, tells us what to do. His vision is of a centrally governed society that is based on scientific ecology, to which the social structure and the application of science are established. Such a society is not only capable of arranging people's relationships with nature but also of organizing production 'according to the rational-use value of the final product rather than by the value added in the course of production' (Commoner, 1972, p287).

Commoner's vision is thus clearly anti-capitalistic. In this view, planning and central government according to rational scientific principles is not an unattainable ideal, but the way to assure that nature is not damaged. Rationality is the establishing of society following the premises of nature, not of capital.

Even though this may today seem equally super-technocratic and naïve, this is not the whole explanation of why ecology is incapable of creating an irreproachable ethics. Alongside the concept of modernism as it is represented by Commoner among others, there exists another 'softer' concept. The latter departs considerably from 'strong modernism', albeit it still manages to stick to the ecological way of thinking, and perhaps this is exactly the reason why it is capable of doing so.

In the following analysis, I will stress the neomodernistic version of ecological thinking – mainly because it is neomodernistic ecological thinking that has won the dominating position in the fight with different concepts of ecology. Eder's formulation has dictated the framework for the institutionalization of ecology in the public debate. Considering it is this kind of thinking that can bring understanding to the visible attempts to further new ecological concepts of regulation, this final aspect has been taken up for further analysis in this book.

That the romantic perceptions of ecology are subsequently discussed is due to the fact that they demonstrate, in an exemplary manner, that it does not have to be technocratic visions about government and control that serve as the Achilles heel, but the idea about an extra-discursive reality reflecting the truth.

Neomodernism in ecological thinking

Neomodernism not only departs from the idea of the possibility of attaining truth, as a perfect reflection of an extra-discursive reality. It also abandons the perception of strong or traditional modernism that knowledge is universal or timeless, and so a *historical dimension* is added to the gaining of knowledge. Truth is not determined by something extra-discursive and original, but by *how* knowledge is constructed in accordance with formal autonomous procedures and preconditions.

The move towards a historical dimension in the construction of knowledge has taken place parallel to the whole development of the modern conception of knowledge – that is, during the last 200 years. According to Bacon, knowledge was something created via a systemic classification and incomplete knowledge, was only seen as the result of *temporary* difficulties. Hegel had already changed this conception and saw knowledge as something created *in* the historical process. To him, the dialectic process was a historically ongoing process. Kant, too, contributed to an inclusion of the historical aspect, regarding categories for understanding the world as originating within ourselves – that is, being man-made – although he perceived this in a static way. Through the 19th and 20th centuries this static viewpoint was gradually dissolved, and with the development of neomodernism, knowledge was regarded as being historical and provisional, not timeless. The scientific character of knowledge was thus more determined by the procedural and institutional conditions for its construction than by the contents as such (Schnädelbach 1984, pp81–91). Popper, in particular, was instrumental for the break-through of neomodernism as distinct from strong modernism, and what also followed – logical positivism (Popper, 1968).

In this way, the whole perspective as regards the creation of knowledge moved from systematization to innovation. The notion that science was a direct reflection of reality decreased. In contrast, science was increasingly put on a par with human knowledge that is fallible, albeit it was considered that the progressive character of science could be assured through correct methods.

Thus three conditions characterize neomodernism in relation to strong modernism:

- It does not consider knowledge timeless and universal, but *historically* determined.
- It underlines *how* knowledge is created or attained and in this respect gives priority to *form* over *content*.
- As a consequence of this the production of knowledge is *not centrally steered*, but is by 'nature' decentralized.

The ethics developed on the basis of this neomodernism, which notably influence ecological thinking, has – via its liberation from the thought of an extra-discursive reality in relation to which evaluations and attitudes must concord – been able to attach weight to procedures and practices for establishing morality and command. Already 'the Kantian turn in ethical thought had focused attention on the *form* of valid ethical judgements – on features such as universality – but had still retained the idea that getting the form right would itself lead to a substantive ethical *content*' (Benhabib, 1992, pp12, 25). However, neomodernism weakens the already degraded interest in content even more by considering the historical binding of moral evaluation real and not just random.

Parallel to this is the uncertainty in obtaining certain knowledge about nature that makes some ecological thinkers adopt neomodernistic views. Instead of pursuing knowledge about nature that can be transposed to a centralized, nationally governed and planned ecological society – a knowledge that they do not believe can be established – these thinkers strive to produce formal and procedural conditions in such a way that a fallible but also privileged knowledge can emerge. So the neomodernistic ecology focuses on the setting up of a framework that creates dynamism in a desired direction, although the direction at the time might not be known. Nevertheless, this is considered more 'secure' and preferable to an indefinable goal that can be reached by planning and management (Szerszynski, 1996, p115).

It is of course possible to argue that the way forward is only accessible through discussion and debate without adopting a neomodernistic point of view. It is also possible to claim that good *does* exist, that moral prescriptions *do* exist and that these are best gained through debate and argument. The latter position is comparable to a genuine modernistic view of a static and timeless truth. But we are on neomodernistic ground if formalization inflicts the debate that by nature is necessary for obtaining a valuable viewpoint, and if 'good', no matter what, *is* what comes out of the debate and not something already existing that is discovered through this process. Finally, form has given precedence over content, the very dilemma that will cause neomodernism to be caught in nihilism, which it originally set out to abolish.

Szerszynski (1996, pp115–118) mentions four central examples of this that will be discussed below. They are not only important as an illustration of the arguments at this point. Three of the authors of these examples play a decisive role in the further presentation of the problematic of this book. Furthermore, as I am neither in agreement with the concepts of the four examples, nor with important aspects of Szerszynski's interpretation of these, the analysis will also provide a critique of these points of view. The critique is developed further and put into perspective in the following chapters. The order of the examples presented is determined by the degree to which they abandon content in relation to form.

Four examples of neomodernism

The first example is an approach to the environmental question with '*deliberative democracy*' as represented by Dryzek (1992) and Miller (1992). To know what we ought to do, according to this viewpoint, we need a new political forum with free access to information and political debate. Technical expertise can never alone determine what ought to be done in a democratic society, nor can the ecologists' intuition. It has to grow from discussions between real and well-founded actors in accordance with common rules for good arguments.

Accordingly, neomodernism maintains that validity of knowledge and the viewpoints are conditioned not by their content, but by the purely formal characteristics of the discussion – an unconstrained, fair and open discussion. The result is valid simply because it *is* the result.

According to Szerszynski, this kind of democratic deliberation to the environmental question follows Habermas' discourse, with its aim of avoiding the naïve universalism of strong modernism. Furthermore, it follows Habermas' view that criteria for testing the validity of statements exist implicitly in every situation where dialogue takes place. Precisely as in the neomodernistic perception of science, where the idea about a timeless, static truth is nothing but a decisive and impracticable ideal, Habermas works, according to Szerszynski (1996, p116), with a decisive ideal, the 'ideal situation for dialogue' and 'unbiased communication'. It is presumed to be the necessary competence for communicative action and thereby can guarantee the non-enforced consensus (Habermas, 1979, p64). Whatever comes out of the debate is not a result of the rhetorical power of conviction but of the inner rationality of the debate.

It is therefore the establishment of social conditions and frameworks for public debate about environmental questions that is the central point of this approach, and the validity of statements are related to those conditions and not to an evaluation of contents.

For this kind of neo-modernist environmentalism, the shift away from content and towards form manifests as an emphasis on procedures and institutions. Rather than attempting to articulate concrete prescriptions of how we should live with nature, it concerns itself with setting up the social conditions for rational public debate.

*   The environmental movement, for example, is valued by Habermas not because of any substantive ethic of nature it might promote (indeed he denies the possibility of such an ethic (Habermas, 1982, p245)), but because of its defence of such communicative spaces within society from colonisation by the instrumental reason of economics and power politics.*

Szerszynski, 1996, p116

In this way, Szerszynski uses Habermas to support his view of deliberative democracy with regard to the environmental question. It is correct that Habermas in the quoted reference refuses to attach anything that concerns the ethic of content to nature in itself. But this does not mean that he eliminates all content from his ethics. To use Habermas as support for a deliberative democratic standpoint like the above is precisely to neglect his insistence on the normative content of the modern. True enough, he does not anchor the normative content of the modern in nature but in *reason* that, according to Habermas has retained a unity he calls *the communicative everyday practice*. Therefore by 'the ideal situation of dialogue' and 'non-distorted communication' Habermas implies the existence of a unity of reason in the communicative everyday practice which he describes as the better argument's constraint-free constraint. Furthermore, the existence of such a form of unity of reason is only possible if attached to a lifeworld different from the differentiated economic system and the differentiated administration, which are both dominated by instrumental reason.

Therefore 'the inner rationality of the debate' that Szerszynski refers to, cannot be displayed in every situation, and every outcome is not valid because it *is* the outcome. As will be shown in more detail in the following chapter, the above concepts in Habermas' theory about the modern imply a completely different understanding of content and form than what was expressed by the deliberative approach to the environmental question. The development of the 'better argument' and 'the communicative reason', different from a mere instrumental reason in a democratic debate presupposes Habermas' distinction between the lifeworld and system as well as a description of how the implied rationales can be separated or how a comprehensive abolition of the built-in contradictions can be established. Habermas' distinction between lifeworld and system is determined in more detail in the following chapter.

Finally, it might be appropriate here - and this is developed further in the next section – to draw attention to the fact that Habermas, at some point in the middle of the 1980s, feared the green movements' anti-modernism and their return to pre-modern conditions (Habermas, 1981c). So it seems ironic when Szerszynski 'credits' Habermas for being of the opinion that the environmental movement supports the neomodernistic view.

The second example is *the free market approach to the environment*, represented by Anderson and Leal (1991), Bennet and Block (1991). They insist that the market mechanism should determine what is environmentally desirable, and not rational debate. In a pluralistic society they consider it to be the task of the state to maintain the framework for the proper functioning of the free market, but not to enforce specific ethical attitudes onto individuals. In particular, they consider marketable rights to environmental goods and nuisances the only way to solve the environmental crisis. This implies, for example, privatizing 'common goods' as marketable pollution permits.

Notwithstanding those differences between the 'deliberative democratic' and the 'free-market' approach, Szerszynski insists on attributing to them a common perception of the existence of 'good':

> *Despite their clear political differences, the deliberative-democracy and the free market environmentalists occupy a very similar position in the neo-modernist spectrum. Both of them reject the idea of substantive ethics or techniques of nature being arrived at through monological deliberation and 'imposed' on society. For both, the good for society can only be the outcome of an actual interactive process governed by abstract, formal rules. For both, the outcome is good simply* because *it is the outcome of such a process. But also, for both, that process 'whether rational debate or market exchange' has an innate rationality that, in principle, will guarantee that the outcome really* is *the best outcome – the good. Both deliberative-democracy and free market environmentalism, then, retain the ghostly presence of a 'real' to which normative statements can and should correspond, even if that 'real' can never be timelessly captured.*
>
> Szerszynski, 1996, pp116–117

I admit that I find this comparison equally naïve, superficial and arbitrary. Considering the above discussion of Szerszynski's reading of deliberative democracy, the comparison might be said to reflect the depth of this reading, particularly concerning the interpretation of Habermas. Szerszynski's lack of distinction between the system and the lifeworld leads to his attribution theory in terms of the economic system, the market, of the creation of normative values as being comparable to the norms that must be valid for a democratic debate. But the question is, is it not the separation of these 'worlds' that is necessary to make clear in which way economic demands are in contradiction with concerns about the environment?

As a third example, which to an even greater extent than the two preceding examples stresses form over content, Szerszynski draws attention to Ulrich Beck's ideas about 'reflexive modernization'. Beck, too, emphasizes the formal social framework for the solution of the ecological crisis – a reflexive societal self-criticism – instead of content-based ethics relating to the environment. Szerszynski compares Beck's formulation of a reflexive modernization of society as an elaboration of the modern project – as a radicalization and generalization of doubt in the modernization process in relation to all dogmatic claims of knowledge – to Habermas' description[16] of communicative action (Szerszynski, 1996, p117).

Generally, however, he does not assign to Beck any recognition of Habermas' theories and understanding of the importance of a rational debate. Indeed, quite the opposite, as we see from the quote below:

> *However, Beck does not seem to share Habermas's faith in the idea that reasoned debate (form) can lead to 'truth' (content), however historically situated. Reflexive modernisation guarantees not that the future is better or worse, but only that it is different (Beck, 1996, p40). Conflicts over risk-definitions, for example, are not settleable* de jure, *by any recourse to objectivity or rationality (pp36–37), but only* de facto, *by the reflex of society riven by epistemic conflicts (pp32–33). Beck rejects critical theories of society such as that of Habermas – theories which impose the content of their ethico-political standards onto society in order to make their critiques – in favour of a purely formal account of a society divided by 'sectional rationalities' (p33). In so far as reflexivity is about 'reflection', rather than just reflex, it is the self-consciousness of humanity becoming aware of the radical contingency of all knowledge claims. While surely correct in its rejection of strong modernist claims to an 'objective' knowledge of nature which can tell us what to do, Beck's position reveals its capture within the modern problematic in its all but abandonment of the 'real' as a constraint on human self-definition.*
>
> Szerszynski, 1996, p117

Given that it is correct that Beck does not accept Habermas' critical theory, it is remarkable that Beck – like Habermas – *divides* rationality in connection with *reflexive* modernity. When Beck talks about this specific form of modernity it is equally remarkable that he is only capable of describing its results as different in relation to something existing, and that he, in Szerszynski's words, almost abandons 'the real', in preference to the radical coincidences of society. In the next chapter I will present a critique of Beck's concept of reflexive modernity and generally demonstrate his lack of understanding of the modernization process, which will form a partial explanation of these shortcomings.

Abandonment of the 'real' is actually present in Szerszynski's fourth example – Martin Hajer's version of *cultural politics* in terms of the environmental question. Hajer gets even with all attempts at arriving at something substantively 'real', including Habermas' belief in rationality in an open debate and in a broader sense the belief in progress. Instead, he envisages a democratic process with a kind of cultural competition between different discourses. In this process all content concerning a determined nature that can function as place of origin for knowledge has disappeared completely, even if seen as a limitless or unattainable goal for knowledge. The only thing left is what Hajer calls 'story lines' about nature –a kind of 'thought tracks' for what the problem is and how one can act. All that is left is merely the autonomy in mankind's actions, once and for all deprived of modernistic illusions about cultural self-knowledge. For Hajer, the question is therefore not 'what we should do' to protect nature, but inversely 'what sort of nature and what sort of society we want' (Hajer, 1996, p259).

This staunch neomodernism of Hajer seems to me to be the most consistent of the four examples. It leads him to consider ecology from a consistently social point of view, and this implies that there is a need for democratizing the decision processes in opposition to a techno-corporative regulation led by experts. This position implies, at the same time, that he has difficulties locating his point of departure in relation to the process of modernization. He thus lacks an explanation of the way in which the concrete modernization influences the possibility of choosing 'what sort of nature and what sort of society we want'. But he formulates a completely independent version of ecological modernization capable of including the participatory tools in the environmental politic of the last decades. His position therefore warrants a separate analysis, which will be formulated in Chapter 4.

These four examples of neomodernistic positions in the environmental question bring the modern problematic to a pinnacle. When the attempt to reconcile language and world is abandoned in favour of the pure autonomy of discourse, modernism becomes a project of formalization. The formalization previously used to guarantee agreement has become a goal in itself. The more one follows this direction, the more content yields to pure form, the closer is the return to 'the world view in the heart of the modern problematic' – a picture of a forlorn mankind that is faced with the task of pure self-assertion in a meaningless world that no longer tells them/us what we should do (Szerszynski, 1996, p118).

In this respect, there are only two ways for ecology to go, and both ways are shaded by the nihilistic emptiness that modernism at one and the same time presumes and abandons, and that none of them can lead us away from. We either have a technocracy dependent on the legitimacy of the abolition of its own fortuitousness, or we are left with nihilism, which has emerged from mankind's free creation and affirmation of opinions in a world that has no meaning in itself (Szerszynski, 1996, pp118, 119).

Romantic ecological thinking

An evident question in this situation is, therefore, whether romantic ecology has any alternative to offer. This question arises because neomodernism leads to a situation where the problems of creating a connection between language and reality have not diminished. In effect, neomodernism has created a gap between language and reality, while romantic ecology does the opposite by reintroducing consciousness into the world.

> *In many ways, the oft-noted romanticist strands within contemporary environmentalism might seem a far more promising place to look for an escape from the modern problematic (cf. Harvey, 1993, pp15–19, 29–31). Romanticism offers a very different picture of the world and the human place in it to that of modernism. It sees nature as filled with meaning and*

value, rather than a neutral backdrop for human projects. It has an emphasis on ethical content, rather than the formalization of ethical language. It focuses not on proportional knowledge, but on immediate experience, the fusion of knower and known. Surely here, if anywhere, we can find the overthrow of the alienated consciousness that lies at the heart of the modern problematic. Perhaps it is through this kind of ecology that we can know what to do.

Szerszynski, 1996, p120

Romantic ecology exists in different variations from which two main forms can be derived: the expressive and the traditionalist. By *expressivist ecology* is understood the notion that individuals can recreate their connection with nature through the regaining of an authentic condition that has otherwise been lost through the artificiality of social existence. This kind of romanticism is a recurring feature from Rousseau to Wordsworth and the American transcendentalists, and is expressed in contemporary environmental movements such as, for example, depth ecology, radical eco-feminism, bio-regionalism and neo-primitivism.

Inversely, by *traditionalist ecology* is understood the belief that a non-alienated existence is possible only through a re-establishment (re-embedding) of a concrete social community and substantive traditions. This kind of collective romanticism is found in Hegel, in the medievalist-inspired English social criticism of the 19th century, to which Carlyle, Ruskin and Morris belong, as well as in the new commentators such as MacIntyre, Walzer and Etzioni. In the contemporary environmental movement is the conviction of the shared mother tongue, which holds that traditional forms of knowledge, by their very nature, are ecologically superior (Szerszynski, 1996, pp120, 124).

The core belief of expressivism is that the 'true self' is in existence, and that humanity has been alienated from the authentic existence of civilization. Where modernism offers progress, expressionism has declined – a fall from a natural, pre-social existence in harmony with the providence of nature to our actual artificial existence. However, by the rediscovery of our natural true self, in tandem with everything else, we can defeat this alienation in our relation to others and to nature.

Deep ecology's (Næss, 1991), the best known and most developed form of expressivist ecology, main aim is to develop an ecological consciousness that no longer endorses the boundaries of this world between one species and another, or between these and the rest of the world. Therefore, depth ecology makes a shift from epistemology to ontology – from proportional knowledge to the recreation of authentic existence.

The denial of subject–object dualism looks like a distinctive placement of oneself outside modernism, and the radical placing of the self inside a nature filled with sense and values seems far from the lonely Gnostic version of mankind trapped in a foreign world (Szerszynski, 1996, p122).

A closer look reveals that depth ecology simply reproduces the way of modernism telling us what we ought to do. It reproduces modernism's strategy of *origin.* Whereas modernism invokes an extra-discursive reality to underwrite abstract, privileged 'knowledge', expressivism is an asocial 'nature' that serves as the final guarantor for an abstract, authentic 'being':

> *As such, expressivism is as vulnerable as modernism to the charge that this strategy can only be carried out at the expense of denying the radical embeddedness of identity and knowledge – as if there is a reality which stands outside culture, history and judgement.*
>
> Szerszynski, 1996, p123

Traditionalist ecology also falls into this trap and reproduces the modernist strategy of *origin*. But traditionalism has a different starting point than expressivism, and also appears to promise a sustainable alternative to modernism. Instead of denying the embeddedness of identity and experience within culture and convention, it affirms it. Like expressivism, it counters the progressive narrative of modernism with a narrative of decline, not in relation to an original, pre-social existence, but rather to the more proximate and concrete condition, in which all the ties of community and tradition have been removed. It recognizes the connectedness and interdependence of all human beings, not *outside* an alienating society as expressivism finds it, but *within* society. Finally, it has no idea of an autonomous, asocial nature with redeeming power; in effect, both nature and humanity have to be 'saved' by being integrated in a substantive tradition.

The work of 19th-century artist and social reformer John Ruskin was an example of this. He created a forceful combination of aesthetics, philosophy and politics by fusing Thomas Carlyle's conservative social philosophy with William Wordsworth's mysticism of nature, which had made its contribution to seeing the English landscape in a specific way, while at the same time he railed against the effects of the Enlightenment's rationalism, capitalism and industrialism.[17] He saw the latter as dissolving the traditional ties that kept society together, creating a world of individuals ruled by market transitions and 'mammonism'. Ruskin believed not only that there were virtues in living with traditions, but that there was an objective moral order from which the increasingly de-traditionalized modern person was being disastrously disengaged (Szerszynski, 1996, pp124–126).

But since Ruskin also acknowledged Wordsworth's perception that the divine experience of the landscape was dependent on the mental and sentimental conditions of the observer – that is to say subjectivity – he had to form a non-subjective ethic as a starting point *within* the modern problematic. He therefore recognized the existence of an eternal holy and moral reality, but that reality had to be mediated through a language that had become detached from it. Ruskin solved this paradox of securing an accurate correspondence between a language understood as representational and a reality understood as being represented in following Thomas Carlyle, and proposed a solution that was literary and artistic in character. Literature and art provided a prism through which eternal moral realities could be discerned (Spear, 1984, pp6, 94).

We thus see how Ruskin also reproduces the modern strategy with *originality*. He accepts the terms of the modern problematic – language and reality being separated. As a modernist, he believes that language and the world can revert to the notion that a timeless 'constant reality' can serve as an anchor to prevent the nihilistic free play of language. However, for him, this is not achieved through purification or formalization, but by way of a substantive aesthetic tradition. Ruskin shares with modernism the view that a transcendent reality – now a moralistic reality – is what lies behind language and culture.

The so-called new communitarians represent a non-realistic traditionalism, inspired by Edmund Burke's 18th-century traditionalism, which does not posit the content of a form of life by reference to a transcendent moral reality (MacIntyre, 1981; Waltzer, 1983). By leaving the realistic strategy, they instead lead traditionalism into a formalist one of *autonomy*.

So traditionalism, too, is caught in the modern problematic. As soon as it leaves the reference to a transcendent reality with which a given form of life must be in concordance, it falls back to a position from which it can only specify the formal characteristics and never the content of the ethic or ecological life. Just as traditionalism cannot tell us what we have to do, but only how we should do it – traditionally. Precisely as was the case for neomodernism, for neo-traditionalism human knowledge becomes just that: human knowledge, severed from any opportunity of correspondence, simply human calling to human in a world without meaning (Szerszynski, 1996, p129).

Summing up, we can ascertain that ecology cannot tell us what we have to do. Our contemporary moral traditions, from which ecological thinking derives, are bound by modernism's understanding of language and the world to the extent that they are incapable of helping us to leave it. Modernist, expressivist and traditionalist ecology all either attempt to assign correspondence to an *origin*, a universal noumenal 'real' lying behind the phenomenal world, or they abandon this in favour of *autonomy* – the pure groundless operation of argument, spontaneity or tradition. To the extent that they do the former, they tell us *what* we have to do, but only insofar as they project a particular frozen vision of social relations onto the 'real' and then interpret from this. To the extent that they do the latter, they cannot tell us *what* we have to do, only *how* we have to do it – rationally, authentically or traditionally.

No matter what, the nihilistic worldview is always there – either suppressed fearfully in the background or thrust triumphantly forward. Ecology, while seeming to promise a re-embedding of human choices and judgements within a framework, which transcends mere human wishes, fails to do so. It always leads us back to the nihilistic condition of self-assertion in a world without purpose and meaning. Ecology, after all, does not seem to be able to tell us what we have to do (Szerszynski, 1996, p130; Milbank, 1993).

A way out of the problematic?

Szerszynski's proposal about where to look for a way out of this situation is mainly based on Wittgenstein and Heidegger. He proposes a way to think about the ecological crisis that emphasizes our homeliness in the world rather than our alienness. First, rather than seeing the world as not existing outside language, we need to see it as constituted through language. Second, just as language cannot be understood only in terms of representation of, and in correspondence with, an extra-discursive reality, just as little can it be understood merely as a human construction. Accordingly, he believes that the consequence must be that 'the human subject is not simply a user of language. It is the language that speaks' (Szerszynski, 1996, pp131–132).

These points of view about how to understand ourselves, and the world we live in, lead Szerszynski to the fundamental viewpoint that we do not use or construct the world, just as we do not construct or simply use language. We are placed in the world – we inhabit it. Our actions and choices are not crafted in a space outside the world, and then exercised on that world, but are woven into the texture of that world.[18]

Therefore he must on the one hand abandon modernism while on the other hand maintain that we have to include all three examined positions into a much larger context without abandoning any of them. Furthermore, he has had to endorse Hajer's idea that the environmental crisis is one of the few remaining places where modernity can still be reflected upon (Hajer, 1996, p265).

With this thesis of Hajer's, Szerszynski confirms the theme that has been the starting point for this examination, namely why modernity is such a core problematic in ecologically oriented sociology. Briefly, this is because a sociological analysis of the environmental question cannot abstain from posing questions about modernity in terms of social organization as a type of society, since its self-destructive behaviour does not give any meaning, and precisely for that reason it nurtures a hope of saving its 'surrounding world' from horror.

What Szerszynski proposes or imagines is probably nothing less than a change of paradigm.[19] But it seems to me that he is himself caught in the very paradigm he wishes to abandon. Even though I can follow Szerszynski the whole way and find that his analysis adds an important contribution to the understanding of the contemporary deadlock in the scientific analysis of the environmental problematic, he only tells half the story. Something is quite simply missing. A change of paradigm must, after all, be motivated by decisive social changes, which, among other things, entail that science needs to be based on new concepts. Szerszynski touches on this when he writes that 'my point is that the nihilistic picture is not the timelessly true human condition, but a historically specific understanding of the world thrust on us due, largely, to a shift in our understanding of language, knowledge and reality at the end of the Middle Ages' (Szerszynski, 1996, pp130–131).

In my opinion, he remains caught in the modern problematic precisely because something hinders him from seeing a historically specific feature of the social organization of modernity – namely capitalism's reduplication of society in concrete and abstract work, matter and value, utility value and exchange value as formulated by Marx, or lifeworld and system as Habermas formulates it (cf. Chapter 3). This reduplication resulted in Marx' thesis about reification: utility value is the matter, the concrete, the content, the environment succumbing to the exchange value's inconsiderate abstraction; exchange value, or simply value, is the core form of the capitalistic society that gradually subsumes all activity and being. For Habermas, the coupled concepts of lifeworld and system led to the formulation of the thesis of colonization: that the system colonizes the lifeworld, where it is not only the economic forms that subsume, as was Marx's understanding, but also the systemic administration based on power. The form or the formal is the central 'core' of modern capitalist society. So it is not so strange that all 'solutions' of the modern problematic end up in, or rather cannot avoid the form, which makes the content secondary.

I have thus suggested that Szerszynski does not realize why contents give way to form, and for that reason he remains tied down in what he has described so accurately with neomodernism as an example. This critique will be further developed in Chapter 3, where the above concepts are discussed, and where I will also try to show that some of the most ardent defenders of modernity only consider half the topic.

Indeed, Szerszynski gets no further than formulating that we do not construct the world, but are placed in it and inhabit it. But this is not a new theory.[20] These formulations correspond precisely to Habermas' critique of what he calls the monological subject-object model of the philosophy of conscience (TCA, I, pp518–533; TKH, II, pp11–68). He means by this that what is excluded is the fact that we, as human cognitive creatures and users of language, are from the beginning embedded in structures of language and intersubjectivity. So we cannot, as the philosophy of consciousness suggests, consider the acting and cognitive subject as isolated and without interlocutor. This is also the decisive point of departure for Habermas in the formulation of a communicative theory of action, as we will see in the next chapter.

Analogous to this, I conclude that Szerszynski is very precise in his description of the modern problematic. However, as regards his suggestions as to how we may be able to get out of it, he does not get any further than, unconsciously or unintentionally, confirming that we have to break with the monological character of the philosophy of consciousness.

But prior to the account of a breach, we will deal with the reactions to the above situation. The loss of meaning and nihilism that accompany the modern conception of the world, which, within the last quarter of a century, once again has manifested such consequences as those described in the introduction to this chapter, have also led to attempts at formulating postmodern viewpoints, or critiques, of the categories of reason in the modern. This has not exactly taken place in a quiet way in the last 25 years, and it has had a determining influence on contemporary sociological thinking and on how it considers the environmental question.

The environmental question's transcending modernity

The account above has shown that not only is modernity's ethical value sphere void of imagination, but the entire project of modernity is exposing its vacuity. Indeed, one might call this a warning shot that highlights the serious issues at stake.

Not surprisingly, postmodern critics attack modernity at its weakest point, when, as seen during the 1960/70s, the belief in the 'good life' behind the world's sparkling façade was impaired. From then on ecology, or nature itself, became the good things of life legitimizing, as discussed above, a continuation of the modern way forward. A belief that continues to the present day. Yet, it is important to keep in mind that such an ecological viewpoint or, indeed, the notion that nature itself is universally good with a universal value of its own in need of no further legitimizing and justifying discourse, is largely upheld by the natural sciences. However, the postmodern critical thinkers discovered long ago what 'dead ends' and dangers such a point of departure holds.[21]

In his thesis on the dissolution of the grand narratives, the French philosopher Jean-François Lyotard (1924–1998) was the first to put his name to such accusations. According to Lyotard, the dissolution of the 'grand narratives' was founded on the notion that the grand or superior narratives of 'truth', 'reason' and 'progress' that used to legitimize politics, justice and social norms had been discredited. Rather than being the source for development in science and technology which improved the advancement of society and people's universal liberation, they turned out to be means of domination and control – and, in special circumstances, the means for political systems of terror (e.g. Stalinism and Nazism). Notably, the political developments in Europe after Stalin, the ever-returning economic crises during the whole of the 20th century, as well as the enormous advance in science and technology, all testify to the fact that development has never been under the sway of human requirements in legitimizing modern advances.

The belief in science and technological development as a source of progress and human liberation has been replaced by *doubt*, a dominating feature in contemporary society. This doubt has not come about because of lack of outcome, but rather because the extensive results of both the sciences and technology in their advance have proved both destructive and suppressive. Progress has not bettered human values by liberating human beings, for example. Indeed, science and technology can no longer be regarded as being the emancipating forces.

Lyotard's main question is, therefore, what sort of legitimacy future development should be given? The question is whether a situation can continue where scientific and technological progress is legitimized merely on the merit of its ability to further the political, economic and technocratic institutions of society?

In posing these questions, Lyotard has, in a fundamental way, brought modern society's values and progress into the debate.

Concurrently, there was a shift in French thinking. The tenets from the heydays of structuralism that prevailed the decade before radically changed to what is now called poststructuralism. Michel Foucault (1926–1984), Jacques Derrida (1930–2004) and Jean Baudrillard (1929–2001) are considered the poststructuralist theorists, to mention but a few of the most well-known names.

Characteristic of the poststructural movement was the principle that it maintained structuralism's approach of reduction in carrying out meaning and subjective analyses, but gave up the intensive scrutiny of structuralism, which by analysing inconsistencies of texts revealed the underlying logic. This critical approach to systems and theories had affinities, on the one hand, with postmodern artistic movements, notably architecture, and on the other hand in the critique of modern social systems and modes of thoughts. Lyotard became a useful reference for many a comprehensive idea as his scepticism of science was associated with often quite fundamental rejections of the ideologies and philosophies of history, 'the grand narratives', 'progression', 'emancipation' and so on, with which Western modernity had supported and sustained itself (Outhwaite, 1994, p121).

In this way, Lyotard has become the exponent for a critique, call it postmodern or not, that rejects modernity's intentions of enlightenment, thus turning its attention against a belief in rationality, whether of a theoretical, practical or aesthetic character, cf. Kant's concepts of rationality also adopted in Habermas' works. In other words, the critique is turned against a belief in reason within the enlightenment intentions of modernity, the sciences, ethics and the arts, adamant that this would lead to universal progress for mankind, the individual and society. A sensational notion with clout akin to modernity's worst manifestations.

The defence of reason

The defence for the modern project came quickly and very succinctly from Habermas in a speech he gave in 1980 when he received the Adorno prize[22] in Frankfurt. Here Habermas adopts the point of view that ultimately postmodernity has manifested itself to be *anti-modern*. The task for critical social science must therefore be to defend modernity, as well as question why the project is in crisis and in what way it has been unsuccessful – in short, turning out to be an incomplete project.

In the speech, Habermas is extremely outspoken in his critique of the antimodern. At the same time, his defence of modernity is almost the very quintessence of what he later substantiates in a much more comprehensive and detailed analysis in *The Theory of Communicative Action* and *The Philosophical Discourse of Modernity*, respectively. A more detailed account of his speech will therefore be given here. This can then be used as a sort of reference for Chapter 3 of this book, especially with regard to the theory of the communicative action.

To Habermas the problem is that modern society's rationalization processes have lead to one-sided modernization, primarily guided by standards of economic and administrative rationality. Also, other aspects of life, such as passing on cultural tradition, social integration and socialization are guided by such standards

– though they should really be guided by another standard, the communicative rationality.

But in the modern project, the project of enlightenment, the very point of issue is that the differentiation of the expert cultures, science, morality and the arts into independent realms with their own internal history and rules which, through centuries, have gradually established themselves right up to the modern epoch, will ultimately lead to further realizations and knowledge in their field. Reflecting back, they will inform and enrich practical forms of life. Referring to Condorcet, Habermas maintains that not only have the arts and the sciences contributed to the control of the natural forces, but they have also added an understanding of the world, selfhood and changes of morality, and furthermore given integrity to the institutions of society; indeed, even provided happiness for mankind.

However, these reversions from the esoteric *higher levels* (Habermas) have not succeeded overall. Up until now, the division between the expert cultures and people in general (the practical forms of living) have been growing further apart rather than getting closer together. At the same time, the cultural rationalization – that is, the differentiation of the realms of value into expert cultures that has taken place has caused a further devaluation of the remaining traditional elements of the lifeworld. And these are being threatened yet further due to the fact that reversions do not work.

It is at this point that Habermas insists on the modern project. Despite mistakes and catastrophic events, especially in the 20th century, the choice is either to continue modernity's enlightenment intentions or let these fall to the ground, allowing the lifeworld to follow 'blind' traditions and remain unaffected by the cognitive potentials that are not part of technical advances, economic growth or rational administration.

Yet, it can be said about some of the modern enlightenment supporters, especially those Habermas calls the 'back troops of enlightenment' (Habermas, 1981b, p454), that they back only single elements that have been differentiated through a process of reason while neglecting all other elements. Thus the latter gets stunted and in effect even allows a reflection back, in a negative way, on the very element that was originally entrusted.

The problems arise because the differentiation of the sciences, the arts and morality entails that by virtue of their being processed by specialists they become autonomous, and thus distance themselves from the mainstream traditions continually being generated through hermeneutic everyday practice. Consequently, not only do the expert cultures become obstinate; they also come to form their own regulations. This leads to false attempts of negation that could be compared to modern enlightenment, which only trust a single differentiated element. As an example of such false attempts at negation, Habermas draws attention first to the Neo-Hegelian notion with regard to the changing and liberating powers of philosophy, which, if materialized, would render itself superfluous, and second to the surrealists' animosity to art in their aim to break with prevailing artistic forms and aesthetics.

However, the false negation of the expert cultures assumes, erroneously, that the rationalized everyday world can be relieved from cultural impoverishment through the mandatory practice of linking up one of the specialized knowledge forms to another. But in effect, this only replaces one one-sidedness and abstraction with another as cognitive readings, moral expectations, expressions and appraisals in the communicating everyday practice are interrelated. The processes in the lifeworld, through which one gains understanding, require a complete cultural handing over *in its entirety* (Habermas, 1981b, p458; Habermas, 1981c, p11).

To Habermas the alternative to the false negation is a differentiated reversion of modern culture in an everyday practice that is given over to vital codes, although these are impoverished by pure traditionalism. But such reversions will only succeed provided that *also* societal modernization can be diverted towards *other* non-capitalist routes, and provided that the lifeworld, itself, can develop institutions that are able to reduce the self-perpetuating dynamics of the economic and the administrative systems (Habermas, 1981b, p462; Habermas, 1981c, p13).

However, Habermas warns that the chances for this may not be good. Overall, the anti-modern attitudes have increased, and the disillusionment with the very failures of those programmes that called for the negation of arts and philosophy and the appearance of the aporias of cultural modernity has given ground for conservative positions. He distinguishes between the young conservatives' anti-modernism, the old conservatives' pre-modernism and neo-conservatives' postmodernism:

> *The* Young Conservatives *recapitulate the basic experience of aesthetic modernity. They claim as their own the relations of a decentered subjectivity, emancipated from the imperatives of work and usefulness, and with this experience they step outside the modern world. On the basis of modernistic attitudes, they justify an irreconcilable anti-modernism. They remove into the sphere of the far away and the archaic the spontaneous powers of imagination, of self-experience and of emotionality. To instrumental reason, they juxtapose in Manichean fashion a principle only accessible through evocation, be it the will to power or sovereignty, Being or the Dionysiac force of the poetical. In France this line leads from Bataille via Foucault to Derrida.*
>
> *The* Old Conservatives *do not allow themselves to be contaminated by cultural modernism. They observe the decline of substantive reason, the differentiation of science, morality and art, the modern world view and its merely procedural rationality, with sadness and recommend a withdrawal to a position anterior to modernity.*
>
> *Neo-Aristotelianism, in particular, enjoys a certain success today. In view of the problematic of ecology, it allows itself to call for a cosmological ethic. As belonging to this school, which originates with Leo Strauss, one can count for example the interesting works of Hans Jonas and Robert Spaemann.*

Finally, the Neo-conservatives *welcome the development of modern science, as long as this only goes beyond its sphere to carry forward technical progress, capitalist growth and rational administration. Moreover, they recommend a politics of defusing the explosive content of cultural modernity. According to one thesis, science, when properly understood, has become irrevocably meaningless for the orientation of the lifeworld. A further thesis is that politics must be kept as far aloof as possible from the demands of moral-practical justification. And a third thesis asserts the pure immanence of art, disputes that it has a utopian content, and points to its illusory character in order to limit the aesthetic experience to privacy. One could name here the early Wittgenstein, Carl Schmitt of the middle period, and Gottfried Benn on the late period. But with the decisive confinement of science, morality and art to autonomous spheres separated from the lifeworld and administered by experts, what remains from the project of cultural modernity is only what we would have if we were to give up the project of modernity altogether. As a replacement one points to traditions, which, however, are held to be immune to demands of (normative) justification and validation.*

Habermas, 1981b, pp463–464; Habermas, 1981c, pp13–14

Habermas admits that such a typology is a simplification, but maintains that it is not completely useless in an analysis of the spiritual and political discussions prevailing at the time. He is particularly concerned that the anti-modernistic ideas with a pinch of pre-modernism added gain resonance among the Greens and other alternative groups.

In connection with the remarks in the quote above on the neo-Aristotelian inspiration of the ecological problematic, it is particularly interesting to note that already in 1980 Habermas feared ecological movements would result in pre- and anti-modern notions – that is, illusions to revert to more ideal conditions. The ecological movement's perspective on how to solve problems is characterized by familiar visions of something that is perceived to be more ideal than the given present, yet without believing in the potentiality of the given present and therefore not believing either that, through co-existence, human beings will be able to distinguish between what is right and wrong, good and bad, beneficial and harmful, and so on. Habermas regards this kind of scepticism as being the root of the neo-conservatives' mistrust in humanity's ability for action and reason. In terms of power, this turns into a counteroffensive with preconceived ideas with regard to the existence of human being, with, for example, Dionysian overtones or sentiments about the powerful primitive man.

It is, indeed, thought-provoking that 20 years into the ecological movements, well after Habermas expressed these views, such notions continue to be upheld when examining ecological aims. In thought and practice they move within a sphere that spans from distrust of the application of modernity's realizations and insights, to visions of an idealized past world or other such reminiscence. In doing so, they avoid questioning the incongruity of considering their own ideas as superior while rejecting the potentials of modernity. Yet, in both instances, the genuine belief applies that certain things are more sensible to pursue than others and hence one should not avoid the modern discourse outlined above.

Sadly, such logic is not commonly accepted and may be appreciated the least where it is actually most appropriate. And here we have reached the key issue of this book, which will be the point of departure when considering the scopes and pitfalls in connection with the actualities of incorporating environmental considerations as a vital factor in social practice. It is obviously not possible to pursue this question without considering whether environmental issues are to be interpreted as a question of rationality, or whether they are to be interpreted as being preconceived, as being something inherent to nature that pre-empts any deviation.

The philosophical debate on this issue, where the postmodern critique of reason is contrasted by modernity's defence of enlightenment based on rationality, has gone on for more than 20 years. It is far beyond the scope of this book to enter into a detailed analysis of such contentions. Instead, I will give account three different renderings of the discourse. I will look at three authors who, independently, at different times and from different angles seek to resolve the position.

First, we have the theologian Troels Nørager's account on the debate in the introduction to his book (1985) on Habermas' construction of modernity in *The Theory of Communicative Action*.[23] Second, in his 1994 book on Habermas,[24] the sociologist William Outhwaite gives a critical analysis of Habermas' more detailed arguments in *The Philosophical Discourse of Modernity* for the positions he originally outlined in his thank you speech. And finally, in his book *Facing Modernity* (1999)[25] we have the sociologist Barry Smart's analysis of the positions, with special emphasis on postmodernism/structuralism.

Two of the above independent renderings clearly endorse the philosophy of reason in their accounts. Nevertheless, they vary considerably in terms of their willingness to embrace the views from the postmodern critique of reason. Notably, these publications are 10 years apart. In contrast to these, the third account comes from a position that is closer to a poststructuralist approach, and thus cannot be described as following points of view that adhere to Habermas' theories. Significantly, this account is a comparatively recent one and as such benefits from the contemporary rendering of the conflict, historical experiences included.

Nørager

Troels Nørager was the first to give his opinion on the subject, in the middle of the 1980s, when the debate reached a boiling point.

He sees three different meanings of the postmodern:

1   As a concept within aesthetics, where postmodernism is used to signify a number of new tendencies in literature and art that can no longer be expressed in the artistic idiom of modernity and therefore as such has gone further, that is, post.

2   As a concept that has been extrapolated in order to incorporate general contemporary societal conditions, yet without indicating which concrete phenomena of society warrant the nomination of being postmodern.
3   In a narrower sense of the word, the philosophical variant of the postmodern consciousness, a postmodern philosophical critique of modernity as introduced by Lyotard (Nørager, 1985, pp16–17).

This division is still largely valid today. It can be useful to stress that while the first and possibly also the third reading include elements that cannot be expressed in the artistic idiom of modernity or in the philosophical discourse of modernity, this does not mean the second meaning has any materialized societal reality. The examples of the false negations of the expert cultures, as referred to earlier, are precisely what give cause for further contemplation.

Of the three renderings, Nørager is by far the most radical in his view on poststructural or postmodern critiques of modernity. He considers the critique a direct attempt to replace the concept of pure reason with the concept of power, or expressed in a different way, that the alternative for a theory based on reason is a theory based on aesthetics.[26]

Various approaches to the critique of the concept of reason in modern philosophy and social theory share reference to Nietzsche's view on historicism and his ideas regarding the will to power. They also disregard modernity's inherent *counterdiscourse*, which right from the start formed part of the project of enlightenment, and which by Hegel himself was explicitly framed as being the *dialectics of enlightenment* (Nørager, 1985, pp21, 27).

With regards to the dialectic of enlightenment, Hegel emphasizes the dichotomy of modern society insofar as it consists of both liberating and alienating elements. Hence, right from the start, the attempt of enlightened thinking, to introduce what Max Horkheimer called 'bringing sensibleness to the world', was accompanied by a counterdiscourse that emphasized the negative aspects. Indeed, critique of reason is not a novelty but as old as reason (enlightenment) itself. What is new is only the struggle towards totalization that Nietzsche launched (Nørager, 1985, p28).

Nietzsche embarked on his critique of reason around 1870, when *historicism* was the dominating principle of informed understanding insofar as it considered all cultural phenomena to be determined by history and, as such, as being relative and contingent. To be informed and to be sensible implied taking a sceptical and objectifying attitude towards historical and cultural phenomena. Nietzsche's critique attacked the time's tendency of levelling everything of value. Instead, he wanted to see 'a conquest of nihilism' based on 'a reappraisal of all values'. Indeed, nihilism is not, as is so often claimed, discovered by Nietzsche, but rather a result of historicism's levelling of all values.

Nietzsche finds historicism dangerous, because it breaks down 'the will to live' and flattens the grand and the powerful.[27] It is, in fact, the effects of historicism, not its epistemology that he criticizes. In other words, he acknowledged historicism's relativism, albeit radicalizing this into a genuine and perspective epistemology. To this he attaches an alternative theory of history, where the 'will to power' is the deciding factor. According to this perspective the various 'truths' are merely more or less arbitrary – effects of the will to power. Thus it becomes a *theory of power* which (as Foucault later has it) is chosen in order to replace the 'rational' critique of the dialectic of enlightenment (Nørager, 1985, p25).

Nietzsche's disreputable 'superman' is the ideal man – a personality that is brave enough to expose 'nihilism' and strong enough to replace this with other and better values. These new virtues are upheld alone by way of reason, the 'other'. Thus he adopts the line of tradition in Schiller's Kantian critique – that is, he seeks the alternative to reason in 'the aesthetic', radicalizing this to embrace everything.

Nietzsche's anti-humanism lies in the fact that he does not see reason as being other than the outcome of the will to power. His aim is to break the framework of Western rationality, and he therefore leaves behind the dialectics of enlightenment, giving preference to a concentration on reasons 'other'. This, according to Nørager, is:

> *that which radical critique of reason considers detached and displaced by reason: the myth and the 'God who is coming'; notions that by Nietzsche, the classical philologist, is taking the guise of the libidinal passion of the Dionysian figure. It is precisely through the Dionysian figure that it becomes possible to steal a glimpse of the paradigm for an irrational aesthetic-sensual overcoming of reason. In other words, Nietzsche's view of modernity is in favour of the aesthetic experience which opens up for Dionysian connotations and signifies that also the will to power has an aesthetic core.*
>
> *By over-bidding the concepts of modernity with a total and uncompromising critique of reason, Nietzsche surpassed the horizon of reason and discourse. It goes without saying that for this he paid a price, viz. being unable to justify the aesthetic criteria of his critique. And, according to Habermas, this weakness is evidenced especially 'in the dilemma of a self-contained critique of reason that has become total'.*
>
> *In his latest book, Habermas deals with Nietzsche under the headline of 'Eintritt in der Postmoderne', the critical account of which is evidenced by two circumstances in particular: partly the veritable renaissance of Nietzsche in the latter years and partly by the neo-structuralist anti-rational philosophers (Foucault, Deleuze, Lyotard, Baudrillard) who all explicitly acknowledge Nietzsche's influence.*
>
> Nørager, 1985, pp25, 26

Martin Heidegger and Georges Bataille are the intermediate theorists between Nietzsche and the poststructural philosophers. Both of them relinquish their belief in the dialectic of enlightenment, constructing in its place a taut suspension between what is rational and what is 'the other', which as such is not a dialectic contradiction that is adopted with the intention of being negated.

Heidegger attempts to outdo Nietzsche in his reconstruction of Western philosophy by critiquing the subject-centred reasoning that has replaced 'the other' and more importantly: the ontological issue that summarizes the issue of the existence of 'being'.

Likewise, Bataille returns to the early phases of civilization to isolate the rudimentary understanding, which since then has been suppressed and rationalized away. For him the normative notion has not merely been the sentiment to be, but rather conceptions of sovereignty – that is, the irrational excessive experiences that used to converge into religious rituals, sexual orgies and so on (Nørager, 1985, pp26–27).

Nørager's conclusion in the continuation of the previously mentioned chapter by Habermas in *The Philosophical Discourse of Modernity* is:

> *The postmodern philosophers continue thinking in the matrices developed by Heidegger and Bataille among others. Thus, Habermas considers Derrida a productive developer of Heidegger's philosophical mysticism (the idea of Seinsgeschick), just as Foucault is greatly indebted to Bataille's general theory on excessive desire. The consistent overall concept among the Nietzsche-inspired representatives of a critique of reason is that the counterpoint to reason is the conceptualized vague and unique intuition: 'the being' for Heidegger, 'the sovereignty' for Bataille, 'the sacred origin' for Derrida and 'power' for Foucault.*
>
> Nørager, 1985, p27

In the above Nørager has outlined the trend. It is a direct confrontation. The critics' counterpoint to reason is vague, albeit a *universal* foundation of power. The rationale of the Enlightenment is not an unmistakable entity. However, provided we maintain the counterclaims to enlightenment in the dialectic sense of the word, we can continue to employ sensible reasoning and thus provide the world with the hope that, in the last instance, reason will ultimately prevail. Adopting Habermas' argument, Nørager maintains that this is so very important as there is no other authority which we can appeal to. This applies not only for scientific discourse, but also for communicative actions and ethical conflicts in everyday life.

Like Habermas, Nørager is quite clear about the fact that the various nuances and the many different problems raised in the poststructural and postmodern critique disappear during such a direct confrontation. However, he maintains relating to this, the normative philosophical debate on the concept of rationalization has primary status. Indeed, he stresses this argument by ascertaining that within the last 10 to 15 years (in 1985) the outlined critique of reason has gained a considerable foothold without being able to establish its own place and status – for example in the form of a contemporary postmodernistic diagnosis of society. The critique of reason has simply been accepted, and for him that is the essential problem and the very reason to engage in Habermas' critical discourse against it the subject (Nørager, 1985, p29).

Outhwaite

William Outhwaite's critical analysis of Habermas' more detailed arguments in *The Philosophical Discourse of Modernity* regarding the positions in his thank you speech does not take nearly as sharp a line as Nørager does. In many ways, Outhwaite is much more understanding with regard to the poststructural position. Seeing its positive contribution to the discussion, he is at the same time open to the weaknesses of Habermas' assertions.

Notable, however, is the fact that his contribution comes ten years later than Nørager's and ten years after Habermas had disclosed his views in *The Philosophical Discourse of Modernity*. For Nørager, both the situation itself and Habermas' book were quite new. This may be a contributing factor to what might be described as an awkward onset, but which, at the time, nevertheless was in line with Habermas himself and which due to its distinct profile has merit.

Outhwaite starts by stressing that Habermas reacted very pointedly against all that he considered to be superficial and irresponsible attacks on the Enlightenment's rational and human ideals. The engaging and provocative exaggerations from Paris reminded Habermas of the more obscure intellectual and political movements of the German counter-enlightenment beliefs. Also by linking the poststructuralists to the 'new philosophers' of the ultra-conservatives, the ones Habermas in the above quote calls the 'neo-conservatives', made poststructuralists look even more suspect.

By drawing attention to this, he signals that he considers Habermas' immediate reactions far too condemning, disapproving and too authoritative. Indeed, he sets himself the task of finding out what knowledge Habermas subsequently gained from the poststructural discourse.

Outhwaite points out that one way to see Habermas' sensitive reaction to the critique of reason was that Habermas had an appreciation of the modernization theories of the 1950s, which considered modernity separate from its modern European origin and turned 'it into a spatially and temporally neutralized model for all processes of social development' (Habermas, 1987a, p2). The modernization was treated as an automatic evolutionary process and thus modern culture is increasingly becoming separate – it is washed up and its possibilities exhausted, it 'is crystallised' as Arnold Gehlen calls it (Habermas, 1985, p11). Whereas:

> *Gehlen's neo-conservative version of the postmodern or 'posthistory' implies that we should simply make do with what we now have, a more anarchic or subversive account of the postmodernity aims to transcend modernity's instrumental or technical rationality, its will to power. Habermas's suspicion – and this is what drives his sometimes excessive anxiety about contemporary intellectual trends – is that these sceptical backward glances are merely restating anti-modern themes of the 'counter-enlightenment'.*
>
> Outhwaite, 1994, p122

The theory of modernity is introduced by Hegel, who in the Introduction to *The Phenomenology of Mind* describes this as 'something new is on the way' – that is, that we are on our own, free to make our own history (Outhwaite, 1994, p122). For Hegel the deciding factor of modernity is therefore the principle of the freedom of subjectivity. However, Habermas argues that for Hegel 'subjectivity does possess an unexampled power to bring about the formation [Bildung] of subjective freedom and reflection and to undermine religion [...]. But the principle of subjectivity is not powerful enough to regenerate the unifying power of religion in the medium of reason' (Habermas, 1987a, p20).

Habermas stresses that, at the beginning of his philosophical career, Hegel had recognized this problem, but that his later illusory solution, provided by concept of the absolute knowledge, was conceived because he thought the overcoming of subjectivity within the boundaries of the philosophy of the subject (Habermas, 1987a, p22). Thus, the true reason of the enlightenment is seen as an illusory phenomenon with a narrow, and ultimately authoritarian and subjective, understanding of rationality (Habermas, 1987a, pp55–56). In this sense, we 'remain contemporaries of the Young Hegelians' (Habermas, 1987a, p53), and subsequent thinkers down to Adorno, Gehlen and Foucault follow three lines of development:

> Left Hegelian *critique, turned toward the practical and aroused for revolution, aimed at mobilizing the historically accumulated potential of reason (awaiting release) against its mutilation, against the one-sided rationalization of the bourgeois world. The* Right Hegelians *followed Hegel in the conviction that the substance of state and religion would compensate for the restlessness of bourgeois society, as soon as the subjectivity of the revolutionary consciousness that incited restlessness yielded to objective insight into the rationality of the status quo [...] Finally, Nietzsche wanted to unmask the dramaturgy of the entire stage-piece in which both – revolutionary hope and the reaction to it – enter on the scene. [...] Reason is nothing else than power, than the will to power, which it so radiantly conceals.*
>
> Habermas, 1987a, p56; Outhwaite, 1994, p124

If this passage, as Outhwaite writes, is a somewhat brisk exercise in distanced intellectual history, it is not intended to be so on Habermas' part. But Habermas stresses that we cannot step out of the discourse of modernity, and he would want to include a 'participant's perspective' on the problems inherent in these three positions (Habermas, 1987a, p59).

It is the first and third positions, which are of most interest in this respect. Left Hegelianism develops into a neo-Marxist 'praxis philosophy'.[28] However, whereas both left and right Hegelians basically accepted the superiority of modernity to traditional ways of life, Nietzsche both generalizes (to earlier historical periods) and undermines the rationality which had been imputed to modernity. 'Nietzsche owes his concept of modernity, developed in terms of his theory of power, to an unmasking critique of reason that sets itself outside the horizon of reason' (Habermas, 1987a, p96). 'Habermas sees an ambivalence in Nietzsche, again no doubt arising from the Hegelian end-of-philosophy problematic, which develops into a second major branching point in modern philosophy' (Outhwaite, 1994, pp124–125):

> *Nietzsche's critique of modernity has been continued along both paths.*
> *The sceptical scholar who wants to unmask the perversion of the will to*
> *power, the revolt of reactionary forces, and the emergence of a subject-*
> *centred reason by using anthropological, psychological and historical*
> *methods has successors in Bataille, Lacan, and Foucault; the initiate-*
> *critic of metaphysics who pretends to a unique kind of knowledge and*
> *pursues the rise of the philosophy of the subject back to its pre-Socratic*
> *beginnings has successors in Heidegger and Derrida.*
> Habermas 1987a, p97; Outhwaite, 1994, p125

Before Habermas follows these directions in Nietzsche's critique, he refers to 'Horkheimer and Adorno's ambiguous attempt at a dialectic of enlightenment that would satisfy Nietzsche's radical critique of reason' (Habermas, 1987a, p105) in the book, *Dialectic of Enlightenment*. He also stresses the argument of this book that 'reason remains subordinated to the dictates of purposive rationality right into its most recent products – modern science, universalistic ideas of justice and morality, autonomous art' (Habermas, 1987a, p111).

Regarding this astounding oversimplification of modernity, Outhwaite quotes from Habermas 'does not do justice to the rational content of cultural modernity that was captured in bourgeois ideals (and thus also instrumentalized along with them)' (Habermas, 1987a, p113). Also, such a critique of ideology 'outstrips itself' in a Nietzschean manner that makes one 'insensitive to the traces and the existing forms of the communicative rationality' (Habermas, 1987a, pp127, 129; Outhwaite, 1994, p125).

In other words, it is not Horkheimer's or Adorno's understandings of the dialectic of enlightenment we should consult for an understanding of modernity, just as, based on their arguments, we should not favour a rationality concept within modernity in opposition to a critique of reason.

In his further analysis of Habermas' accounts of the Nietzsche-inspired critique of reason, Outhwaite only briefly outlines the critiques of Heidegger, Derrida and Bataille, while his engagement with Habermas' account of Foucault is more substantial.

Habermas approves of Heidegger's critique of the subjectivism of Western metaphysics – though, as Outhwaite continues, Habermas sees Heidegger's view on communicative rationality, like his critique of modernity (which had been a strong impulse in Habermas' own early thought), as set against the background of an overblown conception of philosophy and a messianic mysticism reduced to absurdity in Heidegger's nasty and brutish, if short, identification with Nazism and his subsequent 'turn' to a 'philosophy of origins' (Outhwaite, 1994, p126).

Against this, Habermas insists on the possibility of less dramatic but more secure ways 'out of the philosophy of the subject' (Habermas, 1987a, p137).

According to Habermas, Derrida too is drawn into 'a philosophy of origins'. He develops a critique of Western metaphysics in the form of a critique of the primacy accorded to speech and presence. But rather than analysing the production of meaning in intersubjective terms, Derrida sees these as 'the world-constituting performances of subjectivity' (Habermas, 1987, p172). Derrida's thoughts are 'therefore characterized by an inverted fundamentalism'; he 'inherits the weakness of a critique of metaphysics that does not shake loose of the intentions of first philosophy [philosophy of origins, Ursprungsphilosophie]' (Habermas, 1987a, p167; Outhwaite, 1994, p126).

Habermas' critique of the surrealist George Bataille, according to Outhwaite, is explained by his role in transmitting Nietzschean influences to a later generation of thinkers, notably Foucault (Habermas, 1987a, pp238–239). However, Bataille, according to Outhwaite, is in his own right an important figure in the philosophical discourse of modernity, and shares Horkheimer's and Adorno's suspicion to the self-domination of Western rationality, especially in its ethical dimension. He therefore looks for a way out which parallels Heidegger's. However, for Bataille transcendence takes the form of transgression, excess, waste, and at the limit, ritual sacrifice. But even though he has one foot in philosophy, he rejects the systematic pursuit of knowledge as something also trapped in utilitarian calculation (Outhwaite, 1994, p127).

For Foucault, 'the radical critique' of reason takes the form of an archaeological and genealogical orientated 'historiography of the human sciences'; a 'kind of antiscience' (Habermas, 1987a, pp247, 242) that anatomizes their will to power both at the empirical level, in medicine, psychopathology, criminology, penology and so on, and at the metatheoretical level of the constitution of their basic conceptual orientations (Outhwaite, 1994, p127). However, as Habermas notes, this is only part of the story: 'In the 1970's objectifying approaches no longer dominated the field in the human sciences; they were competing instead with hermeneutic and critical approaches that were tailored in their forms of knowledge to possibilities of application other than manipulation of self and of others' (Habermas, 1987a, pp272–273).

The fundamental problem in Foucault's thinking is the paradox of self-reference, where the attempt to step out of modernity in a genealogical historiography, grounded on the theory of power ends up as being precisely the 'presentistic, relativistic, crypto-normative illusory science that it does not want to be'. 'The internal aspects of *meaning*, of *truth*, *validity* and of *evaluation* do not go without remainder into the externally grasped aspects of practices of power' (Habermas, 1987a, p276).

Outhwaite draws attention to three different critiques that Habermas has raised concerning Foucault. First, he cannot undercut the hermeneutic predicament in his search for a real history of underlying practices that goes below or behind the self-understandings of actors. Ignoring this problematic is to fall victim to it: 'The unmasking of the objective illusions of *any* will to knowledge leads to agreement with a historiography that is narcissistically oriented towards the standpoint of the historian and instrumentalizes the contemplation of the past for the needs of the present' (Habermas, 1985, p327). Nietzsche rides again, Outhwaite writes in short (1997, p149).

Second, genealogical historiography succumbs to 'relativistic self-denial' (Habermas, 1987a, p281; Outhwaite, 1994, p128):

> *if the truth claims that Foucault himself raises for his genealogy of knowledge, were in fact illusory and amounted to no more than the effects that this theory is capable of releasing within the circle of its adherents, then the entire undertaking of a critical unmasking of the human sciences would lose its point.*
>
> Habermas, 1987a, p279

Foucault flirts with a Lukácsian argument to the effect that genealogy recovers subjugated or disqualified knowledge-forms, but he cannot give these the kind of 'cognitive privilege' that was afforded to the proletariat in Lukác's philosophy of history (Outhwaite, 1994, p128).

The third criticism is that Foucault's apparently value-free or supra-normative position resists the demand to take sides and masks a very clear critical standpoint, namely that of 'a dissident who offers resistance to modern thought and humanistically disguised disciplinary power' (Habermas, 1987a, p282). But Foucault cannot ground resistance and critique without moving on to the terrain of normative argument. Of this we have only fragments (Outhwaite, 1994, p128).

Based on these criticisms, Habermas' main attack takes up Foucault's attempt to eliminate 'the categories of meaning, validity and value [...] not only on the metatheoretical, but also on the empirical level', which leaves Foucault 'with an object domain from which the theory of power has erased all traces of communicative actions entangled in lifeworld contexts' (Habermas, 1987a, p286). This claim is illustrated with reference to the classic sociological problems of social order and the relation between the individual and society. Following Axel Honneth's argument in *Critique of Power*, he asks how Foucault can explain the way in which permanent power struggles can lead to stabilized networks of power or how socialization can mean individuation as well as subordination, or that the bourgeois constitutional state is more than just 'a dysfunctional relic from the period of absolutism' (Habermas, 1987a, p290). Foucault's neglect even of penal law means that he overlooks not only the possibilities of law-based counter-movements, in which he was himself active, but also, more fundamentally, the fact that 'it is the legal means for securing freedom that themselves endanger the freedom of their presumptive beneficiaries' (Habermas, 1987a, p291; Outhwaite, 1997, p129).

After this elaborate critique of Foucault, which Outhwaite presents almost word for word and without comments and reservations, he does, however, remark on the fact that it is not easy to separate out the rhetoric underlying much of this discourse from the more substantive underlying claims contained in it. He therefore shares Richard Bernstein's opinion that Foucault ought to be given a more sympathetic reading:

> *Instead of claiming that Foucault is flatly contradicting himself on the question of the subject, truth and freedom, we can read him in a different way – as deliberately using hyperbolic rhetorical constructions in order to compel us to disrupt and question our traditional understandings of these key concepts. And he effectively does this by showing us the dark ambiguities in the construction of these concepts and the role they have played in social practices.*[29]

Referring to Honneth, Outhwaite is of the opinion that such a reading brings Foucault closer to Adorno and the tradition of critical theory and reveals him as a thinker whose focus on social conflict is a crucial counterpoint to Habermas' communication theory (Outhwaite, 1994, p129).

Pointing out that Habermas is not completely alien to this idea, Outhwaite writes that Habermas has suggested that Foucault's 'acute diagnosis' of the 'basic conceptual aporias of the philosophy of consciousness', together with those of his own philosophy of power, points the way for his own project of replaying the philosophical discourse of modernity so as to find 'other ways out of the philosophy of the subject'. By this he is thinking of a model in which, 'participants in interaction [...] coordinate their plans for action by coming to an understanding about something in the world' rather than oscillating between the inflated knowledge of the human subject and a radical scepticism about reality. In the reconstruction of these practices, 'the ontological separation between the transcendental and the empirical is no longer applicable'. Thus, the relation between the unconscious and the conscious, and the making conscious of what is unconscious, ceases to be seen as 'heroic exertion' of the subject, but rather as part of the process of coming to understanding (Habermas, 1987a, pp295, 296, 298; Outhwaite, 1994, p130).

Such self-reflection gives rise to two distinct procedures: (a) the rational reconstruction of formal rule systems, and (b) a more totalizing process of methodical self-criticism, which has a bearing on all forms of life. This does not mean, 'that the purism of pure reason is resurrected' (Habermas, 1987a, p301). Habermas' aim is a critique that – in opposition to totalizing critiques of rationality and logocentrism – is less dramatic and:

> *starts from an attack on the abstractions of the surrounding logos, as free of language, as universalist, and as disembodied. It conceives of intersubjective understanding as the telos inscribed into communication in ordinary language, and of the logocentrism of Western thought, heightened by the philosophy of consciousness, as a systematic foreshortening and distortion of a potential always already operative in the communicative practice of everyday life, but only selectively exploited.*
> Habermas, 1987a, p311; Outhwaite, 1994, pp130–131

This points to an analysis that focuses not on judgements and sentences but on speech acts, in which the validity claims of truth, normative rightness and trust-worthiness are equally important, in contrast to the conceptions of language in which language is either just a factual representation or merely rhetoric. The phenomenological language concept must be expanded to include not only background knowledge 'but also normatively reliable patterns of social relations ... and the components acquired in socialization processes' (Habermas, 1987a, p314). Thus, rationality is not just to be understood as the knowing (and purpo-sively acting) subject, but in procedural terms as a capacity to respond to the full range of validity-claims. 'Communicative reason finds its criteria in the argumen-tative procedures for [...] redeeming claims to propositional truth, normative rightness, subjective truthfulness and aesthetic harmony'. It thus 'recalls older ideas of logos' in its orientation to consensus and 'a decentered understanding of the world' (Habermas, 1987a, pp314, 315; Outhwaite, 1994, p131).

Having presented this long and detailed discourse of opposing radical, in particular the French, critique of reason, it may seem paradoxical when Outhwaite concludes that in latter years – from 1994 – the steam of the critique has somewhat dispersed. Once the noise on the translation channel has been filtered out, many of these positions seem much closer than their protagonists believed (Outhwaite, 1994, p136). In this connection he refers to Manfred Frank who maintained that the prima facie opposition between Habermas' model of the harmonious pursuit of communicative consensus, free from violence, and Lyotard's postulate of irreconcilable conflicts is not necessarily as stark as it appears. He sees Lyotard's model as accentuating the conflicting character of the dialogue in a way which offers a useful corrective to Habermas' model, rather than a root-and-branch alternative.[30]

But then his elaborated account of these seemingly antagonistic points of view may in reality have the more indirect purpose to sharpen Habermas' argument thereby making more accessible his own conclusion that Habermas is right to deny that he is 'advocating a linear continuation of the tradition of the Enlightenment' and that his positive ideal of a philosophy which is post-metaphysical yet not post-rational remains both attractive and plausible (Outhwaite, 1994, p136).

Smart

In his analysis Barry Smart has called the French postmodernist/poststructuralists 'the archaeologists of modernity' (Smart, 1999, p38). He has in this way effec-tively stressed that in terms of modernity they hold a different point of view, and as such theoretically, they can be described as having been capable of exceeding the framework of modernity. Smart stresses their shared critical approach to a number of central themes in the discourse of modernity:

> *(i) the crisis of representation and associated instability of meaning; (ii) the absence of secure foundations for knowledge; (iii) the analytic central-*

ity of language, discourses and texts; and (iv) the inappropriateness of the Enlightenment assumption of rational autonomous subject and a counter, contrasting concentration on the ways in which individuals are constituted as subjects.

Smart, 1999, p38

For Smart the essence of their work is that we live in a time where Western metaphysics is under closure – a metaphysics that has been 'dominant throughout the world in its final form, scientific and technical rationality'. Or, as he also states, the works of these writers have resulted in an understanding of modernity as that of being in 'the last phase of metaphysics', from which he further deduces that postmodernism 'simply is a metaphorical expression of such an ending after which there will be no new beginning' (Smart, 1999, pp39–40, with quotes from Schirmacher, 1984, pp607, 605).

Consequently, it is not possible to justify a political practice or ethical decisions from any theory or analysis of the social situation. This does not render theory or analysis superfluous, but theory cannot provide programmes for legislation or governing.

Instead, theory and analysis should contribute to the cultivation of reflexive processes that lead to a form of plurality of various different interests, traditions and cultures, thereby constituting responsible subjectivity (Smart, 1999, p63), namely creating or maintaining a societal integrating factor in the midst of all the individualized multiplicity.[31]

Thus Smart confirms what has been clear since Hegel that, in the last instance, the problem of modernity is to create coherence in society or, expressed in a different way, empower those elements of society that are able to reconcile individual subjectivity with society. He also confirms that this problem has been accentuated further by the development that gave rise to claims of postmodernism or merely to a postmodern diagnosis of contemporary society.

The defence for a modern rationality

The problem of coherence in society arises from the fact that modernity has an undermining effect on the unifying power of religion. Despite civil wars and wars in general, nation states have played a considerable role in terms of social integration. In the latter part of the 19th and the whole of the 20th century, a decisive factor for social integration has been the spirit of solidarity within classes and the mutual acknowledgement between the parties in the class struggle.

What pivots the problem today, and this becomes clearer day by day, is the fact that globalization is dissolving these structures and creating a situation where total individualization prevails, allowing subservience of everybody to the dictates and demands of market forces. Even fascist dictatorship – quite apart from its general practice of coarse violence against opponents and the general dirty conduct of totalitarianism – may seem a desirable alternative to this involuntary and relentless subjugation, as such regimes in effect are protective powers for the masses against the capitalistic cannibalism of globalization.

If fascism is to be seen as the savagery and the totalization of the will to power with its consequent catastrophe to people – and when modern technocracy becomes totalized in the name of common sense and rationality as the counterpart to modernity, and when it becomes one-sided in relation to a specific potential of reason and a disaster to mankind insofar as it leads to system violence and, by stealth, to subjugation – well, then, indeed, do we have two outcomes of loss of meaning and nihilism, the very task modernity set out to avoid.

As far as I can see there is only one way forward: continued modernization in the name of reason, where the three different elements of rationality are recognized as an entity. In other words, with a view to past modernity, the aim is a new rationality. Habermas maintains that his theory of communicative rationality includes such an aim. In the next chapter, we will analyse this claim and relate this to other notions of modernity.

Indeed, Habermas has stressed that the complexity, the differentiation and decentralization of modern society, where the state is no longer the centre of the functions of society and where everything seems peripheral, is a serious threat for our own self-knowledge. Such self-knowledge can be sustained only when society is at the centre and holds out a possible future. Even a decentralized society needs a frame of reference that is the projected unity of an intersubjectively former common will (Habermas, 1988, p181). This problematic is the very centre of the debate in this book and will be dealt with further in the following chapters. The dimension that is added here to the analysis of the problematic of integration/disintegration is the concept of modernity in relation to modern society. This opens up for not only a philosophical but also a sociological approach to the analysis.

My inclusion of this elaborate discussion of the philosophical discourse of modernity,[32] which Habermas took up following his main account on *The Theory of Communicative Action*, is tied to the fact that I wish to clarify the assumptions for the central analysis of this thesis as it forms an important part of this book. It will become clear that coupled to this concept there are two vital elements: namely *rationality* (in the first instance translated to mean reasoning) and *communication*. This explains why Habermas, rather than for example Foucault, forms the starting point. Or expressed in a different way, why the philosophers of reason are taking precedence over the discourse of the critique of reason.

The above analysis has shown that the early interpretation by Nørager, who considers Habermas in direct opposition to the French poststructuralists, may, indeed, be in agreement with Habermas' own orientation of understanding. At this stage, very pointedly the problematic is considered from different aspects, either that, in the last instance, *reason* would prevail or that, ultimately, *power* would rule. Logically, interpreted in this vein, the latter aspect is not compatible with the practice of environmental assessments, which will embrace specific environmental considerations seen from a rational point of view.

Outhwaite has a somewhat softer approach to the different representations. First and foremost, his perspective takes a detached view of both the metaphysics and the philosophy of the subject. He adds to this Habermas' striving for rationalism, which, considering the fact that the philosophy of the subject has been relinquished, amplifies that intersubjectivity achieved through speech acts may also bring about a validation for the claims of proportional truth, normative rightness, subjective trustworthiness and aesthetic harmony.

Smart, to a greater extent than Nørager and Outhwaite, primarily considers the problematic from a critical point of view concerning modernism. He also sees an end to metaphysics – albeit as a final stage of modernity. This, of course, is in sharp contrast to Habermas, who wants to continue the modern project, but without metaphysics. Once again, the question must be posed whether, in fact, these positions are that far apart, as Habermas does emphasize that society as a central ruling subject is no (longer) possible. He believes it is the communicative coordinated processes in their full validity sphere that are the deciding factors of action – both in the realm of society as well as for the individual. However, Smart's emphasis that theory can no longer justify political practice or ethical decisions, but instead can contribute to the cultivation of reflexive processes, is close to Habermas' understanding.

By introducing further comparisons or rather carrying out further studies of potential similarities, it becomes obvious that Habermas has gone much further in his analysis of the conditions under which, to use Smart's own words, cultivation of the reflexive processes can be carried out. These conditions also include opportunities as well as barriers as to whether such cultivation can, indeed, happen. In the following chapter on modernity in terms of the notion of social structure, we will throw more light on these issues and also we shall analyse Habermas' understanding of modernity in more detail.

So far we have ascertained that, first, some supporters as well as some critics of the philosophy of reason relinquish both the metaphysics as well as the philosophy of the subject, and second, on the subject of the excellence of the modern project, Habermas made his defence more comparable to the sceptics of the discourse on reason, by relinquishing the so-called praxis philosophy.

In real terms, giving up metaphysics only means relinquishing the idea that by applying theories we can predict something about the future – especially something general about it – the character of which can then subsequently be confirmed by experience and in this way gain new knowledge with a validity, which are independent of time and place – that is without historical and spacious limitations.

Whereas Habermas gives up the praxis philosophy, this does not mean that he distances himself from the principle of consolidating rational practice in history, body and language. The problem is that despite everything it is dominated by the philosophy of the subject in the form of a philosophical anthropology, where history, society and body are understood dualistically: either as preconditions given for the subject or as the products of the subject: 'Thought that is tied to the philosophy of the subject cannot bridge over these dichotomies but, as Foucault so acutely diagnosed, oscillates helplessly between one and the other pole' (Habermas, 1987a, p317). Also the language is understood dualistically: either as a tool to create meaning or as something that happens behind one's back. Thus 'any interaction between world disclosing language and learning processes in the world is excluded' (Habermas, 1987a, p319). (See also the previous passage on the disjunctive understanding of language, and my critique of Szerszynski.)

However dualism is not part of Habermas' theory which, unlike Marx's praxis philosophical stand regarding societal work, is based on communicative action. For Marx, the communicative action is separated from the lifeworld, and the difference becomes more pronounced when 'the reproduction of the lifeworld is no longer merely routed through the medium of action oriented toward reaching understanding, but is saddled on the interpretive performances of its agents' (Habermas, 1987a, p342). As regards culture this means:

> *a condition of the constant revision of traditions that have been*
> *unthawed, that is, that have become reflective; for society, a condition of*
> *the dependence of legitimate orders upon formal and ultimately discursive*
> *procedures for establishing and grounding norms; for personality, a condi-*
> *tion of the risk filled self-direction of a highly abstract ego-identity.*
>
> Habermas, 1987a, p345

All points towards a situation where the reproduction of life forms are decreasingly secured by traditions, being replaced by 'a risky search for consensus, that is, be the cooperative achievements of those engaged in communicative action themselves' (Habermas, 1987a, p344).

Thus the problematic from *The Dialectic of Enlightenment*[33] can also be surpassed, because subjectivity, as the principle of modernity, is no longer considered the deciding factor for the normative contents of modernity. Neither is it solely up to self-reflection – which derives from subjectivity, but which simultaneously seeks to exceed its constraints – to show that it can act as the power of conciliation. Neither is the notion of reason derived from the structures of linguistically generated intersubjectivity and concretized in terms of rationalization processes in the lifeworld, an equivalent for the concept of an intrinsically rational praxis deployed in the philosophy of history (Habermas, 1987a, p348).

By giving up the concepts of the praxis philosophy, Habermas avoids regarding society as a self-referential subject-writ-large, which also includes individual subjects:

> *As soon as we give up praxis philosophy's understanding of society as a*
> *self-referential subject-writ-large, encompassing all individual subjects,*
> *the corresponding models for the diagnosis and mastery of crisis –*
> *division and revolution – are no longer applicable. Because the successive*
> *releasing of the rational potential inherent in communicative action is no*
> *longer thought of as self-reflection writ-large, this specification of the*
> *normative content of modernity can prejudice neither the conceptual tools*
> *for diagnosing crises nor the way of overcoming them.*
>
> Habermas, 1987a, p348

In *The Theory of Communicative Action*, Habermas' answer to these problems is that the necessary impulses from the lifeworld will step in and influence, even control the functional subsystems. However, if this is to be realized it demands that 'autonomous public spheres' are developed, defined as public formations, 'which are neither bred nor kept by a political system for the purposes of creating legitimation' (Habermas, 1987b, p364).

The following discourse of this book aims to uncover the scope for procuring such a superior view on the process of environmental assessment. They include society's constitution of a superior framework for this as well as the actual terms for interpreting and practising environmental assessment, according to this form of understanding.

Environment, subject and society

The institutionalization of environmental issues in the public debate and in the political apparatus has meant that questions are evaded as to whether the environment should be protected or whether special environmental considerations should be undertaken for particular actions and decisions. The institutionalization itself is a confirmation of these questions. That this is not synonymous with giving an answer on *how* this should be effected is in a way obvious because, ultimately, this will depend on the actual circumstances. Nevertheless, developments over the last 25 years have shown that the answer to the 'how' is not merely a diversion from the concrete, but the exact opposite insofar as the most abstract issues need to be included – considerations such as societal meaning and aim or, indeed, whether a goal can be set for society's development. Such problematic is profoundly modern, and this is precisely what the environmental problematic has also proved to be.

Consequently, all attempts at having a new central steering subject, such as, for example, ecology steering societal development, to regulate modern society, prove impossible. This is because such a subject cannot exist within contemporary modern society. Analogically speaking, it serves no other purpose than personal satisfaction or moralistic 'self-torture', when people use their acquired individualism of modernity to making environmental issues the leading thread in their personal actions. This in no way alters society's institutionalized practices, and furthermore such actions will only be practicable to a limited degree.

The institutionalized practices of modern society are linked to the modern differentiation of the economic- and administrative systems as well as to the expert cultures. Thus society's various systematized spheres are divided and sealed into autonomous aims and actions, hence losing any chance for a core societal subject-writ-large.

The fact also that the environmental problematic is exclusively modern means that we do not understand it without an analysis of the differentiation and the impact. In effect, we are unable to outline any answers as to how we should respond to this problematic. At this stage, the only thing we can establish is that, as outlined above, 'solutions' can neither be defined in central crisis management terms nor established in subjective terms.

Thus, we are back to the modern problematic with its challenges with regard to societal actions. These can neither be conceptualized nor predicted either centrally or theoretically. Nor can they be based on subjective merits or values. Both the poststructuralists' critical vóices and modernity's defenders agree on this point, and their philosophical response is a rejection of both the metaphysics as well as the philosophy of the subject.

Habermas' rejection/critique of the philosophy of the subject indicates a way out of the modern problematic, which is something entirely different from what Szerszynski calls formalization. Szerszynski does not realize this as, apparently, he has not seen clearly the problematic of the philosophy of the subject. Habermas' solution to the modern problematic is not to steer us beyond modernity, but rather to re-establish the benefits of the differentiated expert cultures in an unbroken form or as an entity. That is, he affirms, to put the three forms of rationality into an entity, which is to be practised via their return to the lifeworld, cf. his critique on 'the false programs of the negation of culture'.

Actually, one should not talk about Habermas' way out of the modern problematic as, in reality, he looks at this from a different perspective. For Szerszynski, the modern problematic is a question of how a true connection is established between language and an extra-discursive reality. In other words, the establishment of a true connection in the situation where language is understood disjunctively is in contrast to pre-modernity, where language was understood conjunctively. He deals with this problem by negating it. Habermas' problematic is of a different character. He considers the differentiation of the modern expert cultures a problem, in cases where benefits or insights are not leading back to everyday culture. They only do so partly or singularly. The reality is that it is the cognitive instrumental rationality that reflects back to everyday life in a singular manner, whereas the moral-practical and the aesthetic-expressive rationality are suppressed by instrumental dominance, and as such is only partly utilized in everyday life. Thus the potential of rationality is lost, and that is a problem in a society where continued modernization is becoming increasingly dependent on such forms of rationality. Significantly, Habermas' problem is not external to the processes of modernity, but an internal one. He does not break away from modernity, but creates a complete modernity.

Other authors have also reacted to the modern problematic on the basis of the philosophy of reason, as outlined above.

In the 1980s, both Ulrich Beck and Anthony Giddens began to talk about reflexive modernization. Taking into account what is related above, such notions are easier to understand. Yet it is also revealed that their understanding is lacking. When they say that modernity itself has become reflexive – in Beck's terminology that it has moved from simple modernization to reflexive modernization – they do not recognize that modernization in itself means that a differentiation of the expert cultures (science, morality and the arts) imply an emancipation from tradition. This entails becoming more reflexive in character and thereby developing further. It is the detachment itself that makes reflexivity possible. In other words, when relieved from traditional actions and traditional ways of thinking, they can become reflexive on their own terms.

In the same period, Zygmunt Bauman starts talking about the ambivalence of modernity.[34] Thus he is resuming the dialectic of the enlightenment without realizing that in so doing he gets ensnared into the philosophy of the subject, and consequently is unable to surpass the problems of modernity without calling on the notions of postmodernity.

The next chapter will deal with the notion of modernity as a concept for society. This is essential for our understanding of why 'models of solutions' that emphasize communicative actions are presented in modern society. At the same time, it also becomes apparent that it is not only a matter of our understanding of why, but just as much a matter of the contents of the communicative actions. The issue is how this may come to indicate a renewal of the modern project, rather than becoming an extrapolation of modernity's cognitive-instrumental narrow-mindedness and controlling practices. It will become clear that this renewal is not some cleverly construed scientific scheme developed by experts and modern management. It is, indeed, an element that was included from the very beginning of modernity, which, however, capitalism's emphasis of cognitive-instrumental values knocked over and prevented from developing in full. In other words, we are talking about the liberation of latent elements in the modern structure – or expressed in another way – an emancipation process.

Notes

1   For example, in 1962, Rachel Carson published the famous work *Silent Spring* about DDT pollution and the extensive dissipation of the poisonous substance through food and foodstuffs, in ecosystems around the world, in *The New Yorker*, 16 June, 23 June and 30 June, 1962.
2   See for example Giddens, 1994, p11 and below.
3   In Danish there is a play on words: the Danish word for value is *værdi* which can also replace the word for currency, *valuta*.
4   To cite but a few: Beck, 1997; Lash, 1996; Hajer, 1995; Aagaard Nielsen, 1999; Mol, 1995; Spaargaren, 1997.
5   Horkheimer and Adorno, 2002.
6   *The Theory of Communicative Action*, vol 1, p1. In the following this work will be referred to as TCA 1 for volume 1 and TCA 2 for volume 2, followed by the number of quoted or cited page.
7   Cf. Eder, 1996, p213. He mentions, as an example of the latter, Beck's risk society that creates new and socially contingent identities, instead of the well-established class culture of the earlier industrial society. Furthermore, he underlines comparable arguments from Giddens, 1991. In the next chapter we are analysing both authors' views more closely.
8   Eder, 1996, p216. Eder has taken the concept of the lifeworld from Habermas. The following chapter looks into the details of this concept.
9   Cf. Spaargaren and Mol, 1992; Mol, 1995; Spaargaren, 1997 and Hajer, 1995.

'10   Cf. Plato's doctrine about ideas, where objects are shadows of their eternal and unchangeable ideas, and in which cognition is called 'anamnesis' – memory of the archetype.Plato differentiated ideas about truthfulness, goodness and beauty, a distinction that will play an important role in the discussion of rationality in Chapter 3.

11   The account is primarily based on the above article by the sociologist Bronislaw Szerszynski: 'On knowing what to do: Environmentalism and the modern problematic'; see Szerszynski, 1996. When Szerszynski's sources have been studied independently by me, I refer directly to the author concerned. Otherwise I refer to Szerszynski. This is, of course, most important when I do not agree with his interpretations and conclusions, which is clearly the case as regards his four examples of neomodernism. In discussing these, I first mention his views and subsequently describe in what way I disagree. Concluding the presentation, I will first of all refer to his specific way out of the dilemma of the modern problematic, and then describe how, in my view, he locks himself in. In short, I find his article very inspiring, even if I disagree with his conclusion.

12   The English mechanical materialist Thomas Hobbes (1588–1679) is known for his theory of the state, in which he calls the state Leviathan with reference to Job's Book in The Holy Bible, Chapters 40–41.

13   The materialist and empirical Francis Bacon (1561–1626).

14   Another English empiricist, John Locke (1632–1704), who dissociated himself from Hobbes' absolutism.

15   The concept of morality referred to here is based on Kant's categorical imperative: that you should only act following the maxim of what you wish/want to have as general law. The autonomy presupposed here, the individual subject's will to do what is right, is precisely what Habermas critiques, giving the ethics a foundation where the capacity of critical reflection is anchored in a linguistic intersubjectivity. Thus for Habermas, autonomy is replaced by intersubjectivity. Cf. Chapter 3. See also Nørager, 1985, pp132, 135, and Habermas, 1987a, pp294–335. As will be shown in Chapter 3, Habermas thus distinguishes between moral prescriptions of universal character and ethics that are bound to culture – that is, locally anchored

16   Szerszynski uses the English word 'description', whereas Habermas' own terminology probably would have used the concept 'Bestimmung', which should be translated as 'definition' in the sense of criteria which uniquely identify a social phenomenon or a concept in social science.

17   An example is the landscapes created by the gardener Gertrude Jekyll and the architect Edwin Lutyens in the decades before and after the turn of the 20th century. In the UK the same currents also lead to the Arts and Crafts movement. In Denmark a similar movement was named 'Skønvirke' (Acting for Beauty).

18   Here Szerszynski is using Kolb, 1986, pp132–133.

19   Following Thomas S. Kuhn's famous dictum about change in scientific framework; see Kuhn, 1996.

20   This was already the case with the German idealists of whom Hegel was a front figure, and later on, Adorno and Walter Benjamin of the Frankfurter School represented such viewpoints; cf. Habermas, 1985, pp34–64.

21   That it is not only the modern philosophers who have seen through this is revealed in Habermas' critical writing on the green movements in his defence for the modern project, see next note.

22   Habermas, 1981, 'Die Moderne – ein unvollendetes Projekt', in *Kleine Politische Schriften I-IV*, Suhrkamp Verlag, Frankfurt am Main, pp444–464.

23   Nørager, 1985.
24   Outhwaite, 1994.
25   Smart, 1999.
26   See Nørager, 1985, p25, where he stresses that since the first critique of reason, found in Schiller's Kantian critique, there has been a firm tradition for seeking alternatives to the sensibleness of the aesthetics as a basis for a new 'mythology'. Nørager refers at this point to Bohrer, 1983, p15.
27   Nørager refers to how Richard Wagner's musical recreation of medieval German heroic poems served for a long time (until Nietzche broke away from Wagner) as an example for Nietzche's aesthetic visions (Nørager, 1985, p25, fn23).
28   Outhwaite stresses in his note 5 to Chapter 8 that by this term Habermas means not only neo-Marxists, but also such thinkers as Alfred Schutz, Helmuth Plessner, Martin Heidegger and Jacques Derrida.

     See also Nørager's comments on the Marxist notions of production that 'have roots' among others with Hegel and the German idealists. Also deriving from this is the notion that part of expressionism – which founded such normative ideas that the individual should realize himself through work – provided alienation can successfully be resolved. The problem of the production paradigm (which remains the deciding factor in the so-called 'praxis philosophy' is twofold: first, it suggests a craftsman-like activity that has very little in common with modern industrial works, and second it mixes up two different things, namely work (understood as an instrumental relation to nature) and interaction, understood as 'a linguistically mediated interaction with other individuals' (Nørager, 1985, p13). I return to this critique of the praxis philosophy in Chapter 3.
29   Richard J. Bernstein, 'Foucault: Critique as a philosophical ethos', in Honneth et al, 1992. Quoted from Outhwaite, 1994, p129.
30   Frank, 1988, p64.
31   We will come back to Smart's analysis in the following chapter, where the theories of reflexive modernity will be examined.
32   Habermas, 1987, originally in German; Habermas, 1985.
33   Horkheimer's and Adorno's famous combined work with the title *The Dialectic of Enlightenment* – see Horkheimer and Adorno, 2002.
34   Bauman, 1991.

Chapter 3

Modernity and Reflexivity

How the concept of modernity entered sociology

Over approximately the last 20 years, modernity has once again become modern. To be more precise, initially it was not actually modernity that became modern, it was postmodernity. For, as we saw in the last chapter, it was the assertion of a postmodern condition that brought the concept of modernity to the fore. Perhaps precisely because postmodern was conceived by means of a 'post'. Whatever the reason, there have been two trends or viewpoints since the 1970s, one of which has finally prevailed.

On the one hand, in the early 1970s, society was said to be a mix between capitalism and socialism, or it was called late capitalism. However, later in the 1970s and in the 1980s such terms gave way to the term 'capitalist crisis society'. In the same breath, the belief that the future and the passing of time would bring progress changed from quiet expectation (late capitalism!) to deep scepticism[1] – while nostalgia for the bliss of prosperity and the issue of how to recover it used to dominate and instil fear of the future with a sense of doom prevailing. For instance, seemingly insurmountable and increasingly global environmental problems combined with anxiety about technology rendering human labour superfluous feed into this fear.

Yet society was called modernity. Modernity had been talked about since the latter decades of the 19th century. However, during the 1970s and 1980s, the term reappeared in the shape of a concept describing the very nature of society. This formulation of new forms of modernity was introduced from 1979 to 1981. Lyotard asserted a postmodernity existed that highlighted the need to consider technology and science in new ways that questioned the values and directions of society (Lyotard, 1979). Habermas presented modernity as an (admittedly) incomplete project (Habermas, 1981c). Berman, an American, put forward his own critical studies on the concept (Berman, 1982).

It may be characteristic that the use of the concept of modernity gained momentum in tune with the 1980s affirmation of the fact that the crisis of the 1970s was anything but a temporarily passing phenomenon. In addition, in the years around 1989, the authoritarian socialist systems of Central and Eastern Europe collapsed, presumably advanced by the crises of the West and the consequent enormous rationalization that this had caused in Western capitalism. The socialist systems did not embrace a similar 'cleansing mechanism' and were consequently left behind to a degree that shook the political structure and made it collapse like a house of cards. This situation was left to a combination of capitalism and democracy. Somehow the crisis of the West seems to have caused the collapse of the East, while the collapse of the East dissolved the crisis of the West.

Right from the early 1990s, all talk about capitalism and crisis had subsided, even though capitalism itself, including its combination with globalism, was as rife as ever as an increasingly dominating force. Simultaneously, no one wanted to comment on when the crisis of capitalism had ceased or, indeed, whether it had ceased at all. Modernity was not merely a phenomenon of societal development, but signified the actual societal form of the West. The concept of modernity excelled and became synonymous with contemporary capitalism, not in a negative sense of the word, but rather as a final victory for the entire Western free world and its increasing global dominance.

It may therefore seem paradoxical that the re-introduction of modernity as the concept for contemporary societal development and condition, in Ulrich Beck's writings, is linked to the contrasting concept of *risk society*, which, according to him, is further characterized by the fact that modernity has become *reflexive* (Beck, 1992, pp11, 19).

He shares this position with a number of other contemporary authors. However, similar twofold views in relation to modernity – seeing it as progression or an improvement of a historical condition and seeing it as a situation more prone to danger and risk – were implied right from the start when the concept was first introduced almost 150 years ago. Similar kinds of interpretations can be found as early as Baudelaire's detailed accounts (1821–1867), followed by Marx (1818–1883) and Nietzsche (1844–1900). As discussed in Chapter 2, Hegel conceded to a dialectic outlook on modernity. Indeed, all these authors shared the ambition to define to what extent the emerging contemporary society was new in relation to past societal traditions, religious ties and historical self-determination.

Baudelaire was the first writer to use the concept of modernity, which, to him, meant the condition of a new form of society that was fluid, passing and random. In his view, the novelty of society was the emancipation away from all the previously binding traditions, religions and historical terms. The poet sticks his head out when, instead of characterizing this phenomenon in a negative way, he defines it as the very core of fluid beauty itself.[2]

Similarly, Marx was not merely alarmed by society's capitalist forms of production, but also fascinated by its potential. For Marx, the new society meant a constant revolutionization of production, a continuous intrusion of all social relations, insofar as all fixed and static circumstances were to be discarded and that all that was permanent had to disappear into the clear blue sky.[3] In his analysis, Marx aimed to reveal the capitalist laws of production and show that the mode of production, which created these laws, was a temporary historical condition of society. A basic characteristic of this mode of production was also the fact that it hid its own temporality. It hides and distorts all social relations as well as its own historical and passing character. It conceals all social relations and exposes them as relations between material things. This phenomenon is described by Marx as fetishism or reification.[4]

It could be said that Marx's analysis of commodities as being the core element of the economy and the real product of labour denotes the general abstraction of modernity.

Of the above three philosophers, the most pessimistic viewpoint on modernity is found in Nietzsche's philosophy. According to Nietzsche, the immediate issue is modernity, which transforms all values and in so doing is creating a world of masks and simulacrum.[5] He refers to modernity as being decadent. Life in modernity is no longer a genuine entity. It is complex, calculating, contriving – an artefact. Yet, despite this, Nietzsche also sees modernity as liberation from past traditions, religious ties and historical contingencies. It is the rejection of one ideology that makes way for the enforcement of another.

This very brief account of the first and original interpretations of the concept of modernity in terms of modern social life will hopefully suffice in order to appreciate the sharp contrast between the former and later accounts of modernity regarding the promise of liberation, the creation of something new and exciting, or something modern that is up-to-date and suitable in relation to the ties and ignorance of the past, as it is often expressed within the arts, such as for example literature and architecture.

However, the original meaning of the concept did not imply a blind belief in the future or confidence in a bright modern time ahead, but rather pointed to a twofold perception of these developments. Doubts with regard to the liberating value of modernity prevailed right from the outset. Emancipation and enforced artificiality, fetishism and randomness were depicted to go hand in hand. Besides this double meaning, other characteristics accompanied them, such as constant revolution, reshaping and renewal. Yet, significantly, not only can this be described as characteristic, in addition, it also holds the former double meaning.

The lack of endorsement of these two perceptions of double meaning is found among analytical scholars of modernity that had appeared before the world was to run amok with Nazism and a World War that destroyed any talk about modernity, technology and scientific progress. Incidentally, all from the same spatial starting point.

The place of origin was Berlin, the grand city where, at the turn of the century – a few decades before the madness of Nazism gathered pace – three authors analysed the concept of modernism. They were George Simmel (1858–1918), a sociologist, Siegfried Kracauer (1889–1966), a sociologist and philosopher, and Walter Benjamin (1892–1940), a literary critic and cultural theorist.[6] They all focused on two aspects of modernity that prevailed at the time: the modern metropolis and social relations under capitalism. They regarded the metropolis and the capitalist economy as the main factors that decided modern social life. For them, modernity meant a metropolitan labyrinth of human co-existence where capital and money created a form of life that was socially differentiating and impersonal although, at the same time, also liberating.

Both Kracauer and Benjamin considered not only Berlin but also Paris, especially after the Nazis seized power, the exponent for this form of modernity. While acknowledging its liberating factors and considering the city the place where fragments of modernity are present in all forms of progression, their analyses aimed to alert the world of the false pretences and reveal its deceiving effects. Modernity is thus also an illusion and deception that signifies prosperity and renewal, but in such a way that it blocks insight into its negative impact.

The antithesis was the calamity of the Second World War and the conclusive atom bombs, which prescribed the 1950s lacking belief in a future of science and technology. Indeed, the fear of what technology might bring prevailed right up to the 1960s.

However, equally characteristic for the late 1960s was the rejoicing in a new belief that no limits could confine the future. But the rejoicing was marred by short-sightedness. When something was good for nothing, all one had to do was to create something new. Therefore the horizon of decisions lacked foresight, not due to a lack of conviction or inability in terms of taking long-term views, but more due to a lack of appreciation of the necessity to do so. From a historical perspective, the 1960s could be likened to a 'narcotic ecstasy'. The more intense and consciousness-expanding the experience, the more acute also the symptoms of withdrawal.

The sudden and heavy economic downturn and crisis in Western Europe from the middle of the 1970s onwards gradually influenced the political and cultural situation and led to an identity crisis and a cultural vacuum for many groups of people. Past political ideals and cultural values lost impact, and it became increasingly difficult to aspire to new utopias and goals.

The left wing's expectations of socialism as a political alternative collapsed despite the crisis of capitalism, and despite the fact that the right-wing groups had not succeeded either in their attempts to establish alternative movements. The latter was perhaps due to lingering memories about the 1930s fascist movements that were hard to shed, thus causing a paralysing effect on all initiatives from that quarter.

While the left wing's belief in a total collapse of capitalism and a radicalization of broad masses of people did not materialize, the modernization and rationalization processes within the capitalist production processes continued recklessly with unimpeded force. People in general adapted to the new terms, becoming de-politicized in a traditional sense, while also, in defiance of traditional political and class divisions, the engagements of popular movements gained ground, in particular, peace movements and, as we have seen already, environmental movements.

Whereas the state had previously been seen as the guarantor of the common good, a large part of the public now considered the political institutions powerless due to the domination and all-encompassing effect of the market forces.

In response to this situation Lyotard asserted his diagnosis of a societal condition that supersedes modernity, while Habermas sees modernity as being incomplete insofar as it needs to be reinstated in order to counteract antimodernism and conservatism, - and this even despite any negative effects or, indeed, despite Ulrich Beck's claims that modernity has ruptured. Beck's thesis is that a new form of modernity has developed – that is, reflexive modernity, which, among other things, attests the effects of a kind of modernity that is beginning to prove destructive both to the environmental and cultural foundations of society as well as having invoked risks that jeopardize the socially accepted norms of safety and security.

Also other sociologists talk about modernity's reflexive character, about reflexive knowledge and reflexivity in society. Anthony Giddens believes that reflexivity in modern society entails a critical evaluation of the social practices, which, in the light of the incoming information about the same practices, transform them, thus causing a change of their fundamental character (Giddens, 1990, p38).

The sociologists Barry Smart and Scott Lash also bring reflexive modernity into the debate. However, contrary to both Beck's and Giddens' points of view, but above all contrary to Beck's claim of a breach within modernity, Smart and Lash consider reflexivity as being part of modernity as such. Finally, Niklas Luhmann's talks about the cybernetic and self-referential societal systems of another order that are able to reproduce the elements that they themselves consist of (Luhmann, 1987; 1993).

These different assertions will be discussed and analysed later in this chapter. All that is established, at this point, is that the concepts of modernity, whether of a reflective character or something else, have gained prevalence in sociology and its theories – indeed, they play a very vital role. This account does not aim to give an analysis of the historical and scientific genesis and the development of modernity. Such a task would be far too extensive. However, modernity and reflexivity are irrevocably linked to an analysis of the actual condition of a society, and the consequences of this will be examined in the remaining part of this chapter.

That the various authors immersed in the question of modernity and reflexivity have no homogeneous attitude to the concept has already been suggested, and this will become clearer as the following account unfolds. How the concepts are applied is imperative to this debate. The purpose is to reach an understanding as to how the various perspectives may be useful for the analysis of various societal contexts from within which planning and environmental assessments are effected. It should hopefully become clear which areas need to be supplemented with further accounts. The following analysis also has the purpose of explaining to what extent existing concepts are useful in determining the characteristics of specific forms of society. From this, a basic framework should transpire for determining the characteristic forms of action in which planning and environmental assessment usually become embedded.

Communication and modernity – Habermas' 'Theory of Communicative Action'

Two authors in particular have been interested in the communicative aspects of modernity, namely Habermas and Luhmann. Both theorists consider communicative action the core of modernity, and it is the detachment of the communicative practice away from the immediately contextual aspects that enables modernity. In their respective comprehensive theory and system constructions, they specify how they understand the concept of modernity per se. Habermas takes his a point of departure in modern philosophy and sociology. Luhmann, on the other hand, pursues the sociological systems theory, where scientific ideals are inspired by the exact sciences.

Therefore in the further analysis presented here, Habermas' theories will be explored in some depth. Of the two theorists, he is the one who puts forward the most comprehensive theory on modernity as a social concept. Indeed, the main objective of his work aims to identify a theory of modernity. And, in contrast to Beck and Giddens, who both concentrate on examining the more specific consequences of modernity on environmental and personal issues, Habermas focuses on developing an understanding of the process of modernity itself, and the changes involved. Furthermore, Habermas sees reflexivity as a common aspect of modernity, rather than, as in particular Beck does, a manifestation of a specific stage of development of modernity. Indeed, Giddens shares Beck's view of a specific radical modernization process, which he calls 'late- or high-modernity'.

In 1980, Habermas pointed out the importance of defending what he called *the modern project*, which he considered was being attacked by the neo-conservatives and specific ecological movements ('green' lobbies and environmental fundamentalists) alike. The reason was, as previously mentioned, that he saw no alternative to modernity, even though he recognized that the modernization process under capitalism had a twofold effect. On the one hand, it broke away from traditional values and beliefs, in holding out more universal promises, yet, on the other hand, by destroying handed down ways of life and cultural traditions without replacing these with more developed forms, it resulted in impoverishment. Habermas will thus continue the modern project, because it, until now, has been an *incomplete* project only, where the cognitive-instrumental reasoning dominates. As such it has only partly been a rational project.

The question is how he can fulfil a modern project that contains all forms of rationality, and what, to him, will modernity then entail? The question also arises – why modernity has not succeeded so far? Why did the philosophers of the enlightenment get it wrong, and why did the utopian modern socialist undertakings not succeed either?

According to Habermas, an adequate answer to these questions is dependent on a shift of paradigm in terms of modernity being based on a theory of communicative action rather than on the subject-object model of the philosophy of consciousness. The theory of communicative action has three dimensions or poles in contrast to the two-dimensional philosophy of reason. The theory is about two or more communicating participants who seek a mutual understanding of statements that relates to a world of language, whether relating to the external social world or the individual's subjective world. In contrast, the subject-object relations of the philosophy of consciousness are based on monological thinking that excludes the deciding role of intersubjectivity and language.

Habermas has been consistent in his belief that it is possible to have a society that is ruled by reason and that, in the last instance, such reasoning is normatively accomplished in language, as reaching understanding is the inherent telos of human speech (TCA 1, p287).

As we have seen, Szerszynski's analysis of the modern problematic found that it was necessary to find a scientific paradigm beyond the subject-object way of reasoning. His work asserts that we do not use or construct the world or language but that we are placed in this world with its accompanying language. However, he does not manage to point to any accomplished alternative. Similarly, we have seen that postmodernism and poststructuralism also aimed to shift the paradigm, albeit this shift was understood as having surpassed modernism.

Finally, Habermas refers to the systems theory claim of a new paradigm, put forward in Luhmann's concept of self-reflection.[7] Habermas rejects this as untenable, as all that is happening is a displacement from the subject-object relation to a relation between the system and its surroundings. However, by way of extrapolating the subject-object relation with the communicative relation, one can show that to some extent the systems theory is also a form of philosophy of the subject in sociological guise, and that communicative action cannot be reduced to being a relationship of system and surroundings (Habermas, 1987a, pp353ff, 368ff).

In the following, I will give an account of the main elements of Habermas' theory of communicative action. The aim is to highlight the main elements only, without including an account of Habermas' discursive form. It is crucial for the problem of this book that the theory is not confined to being a theory of action in the narrow sense of the word. The theoretical problematic of action constitutes a part of a superior theory of rationality and modernity. By way of introduction, Habermas himself emphasizes that the theory of communicative action opens up three thematic complexes:

> *First, a concept of communicative rationality that is sufficiently sceptical in its development but is nevertheless resistant to cognitive-instrumental abridgments of reason; second, a two-level concept of society that connects the 'lifeworld' and 'system' paradigms in more than a rhetorical fashion; and finally, a theory of modernity that explains the type of social pathologies that are today becoming increasingly visible, by way of the assumption that communicatively structured domains of life are being subordinated to the imperatives of autonomous, formally organized systems of action. Thus the theory of communicative action is intended to make possible a conceptualization of the social-life context that is tailored to the paradoxes of modernity.*
>
> TCA 1, pxlii.

Thus, Habermas' account in *The Theory of Communicative Action* follows the line of giving *an introduction* in which he establishes the concept of rationality, which forms the basis of his theory. Then a *first and second intermediate reflection* follows, in which this basic concept of the communicative action is discussed from the three thematic complexes: (a) the concept of communicative rationality, (b) the two-level societal concept that connects the paradigm of the lifeworld and the system, (c) a theory of modernity and its paradoxes, and finally a *conclusion*, that connects the theory-historical and systematic analyses. To facilitate reading and interpretation of these sections Habermas gives an account of social history, in particular Max Weber, George H. Mead, Emilie Durkheim and Talcott Parsons.

Nørager puts forward and demonstrates four points, giving an account of Habermas' main theses and demonstrating how Habermas has amplified or rejected existing theories in order to redeem these theses. Nørager's first point is that *the theory of social action*, Weber's one-sided focus on 'purposive rationality', needs to be ousted giving way to a concept of social action that is founded on a comprehensive theory of communication. Second, it needs to be pointed out that *societal rationalization* relates to a rationality potential that incorporates what Habermas calls 'the basis for validity of speech'. Third, Habermas must demonstrate that as far as the question of *the foundation of the normative* is concerned, action oriented to reaching understanding (performative or illocutionary) is more fundamental than strategic action (perlocutionary). Finally, the fourth point, with regard to a theory of modernity it is necessary to show how speech acts are gradually taking over action coordinating functions and in so doing are also gradually contributing to strengthening and stabilizing interactions (Nørager, 1985, p94).

We have now reached the crux of why, in particular, Habermas' theories are so important for this book. This can be summarized in three points:

1   The first point concerns to what extent one can *conceptualize social life-contexts*, which takes into account modern paradoxical issues. How does Habermas understand the modern as a concept of society, and in what way can modern society's specific life forms be identified and thus, at a higher level, help to identify the potentials with regard to environmental politics?

2   The second point is a determination of the concept of rationality in the modern age. What are the implications of the reduction of rationality to cognitive-instrumental rationality? Do possibilities exist that include all the aspects of rationality, and how can this be achieved?

3   Finally, in terms of the concept of the communicative action, combined with a matching concept of rationality, the third point is an analysis of the feasibility for *carrying out strategic environmental assessments in a form that surpasses technocratic manipulation*, understood in the sense of being able to carry out environmental assessments that are free not only from political ties but also from any interference from politicians who operate under the auspices of political dispositions with technocratic arguments.

The social evolution and societal rationalization

In *The Theory of Communicative Action,* modern society is viewed to have developed as a result of a social *evolution,* in which *rationality* is continually progressing in the historical process. According to Habermas, besides modern society, the stages of this social evolution are *tribal societies and traditional societies or societies organized around a state* (TCA 2, p154). In this respect, he is coupling himself to the general convention that has developed in sociology.

Yet, he does not adopt the evolutionary theories uncritically. In respect of Max Weber's theories, which relinquish both the philosophy of history and the theories of evolution in a Darwinian sense, Habermas concurs with Weber's attempts in following the process of rationalization of a religious worldview as distinct from the development of science (Nørager, 1985, p53). In fact, the latter was the philosopher of history Condorcet's view, and indeed Habermas is quite critical about this, as he is also critical of another variant of the philosophy of history, namely historical materialism despite the fact that his own view of the social evolution could be argued to have some association with both of these (Outhwaite, 1994, pp58–59).

Condorcet, supported by a boundless faith in the rationality of the mathematical sciences – for example Newtonian physics – is energized by an optimistic belief in the future in the belief that methodical advances in scientific knowledge will ensure spiritual and cultural progression. In modernity, the perfectionism of the human faculty is not limited by a telos inherent in it, as in the tradition of Aristotle, but is heading towards unimpeded, uninhibited fulfilment. Perfectionism is thus interpreted as the mastery of the external and internal forces of resistance in our minds (TCA 1, p146).

With regard to Condorcet's theories, Habermas draws attention to four points, which determine a change in the historic-philosophical interpretation of modern age. They are a belief in (a) the linear concept of future progress, (b) the universal reasoning of the human spirit, (c) a pre-critical concept of nature that presupposes a unity of theoretical and practical reason, and finally (d) that the human accumulation of knowledge automatically has empirical consequences and results in empirical progress (TCA 1, pp148–152).

In contrast, as we have already seen, Habermas: (a) denies a linear concept of history, (b) argues that reason is linked to a kind of intersubjectivity in language rather than merely dependent on the individual, (c) links the theoretical and practical reasoning to two different expert cultures that differentiate modernity – that is, the cognitive-instrumental and the moral-practical aspects respectively – and finally (d) considers it the task of modernity to revert to the comprehensive potential of reason of the expert cultures back to the lifeworld as a cultural transmission in its entirety.

Habermas' dissociation from historical materialism is primarily due to the determinism that is attached to it, but he has also suggested a differentiation between work and interaction, and argues that historical materialism focuses too narrowly on the first category, as a source of learning. His argument is that there is a parallel between individual and social development, between 'the reproduction of society and the socialization of its members'[8] and furthermore there is good reason to believe that the 'learning processes also take place in the dimension of moral insight, practical knowledge, communicative action, and the consensual regulation of action conflicts – learning processes that are deposited in more mature forms of social integration, in new productive relations, and that in turn first make possible the introduction of new productive forces'.[9]

Yet, Habermas does not relinquish historical materialism.[10] On the contrary, he sees himself as reconstructing historical materialism, as it is the most suitable theory about the historical development of society as a learning process. He affirms the Marxian view of the primacy of production albeit in the sense that culture is part of the superstructure. He also draws attention to the fact that Marx himself conceived historical materialism as a theory of social evolution (TCA 2, p343).

The reconstruction of historical materialism does not need to assume a species-subject that undergoes evolution as evolution is sustained by societies themselves and the subjects acting in them. Furthermore, empirical substances don't necessarily develop in a linear or irreversible fashion, unlike the patterns of higher levels of social evolution that can be rationally reconstructed. Nor can teleology be imputed to history. Social development must be judged by the stage of development of the productive forces and by the maturity of forms of social intercourse (Habermas, 1981d, pp205, 207; TCA 2, p383).

Within this understanding, Habermas' thesis emphasizes that the perception of action rationality determines the perception of societal rationalization. Furthermore, this needs to be based on a communication-theoretical concept of social action. However, the existing action concepts that Marx, Max Weber, Horkheimer and Adorno take as basic are not complex enough to capture all the aspects of social action to which societal rationalization can be attached (TCA 1, p145).

The problem in Weber's analysis of the rationalization of modern Western society is that it is based on purposive-rationality to a great extent. Such a perspective is too narrow. Weber's concept of rationalization is not, as is often claimed, too wide and diffused. On the contrary, it is too limited and therefore not suitable for illustrating substantively rational society, which is a lost utopia for Weber (Outhwaite, 1994, p75). In comparison to Marx's view, Weber sees the institutional framework of the capitalist economy and the modern state in a different light: not as relations of production that fetter the potential for rationalization, but rather as subsystems of purpose-rational action where Western rationalism develops at a societal level (TCA 1, p144). In other words, it is first and foremost the capitalist economy and the state that Weber is concerned with in his theories on rationalization.

In contrast, Habermas suggests a broader rationalization concept that includes action orientation and worldviews. The aim of this is that 'the aspects of rationality of action that we found in communicative action should now permit us to grasp processes of societal rationalization across their whole breadth and no longer solely from the selective viewpoint of the rationalization of purposive rational action' (TCA 1, p335).

The action theory must therefore be linked to the concept of society, and Habermas develops this by introducing and applying a concept of the lifeworld that incorporates action orientations as well as worldviews:

> *It is only with the turn back to the context-forming horizon of the lifeworld, from within which participants in communication come to an understanding with one another about something, that our field of vision changes in such a way that we can see the points of connection for social theory within the theory of communicative action. Then communicative action becomes interesting primarily as a principle of sociation [Vergesellschaftung]: Communicative action provides the medium for the reproduction of lifeworlds. At the same time, processes of societal rationalization are given a different place. They transpire more in implicitly known structures of the lifeworld than in explicitly known action orientations (as Weber suggested).*
>
> TCA 1, p337

But the circumstances are, in effect, that 'every theory of society that is restricted to communication theory is subject to limitations that must be observed. The concept of the lifeworld that emerges from the conceptual perspective of communicative action has only limited analytical and empirical range. I would therefore like to propose (1) that we conceive of societies *simultaneously* as systems and lifeworlds. This concept proves itself in (2) a theory of social evolution that separates the rationalization of the lifeworld from the growing complexity of societal systems' (TCA 2, p118).

Before proceeding further with the elements of the theory of communicative action, the principal point of which is a theory of modernity, we can now outline an overall theoretical framework for such a theory. Modernity is the result of a societal evolution with advancing rationalization. Such a rationalization does not focus on society per se, but rather on that part of society that represents the lifeworld. Society can therefore be understood as a unity of system and lifeworld.

Thus the concept of societal evolution has been given a more explicit formulation, and the core consideration of rationality is shifting from purposive-rationality within the capitalist economy and the state to the communicative rationality within the lifeworld. However, the total reproduction of society cannot be explained solely from the theory of communicative rationality, indeed understanding is reliant on the relationship between the lifeworld and the system.

The rationalization of the lifeworld

The rationalization of the lifeworld has not yet been given any substance, nor has Habermas' own understanding of rationality and the lifeworld. At this juncture, I shall refer to some of his preliminary definitions and use of concepts, which will enable a further analysis of specific elements of particular interest for the problematic of this book. Next, the broader elements of the theory will be addressed: forms of action, the concept of communicative rationality, the lifeworld, and systemic components. Thereafter, the evolutionary process can be deciphered, and based on this the theory of modernity, and how its pathologies effect the forming of life connections.

As Habermas wants to derive a concept of societal rationalization from the theory on communicative action, before he has properly developed the latter, he is obliged to introduce a preliminary concept on rationality. He outlines this as 'a disposition of speaking and acting subjects that are expressed in modes of behavior for which there are good reasons or grounds. This means that rational expressions admit of objective evaluation' (TCA 1, p22).

As part of his account of the lifeworld and its rationalization Habermas applies what he calls *cultural interpretive systems* or *worldviews* that reflect the background knowledge of social groups and guarantee an interconnection among the multiplicity of actions. Based on these preliminary concepts of the lifeworld, he wants to 'inquire into the conditions that the structures of action-orienting worldviews must satisfy if a rational conduct of life is to be possible for those who share such a worldview' (TCA 1, pp43–44).

The rationality of worldviews is not measured in terms of logical and semantic properties but in terms of the formal-pragmatic basic concepts they place at the disposal of individuals for interpreting their world. This statement leads him to give an indirect reason why there is a need for a theory of communicative action. We could namely in relation to the above outlined concepts built into the world-views speak of the 'ontologies', providing that this concept from the tradition of Greek metaphysics is not restricted to a special world-relation – that is, to the cognitive relation to the world of existing things. There is no corresponding concept of philosophy that includes relations to the social and the subjective worlds as well as to the objective world. Here it is this lack that the theory of communicative action is meant to remedy (TCA 1, p45).

An analysis of the modern and the mythical worldview leads Habermas to an introduction of the concept of the lifeworld, correlating the processes of reaching understanding where they are played between three worlds: the objective world, the social world and the subjective world:

> *Subjects acting communicatively always come to an understanding in the horizon of a lifeworld. Their lifeworld is formed from more or less diffuse, always unproblematic, background convictions. This lifeworld background serves as a source of situation definitions that are presupposed by participants as unproblematic. In their interpretive accomplishments the members of a communication community demarcate the one objective world and their subjectively shared social world from the subjective worlds of individuals and (other) collectives. The world-concepts and the corresponding validity claims provide the formal scaffolding with which those acting communicatively order problematic*

> *contexts of situations, that is, those requiring agreement, in their lifeworld,*
> *which is presupposed as unproblematic.*
>
> TCA 1, p70

While acknowledging that this is as yet a preliminary concept of the lifeworld, the rationalization process of this can nevertheless be defined as follows:

> *The lifeworld also stores the interpretive work of preceding generations. It*
> *is the conservative counterweight to the risk of disagreement that arises*
> *with every actual process of reaching understanding; for communicative*
> *actors can achieve an understanding only by way of taking yes/no*
> *positions on what is in principle criticizable validity claims. The* relation
> between these weights changes with the decentralization of world-
> views. *The more the worldview that furnishes the cultural stock of*
> *knowledge is decentered, the less the need for understanding is covered* in
> advance *by an interpreted lifeworld immune from critique, and the more*
> *this need has to be met by the interpretive accomplishments of the partici-*
> *pants themselves, that is, by way of risky (because rationally motivated)*
> *agreement, the more frequently we can expect rational action orientations.*
> *Thus for the time being we can characterize the rationalization of the*
> *lifeworld in the dimension 'normatively ascribed agreement' versus*
> *'communicatively achieved understanding'. The more cultural traditions*
> *predecide which validity claims, when, where, for what, from whom, and*
> *to whom must be accepted, the less the participants themselves have the*
> *possibility of making explicit and examining the potential grounds on*
> *which their yes/no positions are based.*
>
> TCA 1, pp70–71

Habermas outlines four formal conditions that cultural traditions must exhibit 'if rational action orientations are to be possible in a lifeworld interpreted corre-spondingly, if they are to be able to consolidate into a rational conduct of life:

1   The cultural tradition must make available formal concepts for the objective, social and subjective worlds; it must permit differentiated validity claims (propositional truth, normative rightness, subjective truthfulness) and stimu-late a corresponding differentiation of basic attitudes (objectivating, norm-conformative and expressive). Symbolic expressions can then be produced on a formal level at which they are systematically connected with reasons and accessible to objective assessment.
2   The cultural tradition must permit a reflective relation to itself; it must be so far stripped of its dogmatism as to permit in principle that interpretations stored in tradition be placed in question and subjected to critical revision. Then inter-nal interconnections of meaning can be systematically elaborated and alternative interpretations can be methodically examined. Cognitive activities of the second order emerge: learning processes guided by hypotheses and

filtered through arguments in the domain of objective thought, moral-practical insight, and aesthetic perception.

3   In its cognitive, moral, and evaluative components the cultural tradition must permit a feedback connection with specialized forms of argumentation to such an extent that the corresponding learning processes can be socially insti- tutionalized. In this way cultural subsystems can arise – for science, law and morality, music, art, and literature – in which traditions take shape that are supported by arguments rendered fluid through permanent criticism but at the same time professionally secured.

4   Finally, the cultural tradition must interpret the lifeworld in such a way that action oriented to success can be freed from the imperatives of an under- standing that is to be communicatively renewed over and over again and can be at least partially uncoupled from action oriented to reaching understand- ing. This makes possible a societal institutionalization of purposive-rational for generalized goals, for example, the formation of subsystems, controlled through money and power, for rational economics and rational administra- tion' (TCA 1, pp71–72).

In relation to the subsystems, mentioned under 3) and 4), he adds that Max Weber regarded these as a differentiation of spheres of value that for him repre- sented the core of the cultural and societal rationalization in the modern age. If we employ Piaget's[11] concept of decentration as a guiding thread in this way, in order to clarify the internal connection between the structure of a worldview, the lifeworld as the context of processes of understanding and the possibilities of a rational conduct of life, we again encounter the concept of communicative ration- ality (TCA 1, p72).

We have now reached the core of the concept of rationality, its relation with communication and a wider understanding of modernity as a concept of society. It should also be noted (point 2 above) that reflexivity comes in right from the very beginning of the historical process of modernization. The possibility for reflexivity is one of the preconditions for the process of modernization. The concept of rationality which Habermas introduces with reference to 'good reasons' is indeed a cognitive conception linked to epistemology or truth rather than pure procedural considerations. The consequence of this approach to rationality which is linked to communicative action is the emergence of a more comprehensive concept of rationality which is orientated to 'argumentative speech'. Such a concept is decisively different from a cognitive- instrumental understanding of rationality that is linked to teleological action, where the objective is either manipulation of or adaptation to the surroundings (TCA 1, pp10–11, 22; Outhwaite, 1994, p70).

Communicative action and rationality

The concept of communicative rationality needs to be analysed in the light of achieving understanding in language. This points, 'on the one side, to different forms of discursive redeeming validity claims [...]; on the other side, it points to relations to the world that communicative actors take up in raising validity claims for their expression. Thus the decentration of our understanding of the world proved to be the most important dimension of the development of worldviews' (TCA 1, p75).

These validity claims are connected with the cognitive processes in between three worlds, described above, which the speaker relates to: the objective (physical) world, the social world (roles and norms), and the subjective world (inner experienced/internal world). Communication relates to one, two or all three worlds, but the very option that one is able to refer to all three worlds endorses the perception of their differentiation as being a core element of modernity. Habermas writes:

> *Cognitive development signifies in general* the decentration of an egocentric understanding of the world. *Only to the extent that the formal reference system of the three worlds is differentiated can we form a reflective concept of 'world' and open up access to the world through the medium of common interpretive efforts, in the sense of a cooperative negotiation of situation definitions. The concept of a subjective world permits us to contrast not only our own internal world, but also the subjective worlds of others, with the external world.*
>
> TCA 1, p69, cf. also point (2) above

Based on these three world relations, Habermas distinguishes between four concepts of action, each having their own claim of rationality attached. These are the concepts of *teleological action, normatively regulated action, dramaturgical action* and *communicative action,* where the concept of communicative action is the basis from which all the others evolve. The first three types of actions are thus limiting cases of communicative action. Finally, a fifth form of action is introduced, namely *strategic action,* which is an expansion of the teleological action. Strategic action occurs when 'there can enter into the agent's calculation of success the anticipation of decisions on the part of at least one additional goal-directed actor' (TCA 1, p85).

Linked to the concept of communicative action, there comes into play the additional presupposition of a linguistic medium. At this level of concept formation, the rationality problematic moves into the perspective of the agent himself, as there is a need to make clear in what sense achieving understanding in language is thereby introduced as a mechanism for coordinating action (TCA 1, p94).

Strategic action *can* be understood to mean, 'that participants' actions, directed through egocentric calculations of utility and coordinated through interest positions, are mediated through speech acts'. In both normatively regulated and dramaturgical actions 'we even *have* to suppose a consensus formation among participants that is in principle of a linguistic nature. Nevertheless, in these three models of action language is conceived *one-sidedly* in different respects' (TCA 1, p94):

> *The one-sidedness of the first three concepts of language can be seen in the fact that the corresponding types of communication singled out by them prove to be limit cases of communicative action:* first, *the indirect communication of those who have only the realization of their own ends in view;* second, *the consensual action of those who simply actualize an already existing normative agreement; and* third, *presentation of self in relation to an audience. In each case only one function of language is thematized: the release of perlocutionary effects, the establishment of interpersonal relations, and the expression of subjective experiences. By contrast, the communicative model of action which defines the traditions of social science connected with Mead's symbolic interactionism, Wittgenstein's concept of language games, Austin's theory of speech acts, and Gadamer's hermeneutics, takes all the functions of language equally into consideration.*
>
> TCA 1, p95

Teleological action presupposes one world – the objective world. This is also the case for the concept of strategic action. The point of departure for the communicative action is in language as a medium among other media by which each actor 'is oriented to his own success and behaves cooperatively only to the degree that this fits with his egocentric calculus of utility' (TCA 1, p88). Based on the interpretation of the situation and the conceptual rationality, decision-making follows. In other words, it is judged according to its effect. 'The rules of action embody technically and strategically useful knowledge, which can be criticized in reference to truth claims and can be improved through a feedback relation with the growth of empirical-theoretical knowledge. This knowledge is stored in the form of technologies and strategies' (TCA 1, p333).

Normative regulated action presupposes two worlds – the objective world and a social world. The point of departure of communicative action presupposes 'language as a medium that transmits cultural values and carries a consensus that is merely reproduced with each additional act of understanding' (TCA 1, p95). Members of social groups that are oriented to the same kinds of values, and through their mutual consensus of norms as rooted in common behavioural expectancy bring about this action. 'Normatively regulated speech acts embody moral practical knowledge. They can be contested under the aspect of rightness. Like claims to truth, controversial claims to rightness can be made thematic and examined discursively. In cases of disturbance of the regulative use of language, practical discourse offers its services as a continuation of consensual action with other means. In moral-practical argumentation, participants can test both the rightness of a given action in relation to a given norm, and, at the next level, the rightness of such a norm itself. This knowledge is handed down in the form of legal and moral representations' (TCA 1, p334).

Dramaturgical action presupposes two worlds, namely an internal world and an external world. The point of departure of the communicative action presupposes:

language as a medium of self-presentation; the cognitive significance of the propositional components and the interpersonal components and the interpersonal significance of the illocutionary components are thereby played down in favor of the expressive functions of speech acts.

TCA 1, p95

Dramaturgical actions embody a knowledge of the agent's own subjectivity. These expressions can be criticized as untruthful, that is, rejected as deceptions of self-deceptions. Self-deceptions can be dissolved in therapeutic dialogue by argumentative means. Expressive knowledge can be explicated in terms of those values that underlie need interpretations, the interpretations of desires and emotional attitudes. Value standards are dependent in turn on innovations in the domain of evaluative expressions. These are reflected in an exemplary manner in works of art.

TCA 1, p334

Finally, *communicative action* presupposes three worlds, an objective world, a social world and a subjective world:

Only the communicative model of action presupposes language as a medium of uncurtailed communication whereby speakers and hearers, out of the context of their preinterpreted lifeworld, refer simultaneously to things in the objective, social, and subjective worlds in order to negotiate common definitions of the situation.

TCA 1, p95

As regards the latter point of the relations to the world – that is, the subjective world – communicative action presupposes language as a medium of communication that serves reaching understanding where the actors in relating to the world raise validity claims, which can be either accepted or contested. Three validity claims with an utterance are involved, namely that the statement is true, that the speech act is right with respect to recognized normative contexts, and that the manifest intention is meant the way it is expressed (TCA 1, p99).

In other words, Habermas insists that we can maintain rationality in all communicative actions, and not just in teleological action. But there is a risk that the rationality problematic gets displaced. It should not be placed 'in the orientations for action, as it does in Max Weber's theory of action – but in the general structures of the lifeworld to which acting subjects belong' (TCA 1, p328). The claim is simply that it is not the words nor the orientations for action per se that hold meaning; in fact what determines the interpretations of utterances depends on the speakers and the hearers *collective* background and context. It is the actors' lifeworld that determines the interpretation of their actions rather than the mere utterances. It is only with the turn to the context-forming horizon of the lifeworld, from within which participants in communication come to an understanding, that communicative action is understood as principle of sociation (TCA 1, p337). At the same time, the processes of societal rationalization gain another status. They are no longer understood as processes that aim to maximize economic and political system goals, as they are by Weber. Instead, societal rationalization is understood as a process where the starting point is the decentralization of the lifeworld's worldviews and a process, in which less and less is unproblematic shared knowledge and practice. Indeed, understanding is increasingly based on communicative action rather than being normatively motivated or handed down.

To facilitate a complete overview of the many categories of action orientations, validity claims, world relations, functions of speech, and so on, I have shown Habermas' two figures that illustrate *the pure types of linguistically mediated interaction* (Table 3.1) and *the various aspects of rationality of action* (Table 3.2), respectively. With Weber as the starting point, utilizing Austin's[12] and Searle's[13] classifications of speech acts, Habermas fundamentally distinguishes between three pure types of communicative action within a twofold system of orientation to success versus orientation to reaching understanding and social versus nonsocial characteristics. The three types of action are as follows:

1   *Instrumental action*, which is oriented to success and is nonsocial, following technical rules of action and assessing the effects in relation to circumstances and events.
2   *Strategic action* is oriented to success and is social, following rules of rational choice and assessing the effect of influencing the decisions of a rational opponent.
3   *Communicative action*, which is oriented to reaching understanding and social, as the actions of the agents involved are coordinated not through egocentric calculations of success but through acts of reaching understanding (TCA 1, p285–286).

As previously seen, the intention is to show that action oriented to success must be considered to have derived from action oriented to reaching understanding.

In considering these three types of action, he distinguishes between four linguistically mediated interactions, three of which are described as being pure types of speech acts. They are *constantative, regulative* and *expressive* speech acts. These three are based on their so-called illocutionary effects, while the fourth type of the linguistically mediated interactions, the strategic action, is based on its perlocutionary effects.

Finally, the communicative model of action does not equate action with communication. It describes a type of interaction which is coordinated through actions of speech, yet without concurrence. There are different ways of coordination, which lead to different types of social actions:

> *as the interlacing of egocentric calculations [...]; as a socially integrating agreement about values and norms instilled through cultural tradition and socialization; as a consensual relation between players and their publics; or as reaching understanding in the sense of a cooperative process*

of interpretation. In all cases the teleological structure of action is presup-
posed, inasmuch as the capacity for goal-setting and goal-directed action
is ascribed to actors, as well as an interest in carrying out their plans of
action. But only the strategic model of action rests content *with an expli-*
cation of the features of action oriented directly to success.

TCA 1, p101

Table 3.1 *Pure types of linguistically mediated interaction*

Formal pragmatic features, types of action	Characteristic speech acts	Functions of speech	Action orientation	Basic attitudes	Validity claims	World relations
Strategic action	Perlocutions imperatives	Influencing one's opposite number	Oriented to success	Objectivating	[Effectiveness]	Objective world
Conversation	Constantives	Representation of states of affairs	Oriented to reaching understanding	Objectivating	Truth	Objective world
Normatively regulated action	Regulatives	Establishment of interpersonal relations	Oriented to reaching understanding	Norm-conformative	Rightness	Social world
Dramaturgical action	Expressives	Self-representation	Oriented to reaching understanding	Expressive	Truthfulness	Subjective world

Source: TCA 1, p329

Table 3.2 *Aspects of rationality of action*

Types of action	Type of knowledge embodied	Form of argument	Model of transmitted knowledge
Teleological action: instrumental strategic	Technically and strategically useful knowledge	Theoretical discourse	Technologies, strategies
Constative speech acts (conversation)	Empirical-theoretical knowledge	Theoretical discourse	Theories
Normatively regulated action	Moral-practical knowledge	Practical discourse	Legal and moral representations
Dramaturgical action	Aesthetic-practical knowledge	Therapeutic and aesthetic critique	Works of art

Source: TCA 1, p334

Early in his account Habermas draws attention to the decentred understanding of the world, or, as we can also say, the differentiation of an objective world, does *not* mean totally excluding the social and the subjective worlds from the domains of area of rationally motivated agreement (TCA 1, p73). Yet, the rationality problematic appears different in understanding the meaning of social actions. For subjective teleological or purposive-rational actions we can pose the question of whether such actions are objectively rational. Our rational interpretations are undertaken in a performative attitude – that is, 'the interpreter presupposes a basis for judgment that is shared by all parties, including the actors' (TCA 1, p103). For normatively regulated actions 'the question of a rational interpretation does not yet arise, since an observer can ascertain descriptively whether an action accords with a given norm and whether or not the norm in turn enjoys social currency' (TCA 1, p104). However, Habermas raises the question whether the norm is justified, and characterizes this as being a rational interpretation:

> *The moral-practical appraisal of norms of action certainly places an interpreter in even greater difficulties than monitoring the success of rules of purposive-rational action. [...] however, I am concerned only to show that normatively regulated actions, like teleological actions, can be rationally interpreted.*
>
> TCA 1, pp104–105

This will also be the case for dramaturgical actions. 'An interpreter can interpret an action rationally in such a way that he thereby captures elements of deception or self-deception' (TCA 1, p105). Altogether this leads Habermas to the concluding claim that communicative actions can always be interpreted rationally:

> *Access to the object domain of social action through the understanding of meaning of itself makes the rationality problematic* unavoidable. *Communicative actions always require an interpretation that is rational in approach.*
>
> *The relations of strategic, normatively regulated, and dramaturgical actors to the objective, social, and subjective worlds are in principle open to objective appraisal, both for the individual actor and for an observer. In communicative action, the very outcome of interaction is even made to depend on whether the participants can come to an agreement among themselves on an* intersubjective valid *appraisal of their relations to the world. On this model of action, an interaction can succeed only if those involved arrive at a consensus among themselves, a consensus that depends on yes/no responses to claims potentially based on grounds.*
>
> TCA 1, p106

For this rational infrastructure of action orientation to reaching understanding to be considered valid – that is, rational – for others than the actors themselves, it needs to be able to be explicated via a non-participating interpreter. However, communicative action can only be interpreted 'rationally' in a sense, which Habermas sets out to explain. (TCA 1, p107). But, first he needs to develop this also for him disquieting thesis in connection with the problematic of understanding meaning in the social sciences. First from the perspective of the theory of science, and then from that of the phenomenological, ethno-methodological, and hermeneutic schools of interpretive sociology (TCA 1, p107).

The inquiry into the basic concept of action theory and of the methodology of understanding meaning will not be expounded upon, aside from pointing to Habermas' conclusion, 'that the rationality problematic does not come to sociology from the outside but breaks out within it' (TCA 1, p136). To bring coherence between the concept of action rationality and societal rationality thus poses the following question:

> It [the problematic of rationality] is centered around a concept of reaching understanding that is basic from both a metatheoretical and a methodological point of view. This concept has been of interest to us both under the aspect of the coordination of action and under that of an interpretive access to the object domain. Processes of reaching understanding are aimed at a consensus that depends on the intersubjective recognition of validity claims; and these claims can be reciprocally raised and fundamentally criticized by participants in communication. In the orientation to validity claims the actors' world-relations are actualized. In referring with their utterances to something in one or another world, subjects presuppose formal commonalities that are constitutive for reaching any understanding at all. If this rationality problematic cannot be avoided in the basic concepts of social action and in the method of understanding meaning, how do things stand with respect to the substantial question of whether, and if so how, modernization processes can be viewed from the standpoint of rationalization?
>
> TCA 1, p136

Significantly, what is referred to is the concept of *societal* modernization. From the outset, sociologists have occupied themselves with this theme. But beyond this, there is also an internal relation between sociology and a theory of rationalization. According to Habermas, if sociology is not to end up as a specialized or particular discipline, its concepts of rationality need to encompass universalistic claims.

For that reason, the rational internal structure of reaching understanding, characterized by way of anticipation 'in terms of (a) the three world-relations of actors and the corresponding concepts of the objective, social and subjective worlds; (b) the validity claims of propositional truth, normative rightness, and sincerity or authenticity; (c) the concept of a rationally motivated agreement, that is, one based on the intersubjective recognition of criticizable validity claims; and (d) the concept of reaching understanding as the cooperative negotiation of common definitions of the situation' (TCA 1, p137), will have to be shown to be universally valid in a specific sense.

Habermas admits that for someone who is operating without metaphysical support and who, strictly speaking, is no longer confident that a rigorous transcendental-pragmatic program claiming to provide ultimate ground can be carried out, this is a very strong requirement (TCA 1, p137). Yet, he ventures one attempt of three possible ways. The first way is the formal-pragmatic development of the concept of communicative action in a propadeutic fashion. In the second way, an attempt can be made to assess the empirical usefulness of formal-pragmatic insights in three areas of research: the explanation of pathological patterns of communication, the evolution of the foundations of sociocultural forms of life and the ontogenesis of capabilities for action. As both ways would require a very great and limitless effort, he chooses the third and less demanding way: 'to work up the sociological approaches to a theory of societal rationalization […] with the systematic aim of laying out the problems that can be solved by means of a theory of rationalization developed in terms of the basic concept of communicative action' (TCA 1, pp139–140).

This choice is not motivated just by reasons of convenience as is evident from the following deliberations: (1) he wants to ascertain what systematic yield can be obtained from the theoretical perspectives developed in the introduction – that is, show their theoretical strength in characterizing the modern society – and (2) to uphold the adherence to the question whether and, if so, how the capitalistic process of modernization can be regarded as a one-sided rationalization process.

The account of Habermas' evolution theory has already answered the latter question (see also Chapter 2, p45). In the following, I have therefore confined myself to giving an account of the remaining main elements of the theory of communicative action.

This restraint is not just an attempt to limit the reception of theory. It is also determined by the fact that I wanted to condense the more detailed accounts to areas that are concerned with the problematic of rationality, and specifically to areas that extend the problematic to include moral-practical and aesthetic-expressive forms of rationality. This includes how historical rationalization of the lifeworld in modernity gives rise to the principle of subjectivity and the necessity of reflexivity. These questions are of special interest for the problematic of this book and important for a critique of other concepts of modernity, which, from the way I understand it, leads to serious misinterpretations of the potentialities of environmental politics.

The uncoupling of system and lifeworld

What is still missing is an account of some elements of theory that can decipher the relations between system and lifeworld, characterize modernity based on the concept of communicative action and finally also identify the pathologies of modernity. The latter is of paramount importance for the understanding of why the one-sided process of rationality calls for a shift of paradigm in order to find a radically different approach to the environmental problematic – other than the current technocratic ones that appear in various guises of 'progress'.

As we have seen, in his critique of Weber's preference for focusing on purpose rationality and action orientations rather than on the general structures of the lifeworld, Habermas concludes that a coupling of the theory of action and the theory of society needs to be anchored by connecting societal rationalization to the lifeworld.

In analysing Mead's and Durkheim's works, Habermas notes the 'basic concepts in which Weber's theory or rationalization can be taken up and freed from the aporias of the philosophy of consciousness: Mead with his communications-theoretic foundation of sociology, Durkheim with his theory of social solidarity that interrelates social integration and system integration' (TCA 1, p399).

However, an analysis of the connection between the stages of system differentiation and forms of social integration is only possible 'by distinguishing mechanisms for coordinating action that harmonize the *action orientations* of participants from mechanisms that stabilize non-intended interconnections of actions by way of functionally intermeshing *action consequences*. In one case, the integration of an action system is established by a normatively secured or communicatively achieved consensus, in the other case, by a non normative regulation of individual decisions that extends beyond the actors' consciousness. This distinction between a *social integration* of society, which takes effect in action orientations, and a *systemic integration*, which reaches through and beyond action orientations, calls for a corresponding differentiation in the concept of society itself' (TCA 2, p117).

As we have seen, Habermas' response to the call for a concept of social differentiation based on a distinction of the systemic and social integration of society, each, respectively, intermeshing and forming a connection with action orientations, is the conception of society as simultaneously system and lifeworld.

From the provisional concept of the lifeworld that Habermas first introduced, he goes on to broaden it into a more developed form, which includes more than just the culturally transmitted worldviews and interpretive patterns. Because, if 'the solidarities of groups integrated via norms and values and the competences of socialized individuals flow into communicative action *a tergo*, in the way that cultural traditions do, it makes sense for us to correct the culturalistic abridgement of the concept of the lifeworld' (TCA 2, p135). This is achieved by introducing the more comprehensive *everyday concept of the lifeworld*, by which the concept is also being emancipated from the phenomenological sociology, which for Alfred Schütz, Berger and Luckmann leads to a reduced concept of communicative action in favour of interpretative and collective understanding, and for Durkheim a societal concept that emphasizes normative integration and finally for Mead the concentration on the socialization of the individual in which the theory of society shrinks to social psychology (TCA 2, p140).

Thus Habermas introduces a concept of the lifeworld that embraces cultural reproduction as well as social integration and socialization:

Under the functional aspect of mutual understanding, *communicative action serves to transmit and renew cultural knowledge; under the aspect of* coordinating action, *it serves social integration and the establishment of solidarity; finally, under the aspect of* socialization, *communicative action serves the formation of personal identities. The symbolic structures of the lifeworld are reproduced by way of the continuation of valid knowledge, stabilization of group solidarity, and socialization of responsible actors. The process of reproduction connects up new situations with the existing conditions of the lifeworld; it does this in the* semantic *dimension of meanings or contents (of the cultural tradition), as well as in the dimensions of social space (of socially integrated groups) and* historical time *(of successive generations). Corresponding to these processes of* cultural reproduction, social integration, *and* socialization *are the structural components of the lifeworld: culture, society, person.*

TCA 2, pp137–138

Within this concept of the lifeworld, *cultural reproduction* ensures continuity of traditions and coherence of knowledge sufficient for daily practice. This is measured by the *rationality* of knowledge accepted as valid. Disturbances of cultural reproduction get manifested in a loss of meaning and lead to corresponding legitimation and orientation crises. *Social integration* ensures the coordination of action and makes group solidarity sufficiently permanent to uphold everyday practice. This can be measured by the *solidarity* of the participating individuals. Disturbances in social integration are shown to be anomalies. Finally, *socialization* ensures that coming generations acquire generalized competences for action and ensures that the individual life histories are in harmony with collective forms of life. This is measured by the *responsibility* of persons. Disturbances of the socialization process are manifested by psychopathologies (TCA 2, p141).

Rationalization of the lifeworld is outlined by Habermas as follows:

... the further the structural components of the lifeworld and the processes that contribute to maintaining them get differentiated, the more interaction contexts come under conditions of rationally motivated mutual understanding, that is, of consensus formation that rests in the end on the authority of better argument.

TCA 2, p145

This process of rationalization of the lifeworld is to be found in a societal situation where rationalization leads to increasing structural differentiation, where cultural traditions are constantly being challenged and renewed, where political forms are more and more reliant on formal legitimization procedures and where individuals become increasingly autonomous. The relation to tradition, institutions and socialization processes becomes increasingly *critical* and *reflexive* (Outwaite, 1994, p87).

Historically, the Counter-Enlightenment that set in immediately after the French Revolution grounded a critique of modernity which today, according to

Habermas, is continued at a comparable level only in French poststructuralism. The common denominator is the conviction that loss of meaning, anomie and alienation can be traced back to the rationalization of the lifeworld itself (TCA 2, p148). By contrast, Marxism accepts the rationalization of the lifeworld, but explains the deformation of this by the conditions of material reproduction. Therefore its theoretical approach neither identifies the lifeworld with society as a whole nor reduces it to a systemic nexus. Accordingly, Habermas gives the following guideline:

> ... *the dynamics of development are steered by imperatives issuing from problems of self-maintenance; that is, problems of materially reproducing the lifeworld; but that, on the other hand, this societal development draws upon structural* possibilities *and is subject to structural limitations that, with the rationalization of the lifeworld, undergo systematic change in dependence upon corresponding learning processes. Thus the systems-theoretical perspective is relativized by the fact that the rationalization of the lifeworld leads to a directional variation of the structural patterns defining the maintenance of the system.*
>
> TCA 2, p148

From this perspective, what binds society together is a web of communicative actions, which can only succeed in the light of cultural traditions. This does not mean systemic mechanisms as they are out of reach of a member's intuitive knowledge. The lifeworld that members construct from common cultural traditions is in co-existence with society. It draws all societal processes into the searchlight of cooperative processes endowing everything that happens in society with a transparency of something about which one can speak – even if one does not (yet) understand it (TCA 2, p149).

Yet, if in this way we conceive of society as the lifeworld, we are accepting the following fictions, (a) the autonomy of the actors, (b) the independence of culture from external forces, and (c) the transparency of communication or the existence of unlimited ways of communication.

Such fictions can only be dissolved when we avoid the identification of society with the lifeworld and so long as we do not assume that the integration of society is solely accomplished through processes of reaching understanding. The reason is that the participants' goal directed actions are coordinated not purely through processes of reaching understanding, but also through functional interconnections that are not intended by them and are usually not perceived within the horizon of everyday practice. In capitalist societies, the market is the most important example of this:

> *The market is one of those systemic mechanisms that stabilize non intended interconnections of action by way of functionally intermeshing action* consequences, *whereas the mechanism of mutual understanding harmonizes the action* orientations *of participants. Thus I have proposed*

that we distinguish between social integration and system integration: *the former attaches to action orientations, while the latter reaches right through them. In one case the action system is integrated through consensus, whether normatively guaranteed or communicative achieved; in the other case it is integrated through the non-normative steering of individual decisions not subjectively coordinated.*

TCA 2, p150

From this account it is clear how Habermas distinguishes between lifeworld and system, and how he sees societal integration as happening through two simultaneous and different forms of integration, linked to those two concepts: *social* and *system* integration.

However, the connection that exists between system and lifeworld in terms of society producing systemic stabilizing connections of action for socially integrated groups can also be considered a *differentiation* process, in which, in the course of social evolution, an uncoupling of system and lifeworld takes place. Habermas calls it a second-order process of differentiation. System and lifeworld are differentiated in the sense that the complexity of the one and the rationality of the other grow and furthermore between each other, namely they become differentiated from one another at the same time (TCA 2, p153).

From the system perspective this means that the systemic mechanisms are increasingly uncoupled from the social structures and modern society attains 'a level of system differentiation at which increasingly autonomous organizations are connected with one another via delinguistified media of communication' (TCA 2, p154). Systemic mechanisms steer a social intercourse largely disconnected from norms and values, within the subsystems of purposive rational economic and administrative action that, on Weber's diagnosis, have become independent of their moral-practical foundations (TCA 2, p154).

Simultaneously, the lifeworld remains the subsystem that defines the existence of the societal system as a whole. Thus, the systemic mechanisms need *to be anchored in the lifeworld*, they have to be institutionalized (TCA 2, p154).

Habermas analyses the process of differentiation right from tribal societies up to the development of modern society. Accordingly, the new systemic mechanisms, created during the process, were first and foremost the state and the medium of money that resulted in modern society's systems of industrial capitalism. In state-organized society, in addition to the political level, a level for legitimizing existing structures arises, where religious worldviews take on ideological functions. Finally, a third level of functional interconnection arises in modern society:

These systemic interconnections, detached from normative contexts and rendered independent as subsystems, challenge the assimilative powers of an all-encompassing lifeworld. They congeal into the 'second nature' of a norm-free sociality that can appear as something in the objective world, as an objectified *context of life. The uncoupling of system and lifeworld is*

experienced in modern society as a particular kind of objectification [...].
What we have already found in the system perspective seems to be
confirmed from this internal perspective: the more complex systems
become, the more provincial lifeworlds become [...]. This should not be
read causally [...]. The opposite is true: increases in complexity are
dependent on the structural differentiation of the lifeworld. And however
we may explain the dynamics of this structural transformation, it follows
the inner logic of communicative rationalization.

TCA 2, p173

More thoroughly, Habermas elaborates his understanding of *institutionalization* in the lifeworld as follows:

Every new leading mechanism of system differentiation must, however, be
anchored in the lifeworld; it must be institutionalized *there via family*
status, the authority of office, or bourgeois private law. In the final analy-
sis, social formations are distinguished by the institutional cores that
define society's 'base', in the Marxian sense. These basic institutions form
a series of evolutionary innovations that can come about only if the
lifeworld is sufficiently rationalized, above all only if law and morality
have reached a corresponding stage of development. The institutionaliza-
tion of a new level of system differentiation requires reconstruction in the
core institutional domain of the moral-level (i.e. consensual) regulation of
conflicts.

TCA 2, p173

Morality and law are specifically tailored to check open conflicts in such a way that the basis for actions oriented to mutual understanding, and with it the social integration of the lifeworld, does not fall apart. They are second-order norms of actions (TCA 2, p174).

However, this account of the evolution of new levels of system differentiation gives rise to problems of explanation. If new levels of system differentiation are only possible when the rationalization of the lifeworld has reached a correspon-ding level, it is necessary to explain 'why the development toward universalism in law and morality *both* expresses a rationalization of the lifeworld *and* makes new levels of integration possible' (TCA 2, p179). Habermas bases such an explana-tion on the analysis of two counter-tendencies that establish themselves on the level of interactions and action orientations in the wake of increasing 'value gener-alization'. Parsons applies the phrase 'value generalizations' to the tendency for value orientations that are institutionally required of actors to become more and more general and formal in the course of social evolution (TCA 2, p179).

In modern bourgeois society this trend gives rise to two opposite tendencies as regards interaction that also reflects the decoupling of system and the lifeworld:

> *The further motive and value advance, the more the communicative*
> *action gets detached from concrete and traditional normative behavior*
> *patterns. This uncoupling shifts the burden of social integration more and*
> *more from religiously anchored consensus to processes of consensus forma-*
> *tion in language. [...]*
>
> *On the other and, freeing communicative action from particular value*
> *orientations also forces the separation of action oriented to success from*
> *action oriented to mutual understanding. With the generalization of*
> *motives and values, space opens up for subsystems of purposive rational*
> *action. The coordination of action can be transferred over to the delinguis-*
> *tified media of communication only when contexts of strategic action get*
> *differentiated out. While a deinstitutionalized, only internalized morality*
> *ties the regulation of conflict to the idea of justifying normative validity*
> *claims – to the procedures and presuppositions of moral argumentation –*
> *a de-moralized, positive, compulsory law exacts a deferment of legitima-*
> *tion that makes it possible to steer social action via media of a different*
> *type. [...] To satisfy this growing need for coordination, there is either*
> *explicit communication or relief mechanisms that reduce the expenditure*
> *of communication and the risk of disagreement. In the wake of the differ-*
> *entiation between action oriented to mutual understanding and to*
> *success, two sorts of* relief mechanisms *emerge in the form of communica-*
> *tion media that either* condense *or* replace *mutual understanding in*
> *language. We have already come across prestige and influence as primitive*
> *generators of a willingness to follow; the formation of media begins with*
> *them.*
>
> TCA 2, pp180–181

This process of media formation is decisive for the lifeworld as an area of coordi-nation of action. Yet, what transpires in the end is the fact that the lifeworld is no longer essential for this to take place:

> *The transfer of action coordination from language over to steering media*
> *means an uncoupling of interaction from lifeworld contexts. Media such*
> *as money and power attach to empirical ties; they encode a purposive-*
> *rational attitude toward calculable amounts of value and make it possible*
> *to exert generalized, strategic influence on the decisions of other partici-*
> *pants while bypassing processes of consensus-oriented communication.*
> *Inasmuch as they do not merely simplify linguistic communication, but*
> *replace* it *with a symbolic generalization of rewards and punishments,*
> *the lifeworld contexts [...] are devalued in favor of mediasteered interac-*
> *tion; the lifeworld is no longer needed for the coordination of action.*
>
> TCA 2, p183

The transition to a society of high cultural values was accompanied by the inven-tion of writing, which was, first of all, used for administrative purposes and later for the literary formation of educated classes and so on. Still, the printing press only gained real cultural and political influence in modern society. Thus, communicative actions expanded, and the electronic media of mass communication has developed this yet further.

The more consensus formation in language is relieved by the media, the more complex becomes the network of media-steered interaction. However, the two different kinds of relief mechanism promote quite different types of multiple communication. The delinguistified media of communication such as *money* and *power* connect up interactions in space and time into more and more complex networks that no one has to comprehend or be responsible for. By contrast, the media of communication, which condense but do not replace the validity claims of interaction, are dependent on technologies of communication, because these technologies make possible the *formation of public spheres*, that is, even concentrated networks of communication are connected up to cultural traditions and dependent on the validity claims of actions (TCA 2, pp184–185).

> *In the end, systemic mechanisms suppress forms of social integration even in those areas where a consensus-dependent coordination of action cannot be replaced, that is, where the symbolic reproduction of the lifeworld is at stake. In these areas, the* mediatization *of the lifeworld assumes the form of a* colonization.
>
> TCA 2, p196

Habermas talks about *forms of understanding* in this connection. He talks about a situation that comes about by way of 'mediatization' of the lifeworld – that is where the system integration interferes with social integrations. But, as we have seen, system integration is institutionalized in the lifeworld, that is, it (the system integration) can only function when it uses the lifeworld as an instrument to procure the necessary legitimization (Nørager, 1985, p174). Nevertheless, for this to have an effect, it needs to remain covert – that is, it is necessary that the individual remains unaware of what is happening. If the lifeworld did not continue to appear independent, it could not provide legitimacy. This mediatization is not readable as an internal or as an external process, that is, it cannot be read of from the intuitive knowledge of individuals or from the system-integrative perspective. It becomes visible only in an analysis of the formal conditions of communicative action (TCA 2, p186). In effect, instrumentalization of the lifeworld takes on the character of objectively false consciousness, which has to remain hidden within the communicative action.

According to Habermas 'this gives rise to a *structural violence* that, without becoming manifest as such, takes hold of the forms of intersubjectivity of possible understanding' (TCA 2, p187). This is being exercised by way of a systematic restriction of communication and prejudges the participants' perception of the relationship between the objective, the social and the subjective worlds:

> *A form of mutual understanding represents a compromise between the general structures of communicative action and reproductive constraints unavailable as themes within a given lifeworld. Historically variable forms of understanding are, as it were, the sectional planes that result when systemic constraints of material reproduction inconspicuously intervene in the forms of social integration and thereby mediatize the lifeworld.*
> TCA2 2, p187 – see also Habermas' Figure 28, p192, on the development of mutual understanding in social evolution

In conclusion, it is important to note that first of all, Habermas talks about the decoupling or uncoupling of system and lifeworld and *later* in his account he talks about the *internal* colonization of the lifeworld. In the introduction to his account of the uncoupling and creation of media of understanding, he also describes this as the irresistible irony of the world-historical process of enlightenment. 'The rationalization of the lifeworld makes possible a heightening of systemic complexity, which becomes so hypertrophied that it unleashes system imperatives that burst the capacity of the lifeworld they instrumentalize' (TCA2, p155).

Modernity defined via the Theory of the Communicative Action

The above concepts and notions can be summarized as characterizing the concept of modernity, which Habermas set out to explain via his theory of communicative action.

In the modern epoch, social evolution has reached a level where the rationalization of the lifeworld is so advanced that not only has a differentiation of independent trade systems and independent government services taken place, but also science, morality and arts are differentiated as being autonomous expert cultures that develop with their own regularities. Within these expert cultures, separate *types of rationality* are formed according to the specific types of action: the cognitive-instrumental, the moral-practical and the aesthetic-expressive.[14]

These types of rationality remain one-dimensional in that they are being weighed by the weight their corresponding action achieves in society. Only actions oriented to reaching understanding with matching communicative rationality comprise all three types of rationality.

Furthermore, modernity is characterized as a social evolution that has reached a level of development where the uncoupling of system and lifeworld is so advanced that the difference between the two kinds of *action coordination, system* and *social* integration respectively, is a reality and mediatization is thus having the effect of *system integration interfering with social integration.*

A consequence of this is that modernity is also portrayed as being afflicted by *cultural impoverishment.* On the one hand, modern life forms oust or break up traditional society's life forms and cultural tradition. On the other hand, however, a weakening of culture is taking place in modern society – that is cultural impoverishment. In other words, the rationality potential achieved by the differentiation of the expert culture will only to a limited extent be of benefit to the lifeworld.

Main elements of Habermas' Theory of Communicative Action

Discourse Ethics > rational argumentation defined in the process of social dialogue, in contrast to previous notions of rationality, as monologic and logic reasoning, see also Giddens' concept of dialogical democracies and Beck's ideas on subpolitics (Chapter 3)

The Modern Form of Understanding > form of understanding that hides the twofold-edness of transparency and cultural impoverishment

Cultural Impoverishment > the released potential of meaning not made beneficial to the lifeworld

The Colonization Theory > the contest between different kinds of reasoning that dominate system and lifeworld respectively.

Systemic Crisis Management > the use of economic considerations among an ever-increasing broader arena

Mediatization > the steering of social actions by way of means of media communication which either relieve or replace linguistically acquired understanding

The Public Sphere > controls/makes room for parliamentary processes that take discursive arguments into account and procure signals from the lifeworld to systems.

Despite the irreversible differentiation of reason, the theory claims that *unity of reason* can nevertheless be established through the discursive medium of communication. Yet, at the same time, a number of basic circumstances in modernity are contributing to prevent the establishment of such a unity. Therefore it has to be established pragmatically at the formal level, namely by discursive practices claiming to have universal validity.

Cultural impoverishment may be explained by the existence of a *fragmented everyday consciousness*. But what effect does this have on modern society? It means that, in modern society, false consciousness is created, not by ideologies imprinted onto people, but rather by the fact that basic social knowledge *remains* diffused (caused by among other things cultural impoverishment) and thus the advancement of thorough assessments of what is achieved are prevented, social critiques included.

Habermas' version of the dialectic of enlightenment therefore entails what he calls the *modern form of understanding* that signifies modernity's twofold context of *transparency* and *cultural impoverishment*.

The *modern form of understanding* can be characterized as that of concurrently creating transparency which, in reality, also causes fragmentation within the consciousness of the individual. Transparency arises when the rationalization of the lifeworld is so far that individuals, based on abstract norms and principles, are able to judge social actions and where, by reflection, autocratic principles of cultural traditions are broken; in other words when the substance of basic convictions that are sanctioned by culture and thus need no reasoning have vaporized. This fragmentation exists, because cultural impoverishment allows basic social knowledge to remain diffused.

The characteristic tendency of modernity is that alongside a continued rationalization of the lifeworld, there is also a *colonization of the lifeworld*. System integration takes over, by way of legalizing part of the symbolic (in contrast to the material) reproduction, for instance, by encroaching upon the sphere of the family, such as, for example, schools' increasing involvement in the functions of family life.

Thus modernity can be characterized as a societal condition where conflicts are constantly arising between the media-steered subsystems and the communicative action of the lifeworld. These conflicts are readily apparent when we consider the media-steered subsystems that, for the sake of their own goals of rationality, intervene in the communicative structure of the lifeworld (the symbolic reproduction) and thus colonize communicative reasoning in terms of the communicative process being replaced by systemic principles of validity claims – for example in justifying actions.

In all instances, according to Habermas, there is no other way forward for modernity other than reversing the expert cultures' acquired liberated potential of rationality as a whole in order not to fall under the spell of false negations of culture.

Modernity, according to Habermas' assertions, as an incomplete societal condition, is a predicament that we cannot 'ignore', but need to address in order for it to be 'accomplished'. The crux of incompleteness lies in the one-sidedness of modernization, where instrumental reasoning has prevailed. To get out of this situation we need to acknowledge that we live in a society where communicative rationality plays an increasingly larger role in the societal reproduction. This is, indeed, a rationality that reaches beyond technical and scientific cognition. Nevertheless, Habermas asserts that we have to operate with some concept of rationality if we do not want an 'instrumentalist' society that is allowed to run an even more one-sided course. He does not oppose rationality by ecology. On the contrary, he considers rationality to be superior also when it comes to ecological discussions.

Excursus: An account of the process of modernization based on the theory of communicative action

The process of modernization is the crux of this book. Based on the above account of the theory of communicative action and its modernity, at this point I shall therefore aim to elucidate this process.

As we have seen, according to Habermas, the modernization process consists of a continued rationalization of the lifeworld and an increasing systemic complexity, where the latter is dependent on the former and at the same time they differentiate from each other. Thus we find that a constant differentiation is taking place between normatively regulated and linguistically coordinated action in the lifeworld and a delinguistified action coordination of the system; between actions oriented to reaching understanding and result-oriented actions. The relation between these two 'worlds' is coordinated by the steering media, inclusive of the necessary institutionalization of systems or subsystems in the lifeworld. Such media are operating in two ways, either they replace communication – the so-called steering media of money and power, or in the form of media that condense or relieve communication, the so-called communication media.

Based on the process of differentiation, modernity can be characterized by two factors. First, the differentiation of the value spheres of science, morality and arts to a professionalism that means an increasing differentiation between expert cultures and the broader public. Second, under the capital economy, modernization processes have been found to favour one above the others of these expert cultures: the cognitive-instrumental. These characteristics of the modernization process have been described as being cultural impoverishment and colonization of the lifeworld.

However, it is not the differentiation of value spheres and the consequent one-sidedness of each sphere per se that lead to cultural impoverishment. After all, it must be acknowledged that the differentiation process itself forms part of the progress of civilization, as, for the first time in history, it is possible to assess each value sphere purely according to its own sets of validity claims in terms of truth as well as rightness and truthfulness. In consequence, a further rationalization is made possible, that is the creation or development for a potential for reasoning.

The cultural impoverishment arises because an elitist differentiation of the expert cultures is taking place away from the communicative everyday practice. This means that only some parts of the civilizing progress – that is, the creation of potential reason, return to or are made useful for the lifeworld. Therefore, in terms of societal progress, deterioration and impoverishment take place.

Likewise, it is not the uncoupling from the lifeworld of the media-steered subsystems and their organizations as such that singularly lead to either one-sided rationalization or fetishism in communicative everyday action. What causes the colonization is the systemic movement into fields that in no way lend themselves to a replacement, in which linguistical action coordination is being replaced by instrumental media steering. What we see is the encroachment of economic and administrative rationality into areas of action that, in action coordination, should be governed by linguistically mutual understanding. Cultural traditions, social integration, socialization and upbringing, in particular, are the areas at stake.

In other words, one-dimensional societal modernization has come about due to structural transformation. This is partly caused by the fact that certain forms of action – that is, strategic actions that are based on cognitive-instrumental rationality, have dominated media steering and the differentiation of systems, the economy and the administration. These forms of action, with appurtenant cognitive-instrumental rationality, have increasingly influenced more and more areas of action coordination in the lifeworld. Modernization is synonymous with rationalization of the lifeworld and also growing complexity, which add an increased systemic pressure onto the lifeworld's social integration. System integration is increasingly dominating social integration. Cognitive-instrumental rationality rules over moral-practical and aesthetic-expressive rationalities. Furthermore, this becomes manifest in the light of the cultural impoverishment of the lifeworld linked to societal modernization.

However, in Chapter 2 we also saw that the theory of communicative action, as a critical societal theory, founded its normative basis in communicative action – mutual understanding through language – in the communicative reason. Of course, this unity of reason does not disappear even though a differentiation of the expert cultures and a consequent advancement brought about by their specialization are taking place. Therefore, by way of a counter-movement to the double destruction – that is, the systemic colonization and the professionalization of the expert cultures – it is possible to find a unity of reason, 'not a unity that could be had at the level of worldviews, but one that might be established this side of expert cultures, in a nonreified communicative everyday practice' (TCA 2, p398).

Thus, a contrast to the one-dimensional modernization can be found in communicative everyday practice. Such unity of reason is not an obvious empirical reality, yet it demands some mediation based on, for example, theory-historical perspectives and theories that communicate with one another (TCA 2, p398). Indeed, this implies that some elements of a unity do exist in the immediate communicative practice of the lifeworld that can practicably be applied, for instance in debates about its suitability in relation to various modernization initiatives, such as, for example, projects, plans or policies. We shall build on these insights and experiences in Chapters 4 and 5.

The theories of reflexive modernity

The theories about a distinctive reflexive modernity have been particularly espoused by Ulrich Beck and Anthony Giddens. They both see the latest decades as a special phase in the development of modernity, which they characterize as reflexive.

While Habermas presents reflexivity as part and parcel of the modernization process itself, Beck and Giddens see it as a qualitative developmental feature within modernity. And just like Habermas and the poststructuralists, the theories of reflexive modernity conceive the crisis of the modern as a result of technical-scientific rationality. To Habermas, this is a problem of domination, in which other aspects of modernity are prevented from being expressed, whereas the theories of reflexive modernity view the crisis as an outcome of the technical-scientific rationality transgressing its own limitations. In plain terms, the theories of reflexive modernity hold that the exploitation of technical-scientific rationality has reached a point where it no longer leads to progress, but generates new problems, including risks and dangers. In this respect, they thus concur with poststructuralism.

However, while the poststructuralists see the transgressions of technical-scientific rationality as a manifestation of the end of modernity, the theories of reflexive modernity consider it an expression of a new development *within* modernity, which is evolving in new manners – that is, towards a new modernity, as the term implies, towards a reflexive modernity.

This delving into modernity itself does not mean, however, that technical-scientific rationality is rejected, nor is it surpassed or supplemented. On the contrary, the theories of reflexive modernity may be said to prescribe an endeavour to develop, reshape or alter the technical-scientific rationality so that it evolves with a new content, or encounters a technical-scientific challenge, producing a new outcome.

For instance, Beck motivates his characteristic of modernity as reflexive by arguing that 'today the same [demystification] is happening to the understanding of science and technology in the classical industrial society, as well as to the modes of existence in work, leisure, the family and sexuality. Modernization *within* the paths of industrial society is being replaced by a modernization *of the principles* of industrial society,' (Beck, 1992, p10) and 'technocracy ends when alternatives erupt in the technoeconomic process and polarize it' (Beck, 1997, p52).

He further highlights the development within modernity, as he writes:

> *it is not the crisis, but [...] the victories of capitalism which produce the new social form. [...] it is not the class struggle but rather normal modernization and further modernization which are dissolving the contours of industrial society. The constellation that is now coming into being as a result of this [...] is that high-speed industrial dynamism is sliding into a new society without the primeval explosion of a revolution, bypassing political debates and decisions in parliaments and governments.*
>
> Beck, 1994, p2

Note that Beck here stresses how the development observed springs from normal modernization and further modernization. Incidentally, also note that he does not specify what he means by industrial dynamism. We shall return to the latter point later.

Giddens also sees the development of reflexive modernity as something that lies in continuation of, yet reshapes, the (simple) modernity experienced thus far:

> *In such modernization [simple modernization], capitalist or industrial evolution seems a predictable process, even if understood in a revolutionary way in the manner of Marx. Science and technological advances associated with it are generally accepted as embodying claims to authoritative truth; while industrial growth has a clear 'direction'.*
>
> *Reflexive modernization responds to different circumstances. It has its origins in the profound social changes [...] the impact of globalization; changes happening in everyday and personal life; and the emergence of a post-traditional society. These influences flow from Western modernity, but now affect the world as a whole – and they refract back to start to reshape modernization at its points of origin.*
>
> Giddens, 1994b, p80

In the following two sections, I shall first present Beck's and then Giddens' perception of reflexive modernity, and the special characteristics each of them attributes to it. Thereafter, I shall criticize a series of aspects of their theories as a whole, albeit with specific reference to each individual scholar whenever warranted by the particularities of their views. After portraying and specifying the modernization process according to Weber and Habermas, I shall – through an overall critique of the theory of reflexive modernity – attempt to reach my own definition of 'reflexive modernity', not merely to seek a different understanding of the term, but also to arrive at useful and tangible concepts, which – informed by Habermas' definition of modernity – may contribute to spotlighting the opportunities in society for environmental policy-making, in particular regarding the tool of environmental assessment. The reason for placing my own definition of 'reflexive modernity' between inverted commas is that my critique will dispute the existence of such a distinctly reflexive modernity, or of a distinctly reflexive phase in the evolution of modernity.

Risk society and reflexive modernity

Ulrich Beck situates his *risk society* thesis in close conjunction with his concept of modernity, and to the particular *break* within it, which occurs, he argues, with *reflexive modernity*. Beck has been highly instrumental in placing the concept of risk at the centre of basic social scientific analysis, whereas it used to belong to the realm of technical- and natural-scientific probabilistic categories. Furthermore, Beck's characterization of the society that he calls reflexively modern as a *risk society* – that is, as a society that brings about risks to those who live in it – is almost tantamount to characterizing the risk society as the antithesis of the concept of society, a kind of *anti-society*. Verging on a statement about the end of society, it becomes even more powerful by featuring *individualization* among the decisive elements that characterizes this society, thus expressing an emphasis on the category of individuals, as opposed to collective aspects, such as class or indeed society.

Therefore, it is understandable that the thesis about the risk society has created a stir among wide circles of researchers and administrators, who see this as placing their functions in an entirely new setting. Among environmental researchers, the thesis has naturally drawn particular attention, perhaps primarily because it inserts the environmental issue directly into the general debate in society, leaving no doubt that – notwithstanding the individualization thesis – the state of the environment is the outcome of systematic social forces, and is not individually or randomly caused by big-business fat cats, particularly evil or careless persons, enigmatic sunspots or other spectacular natural phenomena.

In relation to the present book, the presentation of Beck's position will, quite logically, concentrate on his definition of two stages of modernization of society, and on the break in the form of modernization, which he believes to have identified in this manner.

The thesis about the risk society is first presented by Beck in the book *Risikogesellschaft:Auf dem Weg in eine andere Moderne*, published in 1986. Here, he also makes his first claim as to the existence of reflexive modernity as a break within modernity. However, what he means by reflexive modernization and risk society is, in fact, much more clearly expressed in his later article from 1994 entitled 'The reinvention of politics:Towards a theory of reflexive modernization' (Beck, 1994, p1). Incidentally, it is worth dwelling on the title, as he uses it to stress, first, that he is still only moving *towards* a theory of reflexive modernization, just as he was in 1986, and second, that his theory seeks to shed light on the position of *politics* in the society that he describes as reflexively modern. In other words, in addition to saying that he is only working towards a theory, he also says that, in fact, the theory he is searching for is not about the type of society as such, but about the meaning of politics within it, even if he actually claims elsewhere that his definition is of an epochal nature (Beck, 1994, p7).

Beck introduces his article with three different explanations of what he understands by reflexive modernization:

> *reflexive modernization means first the disembedding and second the re-embedding of industrial social forms by another modernity.*
>
> Beck, 1994, p2

> *This new stage, in which progress can turn into self-destruction, in which one kind of modernization undercuts and changes another, is what I call the stage of reflexive modernization.*
>
> Beck, 1994, p2[15]

> *Reflexive modernization, then, is supposed to mean that a change of industrial society which occurs surreptitiously and unplanned in the wake of normal, autonomized modernization and with an unchanged, intact political and economic order implies the following: a radicalization of modernity, which breaks up the premises and contours of industrial society and opens paths to another modernity.*
>
> Beck, 1994, p3

He supplements these descriptions, or explanations, by stressing in various manners that the change away from what he calls simple modernity (see below) does not take place as a transition that is chosen, but as a process that is deaf and blind to its own effects and hazards. The changeover is undesired, unseen and compulsive (Beck, 1994, pp3, 5–6).

This confirms my conviction of essentially differing from Beck, which springs from a sensation that something is lacking. Evidently, a shift in societal epoch or social forms is not something that is *chosen*, or something that is *willed* by any society, although individuals may well wish for a particular development and work alongside others to realize particular interests.[16] It is something that takes place at a structural level. However, I choose to see Beck's depiction of the process as deaf, blind and unwilled as a consequence of his failure to look at the forces driving the development that he describes.[17] I shall return to this view as one major point in my critique of his identification of a break within modernity.

Beck's definition of the *risk society* elaborates on the identification of a transition from simple to reflexive modernization:

> *This concept designates a developmental phase of modern society in which the social, political, economic and individual risks increasingly tend to escape the institutions for monitoring and protection in industrial society.*
>
> Beck, 1994, p5

The development to reach this state of affairs takes place in two successive phases. In the *first phase*, effects and self-threats are systematically produced, but are not subjected to public debate or political conflict. In the *second phase*, the dangers of industrial society start to predominate in public as well as private political conflicts and debates, as the institutions of industrial society turn into producers and legitimators of dangers beyond their control (Beck, 1994, p5).

It is in the transition to the second phase that Beck finds a *break* occurring within modernity. He uses the term 'break' (*Bruch*) instead of *post*modernity, as he considers the latter to signal the end of modernity, which he refutes to be the case. This is why he talks about a break within modernity, in which modernization taking place *within* the framework of industrial society is replaced by modernization of the very *principles* on which industrial society is founded. In this sense, he distinguishes between modernization of *tradition* and modernization of *industrial society*, that is, between *classical* and *reflexive* modernization (Beck, 1992, p11).

This break has not been widely acknowledged, according to Beck, mainly because of a myth that has held sway over social thinking throughout the 19th century, and which casts a long shadow into the latter third of the 20th century. It is the myth of the developed industrial society's *thoroughly modernized* character, a culmination of modernity whose superseding cannot be meaningfully envisaged. One of the most striking manifestations of this myth is the 'joke' about the end of history. In contrast to this myth, Beck perceives developed industrial society as expressing only a modernization of tradition – that is, what he categorizes as classical modernization (Beck, 1992, p11).

However, since the modernization trend of a reflexive nature, which he wishes to outline, is coming only faintly into view, or is still in embryonic form, it can only be depicted by analysing a series of specific areas, and the picture is too complex to foreshadow which fields of established thinking in industrial society will succumb to such modernization raised to the second power. Therefore, the account of the risk society, in the book of the same title, relies upon two perspectives.

The *first perspective* is an interplay between continuity and break, exemplified by wealth production and risk production.

In industrial society modernized only in the simple form, wealth production predominates over risk production, but this is turned on its head in the risk society, as productive forces lose their innocence. The greater power and wealth are increasingly overshadowed by the production of risks, which can no longer be legitimized as latent side effects. When risks are universalized, while being subjected to public criticism and an (alternative) scientific exploration, they lose their latent status, taking on a new and central meaning in the social and political discussion. While in the 19th century and first half of the 20th century, industry-related and occupational hazards could be attributed to certain localities and specific groups, risks in the latter half of the 20th century present an increasingly globalizing trend, which covers both production and reproduction, and which contains supra-national and non-class-specific global hazards (Beck, 1992, pp12, 13).

The *second perspective* focuses on immanent contradictions between the modern and the countermodern in industrial society. Beck illustrates this in a series of spheres (Beck, 1992, pp13–14):

On the one hand, industrial society is constituted as a macro-group society, a class-divided and stratified society. On the other, the classes are based upon the validity of social-class cultures and traditions, which are indeed being *de*-traditionalized as a consequence of society's modernization towards the welfare state.

On the one hand, the intimate relations in industrial society are prescribed and standardized in keeping with the ideal of the nuclear family. On the other, the nuclear family is based upon ascribed 'feudal' gender roles for men and women, which are just starting to disintegrate along with the modernization process.

On the one hand, industrial society is perceived within the categories of (wage) working society. On the other, a series of current rationalization measures are indeed challenging this ordered pattern of that society.

On the one hand, science, and hence methodical doubt, is institutionalized in industrial society. On the other, this doubt is (to begin with) confined to outer manifestations, to the research objects, whereas the foundations and consequences of scientific endeavour remain shielded from this inner scepticism.

On the one hand, the ideals and various forms of representative democracy are taking root in industrial society. On the other, the validity domain of these principles is shrinking.

Reflexive modernization is an opportunity for dissolving the countermodern element in the modernization of industrial society, and hence an opportunity for freeing *the principles of modernity from the halfway house that occurs in industrial society*. Under reflexive modernity, we thus become witnesses to a change in the foundation for change (Beck, 1992, p14).

Risk society is the concept applying to the stage of modernity characterized by the production of dangers not only being present, as it has been part of industrial society from the outset, but becoming a dominant feature in society. This calls for limitations in production, and for redefining standards and norms concerning potential hazards.

The problem is, however, that the hazards cannot be determined scientifically. The definition of danger is a cognitive and social process. Accordingly, the degree to which modern societies are confronted with their own foundations and with the limits to their own construction stops short of prompting them to change or to react to the consequences of their own conduct. In this sense, the reflexively modern society is epoch-making and transformational in three regards:

- The resources of nature and culture upon which society is built are dissipated or squandered.
- The threats and problems being produced by society defy fundamental social ideas of safety.
- The collective and group-specific sources of meaning suffer from fatigue, break-up and decline, stepping up the pace of individualization (Beck, 1994, p7).

Therefore, risks and opportunities are coupled together. They are constituted as what might be conceived as communicating vessels, where further communication contains or reinforces one of them, but always accompanied by the other, which articulates new opportunities or risks on the basis of the first.[18]

Two particular phenomena are typical expressions of this in the society of reflexive modernization: *the return of uncertainty and the individual's return to society*.

The return of uncertainty is essentially manifested by what is called today's ecological crisis. The metamorphosis of unforeseen side effects of industrial production into focal points of a global ecological crisis is no longer perceived merely as a problem of our surroundings, a so-called environmental problem, but as a deep institutional crisis affecting industrial society (Beck, 1994, p8). The uncertainty expresses the unpredictability of this society. Neither its technical nor its social processes can be calculated or predetermined with any certainty. Knowledge cannot be seen as certain, or as something beyond being refuted or overridden by new knowledge. The uncertainty also reflects the dual nature of social processes: on the one side, controlled experiments and processes, including productive processes; on the other, uncontrolled consequences or outcomes, which may in turn feed their effects back onto the original activity. Good for something, bad for something else, but never one thing or the other.

Beck also calls the individual's return to society *individualization*. It occurs in two variants. First, through individualization of each person's adaptation to the forms of life in society. This adaptation becomes an individual phenomenon in contrast to the collective or class-specific forms of life that characterize the classical industrial society. It does not imply that each person chooses freely and has all possibilities, but first and foremost that the individual must create his or her own biography within the scope of reflexive modernity (Beck, 1994, p15).

The second form of individualization arises from the advance of subpolitics, which is detached from the political processes of the established political-institutional system and of the corporate system (Beck, 1994, p22). Subpolitics springs from subpoliticians acting outside the corporate system, for example, professionals, technical intelligentsia from companies, organizations, research institutes, and so on, or from citizens' initiatives, public exposure, and other ways. Moreover, subpoliticians are often individuals acting on their own initiative. Subpolitics means shaping society from the bottom up.

Individualization is an expression of individuals in society being left to their own devices with regard to: (a) assessing the situation that forms the background to action; (b) taking on responsibility for acting; and finally (c) bearing the consequences of an action, even when the opportunities or scope for action have been externally imposed, in other words, individual responsibility for doing something that does not lie within free choice, but is externally structured.

Thus, in reflexive modernity, not only does society's production of risk become predominant. It is also left to each individual to live with the uncertainties that this entails, since the institutions that used to form a collective shield are disappearing. Consequently, individualization also spells the impotence of the individual.

However, Beck does not suggest that the risk society differs from industrial society in how it deals with risks, or in the greater extent and range of these as a result of new technologies and rationalizations. The pivotal point is that reflexive modernization radically changes the framework conditions of society, since 'scientization' brings the latency phase of risk threats to an end, making previously invisible hazards visible. The triumph of the industrial system blurs the boundaries between nature and society (Beck, 1992, p154).

Beck presents the consequences of this as concerns science and politics, since he wishes to illustrate the thesis: 'reflexive modernization which encounters the conditions of a *highly developed* democracy and an *established* scientization, leads to characteristic *unbindings* [*Entgrenzungen*] of science and politics' (Beck, 1992, p154). He also characterizes these unbindings as, respectively, a generalization of scientific knowledge production and a generalization of the political.

Generalization of science

The distinction between modernization of tradition and modernization of industrial society leads Beck to differentiate between two constellations in the relationship between science, practice and public participation, namely primary and reflexive scientization.

In its initial phase, science relates to the 'already given' world of nature, man and society – that is, reflexive in a simple form. In the reflexive phase, however, the sciences are confronted with their own products, shortcomings and side-effects, that is, they encounter a second creation in civilization (Beck, 1992, p155).

The first phase is a semi-scientization, in which the demands of scientific rationality for cognition and information still elude methodical application of the scientific doubt. Conversely, the reflexive phase stands for consistent scientization, which extends scientific doubt to encompass reflection upon the immanent basis and external consequences of science.

This has very far-reaching repercussions, since the scientific demands for truth and enlightenment are demystified,[19] and the sciences are no longer only in the spotlight as a means of solving problems, but also as a cause of problems. At the same time, it de-monopolizes the claims of science to cognition (Beck, 1992, p156).

A consequence of this de-monopolization is that science becomes, simultaneously, more *necessary*, and yet increasingly *inadequate* as regards an obligation towards society to define the truth.

The necessity springs from the rising reflexivity in the cognitive process. The continuous questioning of one's own premises and foundations necessitates production of new knowledge. Conversely, the widespread acceptance of scientific fallibility will foster a search for other means of substantiating decisions (Beck, 1992, p156).

This gives rise to a situation in which the access to truth and reality is replaced by decisions, rules and conventions, which could just as well have been differently shaped (Beck, 1992, p156). This applies, for instance, to national decision-making systems for authorizations to release genetically modified organisms, which are characterized as secure and controlled, because the decision has adhered to certain procedural requirements and criteria.

This trend is assisted by the fact that, the more it becomes impossible to *calculate* the effects – that is, control them rationally through the setting of targets – the more it becomes possible to assess them (Beck, 1992, p172). Consequently, for the sciences to be able to contribute to controlling their own practical risks, what really counts is not that they seek to influence the applications of their own results. What matters more is what kind of science is conducted with a view to discerning the seemingly indiscernible consequences.

In this scenario, science may react with an internal reduction of the external uncertainty in three areas: (a) replacing the amelioration of symptoms with the elimination of causes, (b) preserving or recovering the capacity to learn from practice, and (c) resuming and expanding the capacity to specialize in relation to the context, as opposed to isolated contemplation.

The trend towards generalization of science, as a result of reflexive modernization, may thus, according to Beck, contribute to enabling scientific self-restraint (Beck, 1992, p181).

Generalization of the political

To shed light on how the intensified risk scenario within reflexive modernity leads to a fundamental change in the political, Beck presents four theses (Beck, 1992, pp183–186):

1   Technological innovations enhance collective and individual welfare. This is the increase in living standards that legitimizes the adverse side effects (obsolete skills, risk of unemployment, health hazards, environmental destruction, and so on).
2   The aversion to politics is not only concerned with politics itself, but springs from the *discrepancy* between, on the one hand, the official political power, which is becoming increasingly impotent, and on the other, the wider changes

in society, which do not result from decision-making, and which take place outside the political sphere.

3   Technological and economic development is placed somewhere between politics and non-politics. It becomes something else again, as it takes on the precarious intermediate form of *subpolitics*, in which the reach and ramifications of social change are inversely proportional to its legitimacy.

4   The political becomes non-political, and the non-political becomes political.

In particular, the development towards what is listed as the third thesis may be characterized by the appearance of a new political culture – in the wake of the crisis of welfare state interventionism and the colossal technological innovations – in terms of citizens' initiatives, social movements, demands for participation in project decisions, and so on.

These subcultures also manifest in an institutionalized public sphere. Within the social sciences as well as the political debate, the term 'participation' has become a key concept, whether to raise hopes or to conjure up ghosts (translated from the original German *Hoffnung* and *Gespenst*, Beck, 1986, p322).

However, the arrival and existence of such subcultures also express an *end to the consensus on progress*, even though this has been highly dominant in the post-war period.

The end of progress as a modern religion is heralded by two historical development processes since the 1970s. Throughout the expansion of the welfare state, politics loses its utopian dimension and comes up against a series of inherent limitations and contradictions, at the same time as the potentials for social change accumulate in the interaction between research, technology and economy. This leads to a shift in power from the political to the subpolitical sphere. Change is not expected to result from legislative debates and new laws, but from the application of microelectronics, genetic technologies and information media. The utopias are replaced by the consideration of unintended consequences. The non-political displaces the leading role of politics (Beck, 1992, p323).

The politicians pretend to preserve the status quo, but assist in creating a society about which they have no clue, while employers and researchers protest that they are not responsible for the decisions that are helping to overthrow the existing social order. The division of powers in the modernization process becomes blurred (Beck, 1992, p324).

In the political shaping of the future, grey areas appear, of which Beck outlines three, none of them mutually exclusive: return to industrial society, democratization of technological development, and 'differential politics'.

He rejects the *return to industrial society* with the simple argument that this would be to project the 19th century onto the 21st. This would be a basic mistake, as it neglects the existence of a contradiction between industrial society and modernity. After all, the project of industrial society was only a semi-modern modernity. In contrast stands the fully modernized modernity: the risk society. To imagine the re-establishment of industrial society's cohesion between economy and politics in the risk society is to overlook that risk definitions[20] *do not* create shared economic interests. Risk definitions do not curb the exercise of political power, but enable it (Beck, 1992, p227). A return to industrial society, however, will force upon us a trivialization of risks, which will form a glaring contrast to the risks that have in fact arisen, hence exposing the impotence of politics.

The model of *democratizing technological development* starts from the premise that technological and economic innovations, which are the driving force behind permanent social change, in principle elude democratic co-influence, scrutiny and opposition. Therefore, the public must be given access to these decision-making processes on the basis of a principle of modernity itself: *democratization*. This well-known tool of the political system must be expanded to areas beyond itself. These notions include, for instance, parliamentary oversight of the technological innovations of businesses, special 'modernization parliaments', in which experts from every scientific discipline examine, assess and approve available projects, in addition to the involvement of citizens in planning the technological development and in decision-making processes concerning research policy (Beck, 1992, p229).

To Beck's mind, the problem with this way of thinking is that it remains bound by the 19th-century industrialization model, which is built upon centralization and bureaucratization as a precondition for democratization. These are conditions that have lost their historical validity, and hence become problematic. For example, it is self-evident that the aim of democratization militates against the reactive nature of public and political discussions concerning research and investment decisions. A demand for democratization implies that issues concerning the opportunities and consequences of microelectronics, genetic technologies, and so on should be debated by the national legislature before deciding on their application. In Beck's opinion, this path would surely place bureaucratic and law-making obstacles in the way of both the companies' rationalizations and the scientific research (Beck, 1992, p229).

Beck outlines a variation of this model in the idea of an ecological version of the welfare state, supposed to counter two fundamental problems, namely environmental destruction and high unemployment. However, the danger of such ecologically-orientated state interventionism, namely authoritarian science and extensive bureaucracy, comes starkly into focus by drawing parallels to the welfare state. The entire model is based upon the misconception that modernity has, or should have, a political control centre. It fails to notice that modernity has lost its centre and is no longer being controlled.

However, if one avoids this error and refrains from insisting on such a centre, starting instead from an expansion of the boundaries of the political, one will understand the examples over the latest decades of citizens' initiatives, media publicity, protest movements and so on, which are testing new forms of democracy (Beck, 1992, p231).

The model of *differential politics* is based upon a recognition that the boundaries of the political have been widened. It considers modernization to have entered a new epoch, the reflexive one. The monopolies created in industrial society have been dissolved. With this understanding, the era of excuses is over, since everything can be controlled and is man-made.

In keeping with this understanding, Beck's suggestion of how to develop the models centres on extending and legally securing particular opportunities for influence through subpolitics. Two pillars will uphold the subpolitical control system: a strong and independent judiciary, and strong and independent public media (Beck, 1992, p234). In addition, history has shown the need for what he calls an institutionalization of self-criticism (Beck, 1992, p234). This refers to institutional settings for what has thus far painstakingly sought to free itself from the domination of the professions and corporate managers, namely alternative expertise, a different working life, internal discussions of enterprises and organizations concerning the consequences of their development strategies, repressed doubt, and so on (Beck, 1992, p234). The slogan for this model becomes: criticism equals progress. For official politics, the 'old' formal parliamentary political system, this will offer a host of opportunities, as its central job will be to fulfil preservative, conflict-solving, discursive and symbolic functions. It will reflect a new division of labour and power between politics and subpolitics, which may secure ongoing societal experiments and learning processes.

Globalization and trust

At the core of Anthony Giddens' writings is reflexivity, from which he derives all his key statements about the current features of modernity. The critical changes in people's everyday life, claims Giddens, do not spring from the central political sphere; indeed, they may only be remotely related to it. Instead, they arise from elementary changes in the functioning and structures of society, which are global in reach, but also impact locally and in the lives of every person. Consequently, in Giddens' world, reflexive modernization is associated with globalization, changes in everyday life, the personal life, and the emergence of a post-traditional society (Giddens, 1994a, p80). A pivotal point of his authorship is thus the link between the global dimension and personal living conditions.

Just like Beck, Giddens talks about the risk society. However, in his writings, this refers to *uncertainties produced* by reflexive modernity. He defines four spheres in which we are faced with high-risk consequences on a global scale, arising from the uncertainties created. He calls it society's creation of crises in these four areas.

First, the social development of modernity leads to a world-wide crisis of ecosystems. This trend is associated with the *industrial* dimension of modernity. Second, it brings about poverty on a vast scale. This is related to the *capitalist* aspect of modernity. Third, it leads to the threat of a large-scale war. This crisis is linked to the *violent* dimension. Fourth and finally, an area of crisis is the advance of repression of democratic rights on a major scale. This trend is connected with modernity's expansion of *surveillance and control systems* (Giddens, 1994a, pp97–101).

The four areas of crisis are thus all linked to an institutional dimension of the reflexively modern society: industrialism, capitalism, the apparatus of force, and surveillance/control.

The crises in these four areas are, according to Giddens, a manifestation of the *radicalization* of modernity. However, he refutes that such radicalization constitutes a break in modernity, or some kind of postmodernity. It is only that modernity is changing at an accelerated pace and, within a given period of time, with more widespread repercussions than before. He thus rejects the use of the concept of postmodernity in the context of social-scientific analysis of societal development, finding it applicable only in the analysis of aesthetic considerations, such as painting, architecture, literature and so on.

To Giddens, the reflexivity of modern society consists in social practices that are constantly examined and reformed in light of incoming information about those very practices, thus constitutively altering their character (Giddens, 1990, p38). However, in what he calls high or late modernity, the development is characterized by extreme reflexivity. By this he means that 'the entry of knowledge into the circumstances of action it analyses or describes creates a set of uncertainties to add to the circular and fallible character of post-traditional claims to knowledge' (Giddens, 1991, p28).

The social sciences themselves Giddens characterizes as formalized reflection (a specific genre of expert knowledge) and they are quite fundamental to the reflexivity of modernity as a whole (Giddens, 1990, p40).

He also distinguishes 'three dominant sources of the dynamism of modernity [...] each connected with the other' (Giddens, 1990, p53), namely:

- the separation of time and space;
- the development of disembedding mechanisms;
- the reflexive appropriation of knowledge.

The concept of disembedding[21] plays a particular role. The term refers to mechanisms that 'lift' social action from local contexts, reorganizing social relations across vast distances in time and space (Giddens, 1990, p53). For example, he characterizes capitalist enterprise as a disembedding mechanism par excellence (Giddens, 1994b, p96).

Giddens does not offer any explanation as to why 'the three sources of dynamism of modernity' enter into force, but uses them exclusively to *describe* a series of conditions in modern society which enable reflexive modernity. Thus, these do not form part of a definition of the dynamics of modernity. The concept of disembedding is a construction which portrays *what* is happening, but does not explain *why*.

Perhaps this is why Giddens resorts to an *image* of the dynamics in modernity, his juggernaut. In Giddens' own words, this illustrative metaphor is produced to replace two earlier images of what life is like under modernity.[22] These are, respectively, Max Weber's bonds of rationality,[23] which are increasingly forcing people into the narrow confines of organized bureaucracy, and Karl Marx's representation of the monster of capitalism.[24] The picture of the juggernaut may aim to give such sensation of dynamism, which would otherwise not be present in Giddens' text. Notice that the picture is of a vehicle.

The description of the juggernaut is graphic:

> *a runaway engine of enormous power which, collectively as human*
> *beings, we can drive to some extent but which also threatens to rush out of*
> *our control and which could rend itself asunder. The juggernaut crushes*
> *those who resist it, and while it sometimes seems to have a steady path,*
> *there are times when it veers away erratically in directions we cannot*
> *foresee. The ride is by no means wholly unpleasant or unrewarding; it can*
> *often be exhilarating and charged with hopeful anticipation. But, so long*
> *as the institutions of modernity endure, we shall never be able to control*
> *completely either the path or the pace of the journey. In turn, we shall*
> *never be able to feel entirely secure, because the terrain across which it*
> *runs is fraught with risks of high consequence. Feelings of ontological*
> *security and existential anxiety will coexist in ambivalence.*
>
> Giddens, 1990, p139

In Giddens' contribution to the book *Reflexive Modernization*, written together with Ulrich Beck and Scott Lash, he addresses what he understands by tradition, including its meaning in early modernization and in *high modernity*, which he also calls reflexive modernity.

Here, he poses the obvious question: has society not been post-traditional for a long time? His answer is no! Because throughout its history, modernity has rebuilt tradition at the same pace as it has dissolved it. He describes this as the 'disembedding' of traditions, which is followed by 're-embedding' (Giddens, 1994b, p94). In the face of the exhaustion of tradition, society finds a new balance between modernity and tradition. In early modernity, for instance, formal truths and concomitant rituals were applied to new areas, most significantly the symbolic vindication of 'the nation' (Giddens, 1994b, pp93, 94–95).

However, reflexive modernity changes this earlier balance, creating a new form in which the balance between modernity and traditions is primarily established through globalization. In the high-modern society, traditions thus exist within one of two frameworks: through *discursive articulation and defence*, or through *fundamentalism*. The latter may arise in response to the failure of the former:

> *Traditions may be discursively articulated and defended – in other words,*
> *justified as having value in a universe of plural competing values.*
> *Traditions may be defended in their own terms, or against a more dialog-*
> *ical background; here reflexivity may be multilayered, as in those defences*
> *of religion which point to the difficulties of living in a world of radical*
> *doubt. A discursive defence of tradition does not necessarily compromise*
> *formulaic dialogue while suspending the threat of violence.*
>
> *Otherwise, tradition becomes* fundamentalism.
>
> Giddens, 1994b, p100

This new balance established by means of globalization explains why the post-traditional high-modern society is an end, and at the same time a beginning. It is a truly new social universe of action and experience. It will logically also be a global society – not a world society, but a society with 'indefinite space' (Giddens, 1994b, pp106–107).

The categories of *trust* and *intimacy* also feature prominently in Giddens' analysis of reflexive modernity. A fundamental element in his presentation is that modern institutions are thoroughly linked to the mechanisms of trust in abstract systems, particularly expert systems. This trust is the condition for the time-space distantiation, and for the far-reaching everyday certainty offered by modern institutions compared to the pre-modern world.

Trust in abstract systems, however, is not conducive to mental satisfaction in the same manner as personal relationships, which leaves the individual psychologically vulnerable in a series of realms – for example, where community relations disappear.

This transformation of intimacy implies: 'an intrinsic relation between the *globalizing tendencies* of modernity and *localised events* in day-to-day life – a complicated, dialectical connection between the "extensional" and the "intentional"' (Giddens, 1990, p123). Furthermore: 'The construction of the self as a reflexive project, an elemental part of reflexive modernity; an individual must find her or his identity amid the strategies and options provided by abstract systems' (Giddens, 1990, p124).

Giddens' answer to the risks of reflexive modernity, with its coupling of globalizing tendencies to the personal and intimate life, and so on, is the need to develop a *dialogical democracy*. This is not just an elaboration upon, or a complement to, liberal democracy. Nor is it an attempt to profile rights and represent interests, but rather the continuation of a kind of cultural cosmopolitanism, whose cornerstones are the connection between autonomy and solidarity (Giddens, 1994a, p112). Dialogical democracy is not centred within the state, but placed in a context between globalization and social reflexivity, where it calls for 'democratisation of democracy' (Giddens, 1994a, p113).

Consequently, dialogical democracy is played out in the space between the personal sphere and the formal political democracy. It becomes a subpolitical practice (cf. Beck), which unfolds in civil society in a series of contexts that, on the one hand, enables the individual to adapt to the risks of reflexive modernity, and on the other, exerts certain pressure on the formal political system, forcing it to incorporate partial elements.[25] These contexts range from: (a) areas of private life, such as the pure relationship in sexual relations, marriage and family, (b) social movements and self-help groups, and (c) organizations markedly influenced by the combination of globalization and reflexivity, to (d) a larger global order.

As an example, it is highlighted how democratization processes within organizations bring about features in defiance of what was, only one generation ago, generally accepted organizational principles. However, Giddens claims that a post-bureaucratic organization may both be well-suited for social reflexivity and react to situations of produced uncertainty much more effectively than command systems. Organizations structured in accordance with concepts of trust will necessarily delegate responsibility and depend upon an expanded dialogical space (Giddens, 1994a, pp122–123).

To Giddens, reflexive modernity is thus tantamount to dependency, and the dangers arising from the modernization of society force individuals to trust both the systems and each of their fellow citizens.

Critique of Beck's and Giddens' concept of reflexive modernity

Above I have repeatedly hinted at criticism towards Beck and Giddens regarding their stress on individualization as a particular characteristic of the *current* stage of modernity. I have referred to the fact that Kant and Hegel already drew attention to individuality as a specifically modern phenomenon in contrast to traditional society. Elaborating on this, I have further expressed scepticism regarding their stress on current modernity's distinctive reflexivity, by highlighting the reflexive character, in connection with the presentation of Habermas, as being present since the beginning of modernity. Finally, I have raised the point that, to my mind, the two authors lack concepts to explain the dynamics of modernity, as both remain descriptive.

I will elaborate on all these points later. One part of this will be to show that their lack of consistency in these areas must give rise to a critique of their concept of rationality, and that they operate with an incomplete concept of knowledge, presenting it exclusively as expert knowledge or, within a narrow understanding, as scientific knowledge.

The characterization of current modernity as particularly reflexive leads, in my view, to a *hypostatization of the phenomenon of reflexivity*, since it is held up as the central manifestation of society's *current* developmental *stage*. Both Beck and Giddens portray general developmental features as specific, and thus end up overemphasizing this specificity. Another way of putting it is that this focus prevents them from seeing the reflexivity of reflexivity itself. This is a rather peculiar consequence, since reflexivity is, actually in my view too, a key concept within modernization theories, perhaps even *the* key concept. Accordingly, I do not set out to question their use of the concept as such. However, their depiction of current modernity as being reflexive to a particular degree distorts their focus on the special features of modernity, so that they fail to come to grips with central sets of problems in the ongoing development. Indeed, it leads them to outright misinterpretations of current developmental features. This further critique will revolve around the modernization concept. The initial critique in this section will concentrate on showing that their concept of reflexivity only covers individual reflexivity, and that this contributes to a deficient characterization on their part of societal dimensions in the current manifestation of modernity.

The reason why so much attention in this presentation is dedicated to the issue of modernity's reflexivity stems from its significance in social practices, and particularly in those relating to the scope for planning and control, in this book specifically as regards the incorporation of environmental concerns. A vast series of questions may be raised to testify to the reach of this concept, the extent to which it expresses a reality, and how this is of the utmost relevance to the subject of the book. How does reflexivity affect the functions in the institutions of society, and how they work together? Because, if everything is operating on a reflexive basis, it has to mean that the premises of individual institutions are constantly being questioned, and hence the foundation for working together will be constantly undermined, or have to be re-established. If the social system is reflexive, does it then follow that each individual is forced to function reflexively? Does it entail that individuals act more as single entities, or do they act as collective units, or in collective ways? Does it imply that society is, to a greater extent, dependent upon the ethics and morals of each individual? Does it conversely mean that each person must acquire values and ethical principles in an individually driven rather than in a collective process? What does this mean for the decision-making processes in society? Can common values, platforms, perceptions and so on, be established to a degree that enables collective decisions?

And one step further: is it possible to conduct planning in a society whose assumptions concerning development are constantly overturned, or established and re-established upon new foundations? Can anything be calculated or predicted at all? No, it cannot, this is precisely the point, one would answer from a consistently postmodernistic viewpoint. How do communication processes work, if knowledge and meaning may be constantly thrown aside by new knowledge and meaning? If knowledge and insights are increasingly bound up with individually driven processes and experiences, how can insights of this nature be brought into, or applied within, societal or collective decision-making processes? This would require at least two things: organization and an opportunity for others to understand/use such knowledge and insights! How can such organization and adequate opportunities for interpretation be put in place? Or *can* such organization and opportunities for interpretation be established at all? Can universal values even exist within reflexive modernity? Is it possible to reach consensus on anything under this mode of social existence? Is there anything that is unambiguous, or is everything ambivalent, as Bauman claims? Or is it more an issue of contradictions, rather than ambivalence?

From the perspective of Beck's and Giddens' views of reflexive modernity, the answer to the bulk of these questions must be no. No, it is not possible, and this is indeed one of the problems of modernity. In contrast to this, the following critique aims to show that such a conclusion can be seen as the corollary of a one-sided focus on individuality, and particularly on individual reflexivity, which means that institutional processes – that is, reflexivity in a collective or structural form – seem to be ruled out. As will appear from the presentation below, this need not be the case. In fact, the possibility of institutional reflexivity, in connection with the individual variant, may lead to another understanding.

Modernization – the dynamics of capitalism

It is striking how little attention both Beck and Giddens pay to the economic dimension in their portrayal of the development of reflexive modernity. This is most probably the main reason why both lack a concept concerning the dynamics in modernity, whether or not this is characterized as reflexive. Although it appears from the occasional formulation that society is capitalist, they do not dedicate any space to analyse or specify what this implies in terms of specifically capitalistic regularities in the development of society.

Already Beck's introductory chapter on the logic of wealth and risk distribution in *Risk Society* feeds the suspicion that Beck is not operating with any concept concerning the dynamics of modern capitalist society. In this chapter, he argues that distribution and its related conflicts are central as long as evident material hardship – 'the dictatorship of scarcity' – is ruling the thinking and action of mankind (Beck, 1992, p20). In brackets he adds, remarkably: 'as today in large parts of the so-called "Third World"'. That is to say, he is implicitly stating that the Western world has abolished want and hardship (in this context we ignore the former so-called socialist bloc, still in existence when Beck first published the book in 1986).

In the 'society of scarcity', the modernization process is driven by the idea that the scientific and technological development can tap some of the hidden sources of wealth in society. These promises of deliverance from undeserved want and dependency underlie the action, thinking and research based upon the categories of social inequality, whether in the class society, stratified society or individualized society. In this regard, according to Beck, two things occur under reflexive modernity: the struggle for our daily bread loses its nature as the overriding fundamental problem; and knowledge that the sources of wealth are polluted becomes more widespread. The latter happens due to dangerous side effects, which are not new, but for a long time remained overlooked in the endeavour to overcome want. Today's risks are caused by industrial *over*production, and the threat it entails is global. It is the general output of the industrial progress machinery, and it is systematically increased along with its development. At the same time, the risks assume a new quality, since their effects are no longer confined to the place where they are created, the business enterprise (Beck, 1992, p22).

Here, not only does Beck, quite uncritically, apply the concepts of liberal economists, namely scarcity and need. He also claims that the scientific and technological development in society is motivated by a wish to abolish hardship and misery, or to open the sources of wealth to everyone, as he puts it. But why did we have to go through century-long class struggles precisely against the technological development of industrial production processes, if these were at the service of abolishing need and poverty among the very groups in society that fought them tooth and nail?

Beck steers clear of addressing the driving force behind the forward march of industrialized capitalism. 'Scarcity' and 'need' are the circumlocution of liberal or conservative economists when referring to this process. It is the conceptual construction they use to avoid the term profit; it is how they underline the liberalistic enrichment motivation and refer to the social class struggle fought in this regard.

A similar charge of elementary shortcomings in the understanding of capitalist dynamics may be levelled at Giddens. As mentioned, he resorts to the image of a vehicle to convey something runaway, a ferocious process dictated by blind forces. His fundamentally deficient comprehension of the capitalist process is evident in his distinction between industrialism and capitalism, and his similarly slipshod use of the concepts of exchange-value and use-value.[26]

Capitalism and industrialism are presented by Giddens as two of modernity's four dimensions, the others being surveillance and military force (Giddens, 1990, pp55–63). He thus views industrialism and capitalism as two *separate* dimensions of modernity. In this manner, his discussion of industrialism becomes purely physical, a claim that the historical development of industrial production would have been possible without its capitalist dimension. He uses the concept of capitalism as a kind of exchange-value, and analyses industrialism as pure use-value, without connecting these two. As a result, his analyses of physical phenomena remain purely material, and he never reaches an account of *where* capitalism (that is, the exchange-value) enters into the picture. This prevents an understanding that the exchange-value, or in its unfolded version just the value, expresses the *societal* dimension of capitalism, and that this is where both the dynamics and the structural compulsion come in: the economic shaping of physical phenomena.[27]

In both authorships, the outcome of this deficient understanding of the dynamics of capitalist society is that they see reflexivity as belonging to a particular stage in the development of modernity, and additionally, that they both associate this with the individual, failing to link it to the *structural* functions of capitalism. To put it in Habermasian concepts, they see reflexivity as solely connected to the lifeworld, and cannot identify its systemic forms.

One may even get the impression that they both see reflexivity as equivalent to dynamism, or perhaps confuse the two.[28]

The vagueness in Beck's use of the term *modernization* is apparent in his own definition of the concept:

> Modernization *means surges of technological rationalization and changes in work and organization, but beyond that it includes much more. The change in societal characteristics and normal biographies, changes of lifestyle and forms of love, changes in the structures of power and influence, in the forms of political repression and participation, in views of reality and norms of knowledge. In social science's understanding of modernity, the plough, the steam locomotive and the microchip are visible indicators of a much deeper process, which comprises and reshapes the entire social structure. Ultimately the* sources of certainty *on which life feeds are changed (Etzioni, 1968; Koselleck, 1977; Lepsius, 1977; Eisenstadt, 1979).*
>
> Beck, 1992, p50, note 1

The next part of this quote was left out in the English-language version, here translated from the original German (Beck, 1986, note on p25):

> *Usually, a distinction is made between modernization and industrialization. For the sake of linguistic simplicity, however, I shall here mostly use the term 'modernization' as a generic concept* (Oberbegriff).

The quote is highly expressive. Just to make sure, he throws everything into the mix, without specifying what he means by changes in, for instance, societal characteristics and lifestyles. To Beck, modernization is something really simple that may conceivably be tantamount to what we understand by modernization in the traditional sense, or in common speech – that is, innovation. On the face of it, modernization is just a technical rationalization, primarily in the productive sector, which rubs off on the social and political world, and so on. He does not work out an actual definition in the manner of Hegel and Habermas. Since the reflexive element thus fails to become integrated into the concept of modernity, he manages to introduce it as a particular phase from the moment he finds himself able to observe its empirical unfolding.

Individualization

This error also surfaces in the discussion of individualization within modernity. In particular Beck's accentuation of individualization as a special characteristic of the reflexive phase of modernity must be seen as resulting from a misinterpretation of how the capitalist crisis, since the 1970s, is dissolving collective structures within the corporate system in favour of the market's liberalistic hegemony. This individualization is not merely rooted in a specific form of modernization in these decades, but must be conceived as a continuation of early modernity introducing the individual as a category. Admittedly, trade unions and nation-state welfare policies have put a brake on individualization for more than a century. But if it is seen as a manifestation of capitalist modernization making productive labour processes abstract, and of the individual diverging from traditional and norm-bound society, it raises more aspects than setting individuals free of collective forms of action and protection, as highlighted by Beck.

Capitalist modernization opens up 'communicative spaces' both within the system and the lifeworld. The systemic media-ruled communications within the economic and the administrative system generate new forms of action-structured subsystems, which also entail a colonization of the lifeworld. Within the lifeworld, individuals are being emancipated to coordinate their actions by means of 'mutual understanding'. Consequently 'individualization' involves a structuring as well as a freeing of the individual's scope for action, both by creating new mechanisms of compulsion and by setting it free from existing mechanisms. In both cases, this takes place through modern reflexive processes, and not solely, as Beck imagines, by means of reflexive emancipation from traditionally existing ties or structures.

Although reflexivity is thus, on the face of it, generating ever-more opportunities for extra-structural social action, it also creates new structures, which Lash has termed information and communication structures (Lash, 1994, p111).

The same mechanisms that drive individualization thus also bring about a systemic build-up, subsystems or systemic expansion, which 'take over' and behave as determinants vis-à-vis each person. In fact, this occurs on two fronts, namely by narrowing down the individual's scope for action, at the same time as the very premises for action are increasingly dominated by systemic demands for functionality and efficiency.

Beck's reflexivity

The further critique of Beck's identification of a distinctively reflexive phase within modernity will elaborate on the above discussion of individualization. The critique sets out to show that Beck's concept of reflexivity is exclusively derived from categories concerning the behavioural forms of individuals, omitting structural concepts about society. This is not intended to ignore the development of consciousness that is necessary for the historical accomplishment of modernity. Before the modern world can emerge, one reality must be the shaping of human consciousness as 'reflexive', as opposed to naïve and taking things at face value – that is, it becomes capable of somehow turning back on itself in a critical process, in which both the manners and conclusions of thinking become subject to reflection (Nørager, 1985, p35). One precondition for this is precisely that the myriad scientific realizations achieved over the past centuries are acknowledged and accepted, in contrast to the repression of these by traditional society.[29]

Although reflexivity, to Beck as well as Giddens, is about individualization, about an individual 'self' being increasingly set free from the ties of society (Beck) and becoming able to create his or her own biographical narratives (Giddens), it also creates the collective 'selves', an element of society acting in opposition to the market's liberated self, and as a new ontological condition for something related to society (Lash, 1994, p111).

Thus, the critique below may in fact apply to Giddens as well, even though he does not see reflexive modernity as the result of a particular break in the development of modernity away from early modernity.

The concept of reflexive modernity signals a process in which modernity itself is subject to modernization. It is a process in which industrial society is reshaped by means of constant changes in its foundations, which are severed by its own dynamism. This is the modernization of modernization. There is no reason to question this dynamic here. It is an elementary principle of modernity. What prompts the critique is Beck's reading of this process as taking place in two stages. Subsequently, the critique will focus on Beck's vision that this reflexive modernity may be reshaped into a *new modernity*, whose development of subpolitics and self-criticism may evolve towards fewer risks and mistakes than under the existing modernity. This is because Beck's vision of such a new modernity is based upon his theories of the risk society.

As we have seen, in his contribution to the book *Reflexive Modernization,* Beck argues, based on new premises, that there is a distinctively reflexive phase in modernity, against the background of the critique levelled at the thesis he presented in *Risk Society* (Beck, 1992, pp10, 9–16).

It is necessary, writes Beck (1994, p5), to distinguish between an initial phase, in which effects and self-threats are produced systematically, but not subjected to public scrutiny or political conflict, and a subsequent phase, in which the dangers within industrial society predominate in public and political debate and conflict. In this manner, the institutions of industrial society become producers and legitimators of hazards beyond their control. If the undesired, unseen and compulsive transition from industrial society to risk society is called reflexivity in order to distinguish it from, and contrast it with, reflection, then reflexive modernization means self-confrontation with those effects of the risk society that cannot be assimilated or dealt with in industrial society, he further argues (Beck, 1994, p6).

However, industrial capitalist modernity has, from the very outset, been characterized by constantly severing its own foundations, by constantly revolutionizing production and all social relations in an unplanned manner, as Beck himself indicates with a reference to the *Communist Manifesto* by Marx and Engels (Beck, 1994, p2). And, one might add, the entire thrust of Marx's *Capital* is about this process, in which capitalist modernity is constantly revolutionizing its own underpinnings and all relations in society. Beck attempts to argue that, in reflexive modernity, it is not the class struggle, but rather normal modernization and further modernization that blurs the contours of industrial society, just as he stresses that what emerges has nothing to do with the now shipwrecked socialist Utopias (Beck, 1994, p2). But indeed the whole point throughout *Capital* is that the capitalist modernization process proceeds in the aforementioned (normal) manner.

Smart levels criticism at Beck's distinction between the two phases of modernity, in which reflexivity brings about the transition, and where reflection on the risks is characteristic of the second phase. Smart sees the steadily growing extent of organized reflection on accumulated evidence of concomitant risks and dangers as a logical outcome of the modernization process (Smart, 1999, p77). Reflection has always been – more or less consciously, and determined by the boundaries of the cognitive, moral and aesthetic dimension – a characteristic of modernization, although it may have become a more prominent feature as the momentum of reflexive modernization has grown (Smart, 1999, p77).

The distinction between reflexivity and reflection suggested by Beck is not, ultimately, analytically required, because the explanations of the consequences of reflexivity and of the ambivalence of modernity offered by Giddens and Bauman already make it clear that the institutions of modernity are destined to constantly defy our attempts at control:

> *The disorder of unintended and unanticipated consequences remains an inescapable feature of modern life, and modern scientific reason, by definition, is continually exposed to the possibility of being reflexively undercut*

or challenged, and is thereby unable to provide us with security of certain knowledge. The notion of reflexivity of modernity advanced by Giddens already encompasses reflection, but not in the form Beck has subsequently criticized for being too optimistic. There is no sense in which Giddens implies that 'more reflection, more experts, more science, more public sphere, more self-awareness and self-criticism will open up new and better possibilities in a world that has got out of joint' (Beck, 1994, p177), ironically if such optimism is to be found it is present in Beck's initial thesis.

Smart, 1999, p77

In this connection, Smart draws attention to an interesting parallel between the theory of reflexive modernity and Lyotard's analysis. In both cases, the scientific doubt is stretched to encompass reflection upon the foundations of science and its external consequences (Smart, 1999, p79).

All the more reason to be surprised that Beck – having so forcefully espoused the view that production of risk is now a significant feature of modernity, and that the technical-scientific development by itself is responsible for this – as a strategy to overcome this situation suggests a regeneration of the project of modernity. Beck's hope is that the unpredictability of the consequences of technical-scientific development can be reduced, or completely avoided, by creating an alternative technical-scientific praxis oriented towards self-control and self-limitation (Smart, 1999, p47).

However, although the need for humanizing the technical-scientific imperative is widely acknowledged, Smart claims, with a reference to Giddens, that the realization of such possibilities would require a transcending of the institutions of modernity that is comparable to a *post*modern social future.

Beck's assertion about a *new and better modernity* – in which the formerly so fatalistic industrial modernity is being universally self-reformed – that is an emancipation from modernity being locked in the industrial notion of science and technology, and in which the era of excuses is over – may thus be criticized for recycling one of modernity's central myths. On the contrary, we must accept that the reality of what is referred to as reflexive modernity is that we do not live with certainty and control, but with contingency. This is increasingly recognized as the logical outcome of modernity per se, as identified by both Giddens and Bauman (Smart, 1999, p48).

Therefore, when Beck argues that self-control and self-limitation must be supplemented by self-criticism, he is merely suggesting what is already considered a central part of modern scientific practice. In addition, self-criticism, even in a multiplicity of forms, cannot provide a guarantee against mistakes, as alternative paradigms and counterscientific views cannot be seen as less inclined to err. To institutionalize the right to criticism may be a necessary part of securing knowledge-based decisions, but in itself, this is not enough to prevent the domination of professional management. This would require a radical opening in the access to information, emphasizes Smart, referring to Lyotard as well as Illich (Smart, 1999, p49).

Wynne has suggested that the model of modern reflexivity and its production of risks could be interpreted to imply that it is lay people's critical reflection regarding modern scientific institutions' lacking ability to adequately control environmental and nuclear risks which brings these institutions into contradiction with their own self-legitimizing promises. This provokes further criticism from independent expertise, along with further erosion of modernity's cultural authority, its knowledge and its formal political institutions. This in turn produces an erosion of modernity through its own internal dynamism. Such a model also encompasses the assertion that science and technology are regularly disrupting the well-known patterns and identities of day-to-day life, emptying it of meaning. The result is an incentive to 'withdraw' or 'take refuge' in informal associations, in lifestyle politics and subpolitics outside the formal sphere (Wynne, 1996, p56).

This distinctive character of modernity is based on a neoclassical rational-choice model of human behaviour. Wynne elaborates on his discussion in the following manner:

> ... *this is based on a rationalistic model of social and cultural response to the experience of science, technology and modernity. In this conception, human response is rooted in an instrumental-calculative standpoint. The modern institutions and culture have failed to live up to their promise and to deeply rooted social expectations because the risks and side-effects are now unacceptably high; so the response is to disengage from and reconstruct the prevailing institutions and political culture. Behaviour and the ensuring redefinitions of identity are driven by instrumental concern about security from ecological risks, and the failure of modern expert institutions to provide that security while pretending to do so.*
>
> Wynne, 1996, p56

I fully agree that this is to attribute too much explanatory weight to the risks, regardless of whether or not the risks exist to the presumed extent. The explanation is far too guided by the 'realist' view that the public reacts in response to the expert institutions' handling of *actual, existing* risks.

Wynne's alternative is to explain the self-rebuttals of modernity, which he calls the reflexive movements, from a more thoroughly hermeneutic perspective. This involves an assessment and interpretation of the trust in expert systems intended to control the risks. In this manner, the public's reaction to risks is not considered to be conditioned by perceptions and evaluations of what are presumed to be objectively existing physical risks. On the contrary, the public's reaction is seen as conditioned by its trust in the ability of expert systems to handle the risks.

Looking at it in this manner, Wynne is thus inserting an interpretative link between the citizens and the risks, between the citizens and the institutions of society. The fact that this link is rooted in the culture, in possible traditions and customs, exempts each individual from responsibility for perception and assessment, thus also displacing the level of reaction or action from the individual to the institutional.

Indeed, the consequence of Beck's approach to reflexivity is a concept of society, in which the characteristics of society are conceived as a result of individual acts – that is, Beck's hypostatization of the existence (and cognition) of risks into a risk *society*. When he further argues that this society is characterized by conflict over the distribution of risks replacing the former society's conflict over the distribution of wealth, he is clearly separating the physical conflict, which constitutes the environmental problem (to Beck), from the social conflict, which in my opinion is built into the environmental problematic. This can be construed as further indication that Beck is individualizing the concept of reflexivity, and hence the concept of society, when this is determined on the basis of reflexive modernity.

In fact, interpreted in the above manner, Beck is contradicting himself in the sense that everything boils down to how people *perceive* the situation. The determination of society's reflexivity is reduced to a question of people's *reflection* on the risks. The corollary must be that the situation can be changed by people *understanding and interpreting it differently*. Therefore, it is hardly surprising that his distinction between the concepts of reflexivity and reflection is of no use (Beck, 1994, pp5–8; Wynne, 1996, p56; Smart, 1999, p77). To Beck, the problem (reflexivity) also becomes the solution (reflection), keeping in mind that his strategy to face the problems of reflexive modernity is a modernization of modernity.

This individualization of the concept of reflexivity leads Beck (and Giddens) to associate this existence of risks logically to the reflexive element, thus seeing reflexivity in society as a threat, hence the risk society as a hypostasis. However, a completely different logic would be to insist that a reflexive view of one's own foundations *must be seen as something beneficial*, as something able to substantiate change for the better, innovation, reflection and so on – that is, that reflexivity is a precondition for change.

In comparison, the structural content of Habermas' concept of reflexivity stems from the duality of a rationalization of the lifeworld and increasing complexity of the system. For modernization to start off, the lifeworld must have been rationalized, and as modernization carries on, it still requires such rationalization of the lifeworld to advance simultaneously. Therefore, the structural content of reflexive processes during capitalization is a kind of reflexivity raised to the second power, for instance during the capitalization of new sectors. In parallel, the rationalization of the lifeworld continues. The logic of this is that the capitalization of new sectors leads to a differentiation of these from the lifeworld, for instance from the culture, and the structural content of this is both a rationalization and a differentiation process.

On the basis of such a position, I shall maintain the need for a *socially structured* concept of reflexivity. Combined with the Marxian concept of the real subsumption of capital, such a concept would establish the understanding that the past 20 to 30 years of the capitalist modernization process has seen the capitalization of society earnestly beginning to enter spheres other than the customary one of production, and that society's reflexive pulse has been accelerating rapidly over the same period. This is the phenomenon which, I shall argue, is often confused with a qualitatively new epoch in modern development. Which, in a way, it really is, but with contents somewhat different from what is outlined by Beck (and Giddens). I shall make this case in a later section.

Already here, however, I want to stress that such a starting point does lead to an entirely different determination of the problem of modernity than the one in which reflexivity is viewed as problematic. Indeed I wish to highlight the necessity of reflexivity within modernity, both currently and formerly. The individual reflexivity must also be considered a benefit. The threat comes from the capitalist modernization process, both its instrumentality, or one-sidedness, and its expansion into reproductive spheres, including parts of public administration. The logical consequence of this is a further differentiation of the lifeworld, with its resultant cultural impoverishment and an attendant rise in systemic complexity, imposing the capitalist purposive rationality.

Accordingly, the capitalist purposive rationality is expanded at the expense of the substantial and communicative aspects and rationales of the lifeworld. For instance, further cultural impoverishment may cause mounting difficulties in gaining the wider population's understanding of an environmental problem, hence making it harder to gather support for the overall need for regulation. This produces an extreme intensification of the Habermasian problematic, namely that this greater or strongly escalating differentiation increases the need for a systemic foundation in the lifeworld, which is, simultaneously, subjected to intensifying colonization that narrows the scope for change.

Summing up, Beck's use of the concept of reflexivity is mistaken. On the one hand, it leads to an erroneous understanding of modernization, or to an unclear definition of this process. On the other, the inadequate understanding of the dynamics, or the lacking concept for these dynamics, leads to confusing the full introduction of modernity with a special phase or epoch within it.

Giddens' understanding of tradition

To Giddens, tradition is routines and habits, of which the routines make sense, whereas the habits are meaningless (Giddens, 1990, p105). In accordance with this concept of reflexivity as an expression of individual practices, he also links these to tradition, and not to societal or structural practices. In his contribution to *Reflexive Modernization*, which he entitles 'Living in a post-traditional society', it is striking that – throughout his lengthy description of the transition from traditional to post-traditional society, to early modernity and then to high modernity – he does not dedicate a single sentence to the economic dimension of this change, completely sidestepping the characteristics of the economy or productive sector in his presentation of the shift between each of the three phases.

As previously stressed, the way in which Giddens construes the concepts of capitalism and industrialism reflect this lacking understanding or acceptance of the significance of the productive or economic dimension (Giddens, 1990, pp55–63). In his distinction between industrialism and capitalism as two (out of four) *different* dimensions in modernity, his analyses remain purely physical, and it never becomes clear where capitalism enters the picture.

When Giddens elaborates on his concept of reflexive modernity (Giddens, 1994b), he carefully stresses that tradition is not merely something that is dissolved in modernity, but that new traditions are also being constantly formed. These may then play a decisive role within a period of time, then a new dissolution occurs, a new tradition may take shape, and so forth. Habermas also stresses the continuous creation of a stream of tradition in the hermeneutic practice of everyday life. However, his point is that this formation is sharply separate from modernity's differentiation of system and value spheres, which is subsequently developed unfettered by the stream of tradition. Giddens' failure to incorporate the economic dimension brings him to omit an analysis of the differentiation of this very dimension, and hence of capitalist production processes being freed from tradition. A production process analysis, and an analysis of the differentiation of the economic sphere, could bring home the point that, as soon as the differentiation has been accomplished 'once and for all', it will *set the terms* for continued development within a particular branch of production. Emerging development processes will not again be based upon the traditional craft methods within that branch. Instead, the processes will be constantly innovated, or revolutionized, conditioned by the capitalist form. This is what makes a difference.[30] The traditions that may arise after this transition do not have the same character as those that are swept away in the processes of differentiation. They are of a different kind, they are casual, temporary, ahistorical and so on. As the capitalist forms of development spread into other parts of society, the same pattern is repeated.

The tradition that is the point of departure for differentiation – or what Giddens calls disembedding – of the economic and administrative system, as well as of science, morality and arts, is a concept to describe something in society which steers the development towards this transition in particular.

This gives rise to understanding tradition as something socially embedded (to use one of Giddens' terms), which is something else and more than just routines and habits. Tradition is far more wide-ranging than Giddens' perception of new patterns of tradition taking shape within a particular area, which last for a while, until new ones are formed. A concept of tradition in the first-mentioned wider form of understanding enables us to relate tradition to a societal epoch. This is replaced by a new societal epoch, whose dynamic principle is capital, that is, the epoch is driven by something in form, or rather something abstract released from content and form, which constitutes the 'invisible' dynamics. This contrasts with tradition, where the content is precisely the guiding principle.

The problem with Giddens' understanding of tradition stems from his lack of distinction between system and lifeworld, even though he uses concepts to describe differentiations. His disembedding and subsequent re-embedding become rather vague when asking where, how and why this disembedding and re-embedding occur. Against this somewhat flimsy description, I insist that the systemic differentiation in modernity has been systematically 'lifted from' tradition, and this is where to find the social dimension in the separation of production and reproduction from forms of reproduction conditioned by tradition.

By comparison, Weber uses the concept of demythologization of worldviews to describe the social rationalization that characterizes the dismantling of traditions. And to Habermas, the same process as well as the continued rationalization of the lifeworld is what replaces tradition by mutual linguistic understanding. To both these authors, this is a social and universal process.

Establishing that *society* as such has been de-traditionalized is decisive for the further analysis of the societal modernization process. As we shall see later, environmental assessments do indeed reflect that society has been de-traditionalized, when looking at the assessment from a systemic perspective. This is precisely what conditions both the possibility and the necessity of incorporating *tradition in another form* into environmental assessment, as a potential of reason in communicative everyday practice.

Rationality

It may seem paradoxical that Beck as well as Giddens fails to reflect on the concept of rationality, since both fundamentally make a case for society's *lack* of rationality. Beck expresses this in his identification of reflexive modernity's risk production, which is now overshadowing the progress. Giddens talks about 'the circularity of social knowledge', which he also calls the reflexivity of social knowledge, by which he understands, for instance, that new knowledge fails to make the social world easier to decode, but, on the contrary, changes it and sends it off in new and unpredictable directions (Giddens, 1990, p153). Already here, one may get the impression that Giddens is thus seeing reflexivity as an obstacle to the achievement of rational knowledge, but this is not a point that he clarifies. For both authors, however – just as oddly against this background – knowledge is primarily construed as scientific knowledge, or as it is also characterized, as expert knowledge. I shall elaborate on this in the next section.

Here, I shall focus on Beck's distinction between a *scientific* and a *social* rationality.

His distinction between these two forms of rationality springs, rather logically, from the way in which he characterizes, respectively, the scientific and society's handling of risks. In the most advanced developmental stages of the productive forces, risks are *invisible* and based upon *causal interpretations*, which is why they exist first and foremost in the *knowledge* one has about them (Beck, 1992, p23). In this manner, they may 'be changed, magnified, dramatized or minimized within knowledge, and to what extent they are particularly *open to social definition and construction*' (Beck, 1992, p23). Risks are thus more vulnerable to definitions and conflicts being driven by vested interests.

At the same time, environmental problems are widely considered something exclusively pertaining to nature, technology, economy and medicine so 'that the industrial pollution of the environment and the destruction of nature, with their multifarious effects on the health and social life of people, which only arise in highly developed societies, are characterized by a *loss of social thinking*' (Beck, 1992, p25).

After establishing such premises, Beck derives two characteristic sets of concepts:

• risk definitions and definitional struggles;
• scientific rationality and social rationality.

Risk definitions are the form in which ethics, and hence also philosophy, culture and politics, re-emerge *within* the centres of modernization – that is, in economics, natural sciences and technical disciplines. However, such definitions presuppose 'a cooperation across the trenches of disciplines, citizens' groups, factories, administration and politics, or – which is more likely – they disintegrate between these into antagonistic definitions and *definitional struggles*' (Beck, 1992, p29).

The concept of *definitional struggles* serves to explain why there is not simply a technical-scientifically predictable cause-and-effect sequence in the implementation of particular activities. It may contribute to shed light on why the endless struggles between different scientific views lead to a breakdown in the technical-scientific form of understanding, because these *definitional struggles* are not merely fought out between different (natural) scientific perspectives, but also between a variety of institutions and groups rooted in society. Not only does this lead to an expansion in the magnitude of these struggles and in the composition of their participants. It also widens their scope from being not merely scientific, but also *political* struggles.

This is the background against which Beck arrives at the concepts of, respectively, a *scientific* and a *social* rationality. The former is expressed in mathematical probabilities, ostensibly based upon experimental logic, although this has long been abandoned and the probabilities narrowed down to those that are technically manipulable. Conversely, the latter is the sphere in which normative conditions as well as economy, politics, ethics and so on, constitute the framework for establishing the rationality. However, Beck states, the distinction between these two types of rationality becomes ever more difficult to sustain, and hence they need to be linked together in constant dialectics. He phrases it in the following manner: 'scientific rationality without social rationality remains *empty*, but social rationality without scientific rationality remains *blind*' (Beck, 1992, p30).

With this formulation, he is himself questioning the distinction between scientific and social rationality. His concept of rationality does not really express more than what is traditional within a technical-scientific form of understanding, namely expediency and effectiveness. Without further ado, this concept is transferred to express expediency at the level of social relations, which he then contrasts with the technical and natural-scientific variant. But that something is expedient in a social context is *normative*, and he does not explain how to take this into account. In this manner, he also refrains from breaking with the illusion that one may define what is socially optimal. He omits to say that the concept of rationality does not belong in this context at all. He creates an artificial contrast that can only be used to foster further illusions. To put it more kindly, his presentation remains within the optics of natural science.

In fact, Beck illustrates this himself. After a protracted explanation of how the class society exposes people differently to the acquisition of material wealth, as opposed to how – in principle – the risk society exposes people equally to the dangers, and of the simultaneous interrelation between these social forms, Beck asks whether the political subject of the class society, that is, the proletariat, corresponds to the political subject of the risk society – that is, everyone! (Beck, 1992, p49). Everyone is more or less affected by tangible and massive dangers. And in the mind, this is easy to repress. Everyone and no one is responsible. Does 'everyone' qualify as a political subject? Is there not a far too hasty and casual inference from the global scale of the risks to common political will and action? Beck asks. And in this manner, he has effectively called into question his own concept of *social* rationality. What does the word 'social' express in this context? It remains vague, or perhaps rather unsaid, most likely because it *cannot* be spelt out.

Similarly, one may say that Beck himself empties his rationality concept of its content on the basis of its other side, the scientific one. For example in the sentence: 'Insisting on the *purity* of scientific analysis leads to the *pollution and contamination* of air, foodstuffs, water, soil, plants, animals, and people. What results then is a covert coalition between strict scientific practice and the threats to life encouraged or tolerated by it' (Beck, 1992, p62). He is thus saying that the raising of scientific standards leads to a reduction in the acknowledged kind of risks, and that this brings about a scientifically legitimized *aggravation* of the actual risks.

This analytical attention to detail, however, raises doubt as to what *Beck* understands by rationality.

His analysis of the concept of *threshold limit value (TLV)* is also incisive, but may be interpreted in the same manner as regards the content of the rationality concept. He underlines two mistakes that underlie all determination of TLVs. First, conclusions are erroneously inferred regarding human reactions on the basis of conclusions from experiments with animals (Beck, 1992, p66). Second, TLVs are based upon the experiment with humans taking place and failing to take place. It does take place to the extent that the muck is indeed passed on to humans and animals in certain doses. It fails to take place in the sense that human reactions are not systematically recorded and utilized. But as he says: 'The mode of action among experimental animals has no validity for people, but it is very carefully recorded and correlated. For the sake of caution, the reactions in people themselves are not even noted, unless someone reports and can *prove* that it is actually *this* toxin which is harming him' (Beck, 1992, p69).

However, with which of Beck's concepts of rationality is it appropriate to assess the effects of humans being exposed to various substances? And would that bring any useful clarification? On this matter, Beck is silent.

The concept of knowledge – expert knowledge and lay knowledge

According to Giddens, reflexive modernity leads to trust in expert systems replacing personal commitment. Conversely, to Beck, reflexive modernity means an increasing independence of expert systems, but also freedom to criticize them.

Moreover, both see insecurity as a crucial concept, and consider reflexivity to be a means of reducing insecurity. However, Giddens focuses on the issue of order, while Beck concentrates on change. As conceptualized by Beck, reflexivity generates insecurity, but may also lead to social change through minimization of environmental damage. Giddens talks about 'ontological insecurity', and uses it to formulate a question about order: how can we maintain order and stability, both personally and socially, in a scenario in which not only environmental but also mental and social damage is widespread? His answer is: through expert systems.

Altogether, this means that Beck considers expert systems as obstacles to achieving security, while Giddens sees them as instruments that may contribute to achieving security. Although they agree overall on the reflexive phase of modernity, they thus arrive at very different views on the effects of this reflexivity. This has to fuel the suspicion that their analysis, in a series of areas, is built upon an inconsistent conceptual and theoretical foundation.

One example of such inconsistency may be the shift in public trust in expert systems. Giddens assumes that previously, in what he characterizes as simple modernity, existed a kind of automatic public trust in expert systems, whereas this is not the case under reflexive modernity, since the public is now faced with making a choice concerning a new dimension of insecurity, arising from expert systems being challenged and contested. However, only because public criticism has not previously been manifested, one cannot assume that this has been an expression of trust. This is indeed what Giddens does (Wynne, 1996, pp48–50).

On the face of it, Beck's concept of the risk society builds upon the idea that modern institutions have become their own accusers, because they have failed to live up to their own visions of management and control due to the escalating risks in the use of science and technology. This implicitly entails that people no longer see the sense in trusting in science and expertise, because they feel betrayed by them.

In Giddens' original understanding, reflexive processes are not the outcome of distrust in expert systems, but are caused by interpersonal reactions to globalization and differentiation (Giddens, 1990). However, since he moves towards Beck's perception in his later understanding of popular trust in expert systems (Giddens, 1994a, b), both can be credited with the view that the transformation of modernity into reflexive modernity means that popular trust in expert systems can no longer be taken for granted.

Wynne critiques both of them for two crucial errors. First, that the unchallenged status of expert systems under 'simple modernity' is matched by the public's trust. Second, that reflexive processes in late modernity, in which the expertise is widely and openly contested, is the outcome of the choices that people have to take upon careful consideration, as they are exposed to a new situation of insecurity – that is when the formerly undisputed expert authority is questioned. In a series of examples, Wynne demonstrates that such trust in expert systems did not, as assumed, exist in early modernity either (Wynne, 1996, pp48–50).

With particular reference to Giddens, Wynne makes the case for a different perception of the relationship between the public and the experts, between lay knowledge and expert knowledge, in a manner that challenges the existence of a shift from a non-reflexive to a reflexive-calculative public reaction to expert systems, and which impinges crucially on the identification of reflexive processes in modernity. In contrast to Giddens, Wynne asserts that the public's reaction to expertise and to its dependency on expert systems is highly ambivalent, and that this is deep-seated socially and in terms of identity.

He substantiates this viewpoint with a reference to the study of a minor accident in Buffalo Creek, USA (Erickson, 1976), and a study of the surrounding inhabitants' reactions to information on risks at a hazardous chemical plant in Great Britain (Jupp, 1989). As it appeared, in none of the cases was doubt raised as to the risks presented, neither between the various experts, nor between the experts and the population. However, closer examination revealed that: (a) there was extensive realism among the public as to the existence of immediate risks; (b) there was widespread distrust in the information presented, and ambivalence regarding the expert institutions and their publicly stated claims; (c) that fundamentally different reasons, compared to what would normally be expected, were behind the public's reaction against the expert systems; and (d) there was considerable unacknowledged elasticity and adaptability to this situation in terms of informally recognized dependency and ambivalence.

Wynne thus suggests that the presumption of the public's trust in expert systems in what is characterized as simple modernity be replaced by a more complex understanding of this relationship, in which ambivalence takes centre-stage, and where trust is largely conditioned by the experience of dependency, possible alienation and lacking scope for action (Wynne, 1996, p52).

The consequence of this concerns not only modernity, but also leads, according to Wynne, to discarding the thesis about the risk society. The transformation to reflexive modernity, as proposed by Beck and Giddens, cannot be correct if it is based on such a false premise. Instead, he suggests a wholly different conception of the character of risks, based upon the cultural dimensions of modernity. Wynne thus does not question the existence of risk and its far-reaching significance for living conditions and an ecological crisis of society, but challenges the thesis of a distinct reflexive phase in modernity. To him, reflexivity is merely a feature of modernity in general (Wynne, 1996, p52).

Furthermore, the critique of Beck and Giddens may be levelled at their concept of knowledge. Both see scientific knowledge as consisting exclusively of propositional or logical truths. Moreover, when addressing the nature of reflexive modernity or high modernity, as well as the possibilities of handling risks, they focus exclusively on expert knowledge rather than lay knowledge. Consequently, they also fail to acknowledge the relationship between these two forms of knowledge, and their significance in the democratization of the political and scientific institutions of modernity.

Although scientific knowledge has a cultural dimension, in addition to holding hermeneutic truths,[31] it cannot stand alone. It needs to be supplemented by lay knowledge, which is precisely what contains the cultural and contextual corrective to logically determined truths, cf. Habermas. Therefore, lay people need to play a decisive role in the determination of universal and human values, which will also be a crucial factor in the development of new forms of regulation.

Contrary to this, Beck upholds the exclusive knowledge of expertise in terms of a counter-expertise. In this manner, he conditions the chances of control and security upon decisions and social practices within the *modernized* modernity – that is, where Beck's subpolitics enters the frame. He is thereby repeating the illusions of modernity.

The recognition of the cultural and hermeneutic dimensions of scientific expert knowledge – that is, that it spreads and imposes particular and contestable normative versions of what is human and social – must also lead to abandoning problematic dichotomies in modernity, such as 'natural' versus 'social' knowledge, nature versus society, and expert versus lay knowledge. Such dichotomies reflect a reductionist understanding of the process of change occurring in modern society. They may be seen as the outcome of a rational-choice reading of social relations. In the writings of Beck and Giddens they also cause, as we have seen, a misinterpretation of the concepts of trust and risk, and hence a misinterpretation of the processes of change in modernity (Wynne, 1996, p75).

Accordingly, one cannot trace a break with 'traditional' scientific perceptions of knowledge, either by Beck nor Giddens. In opposition to this, Wynne has a rather vivid description of the relationship between expert knowledge and the lay knowledge that is expressed in public:

- *Scientific expert knowledge embodies assumptions and commitments of a human kind, about social relationships, behaviour and values.*
- *It also embodies problematic 'structural' or epistemic commitments, for example about the proper extent of agency, control and prediction, or of standardization.*
- *It neglects and thus denigrates specialist lay knowledges.*
- *At a secondary level it then defines lay resistances as based on ignorance or irrationality rather than on substantive if unarticulated objections to these inadequate constructions of lay social identity which the expert discourses unwittingly assume and impose.*
- *Thus a further reinforcement takes place, of tacit public ambivalence about being dependent on social actors (experts) who engender such alienation and social control.*
- *Hence the fundamental sense of risk in the 'risk society' is risk to identity engendered by dependency upon expert systems, which typically operate with such unreflexive blindness to their own culturally problematic and inadequate models of the human.*

Wynne, 1996, p68

Accordingly, not only do these 'two cultures' fail to meet. The dichotomous perception of knowledge means, on the one hand, that efforts are stepped up to convince that conditions are under control, which in reality serves to repress reflexivity. On the other, it adds to the sense of insecurity, alienation and involuntary dependency.

Moreover, the dichotomous approach fails to take into account that lay knowledge is also developed and applied with the objective of controlling certain situations or circumstances, including the attainment of social control. However, it is a form of control that is radically different from the one that springs from a scientific form of cognition. Lay knowledge produces a form of human contextual control that stands in contrast to the scientifically based control of modernity, which is not exercised with a human, contextual, complex and holistic insight. Wynne expresses it in the following manner:

> ... *this idiom of knowledge [i.e. lay knowledge] allows control, but of a contextually dense and multidimensional reality in which adaptive flexibility towards the uncontrolled is still recognized as a necessary attribute, and where the reductive, decontextualized and alienated 'control' of other situations in the 'universalistic' manner of science is pre-empted. That is, this kind of adaptive 'control' is one which is exercised with personal agency and overt responsibility. It is just this property which, as Beck notes (1992), is missing from modernity's particular discourse of control, namely science; and it is the reintegration of the deleted issues of human agency, responsibility and value which may lead to the democratisation, legitimation and epistemic pluralisation of science.*
>
> Wynne, 1996, p70

From this perspective, scientific knowledge may be seen as a 'cheap' systemic substitute for human insight, experience and knowledge. It is functional in a systemic context, but beyond that, i.e. in a wider context that encompasses the lifeworld, it will omit or scrap irreplaceable human insights and values.

It is to avoid such a development that Wynne wishes to involve what he calls human activity, responsibility and values that may lead to democratization, legitimation and epistemic pluralization of science from a hermeneutic-cultural approach. He thus holds on to modernity, seeing the environment and the risk debate as quintessentially bound up with the legitimacy crisis in which modern economic, scientific-technical and political institutions are immersed. Consequently, the environmental debate also needs to be incorporated in a search for new forms of legitimate social order and authority. This search will give rise to new configurations of global visions and local roots able to take in new conceptions of universal knowledge and humane values. An inescapable part of the process will involve lay people.

Not only does Wynne insist on the development of the modern, he also *refuses* to give up the idea of universals, whose determination he does not wish to leave to established scientific institutions, preferring to involve lay people in this. In other words, Wynne does not assert that the contextual or 'local' element always takes precedence, or is superior to scientific or universal knowledge.

A comparison of these points in Wynne and in Habermas springs to mind, perhaps even more so since Wynne's writings do not refer to Habermas. For instance, his assertion of modernity's widespread neglect of the cultural-hermeneutic dimension can be compared to Habermas' distinction between system and lifeworld. His demonstration of a reductionist form of understanding based on a neoclassical rational-choice model is akin to Habermas' identification of one-sided modernization and its practice of instrumental reason. Finally, his observation of the need to supplement scientific knowledge with the cultural and contextual corrective of lay knowledge may be compared to Habermas' three forms of rationality and the normative foundation in the hermeneutic everyday practice of the lifeworld. These parallels will also appear from the presentation in Chapter 5 concerning the involvement of lay people and different publics in the development of new forms of regulation.

Smart agrees with the critique of Beck's one-sided perception of knowledge as expert knowledge, and his corresponding lack of emphasis on the public's role. Smart refers, for instance, explicitly to Lash's critique that Beck is neglecting the meaning of differences in the access to 'networks of information and communication structures', and to Wynne's suggestion that Beck does not attribute sufficient significance to 'the informal non-expert public domain' (Smart, 1999, pp70–71). Beck focuses on expert knowledge, and fails to adequately recognize lay knowledge, since his idea of alternatives to the professional knowledge monopoly consists of alternative groupings of scientists or of science (as in Wynne's critique above). In this manner, Beck overlooks the significance of the interaction between expert and lay knowledge, including the cultural content of expert knowledge. However, 'it is precisely the evidence of degrees of scepticism and uncertainty surrounding the issue of "proper technical know how", and associated measures proposed to counter risks, which has led analysts such as Lash and Wynne to argue that ambivalence is intrinsic to risk society, a conclusion to which Beck (1994) in turn has ultimately been driven' (Smart, 1999, p71).

In this regard, the case could be made that Beck's continued oversight of differences in access to communication structures, and his reference to expert knowledge rather than lay knowledge within his definition of reflexive modernity, is precisely what leads him to suggest alternative knowledge forms and practices. He fails to notice that these are already present in the existing form of modernity, and hence do not provide genuine potential for transcendence, modernization or regeneration into a less problematic modernity.

A more direct refutation of Beck's optimism that institutionalization of self-criticism would enable knowledge of risks and dangers to appear beforehand is identified by Smart in Bauman's thesis on modernity's ambivalence (Smart, 1999, p77). To Bauman, contingency is a logical consequence of modernity, rather than a 'temporary ailment', but it would be a serious mistake – which, in fact, he hints that Beck is making (Smart, 1999, p77) – if this is interpreted as a call for anaemic pessimism or a 'sit-back-and-do-nothing' mentality. Bauman is aiming at the exact opposite by offering 'a careful and balanced analysis of existing conditions and possibilities, a sober assessment of what is involved in living without guarantees, a survey of the opportunities and dangers that are to be found on a site Bauman (1991) identifies as 'postmodernity' (Smart, 1999, p78).

Beck does, however, pay attention to Bauman's position, and in his response to the critique, he places more emphasis on the uncertainties, lack of clarity, disorder and irreducible ambivalences of risk society (Smart, 1999, p78). Instead of following up on the strategy that Beck has put forward himself – that is, instead of presenting an institutionalization of self-criticism and some prospect of how science, equipped with 'proper technical know-how' may challenge science itself, as the appropriate way of detecting and avoiding mistakes – he sets more store by 'the onset of ambivalence', and even recognizes that 'living and acting in uncertainty becomes a kind of basic experience' (Smart, 1999, p78; quotes from Beck, 1994, pp29, 12).

Beck's answer to the ambivalence of modernity is that 'the model for unambiguous instrumental rationality must be abolished' (Beck, 1994, p29), and that our growing dependence on experts has to lead to a 'demonopolization of science' (Beck, 1994, p29). As it appears, this encompasses an alternative to existing forms of control over science, by means of opening the knowledge generation, administration and decision-making processes to non-specialists, that is, a new and different way of dealing with ambivalence, which implies that 'experience is once again made possible and justified in society – also and particularly against science' (Beck, 1994, p30).

However, as it turns out, this alternative 'experience' must be lifted to the status of highly ambiguous alternative science (Smart, 1999, p78). Because Beck suggests distinguishing between two types of science which start to diverge precisely in the civilization of threats:

> *On the one hand, there is the old, flourishing laboratory science, which penetrates and opens up the world mathematically and technically but devoid of experience and encapsulated in a myth of precision; on the other, there is public discursivity of experience which brings objectives and means, constraints and methods, controversially into view. Both types have their particular perspective, shortcomings, constraints and methods. Laboratory science is systematically more or less blind to the consequences which accompany and threaten its successes. The public discussion ... of threats ... is related to everyday life, drenched with experience and plays with cultural symbols. It is also media dependent, manipulable, sometimes hysterical and in any case devoid of a laboratory, dependent in that sense upon research and argumentation, so that it needs an accompanying science (classical task of the universities). It is thus based more on a kind of science of questions than on one of answers.*
>
> Beck, 1994, pp30–31

Such distinction between two types of science raises problems on at least two fronts (Smart, 1999, p79). First, it is not tenable. Beck does not explain his rationale behind separating 'university knowledge' from 'laboratory knowledge', nor which are the limitations of the latter category. Not only is his distinction unconvincing, it is also highly contestable, as it fails to take account of the vast series of complex transformations taking place in scientific research practice. For instance, it should have allowed for the growing significance of industry in university research, expressed in the branching out of universities by means of 'science parks'. And second, it is no longer reasonable to equate 'laboratory science' with instrumentality, positivism or selling out to prominence. On the contrary, this kind of science may be said to increasingly fulfil a significant function of bringing forth paradoxes, or of isolating counter-examples.

Consequently, despite an apparent opening towards more alternative forms of knowledge as opposed to established science and expertise, Beck still leaves us in a situation in which lay knowledge and the role of the common public are unclear, or simply not built into the strategies against modernity's risk production and ambivalence.

The reflexive strategies

Indeed, Beck's view of a scientific transformation within modernity, and his apparent belief that it can be brought under human control, or at least become subject to people-driven change, must be seen as dubious. In the words of Smart:

> *Although there is an acknowledgement of transformations in the world of science in Beck's work, in particular a transformation conceptualized in terms of a shift from primary to secondary scientization, the uncertainty and associated absence of security which are deemed to arise with the reflexive self-doubt of the sciences (Beck, 1997, p172) appear to be regarded as, at least in principle, remedial features which may be alleviated by a reorientation or reconstitution of scientific practice.*
>
> Smart, 1999, p79

This, Smart suggests, may be contrasted to Lyotard's discussion of the transformations of the conditions for science, which highlights rather different aspects, and points to the way in which 'science – by concerning itself with such things as undecidables, the limits of precise control, conflicts characterized by incomplete information, "fracta", catastrophes, and pragmatic paradoxes – is theorizing its own evolution as discontinuous, catastrophic, non-rectifiable, and paradoxical' (Lyotard, 1984, p60, from Smart, 1999, p79). Whether or not this describes a science that may be characterized as postmodern is inconsequential. To Lyotard, modern technical-scientific practice is driven forward by dynamics that are independent of conditions deemed by humans to be desirable, profitable or comfortable. Therefore, we cannot expect to exercise control and management, but we may influence the conditions behind this dynamism.

The modern world of growing complexity depicted by Lyotard is more one to which we are subject, rather than one over which we can exercise much control, but there nevertheless seems to remain a remote possibility that a democratization of access to information and knowledge, or a demonopolization of expertise, might offer a basis for critical reflection and for 'making knowledgeable decisions' (Lyotard, 1984, p67).

Smart, 1999, p79

Given my starting point set out in Chapter 2, I can hardly add my voice to this conclusion with enthusiasm. Nevertheless, it is thought-provoking in relation to a Habermasian perspective, as well as to Wynne's critique of Beck (and of Giddens, incidentally) for focusing too much on expert rather than lay knowledge. Not least because the above quote holds out a prospect that may be desirable, given the premises and aims of this book, and falls within the boundaries of what may be said to be feasible.

Beck's vision of responding through alternative forms of action seems dubious, because elements of such alternatives are already widely included in the practices of the risk society, which nonetheless bring those unwelcome consequences depicted by Beck.

Similarly, Beck's idea of a 'rationality reform' must also be considered problematic. Such an endeavour, Beck envisages, could set standards for a new modernity founded upon the principles of caution and reversibility. Doubt created by critical reflection offers the prospect of reconstituting science, knowledge, critique or morality, albeit in a more modest form, with more testing and openness to unforeseen elements, as well as with the tolerance that springs from an understanding of 'the ultimate final certainty of error' (Beck, 1994, p33).

To characterize the new social structure or order that may be packaged with such a reform as 'new modernity' is problematic. In some measure, this is due to Beck's inadequate determination of the dynamics behind technical-scientific innovations, and particularly because he does not refer to any knowledge other than the alternative scientific knowledge behind such new modernity. Thus, he has failed to sketch out any likelihood that such alternative science may act differently from the so-called established form of science, including which conditions in such a new modernity are meant to enable this.

Another shortcoming of Beck's strategy of subpolitics, as I see it, is that it fails to take into account that reflexivity is also a phenomenon *within* the systems, and cannot simply be said to create problems due to the rapid social transformation that it mediates. Beck implicitly ends up ignoring that such changes may lay the groundwork for creating a better modernization. Adaptability, and the need for it, may well be characterized as a good. The trouble arises because reflexivity must not just unfold on the system's own terms, since this will merely reproduce a practice that generates problems for the surroundings of the system. Therefore, such intra-systemic reflexivity has to be influenced from the outside, so that it does not take place solely on its own systemic terms, but is forced to reflexively integrate conditions of a non-systemic nature in order to end the one-sided and instrumental functionality. The question is where this influence should come from, and how it may affect matters in a desirable manner and direction.

As it turns out, the fundamental flaw in Beck's strategy is that, by discarding lay knowledge and real public participation in favour of a dubious, or at least insufficient, alternative expertise, he retains a one-sided focus on instrumental reason. The reflexivity which he holds out as characteristic of modernity is still reflexivity on systemic terms. How this is to contribute to fundamentally changing one-sided modernization remains a puzzle.

Smart even goes so far as to consider that a rationality reform, such as the one prescribed by Beck, does not represent the characteristics of a new modernity, but of an actual Utopia *after* modernity, referring to Giddens' descriptions of a post-modernity (Giddens, 1990, pp163–173; Smart, 1999, p80). However, I find it hard to see how Beck's strategy may lead to anything other than a continuation of instrumental practices. In reality, it would contribute to further one-sidedness, since it so markedly focuses on the experts, whether they be alternative or not, and hence not only rules out participation by different layers or groups in society, but also keeps knowledge and insights gained from new experiences as the preserve of an exclusive social stratum. In other words, this carries the danger of stratifying society and decision-making processes even further, contributing to barring access, as opposed to democratization, and to an ever-widening scope for mistakes.

A similar critique may be directed towards Giddens' vision of dialogical democracy. First and foremost, he also fails to notice that it is intra-systemic reflexivity that needs to be open to influence. In addition, he also focuses on expert rather than lay knowledge. Finally, once again in the same manner as Beck, he concentrates on individual reflexivity on systemic terms.

This makes it difficult to see what is democratic about the dialogue, when it is first to be conducted exclusively among the experts, or at least on the terms of expertise. It is, in other words, difficult to envisage how the dialogue in such conditions is to 'move downwards' in society, that is, beyond the formal democratic system. Yet another blow to the democratic element springs from his wholly uncritical assumption of trust in expert systems. Thus, he apparently fails to understand that expert systems, including the bureaucracy, are the ones who must demonstrate their trust in the people, and not vice versa. Such trust requires openness and information, as well as susceptibility to criticism from all groupings in society concerning these systems' modes of operation. Without such an open dialogue, it is hard to conceive of any democratic development, whether inside or outside the formal democracy.

Thus, the conclusion concerning Beck's strategy of alternative expertise as well as Giddens' strategy of dialogical democracy is that they both send a signal of hope, but nevertheless remain without critical sting and force for change, because they fail to map out the real dangers of modernization. In other words, none of them is able to demonstrate any actual counterweight to the problematic sides of modernization. This gives rise to an impending danger that they may instead result in *alternative instrumentality and instrumental dialogue*.

Synthesis

Summing up the critique of Beck's and Giddens' reflexive modernity, it is evident that they do not bring us any closer to understanding the ongoing development of modernity. First and foremost, because they take such an uncritical view of the reflexive element in modernity, and rather glibly turn it into something particular to the present phase. In this manner, they miss an opportunity to pinpoint the critical potential which could be identified on the basis of the reflexive element, though not in isolation from the other central characteristics of modernity. As Lash has phrased it, a critical core can only come into sight if the theory of reflexive modernity is 'grasped radically against its own grain', which may well be construed as its need to be held critically to account against its own core, or, as Lash also puts it, 'when it is read counter to its own stated purposes and instead in the context of its unspoken assumptions' (Lash, 1994, p110).

The aforementioned critique of both authors may be summed up in three points:

1   They both use the concepts of *modernity* and *modernization* without providing a clear definition of what they understand by the modernization process. This circumstance may spring from their lack of a concept concerning the dynamics in capitalist modernity, which they fail to understand.
2   Their perception of *rationality* is highly inadequate, and they use the expression 'rational' or 'rationality' with an implicit form of understanding, whose substance of meaning becomes unclear, contradictory or outright incomprehensible. This is the case, for instance, when Beck talks about scientific and social rationality as two distinct forms of rationality which act in contradiction to one another, but without clarifying what social rationality is. To both authors, *knowledge* is first and foremost expert knowledge, while other forms of knowledge are neglected, for example, lay knowledge.
3   They both highlight the individualization within *reflexive* modernity, ignoring the fact that Hegel already defined *modernity* as the formation of the subjective principle and the reflection, thus creating new scope for social action outside existing structures, though also giving rise to *new* structures, such as information and communication structures. Existing reflexivity also contains the collective 'selves' – that is, an element of society as opposed to the market's free agent 'self' – though Beck and Giddens focus one-sidedly on a 'self', which is increasingly freed from social ties (Beck) and becomes able to create its own biographical narratives (Giddens). Finally, they understand reflexivity as a *cognitive* process, and overlook its *aesthetic* dimensions, both in high and popular culture, as well as in everyday life.

Capitalization and modernization

Above, I have criticized both Beck and Giddens for not operating with any explicit concept of the social dynamics in the modern capitalist epoch, although they both stress the tremendous momentum for change in this era. Reading both of them, one might get the impression that reflexivity is a dynamic factor per se.

Conversely, Habermas clearly sees the dynamics of modern society as an effect of the imperatives of the differentiated capitalist economic system.

All authors thus attribute a dynamic, overpowering force to modernity, which generates movement and change. However, is this also an expression of modernization? Put differently, the question could be: is the unfolding of these dynamics equal to what is covered by the term modernization?

Below I shall approach the issue from a slightly different angle than the above, namely the shift from rationalization of culture to rationalization of society described by Weber and Habermas. The sights are still set on clarifying the contents of modernity as regards its dynamism and what is behind it, in what its reflexive processes consist, and what are their consequences for continued modernization. The major perspective of this clarification is an identification of the scope for conducting environmental policy, which is the issue at the heart of this book.

The starting point of Weber and Habermas thus leads us to a continued critique of Giddens, and especially of Beck. Though also Szerszynski, who was drawn upon heavily in Chapter 2, must take some flak.

Above, I presented how Habermas relates his theory of action to a theory of society through the concept of the lifeworld, which implies that communicative action may be perceived as a principle for sociation (*Vergesellschaftung*). In this manner, the development of society is understood as an evolutionary process with a progressive rationalization of the lifeworld and – complementing this – an increasing systemic complexity. Moreover, this process involves a continuous differentiation between the lifeworld and the system, in which the systemic integration not only creates the framework for social integration, but also – through mediatization – increasingly replaces social integration. This is what gives rise to one-sided rationalization of society. Put differently, significant potentials from the rationalization of culture are lost in the transformation into rationalization of society, of which the latter – also at this advanced stage of social evolution – is characterized as the *modernization* of society.

But what is it that is lost, and how does Habermas differ from Weber? Weber's identification of the rationalization of cultural legacies is followed all the way to the differentiation and separation of the three sides of the rationality complex. It is, in other words, about delving deeper into the substance of what – in the section on Habermas' theory – is merely determined at the overall level as part of the presentation of the theory. It has yet to be attributed any defining features in relation to the processes which Habermas has characterized as, respectively, colonization of the lifeworld and cultural impoverishment. My project may be phrased as aiming to make explicit *what* it is that disappears in the modern form of understanding in this area in particular.

The spotlight is thus on the transition from the rationalization of the lifeworld to the modernization of society. The goal is to come up with more detailed contents than what was previously, through the critique of Weber, determined as 'to grasp processes of societal rationalization across their whole breadth, and no longer solely from the selective viewpoint of the rationalization of purposive-rational action' (TCA 1, p335). Or, that the processes of societal rationalization 'transpire more in implicitly known structures of the lifeworld than in explicitly known action orientations' (TCA 1, p337).

Elaborating on this point, against the background of the aforementioned theoretical presentations, has at least two overall aims. *First*, a specification of the contents of modern modernization processes will clarify the differences between Weber and Habermas on this issue, which is certainly not only of theoretical interest, but has crucial practical implications. Indeed, it has been commonplace since Weber's time to equate rationality with purposive rationality, whether it be applied to specific actions carried out by individuals, groups or institutions, or whether it be referring to a desirable outcome for society.

Moreover, such specification may provide the answer to *how* the one-sided modernization of society arises, as Habermas claims it does. This would contribute to mapping out what is lost in one-sided modernization, and hence to the discussion of how to re-establish the lost potentials, or reinserting them into the continued modernization of society, if looking at this with Habermasian eyes. Evidently, this point may also be seen as a factor in the overall objective of this whole book. Thus, the relevance of this issue needs not be stressed any further.

Second, the specification of a series of aspects of the modernization process will enable a continuation of the aforementioned critique of the neomodernism espoused by Beck and Giddens. Since both these authors want to take the modern project further by modernizing it, it becomes even more important to elaborate on the critique of their understanding of modernity.

Below I shall start from Weber's understanding of the modern, not only because his ideas are at the heart of the matter, as hinted above, but also because Habermas builds upon Weber's work, as he sets out to show where Weber errs in his identification of the modern form of rationalization, and how there is thus a potential, based upon Weber, for widening the theoretical scope for understanding the modern (TCA 1, p198).

In the understanding of Weber, Habermas also builds upon Tenbruck[32] in particular. In an analysis of Weber's complete works, Tenbruck shows how Weber applied a variety of meanings to rationality and rationalization, but that his fundamental perception of the rationalization process can only be interpreted as a demythologization process (*Entzauberungsprozess*) in the history of religion.[33] Weber construed this as a millennial process driven by an inner logic that springs from an incessant urge to rationalize religious ideas (Tenbruck, 1975, p675), and not by any of the myriad partial rationalization interests that may be associated with human existence. Only in recent times does this demythologization process lead to what he calls the methodical way of life as a precondition for the emergence of capitalism (Tenbruck, 1975, pp689–690). He subsequently characterizes the further course of rationalization under capitalism as a modernization process (Tenbruck, 1975, pp671, 690, 691).

As depicted above, Habermas' concept of rationalization starts from the lifeworld and the processes between human beings taking place within it in order to achieve the coordination of actions and mutual understanding as regards a given intention or situation. He characterizes this coordination of actions as social integration, as opposed to systemic integration, which is established by means of the system. And it is the relation between these two forms of integration that prompts Habermas to talk about societal rationality.

In this respect, Habermas contradicts other followers of Weber, who all see societal rationality as something arising from the fulfilment of a particular objective for society. Individual or one-off actions may well contribute towards this, but the yardstick is clearly referring to the level of society, and is geared towards measuring a specific result. This is where Habermas expresses his difference when, in the above quote, he refers to the processes of rationalization of society taking on a different status when perceived, as he does, as accomplished by means of the implicit knowledge of the lifeworld, rather than through explicitly knowing action orientations.

The discrepancy is all the more remarkable as Habermas' use of Weber's concept of rational interpretation of meaning is clear. This is also the case in Habermas' presentation of mythical and modern thinking, just as his differentiation of the various areas and the validity of action is deeply indebted to Weber's concept of demythologization of the world and rationalization of action orientations, first at the religious and subsequently at the secular level (Outhwaite, 1994, p75). Moreover, Habermas agrees with Weber's endeavour to draw up a rationalization theory that is non-speculative, that is, freed of the evolutionist view of the history of philosophy, of seeing non-cognitive spheres of value (morality and arts) as areas with their own validity, and of the need to perceive the rationalization of worldviews as universal history.

The difference between Habermas and Weber appears in the transition to the level of modernization and in the development of a methodical way of life under capitalism. This level is covered by Weber's theory of rationalization. He distinguishes between a first phase of rationalization, in which a demythologization of religious worldviews takes place, which lays the foundation for a universal historical development of modern structures of consciousness, and yet another phase of rationalization, in which these modern structures must be socially institutionalized and underpin the specific modernization process concerned. He thus distinguishes clearly between the rationalization of culture and of society.

Even so, despite being a defining feature of Weber's authorship, this is precisely the transition which, against the background of Weber's thorough analysis of action differentiation and rationality aspect, comes across as odd or foreshortened.

The oddity springs from the fact that Weber sees the modernization of society as an expression of the demythologized and modern forms of consciousness being institutionalized in purposive-rational action within the modern capitalist economy and the modern state administration. This serves to complete the rationalization/modernization of society, which, as we have seen, to Weber only expresses the utilization of purposive-rational action at the societal level, in the differentiated economy and the differentiated state administration.

What is noticeable about this, according to Habermas, is that Weber only examines the rationalization of worldviews from the *ethical* perspective, and thus leaves out modern science and arts, even though he presupposes a differentiation of *all three* spheres of value in the rationalization of society which lead to the modern. He does this in the analysis of the Protestant ethic. Moreover, he looks at the demythologization of religious worldviews from a particular historical perspective. He does not reconstruct the perceptions of law and morality with a view to establishing an ethic of conviction (*Gesinnungsethiken*), but solely in order to clarify the emergence of a capitalist economic ethic. This springs from his need to elucidate the cultural conditions under which the transition to capitalism could take shape, and hence how purposive-rational action could be integrated into a system of work for society (TCA 1, p198).

Habermas looks rather differently at the capitalist modernization process, although he follows Weber in the rationalization process up until the differentiation of the three spheres of value: science, morality and art. However, given his dual conception of society as system and lifeworld, he places the rationalization processes of the lifeworld directly under the microscope, and is able to see these processes as a foundation for the differentiation of the three spheres of value, as well as for an economic system and state administration. The cohesion of capitalist modernization processes requires the differentiated systems or subsystems to be *anchored* in the lifeworld. Or, as he also phrases it, they have to be institutionalized in the lifeworld. This is actually contrary to Weber, who sees the modernization process as an institutionalization of particular action orientations, results-orientated ones, within the differentiated systems of the economy and the administration.

Consequently, there is no 'left-over' according to Weber, i.e. there is no potential that disappears. Although a loss does take place, this is of meaning and value in life, which is subordinated to purposive rationality, growing bureaucratization, and the economic dictate. Weber is acutely aware of this, and he formulates it as an outright loss of liberty in his famous thesis on the 'iron cage' of bureaucracy and economic compulsion into which humans are locked. According to Habermas, the loss incurred is completely different, namely of the rationalization potential inherent in the moral-practical and in the aesthetic-expressive dimension. However, this loss is neither total nor definitive, unlike that of meaning and value according to Weber.

By situating the starting point of the rationalization process in the lifeworld, and through the concept of communicative rationality, Habermas opens up possibilities both for immediate preservation of the entire rationality complex in parts of social reality – that is, the lifeworld with the modifications caused by the modernization process, as will be explained below – as well as for a long-term prospect of freeing modernization from cognitive-instrumental dominance, that is, the realization of true modernity.

As for the two forms of integration of action, it is within systemic integration that capitalist modernization is accomplished. However, this is associated with both preconditions and consequences concerning the lifeworld. The premise is that rationalizations occurring in the lifeworld are necessary to enable further complexity of the system. Through these rationalizations, culturally determined coordination of actions is continuously turned into coordination driven by communicative actions. This implies that the *continuous modernization involves processes* in which all three (four including the communicative) forms of action rationality play a part.

However, these processes in the lifeworld – which are coordinated by communicative action as well as by cultural legacies, what is termed *social* integration – are also influenced by systemic integration, as a result of capitalist modernization.

Then how does the phenomenon characterized by Habermas as one-sided rationalization occur in the modern epoch, that is, one-sided modernization? Well, the answer must be sought both within the processes of differentiation, that is, in the processing of cultural legacies in systematic and modern form, and within the anchoring or institutionalization of a subsystem in the lifeworld, or within the consequences of systemic integration interfering with social integration.

Habermas depicts it in this manner:

> *A selective pattern of rationalization occurs when (at least) one of the three constitutive components of the cultural tradition is not systemically worked up, or when (at least) one cultural value sphere is insufficiently institutionalized, that is, is without any structure-forming effect on society as a whole, or when (at least) one sphere predominates to such an extent that it subjects life-orders to a form of rationality that is alien to them.*
>
> TCA 1, p240

In the full-fledged theory, we here recognize the distortion between system and lifeworld manifested in the determinations of the *cultural impoverishment* and the system's *colonization of the lifeworld*. Both of these lead to one-sided modernization of society.

Although Weber and Habermas thus aim at different targets in the identification of the constituent parts of cultural legacies, that is, the cultural sphere of value, it can be observed that they arrive at the same three aspects of the rationality complex in the rationalization of society: the cognitive-instrumental, the moral-practical and the aesthetic-expressive. Habermas reaches these aspects of the complex via his reconstruction of the historical process through the concept of communicative action, and thus in a manner rather different from that of Weber. However, his starting point is clearly the works of Weber and Weber's theory of the rationalization of culture and of society. We thus do not need to follow Weber's derivation of the three aspects of rationality. Habermas' and

Weber's modernization concepts have here been contrasted in order to sharpen the understanding of Weber's modernization concept, and to lay the foundation for identifying what is lost in the rationalization dimension when following Weber's rather than Habermas' concepts.

Both Weber and Habermas recognize that capital has emerged as a new driving force in history and in social evolution, but both are also keen to view modernization as more than just capitalization. At the same time, they both see some highly problematic elements in the modernization process, presenting their respective versions of the 'dialectics of enlightenment'.

According to Weber, capitalization means that the institutionalization of purposive and strategic action, in the economic system and in the state adminis- tration, is mediated and intensified, both in terms of process and of needs. The rationalization of worldviews is gradually replaced by the institutionalization of strategic and purposive-rational action, while rationalization takes on the shape of modernization. This brings about vast gains in the economic system, as well as a tremendous expansion of the possibilities for state administration. However, at the same time it entails huge costs to the forms of life, which become methodical and compelled in response to economy and administration, thus losing their former culturally determined value and meaning. This cultural loss, which is a manifesta- tion of the disarticulation of traditional lifestyles, cannot be replaced by modernity. According to Weber, in the modernization processes and in modernity, rationality becomes purposive rationality, whereas the other elements in the complex, which are the foundation of modernization, are dissolved in this process.

Weber thus also sees modernization as one-sided, which means that one form of rationality reigns supreme over the rationality complex as a whole. In other words, he perceives modernization as the differentiation of all three forms of rationality, but it is only the cognitive-instrumental one that is institutionalized *at the level of society*.

Habermas also views capitalization as a driving force of modernization. However, the gradual rationalization of worldviews and action orientations in the lifeworld is not confined to 'freeing' the aspects of the rationality complex one by one. Partly, they are kept together – 'institutionalized' – in communicative action within the lifeworld. Partly, they are differentiated in independent 'institutions', and lead their own lives with their own rules and validity criteria. This is where Habermas' double-layered conception of society shows its significance. Communicative action is increasingly taking over the functions of cultural legacies, and serves to coordinate action, though now on the basis of the three aspects of the rationality complex, each of which is preserved, being actively integrated into the lifeworld. In their systemic form, though, they are fragmented, and only act individually in accordance with their corresponding 'institutional' form of action. However, this contributes to enabling the growing complexity of the systems. It mediates, so to speak, the intensifying modernization. But as the systemic integration penetrates and takes over, or interferes with, the social integration, and as the mediatization enables both the autonomous reproduction of the subsystems (that is, outside any anchorage or institutionalization in the lifeworld) and coordination within the lifeworld without communicative action, then modernization becomes one-sided.

Thus, capitalization is a driving force in the modernization process. However, modernization is not synonymous with capitalization, partly since modernization takes its point of departure in the lifeworld, and partly since modernization causes the systemic mechanisms to reach back into the lifeworld and condition parts of the lifeworld's symbolic reproduction. Capitalization turns into a kind of catalyst for the modernization process, whose various elements are increasingly influenced by capitalization. Moreover, according to Habermas, the material reproduction of the lifeworld takes place within the capitalist economic system. Consequently, the material reproduction of the lifeworld is dependent on capitalization, and is shaped by it, though this is not tantamount to its symbolic reproduction being governed by it.

Furthermore, it must be stressed that, in Habermas' work, modernization is not confined to differentiation of the capitalist economic system, but is also differentiation of the state administration and the legal system – that is, judicialization. The state administrative system also institutionalizes *purposive rationality*, whereas judicialization institutionalizes moral-practical rationality. However, the state administration also becomes increasingly one-sided, giving prominence to purposive rationality. All the various differentiations presuppose, according to Habermas, that the lifeworld has undergone rationalization, which is why continuous modernization also means continuous modernization of the lifeworld. Thus, capitalization is only one form of modernization.

With this specification of Weber's and Habermas' perception of modernization, I now wish to elaborate upon my critique of Beck's thesis that modernization of society has thus far been bifurcated into a semi-modern society, and that we are currently at the threshold of the next (second half of) modernization, which will provide a chance to redeem the principles of modernity from their separations and limitations in industrial society, as he puts it (Beck, 1992, p15).

Thus far, the critique has primarily been aimed at Beck's diffuse or all-embracing concept of modernization and his use of the concept of reflexivity. It has started from his division of the capitalist modernization process into phases, in which he sees first a modernization of *tradition*, and second a modernization of *industrial society*, equivalent to a distinction between *simple* and *reflexive* modernization.

At this stage, it should be clear that Beck's modernization concept follows the line of Weber's, but does not contain the Weberian preconditions for the modernization process. By modernization, Beck means societal institutionalization of purposive rationality. This is modernization from the perspective of the system. It is thus solely the cognitive-instrumental form of rationality that Beck associates with the modernization process. This entails a true bisection (trisection or more) of the full rationality complex, though it is not the kind of halving to which Beck himself refers.

The preceding rationalization of cultural legacies, the demythologization of worldviews in a process enabling the suspension of traditional ways of life, and which – under capitalism – is continued in the modernization process, all of this has been omitted by Beck. Similarly, in principle, Beck sees society as system, or more precisely, he identifies the system as all of society, and thus has no dual concept, such as Habermas. This is also why he cannot take in the cultural rationalization, which to Weber is a precondition for the modernization process, and to Habermas a continuous process in the lifeworld, even after the systemic modernization has 'set off'. Seen in relation to Weber and Habermas, Beck thus cuts society in two, and this is how he sees the mirror distortion of a semi-modernization.

That Beck's bisection of the modernization process into a simple and a reflexive phase is not merely improbable, but conceptually untenable, is also apparent from the fact that the foundation for modernization processes to occur in the first place is the enablement of reflexive processes, both culturally and socially. According to Hegel, Weber and Habermas, a precondition for the advance of modernization processes is the generation of reflexive processes freed from the 'compulsion' of cultural legacies, and this imposes itself as a condition in society.

This happens when the rationalization of cultural legacies reaches the point where the modernization process sets in. Reflexivity is thus, as repeatedly stressed, something present from the beginning of modernization, and not something made possible by or succeeding a first phase.

Put more bluntly, Beck's bisection of modernization, in time and in linear terms, can be seen as the manifestation of a foreshortened concept of both modernization and industrialization. Because just as modernization can be said to encompass reflexivity as a principle, industrialization can be said to include revolutionizing its own foundation as a principle. As the industrial process physically revolutionizes traditional forms of production, it revolutionizes itself. The mechanism driving this is present from the outset, and not something that is added after the traditional forms of production have changed into industrial ones.[34] Beck's foreshortening of the industrialization concept thus contains the same separation of industrialization and capitalization as in Giddens' authorship, and expresses yet another 'halving', in line with the aforementioned critique of Giddens on this point.

Beck's strategy to overcome the flaws of reflexive modernity – with its risk production, uncertainties and individualization – namely modernization of reflexive modernity, may thus also be conceived as a dubious undertaking, as likewise signalled by the above critique. Because such a pursuit would only aggravate these malaises in society, indeed raise them to the second power, since the modernization of modernity suggested by Beck does not, in principle, contemplate any other form of modernization than the existing one.

The knowledge that Beck wishes to add from alternative expert groups, scientists, interest groups and so on is essentially the same type of knowledge – that is scientific knowledge devoid of a cultural dimension. He thus merely replicates the calamities of modernization thus far, creating one-sidedness raised to the second power, instead of what he claims, to promote liberation from one-sidedness.

Because one-sidedness does not spring from knowledge being practised by particular interest groups; at best, one interest will be replaced by another. It springs from the way of thinking itself, from the one-sided cultivation of the cognitive-instrumental rationality, which in Beck's world is common to both established and alternative actors.

At this point, the suspicion is aroused that Beck first confuses/distorts and then misinterprets Marx's concepts of the modernization process. At any rate, it is thought-provoking that the two-phase model, which he presents, and its attendant understanding of the reflexive element, echoes to such a wide extent features of the Marxian concepts of capital's formal and real subsumption of the labour process. I am not mentioning this striking similarity because I find the Marxian concepts useless or erroneous, on the contrary, it is indeed one of the most enlightening concept pairs ever to be found in sociological literature, in which category I include Marx's presentation of the concept of capital. The reason why I am raising the comparison with Marx's concepts is that this contributes not only to pointing out Beck's errors and their extent, but also to deepening the insights into the reflexive processes in industrial society, or in modern society, and hence to an understanding of the nature of the modernization process, when starting from the industrial-capitalist production processes.

Consequently, here below, I shall insert an excursus on the Marxian concepts of formal and real subsumption. Subsequently, I shall return to Beck and Giddens, elaborating on my former critique and the assertion that they are wrong as to where the dangers lie in the capitalist modernization process, which they so one-sidedly and erroneously attribute to reflexivity.

Excursus: Formal and real subsumption

The capitalization of production, or the transformation of traditional production processes to become dominated by capital, assumes two forms according to Marx: the *formal* and the *real subsumption*. As explained above, capitalization cannot be equated with modernization, but it can be characterized as the engine of modernization, once the other conditions for modernization are historically in place. Even so, these two forms of subsumption mean that capital takes on widely differing physical shapes, with corresponding differences in the work performed and in the external effects that may be caused by the production process, for example through pollution from waste products or various kinds of risks in the distribution or consumption of the products.

The *formal subsumption* of labour under capital is the form common to all capitalist production processes. However, at the same time it is: 'a *particular* form alongside the developed *mode of production which is specifically capitalist,* because the second involves the first, but the first by no means necessarily involves the second' (Marx, 1994, p424).

Thus, when a hitherto traditional area of production is capitalized, it always takes place by means of formal subsumption. The formal element springs from capital entering the field and dominating the productive cycle from beginning to end – that is, start-up of production, execution of the production process, and sale of the product in the market. This happens by investment of money, which functions as capital in the productive cycle, and is once again realized as money in the market. In this manner, the actual *objective* of this process changes from being the product itself to becoming the production of money, not the amount invested, but more. And not by a stroke of good fortune in the market, but by letting the production process convert labour into value, which is realized in the market as a greater amount of money than what was invested. In this manner, the formal subsumption, that is, capitalization in the formal form, changes the objective of the production process, which also becomes purely formal, namely valorization *in the form* of money. The interest in the product itself becomes secondary, and only concerns demand for it in the market.

However, although this formal subsumption of the production process has taken place and changed the latter's actual objective, it has not changed its course and execution, which thus continues as before, or with the same contents. Marx expresses it in this manner:

> *Despite all this, the change indicated does not mean that an essential change takes place from the outset in the real way in which the labour process is carried on, in the real production process. On the contrary, it is in the nature of the matter that where a subsumption of the labour process under capital takes place it occurs on the basis of an* existing labour process, *which was there before its subsumption under capital, and was formed on the basis of various earlier processes of production and other conditions of production. Capital thus subsumes under itself a* given, existing labour process, *such as handicraft labour, the mode of agriculture corresponding to small-scale independent peasant farming.*
> Marx, 1994, pp425–426

This formally subsumed labour process may be changed by intensifying the work, prolonging the labour process, and making the work more continuous and orderly. This will result in greater accomplishment of the aim of this labour – that is, the increase in money – but the form and character of the labour process itself does not change in this manner. This is what Marx calls the production of absolute surplus value.[35]

However, when conditions enable a change in the actual contents of the labour process, so that its objective can be accomplished to an even greater degree, a *real subsumption* of labour occurs. Such change in the real production process takes place solely in order to increase its output in the form of more money, and it will thus be arranged exclusively with a view to maximizing this objective. This consummation of the real subsumption of labour under capital gives rise to shaping the production process contents as dictated by the domination of capital, which will be repeated as soon as the objective of production can be satisfied to an even greater degree. It thus provokes an everlasting revolutionizing of the foundation of the production process, which will, at all times, be conditioned by the goal of maximum capital growth.

What is generally characteristic of formal subsumption *remains valid in this case too, i.e. the direct* subordination to capital of the labour process, *in whatever way the latter may be conducted technologically. But on this basis there arises a* mode of production – the capitalist mode of production – *which is* specific *technologically and in other ways, and* transforms *the* real nature of the labour process *and* its real conditions. *Only when this enters the picture does the real* subsumption of labour under capital *take place. [...]*

The real subsumption of labour under capital is developed in all the forms which develop relative,[36] *as distinct from absolute, surplus value.*

With the real subsumption of labour under capital there takes place a complete [and a constant, continuous, and repeated] revolution in the mode of production itself, in the productivity of labour and in the relation between capitalist and worker.

In the case of the real subsumption of labour under capital, all the changes in the labour process itself, analysed by us previously, actually take effect. Labour's social powers of production *are developed, and with labour on a large scale the application of science and machinery to direct production takes place. On the one hand, the* capitalist mode of production, *which now takes shape as a mode of production* sui generis, *changes the shape of material production. On the other hand, this alteration of production's material shape forms the basis for the development of the capital-relation, which in its adequate shape therefore corresponds to a specific level of development of the productive powers of labour.*

Marx, 1994, pp438–439

In this manner, the real subsumption of the production process under capitalization has created a situation in which the *form* of production, the capital, is constantly striving to find its own adequate *content*, at the same time as it – that is, the form – is totally indifferent to how such content may appear, as long as it complies with the form's demand for increasing output in terms of money. Every *content* is thus dictated by the capitalist *form* of production.

Another piece of the puzzle is that, once this revolutionizing process has commenced – indeed only as long as the formal subsumption has taken place – a scientization of production will be enabled in the sense that – given a certain state of affairs at a given time – it becomes possible to conduct research into how this state of affairs can be changed technologically and organizationally with a view to further satisfying the objective of production. There is merely a manifestation that the development of the labour process has ceased to be rooted in custom and immediate experience, and has become imposed from the outside by means of processes in the wider society, such as technological innovations, scientific discoveries, changes in the market, new demands for the products and so on, which may be systematically utilized in the production process, in pursuit of its objective, or which may systematically impose conditions on the production process, also in relation to its objective.

According to Marx, capitalization expresses how production is subjected to sociation (*Vergesellschaftung*), in the sense that it is forced to adjust to processes and conditions in society instead of relating to individual, random or specific needs and wishes. The capitalized production is itself continuously contributing to creating, reproducing and changing these processes and conditions prevailing in society. In this manner, we see that – even though capitalization cannot be equated with modernization, and rather should be considered as the engine of modernization, not as its foundation – then capitalization in the specifically capitalist form – that is, the real subsumption – means that the principles of modernization, such as individualization and reflexivity, also impose themselves and take on specific appearances in the capitalized material production. Indeed, reflexivity may be said to be the very core principle of capitalized material production.

Similarly, individualization is a characteristic not to be confused with what has just been stated about production being subjected to sociation. Individualization is manifested by 'individualizing' people, making them free agents – free to act as they please, and no longer bound by serfdom or other types of ownership that enables right of disposal over them as individuals. Both the capitalist and the wage labourer need to be free persons. The capitalist must be individualized, so that he can act with a view to accomplishing the objective of his production, namely the production of money, without being bound by other concerns than the concern for himself. The wage labourer must be free of serfdom, but also of property. Because if he were not free of property, he would not be forced to sell his labour to subsist.

In this context, the structures of society manifest themselves by the capitalist being compelled to act as a capitalist – to go along with the current conditions in society in order to increase his capital – and the worker is compelled to sell his labour. But nobody in particular can force the capitalist to be a capitalist against his will, and the worker may choose to lie down and die, or subsist from begging, as long as none of these things are prohibited by the laws of society.

Historically, the two forms of capitalization here presented occur in a very uneven fashion, with vast disparities between different trades, regions and countries. The gist of the matter is that the forms, as described, do not deviate. They assert themselves regardless of the trade or sector of production, and in the aforementioned order, with the occasional exception where no movement occurs from formal to real subsumption. In rare cases, these transitions may take several decades, in even rarer cases centuries. Although we have been witnessing capitalization for over 200 years, the process is far from complete, quite the contrary.

The beginning of formal subsumption can be dated back to the late 18th century in England, in particular in weaving and spinning mills, and within the Central European manufacturing of clothes, watches and metal. It spread rapidly to other trades and nations, so that widespread capitalization in material production, including agriculture, was in motion in the early 19th century in almost all Western European countries and the USA.[37] In this course of events, it is noteworthy that, historically, the real subsumption to its fullest degree occurred rapidly mainly in the processing of primary produce, for example in paper and metal production. Conversely, the real subsumption has been much more gradual in manufacturing, such as the production of machinery, building materials and means of transport, which is consequently – in the post-war years and particularly in the latter decades – undergoing a true revolution in terms of production methods and raw materials.

Characteristically, until recent times, capitalization has also been occurring primarily in the sectors of material production – that is, in industry, which becomes the 'master frame' of capitalized production, and in agriculture – what economists call the primary and secondary sectors. Conversely, the tertiary sector, that of services, was not capitalized for the first couple of hundred years. It is a process that was not been observed to any significant extent until the last decades. It is indeed a defining feature of the current economic development that the service sector is undergoing intense capitalization, including what is sometimes rather characteristically termed the *cultural* industry.[38]

Capitalization and modernization (continued)

Against the background of this exceedingly brief depiction of the two forms characteristic of capitalization, I shall return to my critique of Beck's attempt to distinguish between a *simple* and a *reflexive* phase in the capitalist modernization process. Beck's general identification of modernity with industrial society (Beck, 1992, pp9–11) clearly invites centring such a critical approach on his division into phases, and hence on his characterization of today's modern society. This becomes even more evident as his own division of the social modernization process is tantalizingly close to the concepts of formal and real subsumption, something which Beck is apparently unaware of. Alternatively, it could be interpreted as Beck attempting to employ the Marxian concepts in a different manner, in which case it must be described as less fruitful.

As it appears from this book so far, it is not per se Beck's observation of a greater extent of reflexive action in society that brings forth the critique. The flaws lie in his identification of the causes behind this, in the conclusions he draws concerning the consequences of this, and his corresponding failure to notice the real problem.

The first point of criticism has already been discussed. Beck's division into a simple and a reflexive modernization overlooks the fundamental condition that reflexivity forms part of modernity from the outset. There can simply be no modern developmental features until this precondition of reflexive approaches to one's own foundation has been established as a possibility within the structures of society.

The point in the above characterization of reflexivity in real subsumption is indeed that – although it is an action that needs to be taken by the 'individual' capitalist – that is, the need for it must be thought, understood and carried out by one or more persons – this action has already been structurally inscribed into his very existence (as a capitalist). It forms part of the *social* condition of being a capitalist. Capitalism in the formal subsumptive form can be described as a reflexive conduct, because this course of action – in its transgression of tradition regarding the organization of production processes – presupposes, partly, that a rationalization has taken place within the lifeworld, and partly a modernization of the other constituent parts of society, for example, the legal sphere, enabling new types of ownership.

Therefore, capitalization in the real subsumptive form may be characterized as a reflexive conduct raised to the second power, which continues the modernization process, but requires a parallel, continuous rationalization of the lifeworld.

Beck's explanation of the problems associated with the growing reflexivity of approximately the past three decades holds that a contradiction emerges between the fact that individual persons under developed modernity are capable of acting in a rational and instrumentally calculating fashion, whereas the scientific and political institutions are not. This manifests itself, for instance, in the latter's inability to control the risks and environmental damage, which was supposed to be their responsibility and to legitimize their existence. This paralyses, so to speak, both parties, as the institutions do not know how to act, nor do individuals perceive adequate scope for action, since they are unable to foresee the consequences of their conduct.

However, as previously stressed, I wish to cast doubt on Beck's shift from simple to reflexive modernization, and hence also on his determination of why particular risk problems, and so on, emerge under what he calls reflexive modernity. In opposition to Beck's explanations, I wish to espouse the need for a starting point in the capitalist modernization process. It is the defining features of this that should substantiate explanations of the intensifying social reflexivity that can be observed over the past two or three decades. I find that the two presented forms of capitalization may serve as a model to this effect.

This does not, of course, amount to an empirical examination of actually occurring processes, which is, at any rate, beyond the scope of this book. Therefore, I shall go no further than a reference to these common forms of capitalization, in addition to highlighting their manifestation in connection with three typical developmental features of recent decades, all of which concern increasing capitalization in these forms, and which bring about social structuring of reflexive conduct.

The three developmental features are:[39]

1   A shift from formal to real subsumption in a series of productive areas, which had only occurred partially until the period around the crisis of the 1970s, but through this period and the time after asserts itself with full force, enabled, among other factors, by automation technology as well as by the spread and multiple uses of computers in industrial production.

2   Ever faster shifts in production processes that have long been subject to the real subsumption of capital, but – by means of the global expanse of capitalism and the reasons mentioned in point 1 – are revolutionizing their foundations, with consequent changes in demands regarding the necessary labour, organization and so on.

3   A spreading capitalization of sectors that have not been previously dominated by the capitalist economic system, and which in some cases implies only a formal subsumption, in others also a real subsumption. For example, such capitalization is widespread in the administration, services and cultural industry. New information technologies are playing a crucial role in these processes too.

The reflexive conduct being fostered through these structural developmental features appears to me a more solid foundation for explanation than the individual forms of behaviour portrayed by Beck. Of course, such reflexive conduct must be 'executed' by persons or individuals in various roles. But the gist of the matter is that it has to take on two forms, respectively within the system and in an individual form with roots in the lifeworld. The former occurs in connection with systemic adjustments to the shifting demands of external circumstances. The latter regards the individual adaptation to systemic demands, both as an actor of systemic functions and in the reproduction as an individual relating to the system, as well as in the communicative processes of understanding in the lifeworld.

The three features of recent capitalization all concern economic enterprise. To this could be added the growing share of public administration being reorganized to pursue financial targets, outsourced to municipal or state-owned limited-liability firms, performed by inviting tenders from private corporations, or in some other way being passed on to results-oriented business management. In the first instance, such restructuring should possibly be compared only to formal subsumption, though on the other hand, the whole aim of the exercise is clearly to have the formal framework of capital management change the labour-related content, structuring it according to capital-minded goal orientation that is, analogous to real subsumption.

Altogether, these conditions are a manifestation of the growing predominance of the market or, as others might put it, that the market is encroaching into both civil society and the public sector.[40]

It is important that the focus on capitalist differentiation, which this presentation has used thus far as an example of the expansion of reflexive conduct, be supplemented by the process in which elements from the lifeworld and culture are differentiated and brought into the realm of state administration. This differentiation is driven by bureaucratization, containing a parallel acceleration of systemic and individual reflexivity, as described above concerning capitalization. It is, incidentally, one of Habermas' points that reification, or colonization of the lifeworld, may as well spring from bureaucratization of the administrative apparatus as from capitalization of the economic system (TCA 2, p342; see also below). Both forms of differentiation can be said to contribute to advancing reflexive conduct, although the hallmark of the last decades has been the dominance of capitalization, whereas bureaucratization was more in ascendance from the 1950s until about the mid-1970s.

However, as we have seen above, it is not reflexivity in itself that causes problems, on the contrary, it must be said to contain advantages. The problem in connection with the growing capitalization and/or bureaucratization of new areas of the lifeworld is the cultural impoverishment associated with the differentiation into subsystemic expert cultures, which drain the *lifeworld* of these same elements, because the potential of reason thus extracted is not delivered back as an enrichment of the lifeworld. Since this differentiation is, moreover, driven by capitalization or bureaucratization, it leads to the forms of rationality becoming one-sided within the area concerned, which will henceforth be dominated by capitalist or bureaucratic purposive rationality. This thus determines two developmental features as overall starting points for the determination of specific problems, rather than just the reflexive form of action, as in the works of Beck and Giddens. Namely areas from the lifeworld and culture being differentiated and brought into the capitalist economic or the administrative sphere, which entails, respectively, a *one-sided modernization* within the systems and a *cultural impoverishment* of the lifeworld. The problems regarding continued modernization must be associated with these two developmental features, and not with reflexivity in itself.

Of course, Beck does not deny that reflexive processes may take place under simple modernity. This, incidentally, also applies to Giddens, who even accentuates this explicitly, at the same time as rejecting Beck's theory of a break, because Giddens does not see it as a distinct reflexive phase, but rather as reflexivity becoming the dominant feature of modernity in the 1980s and 1990s. However, as demonstrated, both of them lack an explanation of why reflexivity comes to the forefront in these years, regardless of whether this can be considered a break or not.

Against this shortcoming, I am thus asserting that reflexivity becomes a given condition in society from the moment the demythologization of religious worldviews, the rationalization of cultural legacies and so on, in short, the rationalization of the lifeworld, has come so far that normatively motivated concurrence has been replaced by communicative understanding, that the rationality of communicative action has become so entrenched as to enable the emergence of modern society. This is in line with Habermas' statement about communicative action understood as a principle for sociation (*Vergesellschaftung*) (TCA 1, p337).

Beck confuses the empirical manifestation of the myriad reflexive processes with their enablement. But the fact that reflexive processes became a characteristic feature associated with societal development in the post-war era, and especially over the past two or three decades, does not imply that this trend *specifically* contains the reasons for them. It is merely a manifestation that the development of society requires reflexive action to an increasing *degree*.

This mistake, for which both Beck and Giddens can be criticized, leads Beck to associate the characteristic problems in the same period concerning the environment and risks with reflexive processes, which are turned into the source of the problems. He thus interprets reflexivity as something problematic, when in fact an instinctive appreciation must be quite the opposite. Moreover, he becomes blind to the real dangers in the processes that he is observing. This blindness, however, cannot be entirely traced back to the confusion of empirical manifestations with their enablement, but may also be attributed to a lack of critical concepts to analyse capitalism as such and its effects.

It is not totally accurate that Beck perceives reflexivity as problematic, since he does not interpret it *exclusively* as a negative force. Because reflexive conduct, both personally and institutionally, also forms part of his strategies for *solution*. This refers both to his previously mentioned model for 'democratization of technological development' and his 'differential politics'. Both these contemplate a reflexive approach to the development as a solution, though at the same time, they both raise reflexivity as a problem.

The trouble with the ecological version of the welfare state in the first-mentioned model is, as he sees it himself, that it requires a political control centre that no longer exists in current modernity, which Beck says is reflexive modernity. The trouble with the last-mentioned model is that he presupposes the establishment of new forms of political control centres, although he does not seem to be aware of this himself. There are 'strong and independent courts of law', 'strong and independent public media', and an 'institutionalisation of self-criticism'. In both cases, however, it is noticeable that his models of solution are based on a type of knowledge I would call institutional, scientific knowledge, with an attendant one-sided understanding of rationality in its exclusively cognitive-instrumental form, in line with the above critique.

Thus, in my opinion, not only does Beck demonstrate the same confusion and 'doubleness' concerning the modern development, of which he accuses the scientific and political institutions, among others. His own doubleness, his *on the one hand and on the other*, his problem and solution within the same concept, also shows a clearly deficient understanding of the concepts of modernity. He is an astute observer of some typical trends and behaviours, but his explanations of these, to the extent that they exist, and his identification of the consequences, do not cohere. He is irredeemably drawn to contradict himself.

Basically, Beck lacks an explanation of what he understands by modernization, and on this basis a definition of what he understands by modernization taking on reflexive forms, and why this occurs. His reiterations that reflexive modernity means differentiation of industrial social forms, and their subsequent reestablishment under another modernity, are not, to the say least, particularly cogent. Quite simply, it is too hard to discern the information in this definition.

Furthermore, it appears as if he equates modernization with capitalization. However, as we have seen above, this is a foreshortening of the concept of modernization, which confines the view of society to its systemic part, in addition to confusing particular features of capitalism with characteristics of society as a whole.

This thwarts a perception of the real problems associated with growing capitalization, since these must be seen in relation to a more comprehensive concept of society than merely its systemic part. Two matters in particular must be stressed here with a view to shifting the perspective away from Beck's problematization of reflexivity towards seeing the development as a feature that may indeed place *obstacles* in the way of reflexivity, and which may also lead society's perception of rationality to become one-sided. The last point may be compared to what Habermas has called one-sided modernization.

In the interpretation of Beck, Habermas' concept of society – as system and lifeworld at one and the same time – shows its strength. First, because Beck is evidently observing reflexive phenomena in the system, as he explains – without being aware of this duality of society – through individual reflexive reactions in the lifeworld. Second, because, conversely, he fails to see that the systemic developmental trends towards increasing capitalization of tertiary sectors impose upon the forms of actions in these sectors a purposive rationality, in addition to contributing to cultural impoverishment of the lifeworld. This cultural impoverishment will not foster reflexive conduct, but on the contrary, will contribute to *hindering* reflexivity in the lifeworld.

Possibly, Beck does not associate the issue of cultural impoverishment with the problems of modernity at all, since he does not attribute any status to lay knowledge in the knowledge-developing process, and hence does not attach such knowledge to the models of solutions to one-sided modernization. This is in line with the above critique of Beck for wanting to handle risks solely on the basis of expert knowledge.

When Beck sees an increasing degree of reflexivity in society, I will once again claim that this stems from capitalization spreading at breakneck speed to other sectors in society than those of production. This will precisely lead to growing imposition of the processes of real subsumption within these various spheres of society.

This does contain a positive aspect, namely that it adopts the principle of being reflexive towards one's own foundation.

However, it also has negative consequences, since the capitalization means that capitalist modernization invades ever more areas, which entails a danger of spreading cultural impoverishment, as well as of expanding the one-sidedness of capitalist modernization to ever more corners of society.

In short, it is the systemic forces that impose this pattern, namely increased capital accumulation in an intensive form. The social structures per se have not become more or less reflexive. The attendant problems should therefore not be explained by reflexive conduct, which generally speaking should be interpreted as beneficial. Instead, they should be associated with two overall developmental features in society as a whole, i.e. as system *and* lifeworld, which may be identified on the basis of systemically determined development, namely that: (1) through capitalization, purposive rationality takes over as the dominant factor of action coordination in the area concerned, and (2) capitalization means further differentiation of subsystems, and hence a subsequent impoverishment of the lifeworld.

Thus, when capitalization and bureaucratization encroach into the cultural sector, and also increasingly into science, research, morality and the arts, then these areas *lose* their autonomy and development opportunities on their own terms and regularities, which was precisely what they were 'awarded' in their differentiation in modern society, and which has been part of the strength and development force of modernity. Not only does this give rise to the problem of the potential of reason not being returned to the lifeworld. It also means that these areas are no longer developed autonomously, but are governed by the instrumental *capitalist* rationality. They get new masters, precisely after being freed from their masters in the emergence of modernity. This *reinforces* the one-sided modernization process, and creates further difficulties for transcending its limitations.

Since Habermas' theory has been so widely used as an element in the critique of Beck, it is rightful to raise Szerszynski's critique of Habermas here, not least because on some points *he* places Habermas in the same boat as Beck and Giddens, seeing Habermas as a representative of neomodernism, in which *form* has taken over at the expense of *content*.

As shown in Chapter 2, Szerszynski finds that Habermas' position exemplifies a *deliberative democratic* approach to the environmental question. What characterizes this variant of neomodernism is that the validity of knowledge and views does not hinge on the content, but on purely formal characteristics of the discussion, first and foremost that it is unrestrained, fair and open. The outcome is valid by virtue of it *being* the outcome. Such viewpoints adhere to Habermas' discourse ethics, as Szerszynski sees it, aimed at avoiding the naïve universalism of strong modernism. Moreover, they are in keeping with Habermas' perception that every conversation implicitly contains criteria to test the validity of statements in the 'ideal speech situation'. By adding the competencies necessary for communicative action in this situation, it is possible to guarantee an unforced consensus, which is not the result of some rhetorical cogency, but of the inner rationality of the debate.

After the detailed presentation of the theory of communicative action, it is evident that Szerszynski's interpretation of Habermas' position is exceedingly dubious, this being so for at least three reasons:

First, the concept of communicative action also contains criteria of substantive content. The formal characteristic, which Habermas ascribes to linguistically mediated interactions (TCA 1, p329, figure 16) contain precisely what he calls formal-pragmatic features, such as action orientations (understanding orientations) and validity claims (truth, rightness, truthfulness), which are dictated by content. Moreover, these are equivalent to the listed rationality aspects, which cannot be conceived – neither individually nor as a whole – as neutral regarding content. However, just as crucially, nor are they *autonomous* of content. The reason, truth and so on, of an action is conditioned by the communicative space that surrounds this action – that is, the so-called *world relations* which contain the objective, the social and the subjective world. Furthermore, these worlds are encapsulated in society, which consists of system and lifeworld. The content – in this case reason as a whole and in relation to the expert cultures – is not given by something external to the viewpoint of society. Thus, Habermas' view breaks with the naïve universalism of strong modernism.

However, using this to reduce Habermas' position, including his *discourse ethics*, to something purely formal is a misunderstanding, also given that his is a *defence of reason*. In fact, Habermas insists on distinguishing between form and content, but not in the sense claimed by Szerszynski. The distinction enters the picture, as 'values can be made plausible only in the context of a particular form of life' (TCA 1, p42). Therefore, the validity claims of the various value spheres should not be confused with their casual and changing value contents, even if they make up a system that makes claims to *general* validity. Szerszynski, on the other hand, or rather the deliberative democracy, claims a distinction between form and content within the same form of life.

Second, the theory of communicative action is a theory of society which, in its reconstruction of the course of history, determines the developmental features in the content between system and lifeworld. For instance the relationship between these 'worlds' as a process of differentiation, in which one is rationalized and the other's complexity is increased. In this course of events, the two 'worlds' describe different forms of societal integration, namely system integration and social integration. These forms are not interdependent, but condition one another in terms of content at a given point in history. The content is changed over time, and what is ascribed general validity in the theory is that its categories may determine these developmental features in the course of history.

Finally, it may be stressed that Habermas sees his thinking so much based upon the Marxian one that Karl Marx's stubborn insistence on the connection between form and content, between matter and value, is also maintained in Habermas' theories. In Marx's writings, this starts from the analysis of the commodity form and arrives at the capital form, including how the latter dictates a certain content on the basis of its own exclusive demands. Therefore, it is important to uphold this connection, and this whole section has sought to demonstrate how capitalization conditions the modernization process, hence the above excursus. Just as it is important to distinguish between content and form, it is important not to overlook the form when analysing the content.

True enough, Habermas wishes to replace Marx's law of value with 'real abstractions', since he finds that the latter are better suited to describe the specific features of the capitalist modernization process, especially due to a series of historical trends which Marx could not foretell, for instance, the ability of the modern social state to neutralize class antagonism through mass democracy, as long as it guarantees continued growth. One weakness of the value-theoretical approach is that it does not allow a sufficiently clear distinction between the level of system differentiation and the attendant class-specific forms of institutionalization. This weakens Marx's theory of revolution. Another weakness is how the concept of reification relates to the process in which concrete labour is transformed into abstract labour. In this manner, reification is far too easily associated with a 'nostalgically loaded, frequently romanticized past of premodern forms of life' (TCA 2, p342). The aspect of reification thus cannot be discerned from the structural differentiations of the lifeworld, keeping in mind that Habermas introduces his own concept of alienation in the *modern form of understanding*, as examined above on page 99. Finally, a decisive weakness of the theory of value is that it only enables seeing reification (here in the sense of systemic subsumption of the lifeworld) from the perspective of the labour world. However, precisely in the differentiated economic system and administrative system of modernity, these formally organized spheres of action may absorb communicative life contexts by two means: money *and* power. Reification is just as manifest in public as in private spaces, and may relate to the role of consumer just as much as the one of employee (TCA 2, p342).

So far, I have omitted this widened perspective on capitalist modernization. This does not, however, stem from an attempt at distancing myself from Habermas on this issue, but a necessary limitation in the scope of this book. Nevertheless, in the further presentation of the reflexive forms in Chapter 4, I shall incorporate this perspective concerning the subsumption of lifeworld contexts under money as well as power.

The use of two real abstractions instead of the Marxian value theory frees the Habermasian approach from the baggage of the history of philosophy: a) the abstraction of cognitive structures unfolding from the historical dynamics of the events, and b) the abstraction of societal evolution from the historical concretion of forms of life (TCA 2, p383). Thus, Habermas distinguishes between the *logics* and the *dynamics* of development, and makes what in this context may be equated with a distinction between form and content. However, this is not the same distinction to which Szerszynski is referring.

When the capitalist form assumes dominance and expands into more spheres of life, it becomes of crucial importance to analyse the phenomena in the dual nature of historical concretion and capitalist form. Overseeing this duality leads to new forms of naïvism, which are at best useless, at worst exceedingly dangerous to the survival of reason.

That Habermas does indeed set out to accomplish something by means of his theory may be stated in simple terms. He wishes to show how the capitalist form of modernization allows the spread of instrumental reason and represses all other types of reason, and that recognition of this fact is also a precondition for the continuation of the modern project towards one that is *wholly, integrally* modern. In a society that relies increasingly on a capitalist and an administrative instrumental *form* in all respects, one cannot just stand up and demand content instead, since content is constantly appearing after not being taken seriously. One has to try to introduce content in another manner. As Habermas puts it: 'The only protection against an empiricist abridgement of the rationality problematic is a steadfast pursuit of the tortuous routes along which science, morality, and art communicate with *one another*' (TCA 2, p398).

Reflexivity, knowledge and rationality

Modernization is about differentiation. Although they all use different concepts, this is addressed by Habermas as well as by Beck and Giddens. The modernization process separates or frees certain elements of society from the rest of society, letting these elements lead their own life, on their own terms, with their own regularities and aims. This serves to streamline, target and make them more efficient.

But just as essential as these differentiations – or 'disembeddings' as Giddens calls them – is the fact that they do not merely bring about separation or splits of society into various parts, which then function on their own terms and independently. In fact, one may rather speak of 'doublings'[41] within society and even of society itself. The differentiation process is a doubling process. Marx and Habermas also use the term real abstraction, by which they mean that parts of society are abstracted or set free from a series of specific circumstances, details and particularities, instead making their mark in a 'purer' form, without this becoming something unreal or non-real. There is a separation of something superior, something clearly structured and guiding. It is a kind of distillation. Not as something thought out or as an ideal, but as part of reality: a real abstraction.

The modernization process may thus be characterized as a series of differentiations, emancipations, doublings or real abstractions. But actually, it is not only the modernization process itself, understood as the *transition* from traditional to modern society, that is characterized by these differentiations or separations taking place or 'asserting themselves'. It is also the continued modernization and reproduction of the modernized parts of society. Furthermore, these are not processes that occur historically in a single strike, and at the same time in all institutions and spheres of society. On the contrary, in some cases it will be over the long, tough haul, sometimes a little forth and somewhat back, but nevertheless invariably over several centuries. Finally, the process is carried through as a characteristic of the Western societies of Europe and the USA from about the latter half of the 18th century until today.

The outcome is the realization of a society that has lost its centre and control: what used to make up a core and symbolic unit. This also unleashes a series of fundamental *contradictions* between the various newly autonomous parts in society now functioning on their respective terms and pursuing their respective objectives, which partly creates the continued historical dynamics of society, and partly lays the groundwork for basic conflicts and dysfunctions in society.

This modern non-centred society without control also possesses some content-related features or characteristics which have been presented in this chapter.

The doubling of *society* itself has been portrayed by Habermas as its bisection into *system* and *lifeworld*. Both 'worlds' are integrated through communication, but in the system by means of media – autonomized money and power – whereas in the lifeworld, it happens through culture and linguistically achieved mutual understanding. Admittedly, the system must be anchored or institutionalized in the lifeworld, and the material reproduction of the lifeworld must take place in the system, but the two worlds differ in their aims. There is ongoing colonization of the lifeworld, *and* a continuous impoverishment of culture in the lifeworld. In other words, there are clear contradictions between these two parts of society.

Prior to Habermas' depiction of society's doubling into system and lifeworld, Marx had already presented society's doubling into civil society and state, while characterizing the entire society through the dual nature of the commodity as use-value and exchange-value. Like Habermas, Marx highlighted the contradictions, conflicts and struggles caused by the division of society.

The above presentation has shown how *reflexivity* becomes a key concept in modern society. To Habermas, it is a consequence of the individual's emancipation from existing traditions, norms and culture, which enables a mutual understanding between individuals on an independent basis, and becomes a precondition for systemic purposive rationality. Beck sees reflexivity as particularly linked to a modernization of industrial society, while Giddens perceives reflexivity as a more general modern feature, which comes to the fore in what he calls high or late modernity.

Against the background of Habermas' doubling of society into system and lifeworld, reflexivity could be exercised within a systemic framework, that is, under the premise of systemic objectives or as part of the fulfilment of these. Within the lifeworld, reflexivity will form part of communicative everyday practice.

To the same extent that modernization of society leads to the differentiation and independence of the expert cultures of science, morality and arts, *knowledge* in modern society will also be doubled in terms of expert knowledge and lay knowledge, in knowledge forms related to the expert cultures and knowledge forms rooted in the lifeworld.

This duality of knowledge thus springs from the expert cultures being set free to create knowledge and insights independently of the dogmas and ties of the rest of society, e.g. the preconceptions and value doctrines of religion. However, since the individual in the lifeworld is also given freedom to exercise reflexive conduct, a lay knowledge is equally taking shape independently of expertise. The possibility of these forms of knowledge communicating with each other is present, but their fundamentally different contextual sources bring them to different definitions of validity, truth and authenticity. The split of modernization into different forms of knowledge also gives rise to conflicts over domination and control.

Finally, modernity spawns different manifestations of what is desirable, sensible and rational.

Weber saw rationality as being constricted to purposive rationality in modernized society, and described this as an iron cage, which – at the same time as it affected the effectiveness of society – deprived modern life of any other meaning.

Habermas writes about communicative rationality, which – along with the differentiations of expert cultures under modernity – is split into cognitive-instrumental, moral-practical and aesthetic-expressive rationality. The one-sided modernization is a manifestation of cognitive-instrumental rationality dominating the other forms of rationality in systemic contexts. In parallel, through colonization of the lifeworld and cultural impoverishment, the non-instrumental forms of reason are being displaced, so that these are exercised within the lifeworld in ever-narrower contexts, even though elements of a wholeness of reason will survive in communicative everyday practice.

Beck talks of the division of rationality into scientific and social rationality under reflexive modernity. To him, this springs from the success of science, but also from its claim to a monopoly on objectivity, which turns out to be based on probabilities and risk definitions, but not on actual reality. Under reflexive modernity, the knowledge monopoly held by established and institutional science cannot be sustained, but a kind of alternative scientific spirit emerges, which represents other premises and incorporates the demands and needs of society.

Therefore, Beck does not focus on a split of knowledge into expert and lay knowledge, which need to complement each other, as for instance in Wynne's work, but on the division between institutionalized scientific knowledge and alternative scientific knowledge. According to Beck, social rationality can only be achieved by practising both these types of science in a kind of interaction. To Beck, knowledge remains expert knowledge, and he attributes a much greater role to modernization of modernity through subpolitics based on alternative perceptions of science than to the incorporation of lay knowledge by means of public deliberation.

In contrast to Beck's and others' view of reflexivity as the manifestation of a new type of modernity, intensifying reflexivity has been perceived as a manifestation of the added momentum of the modernization process and its expansion into new areas of society, which had not previously been directly affected, that is, they were only indirectly influenced by the ongoing modernization process, primarily in material production, through the repercussions that modernization in this sector had on the rest of society.

Over the past two to three decades, however, these areas are being directly absorbed into modernization processes, which are, in principle, of the same form as that of modernization since the beginning of modern times, although the physical forms and processes are obviously contemporary.

Accordingly, the viewpoint in this presentation has been that modernization is a continuous process driven by the same characteristics. It asserts itself successively and with time lags in the different spheres and sectors of society, but as an invariable condition once it has been set in motion. Thus, the modernization so far is not only a semi-version that has gone half the way, and is now being supplemented by further modernization of a reflexive kind; on the contrary, one may say that modernization thus far has led to a bifurcation of reason, since the instrumental kind has become totally dominant.

Consequently, the reaction to this cannot simply be further modernization of what has already been modernized, as Beck suggests. It needs to be another kind of modernization based on the wholeness of reason – that it, a modernization different from the one ruled by instrumental reason.

Habermas has formulated a strategy to overcome the domination of instrumental reason, in which the freed potential of reason of the expert cultures is to be returned to the lifeworld: *not* just one by one or in isolation, but, as he puts it, across the whole breadth of cultural transmission.

Against the background of the presentation of Habermas' theory of modernity, and the critique of two other strategies to continue the modern project, one may discern two crucial elements in a strategy to overcome one-sided or instrumental modernization.

First, bringing the potential of reason of expert cultures back to the lifeworld implies a 'realization' of this potential. This means that the potential must be internalized into a concrete whole – that is, realized in the context of the lifeworld, and not merely in relation to the 'new masters', capital and power.

Second, such realization must *not* be confined to being useful as such in the lifeworld. It must also aim to be significant in bringing about an *integral modernization*. The lifeworld cannot simply be 'enriched' by feeding back potential of reason, if the modernization process itself is left untouched. This would merely lead to continued colonization and impoverishment. In other words, two-way communication is required between the system and the lifeworld. It is communication that would, in principle, end the bisection of reflexivity under modern doubling into a systemic form and one attached to the lifeworld, in which the systemic form has taken precedence. It is communication that abolishes the split of knowledge into expert knowledge and lay knowledge, in which the former has always triumphed over the latter. And finally, it is communication that will rise above the division of rationality into three forms, in which the instrumental form is supposed to fulfil all the functions.

Notes

1   Georg Henrik von Wright's book from 1993, *The Myth of the Future*, is a philosophical contribution to this discussion; see von Wright, 1993.
2   Baudelaire, *The Painter of Modern Life and Other Essays*, translated and edited by J. Mayne (1964), London, pp1–40. Reference from Frisby, 1985, pp14–20.
3   Marx, Karl, *The Communist Manifesto*.
4   See, for example, Marx, 1996, pp81–86, 93–94 and Marx, 1998, p263.
5   Frisby, 1985, pp28–37.
6   All three accounted for by Frisby, 1985, pp38–272.
7   Luhmann, 1984. Ref. Habermas, 1987a, p368.
8   Habermas, 1976, p13.
9   Ibid., pp11–12, and Outhwaite, 1994, p59.
10   It is necessary to stress that when I write historical materialism I am talking about a *materialistic* history theory in contrast to an *idealistic* one. This differs clearly from the Soviet Communist Party's understanding of a deterministic, materialistic history theory they called 'the historical materialism'. When Habermas uses the expression of historical materialism this is referring to the former meaning in sharp contrast to the Soviet 'historical materialism'. Also note that he talks about reconstructing the historical materialism.
11   Habermas refers to Piaget, 1973, p190.
12   Austin, 1992.
13   Searle, 1970.
14   See Habermas' later self-critique on this subject, according to which he no longer wishes to confine rationality of art to aesthetic-expressive notions with the ensuing validity claims as regards 'truth', linked to such rationality. In this self-critique, he is inspired by Albrecht Wellmer, see Nørager, 1985, p218. As Nørager has also pointed out, this can have wide implications insofar as it can influence the question of universalizability linked to the theory of rationality – that is, it can cover all aspects

of action. I will not pursue this further in this book, other than note that we can find many other truth-claims on art in addition to those adopted in this book.

15 Please notice his formulation 'what I call'. This is conceived more as a characterization than as an actual definition.

16 That is to say, a society is no subject. This also compares to Habermas' formulation concerning the view in subject philosophy of society as a self-referential 'big subject', which also contains individual subjects (Habermas, 1987a, p348, quoted in this book on page 62, Chapter 2).

17 What Beck cannot refer to is the 'blind market forces', as he does not elsewhere address the concept of capital in the Marxian sense.

18 That is, Beck also expresses himself within the framework of the dialectics of Enlightenment, which is presented in this book on pages 55 and 64.

19 In the original German, Beck uses the term '*entzaubert*'. The English-language version of Risk Society translates this into 'demystified'. Outhwaite uses 'disenchanted', as he refers directly to the fact that Habermas' depiction of the difference between 'mythical' and 'modern' thinking is deeply indebted to Weber's concept of 'disenchantment of the world and rationalization of action orientations' (Outhwaite, 1994, pp74–75); see also the presentation of the 'mythical' and the 'modern' worldview in TCA 1, pp72–113. The translation of *Theorie des kommunikativen Handels* into English uses the term 'disenchantment' for *Entzauberung*, see Habermas, 1984, p198. However, others translate the term *Entzauberung* as 'demythologization', for example, Nørager, 1985, p58. Tenbruck, upon whom Habermas draws in his reading of Weber concerning the demythologization process in the history of religion in Chapter II of TCA 1, pp225–366, clearly interprets the process of *Entzauberung* as one of demythologization. See Tenbruck, 1975, pp663–702. About Habermas' use of Tenbruck, see the present book, pp143–144. In this book, when referring to Beck, *Entzauberung* will be translated as 'demystification', and when referring to Outhwaite, 'disenchantment' will be used. In all other contexts, in particular in references to Habermas and Tenbruck, as well as both these authors' use of Weber, I shall follow Tenbruck and use the word 'demythologization', as I find this much more apt in conveying an understanding of the rationalization of the lifeworld than the term 'demystified'.

20 This concept will be subjected to closer examination in the present chapter's section on the critique of Beck's and Giddens' reflexive modernity, pp117 and, in particular, 129–131.

21 Disembedding is a construct employed by Giddens, first time in the book *The Consequences of Modernity*, in which he writes: 'the disembedding of social systems (a phenomenon which connects closely with the factors involved in time-space separation)' (Giddens, 1990, p17). It may well be comparable to Habermas' use of differentiation (from German *Ausdifferenzierung*). However, there is one conceivable difference between Giddens' use of disembedding and Habermas' of *Ausdifferenzierung*, as Giddens applies it more widely, while Habermas confines his concept to describe particular historical processes. The Danish word *selvstændig-gørelse* (akin to 'making independent/self-determining') may also be used in the sense of freeing a development from the ties of tradition.

22 Giddens, 1990, p139.

23 Weber saw the rationalization process as historically universal. In modern society, it would lead to people – due to bureaucratization – ending up in an *iron cage*, and – due to the capitalist purposive rationality – being exposed to a *loss of meaning*, see for instance Tenbruck, 1975, as well as the present book, for example, pp 76, 78, 143–144.

24   However, the image of Juggernaut is used, precisely, by Marx twice in his *Capital*, volume I (Marx, 1996, pp285, 639). In the editorial notes to the first English edition of *Capital*, vol. I, from 1887, note 223 explains: 'Juggernaut (Jagannath) – a title of Krishna, the eighth avatar of Vishnu. The cult of Juggernaut was marked by sumptuous ritual and extreme religious fanaticism which manifested itself in the self-torture and suicide of believers. On feast days some believers threw themselves under the wheels of the chariot bearing the idol of Vishnu-Juggernaut' (Marx, 1996, p782). Using an asterisk (*), at the bottom of page 139, Giddens writes: 'The term [juggernaut] comes from Hindi *JagannÇth*, "lord of the world", and is a title of Krishna; an idol of this deity was taken each year through the streets on a huge car, which followers are said to have thrown themselves under, to be crushed beneath the wheels' (Giddens, 1990, p139). However, more precisely, as can also be seen from Note 223 above, both Juggernaut and Krishna were incarnations of the universal God of Hinduism, Vishnu, who appeared on Earth in several incarnations, of which ten are particularly important, including Juggernaut and Krishna. See for instance the encyclopaedia *Gyldendals Lexicon*, vol 10, p259. Although Giddens in this way wants the replace an image of Marx by another image of Marx, Marx uses both images to highlight the cruelty of capitalism in all its consequences, and not to replace explanations and concepts concerning the dynamics of capitalism.

25   In Habermasian terms, it becomes the mechanisms that adapt the *lifeworlds of individuals* to the *systems* of reflexive modernity.

26   See, for instance, his description of money on pp22–25 in *The Consequences of Modernity*. This is where he phrases it: 'Money makes possible the generalisation of the second of these [exchange value] because of its role as a "pure commodity"' (Giddens, 1990, p22). He makes this statement with a reference to *Grundrisse*, and construes it as Marx's critical comment on money, which foreshadows Marx's later distinction between exchange-value and use-value. However, in this text, Giddens gets it the wrong way around, so that money comes before the exchange of products, although historically the opposite is the case. Moreover, *Capital* starts off by presenting the dual nature of the commodity, with its use-value and exchange-value, and how one commodity has a value in relation to another commodity.

27   Cf. the present book in its 'Excursus: formal and real subsumption', pp150–154.

28   See also Giddens, 1990, p38, in which he writes: 'The reflexivity of modern social life consists in the fact that social practices are constantly examined and reformed in light of incoming information about those very practices, thus constitutively altering their character.' This could possibly also be read as the information flow turning into the exclusive factor of change.

29   Concerning this process, see Liedman, 2000 [In the shadow of the future: modernity's history of ideas].

30   Marx has defined an exact and highly central concept for this process, the *real subsumption*, to which I shall return in an excursus in the following section of this chapter concerning the formal and real subsumption of production under capital.

31   Wynne uses the term *formulaic* knowledge, by which he refers to performance-related knowledge – that is, linked to the execution and not merely to the logics, 'what is said', the statement as such, but also *the manner* in which it is said, and not merely what is said (Wynne, 1996, p61). This is equivalent to what the philosopher J. L. Austin has characterized as illocutionary speech acts. This terminology has also been used by Habermas in *The Theory of Communicative Action*, see all of section III in TCA I, Intermediate Reflections: Social Action, Purposive Activity and Communication, specifically on p319.

32   Tenbruck, 1975, pp663–702.

33   See Note 19 in Chapter 3 of this book.

34   As we shall see in Chapter 4, this is also one of the mistakes in the ecological modernization process, for instance in the writings of Mol. In his extensive work *Refinement of Production*, Mol comments on Beck's and Giddens' concepts of reflexive modernity: 'Both authors believe that the environmental crisis plays a vital role in the emergence of a phase of reflexivity in modernity, since the externality of environmental effects to the economy is becoming more and more absurd, while it remains far from easy, at the same time, to simply internalize environmental effects into the economy, so that they can be managed and controlled. There is a clear decline in people's optimism about and faith in linear scientization and anticipatory control as instruments for dealing with side effects. Giddens' conception of the "reflexivity" of modernity refers to the situation in which social practices and material relations with nature are continually examined and reshaped in the light of new incoming information about those very practices. This "reflexivity" marks the decline of the (Enlightenment) idea that social and natural environments would increasingly be subjected to rational ordering. It includes the reflection upon the nature of reflection itself via the disenchantment of science, and thus subverts reason and certitude in a fundamental way, resulting in an institutionalization of doubt. But reflexive modernity still rests on the central institutions of modernity; therefore this concept is at odds with ideas in which postmodernity is seen as a stage in which nothing can be known with any certainty and no version of progress can plausibly be defended' (Mol, 1995, p17). To this I can only add that a constant reshaping of social practices and material relations with nature is precisely characteristic of capitalist modernization from the outset, and that the decline in ideas about the rational arrangement of social and natural environments, to which Mol refers, is indeed nothing more than the very *purposive* rationalization of these areas.

35   See for instance 'The Production of Absolute Surplus Value', in Marx, 1996, pp187–316.

36   See, for instance, 'Production of Relative Surplus Value', in Marx, 1996, pp317–508.

37   The chief work on the historical realization of these processes is also *Capital (Das Kapital)*. In particular, Volume I is an indispensable source of historical studies with references to a wide variety of original literature. See Marx, 1996. Another major contribution to the historical studies is Maurice Dobb (1963), *Studies in the Development of Capitalism*, London. A short but highly intelligible and useful piece on the Industrial Revolution in the light of the economic history of the world is Carlo Cipolla: *Economic History of World Population* (1965), Revised Edition. It is useful, because it gives an impression or a sense of how *little* we have still seen of this revolution.

38   Some examples are the outsourcing of cleaning and care for the elderly, as well as the capitalization of sports.

39   The following literature may throw light on various sides of this development: Baglioni and Crouch, 1990; Matthews, 1996; Overbeek, 2002; Ransome, 1999; Sabel and Zeitlin, 1997.

40   See, for instance, Nielsen, 1988.

41   The term 'doubling' is here used in the sense that something that used to be one begins to consist of two different parts, which together make up the former unit, but no longer has the same content as before. Doubling thus does not mean two of the same sort. This is comparable to Marx's expression of society's doubling into civil society and state, and the dual nature of the commodity in terms of use value and exchange value, see for instance Marx, 1996, pp45–49, 51–58, 69–71, 81–85.

Chapter 4

Ecological Modernization

If the way forward lies in continued modernization, an obvious question must be whether the modernization process can be made ecological, thus helping us out of the ecological crisis. Does this contain an alternative to starting from Habermas' concepts of modernity? Can the trend in environmental sociology that calls its project *ecological modernization* carry through the formation of such an integral modernization? Conceptually as well as strategically? Theoretically as well as practically? The champions of 'ecological modernization' hold that the way of modernity is clearly preferable to assorted conservative Utopias or to the dictate of power, whether anonymously or as a worshipped saviour. And they do not suggest that ecology needs to be the goal in itself, but that it is possible to 'ecologize' the modernization of society, thus freeing it of its, by now, acute environmental crisis phenomena.

Therefore, this school of thought in sociology will be subject to an analysis below, against the background of the questions raised by the above analyses of the modern and of ecology. I thus do not wish to take ecological modernization at face value, but to gauge its worth on a gold scale. This is also meant to imply that I consider the above analyses to be highly valuable to the course ahead. To me, they have confirmed that it has long been possible to postulate solutions without a foundation in social analysis.

There is also a chance that the practice based upon the theories of ecological modernization holds scope for significantly overcoming the limitations hitherto faced by environmental polity. Consequently, practices based upon ecological modernization, to the extent they can be identified, should also be subject to assessment.

Another point of such an examination is that ecological modernization as a strategy widely contains the elements that underpin environmental assessment, which is the start and end point of the present book. In this connection, the basic question is: why not simply use this tool as outlined in directives, government orders and so on?[1] And the strategic question is: how do we understand and practise environmental assessment in wider contexts, if it is to contribute to the practical realization of a paradigm shift?

Consequently, an analysis of the practical elements of ecological moderniza-tion, whether or not these are phrased or construed as part of the concept of ecological modernization, will bring us closer to an explanation that there may be exceedingly good reasons why environmental assessment as a tool is being increasingly applied, and has become an evermore central part of environmental regulations in most countries across the globe. However, even more crucially, such an analysis may spark a recognition of the grounds for challenging the normal understanding and use of the tool of environmental assessment. This part of the chapter thus focuses on what I have called the 'institutionalization of environmen-talism in the political apparatus' concerning the practical elements of ecological modernization.

The chapter as a whole will be structured with a view to first analysing the self-perception of ecological modernization at a theoretical level, subsequently – against this background – assessing its identifiable practical ramifications.

Incidentally, such a distinction is not easy to sustain. Buttel (2000) stresses that the concept of ecological modernization encompasses an ample range of usages, and identifies four different forms of application: (a) sociological theories of ecological modernization; (b) a portrayal of dominant environmental political discourses; (c) synonymously with environmental management, industrial ecology, eco-reconstruction and so on; and (d) an expression of nearly every innovation in environmental policy or environmental improvement. However, what really matters, according to Buttel, is that the explosive growth in the interest in ecologi-cal modernization does not stem from clarity in the theoretical arguments of this line of thinking, but from ecological modernization being an effective answer to a series of circumstances and imperatives in the socio-ecological thinking of the 1990s.

In the social sciences, it was seen as necessary to react to the rising influence of radical environmentalist movements, particularly to assess whether radical environmental activism would become a dominant factor of power in society and a necessary forerunner to effective environmental improvements and reforms. Moreover, the concept of sustainable development – which initially seemed so promising to the social sciences – began to manifest its shortcomings regarding the indication of visions for future evolutions and environmental policies. The concept of sustainability was originally developed in a North–South dialogue against the background of experiences concerning primary and renewable sectors in the non-city or rural settings of developing countries. In this context, the concept of ecological modernization provided a platform for new thinking concerning the problems and their solutions, which were mostly related to sectors being transformed in cities in advanced industrial nations. Finally, the advocates of ecological modernization, unlike radical environmentalists, saw the role of environmentalist movements from a fresh perspective by refraining from roman-ticizing them, and by appreciating the elementary roles that science, technology, capital and the state could play in the processes of environmental innovation.

Buttel finds that the first-mentioned form of application is the most signifi-cant and useful. However, in his eyes, the use of ecological modernization in sociological theory has been dominated by concepts from economics and engineering. Therefore, he stresses what he sees as the most essential postulates in a characteristic and coherent perspective on ecological modernization. Here below, these will be mentioned only briefly.

The most challenging environmental problems in the past century have been caused by modernization and industrialization, and will also be so in the century ahead. Therefore, their solutions have to lie in *more* modernization and superindustrialization rather than less. Put differently, capitalism is not sufficiently flexible to allow for a trend towards 'sustainable capitalism', but its imperative of competition may, under certain political circumstances, go hand-in-hand with the achievement of pollution-preventing eco-efficiency within the production processes, and particularly within the consumption processes.

The theory of society has to recognize and directly theorize about the role that eco-efficiency and rationalization may play in environmental reform, just as it has to acknowledge the limits to this, and to what degree it may be induced by the state.

Ecological modernization is, in a sense, a critical answer to radical environmentalism or countermodernity, and the role of the environmentalist movement will shift from being a critical opponent placed at the fringes of society to becoming a critical, still independent participant in the courses of development with a view to bringing ecological change.

The perspective of ecological modernization sees the environment as a potential or, in practice, an increasingly autonomous (or differentiated) arena of decision-making processes.

Finally, and perhaps most fundamentally, ecological modernization is a reflection of the policy options that have arisen in the wake of the state's reconstruction or modernization.[2]

As it appears, these postulates of ecological modernization directly address the core of the problems posed by this book, as they profess the need for further modernization as the main tool, that this form of modernization has to be capitalist, that interests outside industry, state and expertise (science) must be drawn into the decision-making processes, and that the environmental sphere as a decision-making arena has been differentiated, that is, given an autonomy that may assert itself in relation to other interests.

Therefore, the guiding questions in the following analysis are whether the concepts of ecological modernization contain an explicit concept of modernization, and if so which one, and whether the addition of an ecological ingredient to this modernization process will make it more likely that the course of development stops being solely based upon instrumental rationality, in one form or another, also taking root in the two other forms of rationality. As for the issue of a differentiation of the environmental decision-making arena, the analysis must consider whether this has brought about autonomous developmental properties that may also be usefully deployed in practice and on their own terms.

Theories of ecological modernization

The theories of ecological modernization have a relatively brief history, according to most authors dating back to the mid-1980s, when a group of sociologist and political scientists – mainly German – began to use the term in connection with their analysis of industrial actors' technological innovations in the production processes aimed at creating environmental improvements and long-term social changes (Jänicke, 1985; Murphy, 2000). Over the following ten years, a host of theories and strategies were drawn up addressing ecological modernization, which rapidly came to denote a holistic view of social development and environmental protection, setting store by prevention and by a modern society, as opposed to more retrospective or moralizing visions of saving the environment.

Nevertheless, the term ecological modernization as a theory encompasses a vast array of different perceptions of what ought to be the core of a restructuring of society that revolves around, or gives equal status to, the environment. Since I cannot delve into all of them in detail, it may be useful to map them out in more general terms. To this end, I shall use Murphy's revision of the existing literature in the field. He divided the development over time into *five dimensions,* which together characterize ecological modernization theory today (Murphy, 2000, pp2–6; also Mol, 1995, pp27–48).

First, ecological modernization may be described as a *theory of unplanned social change.* Ecological modernization is perceived as the outcome of unique and independent changes, primarily in material production, whose combined impact is social change towards a more environmentally sound society. Above all, Joseph Huber has put his name to this side of ecological modernization, and is indeed credited as its founder with a series of influential works (Huber, 1982; 1984; 1985).

In these, he espouses a kind of superindustrialization that will incorporate ecology, but also take away its innocence. The process is seen as driven by industrial decision-makers themselves, rather than through the state apparatus, just as he attributes a limited role to environmentalist movements compared to previously. He divides the history of industrial development into three periods. The first is the foundation (1789–1848), the second is the construction of industrial society as such (1848–1980), and the third, which he sees as inevitable, is the ecological modernization of industrial society.

In all three periods, the economy and technology are driving forces, but the third period is also driven by the need to reconcile the consequences of human activity with environmental concerns.

The *second dimension* in the development of ecological modernization may be termed *theories of macroeconomic reconstruction with environmental gratis effects.* These are not meant to be alternative but rather supplementary to Huber, and are represented by the works of Martin Jänicke and Udo Simonis (Jänicke, 1985; Jänicke et al., 1985; 1989; and Simonis, 1989a and 1989b).

They stress the need for restructuring national economies in line with ecological modernization, which necessitates both a technological and a sectorial change. For instance by changing from energy- and resource-intensive industries to service and knowledge industries. This involves an element of deindustrialization and phase-out of those technical and economic systems that cannot be adapted to meet environmental objectives. However, they generally argue that the restructuring of major industries can be arranged in a manner enabling them to sustain and increase their contribution to the gross national product, at the same time as they reduce their intake of energy, resources and so on. This kind of restructuring may thus give rise to environmental gratis effects.

A *third dimension* in ecological modernization argues for generally assessing environmental policies in the light of those ecologically modernizing steps that are currently feasible. In this regard, the theory of ecological modernization is construed as the *prescription for a government programme with certain key elements.*

Four such elements may be mentioned. First, that any policy must be based on the fundamental principle that there is no inevitable conflict between economic and environmental concerns, but that these may indeed be mutually supportive. Second, that environmental objectives should be mainstreamed into all policy areas, and this to such a degree that some of them may lose their original character. Third, alternative and innovative approaches to environmental policies must be examined, including economic instruments in environmental policy, as well as voluntary environmental accords. Re-regulation takes centre stage, rather than deregulation. Finally, government-led action is seen as something beneficial that may enhance standards and foster industrial innovation.

The *fourth dimension* sees ecological modernization as *an example of cultural politics and discourse.* This approach to ecological modernization is represented by Dryzek (Dryzek, 1993; 1997) and Hajer (Hajer, 1995; 1996). The most high-profile has been Hajer, with his extensive analysis of political reactions to the problems of acid rain in Great Britain and the Netherlands in his book *The Politics of Environmental Discourse: Ecological Modernization and the Policy Process* (Hajer, 1995).

The cultural-political approach to ecological modernization means that the fundamental problem raised by Hajer becomes the social construction of environmental issues. Therefore, he poses questions such as why certain aspects of reality are singled out as 'our common problems'. At a more general level, his main concern is what kind of society is created in the name of environmental protection (Hajer, 1996, p256).

Hajer's analytical starting point is thus that decisive political issues underlie discursive constructions. The aim of the analysis is to uncover the frequently weak foundation upon which a development trend, such as ecological modernization, is built. The discourse analysis draws on concepts such as story-lines and discourse coalitions and, to Hajer, ecological modernization is based on credible and attractive story-lines such as: environmental regulation turns out to be a plus-sum game, pollution is a question of inefficiency, nature possesses a balance that must be respected, prevention is better than cure, and sustainable development is the alternative to former polluting growth. Crucially, story-lines replace complex specialist questions, and often close a debate which is in fact still open. Or they represent a manoeuvre away from the consensus in the academic discourse, for example in the manner in which ecology is used in the political process, even though the notion of balance in nature was already abandoned by academia in the 1960s (Hajer, 1996, p65).

Hajer thus represents a critical variant of ecological modernization, in which an environmental conflict does not primarily emerge as disagreement concerning which means to apply, whether to act or not, but as disagreement on the meaning of a physical or social phenomenon. In this process, story-lines play a key role, since they determine the interaction between physical and social realities. They are perceived as the drivers of change, and should be analysed in view of the specific discursive practices for which they have been produced. Below, I shall return to some of Hajer's viewpoints.

Finally, there is the *fifth dimension* of ecological modernization seen as an *example of institutional reflexivity and the transformation of society*. This dimension is particularly represented by Mol and Spaargaren. Not least Mol's book *The Refinement of Production: Ecological Modernization Theory and the Chemical Industry* has been a major work (Mol, 1995; Spaargaren, 1997).

Mol's and Spaargaren's joint approach – indeed they have co-authored part of their published works – builds especially on Beck's and Giddens' understanding of environmental risks in modern society, as a premise linked to the reflexive acts of individuals and groups.

Mol sees modernization as an empirical phenomenon that can be demonstrated in the transformation of the institutions of modernity (private as well as public), and he interprets this as their reflexivity being faced with environmental problems. The aim of these transformations is not to live with, but to overcome the environmental crisis, and in this endeavour, the institutions of modernity are both a means and an end.

In Mol's aforementioned chief work, he concludes – against the backdrop of an analysis of the chemical industry's restructuring in response to environmental pressures – that ecological modernization can be perceived as a reflexive (institutional) reorganization of industrial society in its attempt to overcome the ecological crisis (Mol, 1995, p394).

These five dimensions in the literature on ecological modernization show the wide span covered by these theories, and reveal a clear trend towards incorporating more elementary societal – in the sense of socially structural – processes. In the beginning, the theories revolve mostly around the relationship between the environment and economy. Later they evolve into focusing more on the relationship between the environment and society.

After outlining these five dimensions, Murphy concludes that one may distinguish between prescriptive/normative approaches and analytical/descriptive approaches (Murphy, 2000, p5).

The first category encompasses the theories suggesting state intervention in the market explicitly aimed at fostering economic growth *and* protecting the environment. The chief measures to this effect are considered to be obligatory environmental standards that signal the premises for industrial innovation. To this should be added macroeconomic restructuring, which – beyond traditional compulsion and control instruments – favours less resource-demanding production and a series of innovative policy tools, such as green taxes, strategic environmental assessments and voluntary accords. At the same time, it is recommended that industries seek solutions to production problems in cleaner technologies. Altogether, such a programme of environmental protection will also boost competitiveness at both micro and macro level.

Murphy highlights some points of criticism levelled precisely at such programmes, including Giddens' comment that the programmes do not seem to reflect the current interest in risks, and conjure up a far too optimistic vision of the possibilities of science and technology (Giddens, 1998, p58). Furthermore, their focus on the national level seems problematic, especially as it apparently places the emphasis on immediate problems, as well as on everything that is measurable, such as resource consumption, waste materials, emissions and so on, while sidelining more cultural factors and non-human values, such as the conservation of wilderness and desert landscapes. Murphy draws special attention to Christoff (1996, p485) concerning the latter issue.

As regards the analytical/descriptive category, the literature is quite different and more self-critical. An example is the problem in Huber's almost exclusive emphasis on technology and entrepreneurs as determinants of social change, and his almost teleological form of argumentation. Hajer's discursive approach has been criticized by Dryzek (1995) for not recognizing that the environment can be a reality and exist independently of the social construction. Hajer is also charged with not being sufficiently able to demonstrate the influence of environmental discourse in policy-making, compared to more traditional factors, such as the chosen instruments, institutional structures, personnel and resources.

The interpretation of ecological modernization as institutional reflexivity, as construed for instance by Mol, is criticized by Hajer (1995)[3] for being incomplete and faulty. He doubts that the phenomena interpreted in this manner really represent reflexivity, and suggests distinguishing between a techno-corporative[4] regime of ecological modernization and a truly reflexive ecological modernization. While the latter entails a democratic process with a free choice between alternative development options, a techno-corporative regime of ecological modernization will bring expert decisions and less democratic models of decision-making, relying on relatively isolated expert decisions concerning superindustrial answers to environmental problems. The theoretical approach expressed by Mol is akin to a techno-corporative ecological modernization,[5] as Hajer sees it.

Although there is evidently a wide variety of contrasting views on ecological modernization, to Murphy the gist of the matter is that ecological modernization testifies to the headway made by advanced industrial nations in addressing the environmental problems, even if much remains to be done (Murphy, 2000, p8).

The present chapter sets out to introduce some light and shade into the aforementioned viewpoints. While there is acknowledgement of the vast array of policies and measures deployed in order to integrate environmental concerns directly into decision-making processes, questions are nevertheless raised as to the impact of these, both on the developmental form of society and on the state of the environment, in the short as well as in the long term, given the underlying instrumental form of rationality. I am thus entering the field of problems which Hajer extends between what he characterizes as techno-corporative and truly reflexive ecological modernization. Nevertheless, as one may already sense from the foregoing chapter, I am doing so very differently from Hajer, just as I shall not reach the same conclusions.

The above outline of the theory of ecological modernization and its evolution over time is thus pointing clearly to the two last-mentioned dimensions as the most relevant to those problems raised in this book that motivate a closer look at ecological modernization. Accordingly, the question is whether an ecological modernization – in a carefully delimited form – is capable of moving beyond a *one-sided* modernization determined by instrumental reason, creating an integral modernization instead.

Consequently, here below, it is Mol's and Hajer's theories of ecological modernization that will be subjected to closer analysis concerning the specific form of modernization expressed by each of them. The above, relatively broad-ranging mention of the variations in the theory and history of ecological modernization have laid the backdrop and the framework for Mol's and Hajer's versions. Therefore, I shall now more directly approach the specific features within ecological modernization that each of them represents.

Mol's ecological emancipation

As mentioned, Mol's chief contribution to the theory of ecological modernization is the book *The Refinement of Production: Ecological Modernization Theory and the Chemical Industry* published in 1995. Here, his starting point is how sociological theory has incorporated the environmental dimension, and more specifically, its various perceptions of the meaning of environment under modernity, including an interpretation of the concepts postulating a reflexive modernity.

The thesis structuring his presentation is phrased in this question:

> *How, and to what extent, do environmental considerations trigger the ongoing transformation of the central, production-related, institutions of modern societies? Or, to use a different formulation: the aim of this study is to construct a theory on the environment-induced institutional transformations related to the industrial clusters within contemporary Western societies.*

Mol, 1995, p4

Several partial theoretical frameworks have been developed and used to explain specific transformations in the various institutions of modernity, such as theories of technological change, state theories, institutional economics and industrial sociology. However, none of them has placed these institutional changes as a whole within the overall perspective of an ecological transformation of industrial society, and this is what the theory of ecological modernization seeks to establish, Mol notes. He sees the theory of ecological modernization as a 'theory on the nature and extent of institutional reform which centres on the formal concept of an "emancipation", or growing independence, of ecology from other dimensions, especially the economy' (Mol, 1995, p5).

In this, he follows Berger (1988) and Giddens in their view of the relation between environmental problems and institutional changes in modernity, since they envisage that constant restructuring of modern institutions will constitute a living chance of overcoming the ecological crisis. Conversely, he sees Bauman and Pepper (1993) as rather pessimistic and apocalyptic in their view of this crisis, as they consider it unsolvable by means of the institutions of modernity (Mol, 1995, p24).

He thus distances himself from both the neo-Marxist perception of environmental problems (Schnaiberg, 1980) as caused by capitalist relations of production, and from the de-modernization theories (André Gorz, Rudolf Bahro, Otto Ullrich), which place environmental problems in the context of an overwhelming industrial crisis, which can ultimately be overcome only by dismantling the existing modes of production.

Across or in-between these positions, Mol champions a view of industrial society as a cornerstone in modernity, thus forging a link to Giddens' division between capitalism and industrialism (Mol, 1995, pp9, 15). As we have seen, Giddens defends such a bisection, since he sees four institutional dimensions as fundamental to modernity: capitalism, industrialism, surveillance and military force (Giddens, 1990, pp55–59).

Before presenting Mol's arguments in further detail, I shall here briefly elaborate on my critique of Giddens on this point, since Mol uses Giddens uncritically.

Giddens defines the dimension of capitalism and industrialism in the following manner:

> Capitalism *is a system of commodity production, centred upon the relation between private ownership of capital and propertyless wage labour, this relationship forming the main axis of a class system. Capitalist enterprise depends upon production for competitive markets, prices being signals for investors, producers, and consumers alike.*
>
> The chief characteristic of *industrialism is the use of inanimate sources of material power in the production of goods, coupled to the central role of machinery in the production process. A machine can be defined as an artifact that accomplishes set tasks by employing such power sources as the means of its operation. Industrialism presupposes the regularized social organization of production in order to coordinate human activity, machines, and the inputs and outputs of raw materials and goods.*
>
> Giddens, 1990, pp55–56

Although Giddens warns against reductionism that either sees industrialism as a subcategory of capitalism or vice versa, these definitions must be characterized as a somewhat naïve perception of capitalism. Not only does he put forward this distinction in two separate dimensions, but he also considers capitalism to be a special subcategory of modern societies in general (Giddens, 1990, p56). The latter view can be countered by a rather elementary question: where can I find a modern society that is not capitalist? One cannot refer to the former Eastern European socialism and the Soviet Union, partly because this no longer exists, and is thus shown not to be sustainable, and partly because even those societies could, to a great extent, be considered to make use of capitalism, albeit centralized or state-controlled capitalism.

I shall here consider capitalization to be part of the breakthrough of the modern, as in the above concerning capitalist modernization. Capitalism thus did not precede modernization, or vice versa, although a series of developmental features in society may be conceived as preconditions for capitalism to arise and develop. However, these features thus also become preconditions for modernity to develop as a society. Just as some constituent elements of capitalism – such as the exchange of goods, markets and money – date back hundreds, even thousands of years before the emergence of a capitalist society as such, so elements of a modern society also existed many years before, for example, the separation between space and time.

In the context addressed here, the problem arises with the failure to acknowledge the capitalist duality of *value* and *material substance*, when mapping out the scope for action towards *ecological* modernization. Because once such a distinction is made, the field is wide open – as concerns the market and capitalist accumulation – for the implementation of ecological/environmental concerns, based upon purely material or functional criteria. This may therefore be done, in principle, *without* regard for the costs or to a form that is viable under the conditions of the market, since a return on the investment in the innovation carried out is left out of the picture.

Mol does not just follow Giddens in such a distinction between capitalism and industrialism, but further stresses that the theory of ecological modernization focuses primarily on the industrial dimension (Mol, 1995, p41). By introducing this distinction, he has established the *general* conditions for a given innovation, say an ecological one, also under globalized capitalism. Thus, one does not need to let the development of market conditions determine such generalization. Attributing such freedom of action to ecological modernization undeniably gives it an advantage that will be hard to recognize in the empirical reality. Admittedly, on the occasion of his comprehensive research into the chances of implementing ecological modernization specifically within the Dutch chemical industry, Mol has to conclude:

> *It is the substantial consequence of the analytically identified growing independence of an ecological sphere and ecological rationality, and of the institutionalization of ecology in concrete social practices involving the chemical industry. More and more ecological criteria appear in the design, performance and evaluation of production activities carried out*

by the chemical industry, resulting in an enlargement and revaluation of environmental policy, *measures and activities or an ecologizing of existing economic practices [...].* Without any doubt, *empirical evidence in the previous three chapters confirms that both these set of criteria – relating to the economy and the ecology* – are still yet not a par. *In the development of the chemical industry,* economic rationalities and criteria predominate and traditional advocacies remain powerful. *But at the same time, the three sub-sectoral studies elucidated that ecological developments are not* fully *subordinate to or* completely *dependent on economic ones. Different social forces and actors increasingly (try to) evaluate and (re)construct chemical production to* both *economic* and *ecological criteria.* Sometimes *a more or less smooth 'integration' of both dimensions on concrete issues in the chemical industry is settled, [...]. On other occasions* economic and ecological interests still clash. *When there is a conflict, the traditional preference for economic interests before ecological interests is being challenged* in a minority, *but growing number, of instances. [...]* No general prediction can be made *on the outcome of such concrete conflicts in the chemical industry.*

Mol, 1995, pp361–362 (my emphasis)

Accordingly, I will consider this to be *the first utopian characteristic* of the theory of ecological modernization. It assumes, on this point, some possibilities that cannot be found in modern reality, at least not in the globalized economic system of the 1990s and the new millennium. As we saw above, ecological modernization has precisely been criticized for foreshortening the perspective to the national level. On the face of it, in this regard, the concept implies a regression to the protected national economies of yesteryear, in which national state regulation actually stood certain chances of forcing the market towards a desired situation, say, production for the home market. Accordingly, there is some contradiction on this point in Mol's work. In one place he writes that modernity and ecological modernization are essentially a Western project with the resultant geographical delimitation (Mol, 1995, p54). But shortly after, he stresses, as one of six main characteristics of ecological modernization, that ecological restructuring is becoming increasingly interdependent with processes of globalization in the economic and political dimension, and will therefore not remain confined to individual nations (Mol, 1995, p58, point 5).

As it appears from the fifth dimension of ecological modernization theory, Mol's version of this is incidentally based on Giddens' and Beck's concept of reflexive modernization, which he considers to be highly useful. He distances himself from 'simple modernization' by stressing that changes are taking place within the institutions of modern society, and also from de-modernization, which focuses on the dismantling of these modern institutions. However, he also steers clear of a postmodern perception of the institutional order.

Admittedly, Mol does criticize Giddens' and particularly Beck's use of the concept of reflexive modernization for carrying some contradictory meanings, for

instance interpretations of the risk society that do not seem compatible with institutional reflexivity.[6] Nonetheless, Mol insists on the usefulness of the concept
exactly to describe the institutional reflexivity in the current phase of modernity;
because this is characterized by the impossibility of understanding the environment as external to the institutional development and social practice of modernity.
Indeed, the environment needs to be returned to the centre of the theory of the
social. In this exact sense, the theory of ecological modernization is parallel to the
idea of reflexive modernization: 'it emphasizes and analyzes the active and reflexive (re)design of central institutions of modernity in dealing with the ecological
crisis and on the basis of environmental criteria' (Mol, 1995, p34).

At first sight, I am able to follow Mol in this understanding of institutional
reflexivity, in line with my critique of Beck's and Giddens' reflexivity concept in
Chapter 3. However, when he also, elsewhere in his work, characterizes this as
'institutional learning', I beg to differ (Mol, 1995, pp34–49), because, in this
manner, he introduces the assumption that these institutions have an inherent
interest in reflecting on environmental risks, deterioration, options for improvement and so on, and that they are capable politically and practically of reacting
adequately to this. To use Giddens' language, it implies that the institutions within
the industrial dimension are able to act independently of, or autonomously of, the
other dimensions, such as capitalism, surveillance and military force, even when
we here also choose to neglect the exercise of control and power over these institutions at the political level.

I do not mean to claim that the political level is able to control the capitalist
dimension. In absolute terms, the opposite is more likely to be the case. All that I
am hinting at is that the political level may provide a certain setting and preconditions for acting inside and on the basis of the capitalist dimension. As we shall see
in Chapter 5, this is also the factor that nurtures the hope for a different social
practice, enabling a modernization process that is not one-sided to assert itself, at
least in certain sub-areas of situations.

The problem I perceive in Mol's understanding of ecological modernization
as institutional reflexivity becomes evident in his presentation of its core element,
which he terms 'the emancipation' of ecology (Mol, 1995, pp28–34). It is this
emancipation process that expresses reflexivity at the institutional level. In this
connection, he also builds on Giddens' concepts.

Mol's starting point in his presentation of the emancipation of ecology is
Giddens' reproduction of Karl Polanyi's 'process of disembedding' (Giddens,
1990, pp17–29; Polanyi, 1957). This refers to a process in which social relations
are lifted from the local and traditional structures and contexts, and subsequently
rearranged or re-established across time and space, including from a worldwide
perspective.[7] This process leads to the progression of pre-modern society into the
19th century, and may be construed as a differentiation of society into an
economic sphere, a political sphere and a lifeworld. And, Mol stresses, this differentiation meant that economic processes evolved independently of traditional
structures, such as religion, family and kinship, instead following its own regularities and specific economic rationality (Mol, 1995, p29).

It is this independent pursuit of economic rationality that, according to Mol, results in the breakdown and deterioration of nature and environment. In order to recover a balance between nature and modern society, the theory of ecological modernization holds, a kind of re-embedding needs to take place. Since contemporary economic practice is firmly rooted in modernity, characterized by a high level of time–space distantiation and associated with modern technical-scientific and state institutions, no re-embedding can take place as a reversal of the occurred disembedding process or through a return to the conditions of times past in general, as envisioned by some de-modernists. Indeed, a re-embedding must be carried through in the light of the current developmental stage of modernity, by integrating the ecological dimensions and acting within the institutions of modernity.

Such re-embedding will, Mol envisages, lead to an institutionalization of ecology in social practices as well as in the institutions of production and consumption. However, for this to bring about a reorientation of basic economic practices in a more ecological direction, ecology must first be emancipated from the economic dimension of modernity. Such emancipation of an ecological rationality and of an ecological sphere, which may thus become relatively independent of its counterpart in the economy, is a necessary first step for a subsequent integration of the two areas on equal terms. This integration follows two mechanisms: 'ecologization of the economy' and 'economization of the ecology' (Mol, 1995, p30).

The most pressing questions posed by such a vision of ecological emancipation is: how does one initiate it? From where and how are institutions motivated to give equal weight to ecological and economic rationality? And stemming from this, another crucial question to Mol must be: what does he understand by ecological rationality? What are the criteria for such a rationality, and how are these criteria institutionalized in the context of social practices?

On the face of it, answers to these questions cannot be found in Mol's work. However, in addition to stressing that the theory of ecological modernization must be perceived as normative, he wishes to develop a series of criteria or hypotheses about ecological modernization which are to help test its real possibilities, or the extent to which one can empirically verify such features of ecologically emancipated modes of action. Therefore, he emphasizes that the outlined distinction between an ecological sphere and an economic sphere is not made with a view to identifying these empirically, but has an analytical aim. Creating a conceptual space for a relatively autonomous ecological sphere enables the study of the extent to which ecologically rational action has been institutionalized in the central institutions of modernity.

As he lays the foundation for the identification of such criteria, Mol stresses that the theory of ecological modernization does not see the emancipation of an ecological rationality as a process towards such ecological rationality, and an ecological sphere, becoming dominant over or in replacement of the economic rationality and the economic sphere. They are all seen as having their reality and legitimacy independently of each other, and pursuing different objectives (Mol,

1995, p35). Rather it is a process that should lead to ecological rationality catching up with the longstanding dominance of economic rationality, without implying the end of the latter.

However, before he singles out the criteria for identification of emancipatory developmental features, Mol points to the changed role of the state. From the perspective of ecological modernization theory, Mol sees two possibilities in particular for overcoming the limitations and shortcomings thus far in the environmental policy-making of the bureaucratic state (Mol, 1995, p46). *First,* a transformation of official environmental policy from being remedial and reactive to becoming preventative and proactive, from an exclusive to a participatory policy, from a centralized to a decentralized one, from a tyrannically overregulated policy to one that creates favourable and sound conditions for environmentally appropriate conduct and practice by producers and consumers.

Second, a transfer of responsibility, initiatives and task from the state to the market. This will hasten the ecological transformation process, first and foremost because the market, compared to the state, is seen as a more efficient mechanism to coordinate the management of environmental problems.

These two possibilities should not be conceived as a new kind of laissez-faire, but as a transformation in the relationship between state and society, and a different emphasis in the guiding role of the state. The state should stimulate self-regulation, either through economic incentives or through the civil sphere in terms of citizens' groups, environmental NGOs and consumer associations. In this manner, ecological modernization theory aims to relieve the welfare state of some of its environmental management tasks, enabling it to concentrate on what cannot be transferred to the market (Mol, 1995, p47).

The criteria for identification of the theory of ecological modernization, with its possible empirical realities, is formulated by Mol in what he calls the six synthesizing 'hypotheses' about institutional development in modern society since the early 1980 onwards (Mol, 1995, p58):

1   The design, performance and evaluation of processes of production and consumption are increasingly based on ecological criteria, besides economic criteria, among others.
2   Modern science and technology play a pivotal role in these ecology-induced transformations, which are no longer limited to the introduction of add-on technologies or process-integrated adaptations, but include changes in product chains, technical systems and economic sectors/clusters.
3   Private economic actors and economic and market mechanisms play an increasingly important role in processes of ecological restructuring, while the role of state agencies changes from bureaucratic, top-down dirigism to 'negotiated rulemaking' and the creation of favourable conditions for such transformation processes.
4   Environmental NGOs change their ideology, and expand their traditional strategy on keeping the environment on the public and political agendas towards participation in direct negotiations with economic agents and state

representatives close to the centre of the decision-making process, and the development of concrete proposals for environmental reform.

5   The process of ecological restructuring is becoming increasingly interdependent with processes of globalization in the political and economic dimension and will therefore not remain confined to the one-nation state.

6   Alternative de-industrialization initiatives for limiting ecological deterioration are applied only to a marginal extent due to limited economic feasibility and poor ideological and political support, among other factors.

I shall consider these six 'hypotheses' and the idea of an emancipation of ecology as Mol's specific contribution to the theory of ecological modernization, and also as his particular interpretation of it.

However, from the above, we may note that Mol prescribes an emancipation of ecology from the economy with a view to distilling an ecological rationale that is independent of and on equal terms with the economy, *without* specifying *what* he understands by such rationale. At the same time, his six hypotheses only address *how to act.* We thus arrive at the fact that, on this point, he truly represents what Szerszynski characterizes as a neomodernistic strategy towards environmental concerns.

Since Mol also, at the theoretical level, insists on the possibility of emancipating from the economy an independent ecology and an ecological rationality, and in this sense thus assumes the objective existence of ecological knowledge, one may here observe a certain contradiction between a modernistic and neomodernistic standpoint, which I shall raise.

Mol has thus failed to move further with his insistence on an institutional reflexivity rather than an individual one, the latter being held up – he argues, and in my opinion correctly – by both Giddens and Beck.

Consequently, I here wish to point to the *second utopian feature* of ecological modernization theory in Mol's version, namely that it insists on continuing the modernization process, whose self-perception will lead to a form of modernization different from the one thus far, where the pursuit of an economic rationality has given rise to environmental problems. However, the different form of modernity implies partly that the economic rationality is to be preserved, partly that it must be supplemented with a form of rationality, the ecological one, to which no content can be attributed (cf. Szerszynski's modern problematic). Furthermore, it has to resort to pre-modern definitions of *autonomy or origin*, and hence breaks with its own assumptions, namely a continuation of modernization, and not a de-modernization.

The two utopian features of ecological modernization outlined and criticized may be supplemented by a slightly more specific critique, if I express myself more directly concerning some of Mol's ideas presented above. In Giddens' version of dis-embedding and re-embedding, which Mol uses quite uncritically, it may be hard to grasp what he means by something being lifted from its traditional context and structure, and subsequently re-established across time and space, and so on. 'What is going on here, if we are to understand this as a social or societal process?' most people might well ask.

If we apply Habermas' and hence also Weber's understanding of the rationalization process, it becomes less mystical, and we should be able to pinpoint the crucial shortcoming in the works of Giddens and Mol. Habermas talks of rationalization of the lifeworld, and Weber about the rationalization of religious worldviews, which in both authorships leads to a capitalist modernization process. As we have seen, this process entails the differentiation of an independent economic system, a state administration, and a differentiation of science, morality and arts. This gives rise to the creation of a potential of reason. However, what is specific to the capitalist modernization process is that only the purposive rationality in the cognitive-instrumental form is returned to the lifeworld to enrich it, to make it more reasoned. Hence the whole wretched business, or as Habermas puts it, hence 'the one-sided modernization process' with all its imbalances and environmental problems.

According to Giddens, and hence Mol, the re-embedding is devoid of problems, or differently phrased, it is not raised as a point of criticism that such a re-connection should cause significant trouble or be subjected to systematic barriers. This is in line with what the cultural pessimists term alienation, and what Habermas instead calls the modern form of understanding. Mol *assumes* that the re-embedding occurs, or *can* occur as described through a normative formulation.

Moreover, we observe the problem in Mol's thinking – as well as among the other exponents of ecological modernization theory – that they do not operate with an explicit concept for what they mean by modernization. Put differently, what is to them the epochally specific social process that modernizes society?

If we only look at ecological modernization theory in its ideal intention, there is no doubt that an ecological or environmental parameter can be, and in fact is being, implemented in the economic decision-making process. However, seen from a wider and long-term perspective, this remains within the framework of an economic rationality, for example in the shape of market concerns and PR management. At least Mol owes us an explanation of why the agents should move beyond this towards *further* ecological considerations. And he owes us documentation that this is actually taking place at an institutional level or to an institutional extent.[8]

This still leaves us with the problem that the addition of physical nature and man-made environment as a parameter in economic decision-making processes *does not* transcend *instrumental reason*, and hence a one-sided modernization process continues.[9]

Hajer's ecological modernization discourse

Hajer also acknowledges that the way in which institutions work creates a fundamental problem. However, in contrast to everyone else on the subject of ecological modernization, he questions whether it is right to talk of an *ecological* crisis or, put differently, whether an ecological crisis should be the starting point for a theory and practice of ecological modernization. Nor does he find that the problem can be solved by adding to the modernization process an element of *ecology* to any wider or lesser degree.

Instead of ecological crisis, he prefers to talk of ecological dilemma. Actually, this is not a new historical phenomenon, as society has always had to decide on what actions are acceptable and unacceptable, what is ecologically and socially feasible, and what is not. In this choice lies the ecological dilemma, because there will always be both pros and cons when the question is seen in its proper social context.

Therefore, the fundamental problem of modern society shall not be solved by making modernization ecological, but by recognizing that the ecological dilemma is culturally determined, and can only been given more or less *socially* acceptable solutions. There is no objective truth that can lead us to this. On the contrary, we find ourselves in a discursive reality as a result of complicated social processes.

This is the position that Hajer characterizes as 'cultural politics and discourse', which he contrasts with the view of ecological modernization as 'institutional learning' or as a 'technocratic project'. In the former position, the problem is perceived as a question of getting a grip on a 'nature out of control', and in the latter, it is viewed as a question of getting on top of 'technology out of control'. In both cases, the aim is to add pure ecology to modernization. This is assumed to be possible, because such an ecology can be objectively identified (Hajer, 1996, pp248–260).

In view of such a position of discursive theory and social constructivism, it is not Hajer's intention to look into what lies behind the metaphors of ecological discourse. Rather he wishes to:

> try to encircle them to be able to challenge them scientifically, and to enhance consciousness of the contingency of knowledge about ecological matters. What is more, it [the position] would investigate the cultural consequences of prevailing story-lines and would seek to find out which social forces propel this ecomodernist discourse-coalition. Once the implicit future scenarios have been exposed, they might lead to a more reflective attitude towards certain environmental constructs and perhaps even to the formulation of alternative scenarios, the socio-political consequences of which would present a more attractive, more fair, or more responsible package. Hence the central concern of this third interpretation [of ecological modernization] is with cognitive reflectivity, argumentation and negotiated social choice.
>
> Hajer, 1996, pp258–259

In such an arrangement of open debate and free choice, it is incumbent upon the theory to open 'the black boxes of society, technology and nature' (Hajer, 1996, p259). From this perspective, it is not credible that nature can be understood and handled by 'framing it' in a new 'ecological language', for instance by giving priority to economy and system ecology, because it does not recognize the existence of such a 'pure' language. Alternatively, it will contrast different languages and forms of knowledge (e.g. expert knowledge versus lay knowledge), and in this manner gain a deeper insight into the nature of ecological problems.

The radical consequence of such a viewpoint, in particular for science, will be that what is characterized as ecological crisis is turned on its head: the debate will no longer be about protecting nature, but about what nature and what society we want for ourselves (Hajer, 1996, p259). If people, after deconstructing for instance the naturalistic and realistic assumptions of a biosphere discourse, become aware of its political and economic motivations, and hence become forced to take their own naturalism seriously, it may stimulate their interests in the myriad ways in which we create, destroy, change and recreate 'nature' and 'human nature'. If technology were not seen beforehand and by itself as something problematic, but as a potential force to reconstruct social relations between nature, technology and society in relation to one's own needs and preferences, it could lead the debate to shed its simplistic mould of modernity versus anti-modernity, and instead give rise to a debate about a recreation of society. One consequence would be that the debate would no longer focus on environmental issues, but instead on the conceptualization of different techniques, on the application of certain techniques, and on the preferred way of socializing nature, Hajer hopes (Hajer, 1996, p259).

However, from this position it may seem strange that Hajer considers himself to be part of the discourse of ecological modernization. From the above presentation it is clear that he rejects its core point: an *ecological* reconstruction of the modernization process in the view of an objective reality and drawing on a correspondingly universal ecological language. Authors such as Buttel and Murphy also mention that Hajer in many ways does not belong within the self-perception of ecological modernization.[10]

Indeed, Hajer may be said to represent a consistent neomodernism which stands in stark contrast to other theory in the field of ecological modernization, primarily because he consistently writes off the existence of an objectively existing ecological knowledge, as is more or less explicitly assumed in the other literature on the subject of ecological modernization. In addition, and as a corollary of this, because he claims that there is a discourse-theoretical standpoint, according to which knowledge and insights are achieved through the so-called story-lines. And finally, because he insists that the production of knowledge is not centrally manageable, but has to be a decentralized process. The two latter conditions, however, are much more ambiguously presented among the rest of the exponents of ecological modernization theory. I shall elaborate on this below.

However, whether ecological modernization be characterized as strong modernism or as neomodernistic, it is noticeable that Szerszynski offers an option between two roads to ecology on a modern basis: either a technocratic path or a development built on human self-assertion, in which the real has been abolished, and where humanity awards itself the role of freely creating and asserting its own meanings in a world which has none of its own (Szerszynski, 1996, pp118–119).

In somewhat simplistic terms, Mol and Hajer represent two such development paths, Mol the one of technocracy, Hajer of nihilistic free creation. In addition, the difference between the two apparently lies in the fact that Hajer seems conscious of his position, whereas Mol looks split between a modernistic and neomodernistic way of thinking.

Hajer's version of ecological modernization theory also diverges clearly from Mol's by explicitly distancing itself from what he calls a techno-corporative regime in the practical accomplishment of ecological modernization. Here, I shall elaborate on what he sees as the alternative to such a techno-corporative regime, and what other visions he identifies in the discourse of ecological modernization.

Hajer's social constructivist and discourse-analytical foundation brings him to focus on conflicts concerning the meaning of physical or social phenomena, and on the story-lines playing a key role in this, since they determine the interaction between physical and social realities. When, based on this position, he takes a critical stance towards an understanding of ecological modernization as institutional reflexivity, questioning whether this represents reflexivity in practice, it is because he takes reflexivity to mean something completely different.

In his form of understanding, the ecological crisis is a 'discourse of self-confrontation', which calls for a re-assessment of the institutional practices that have provoked it. Moreover, Hajer, has defined reflexivity as an essentially discursive quality. 'Reflexivity is a quality of discursive practices that illuminates the effect of certain social and cognitive systems of classification and categorization on our perception of reality' (Hajer, 1995, p280).

His analysis of the ecological modernization in Holland and England in the 1970s and 1980s, as a reaction to acid rain problems, revealed that very different understandings prevailed – both in the general public and within the various political apparatuses – of how the systems and categories introduced also had negative effects in the shape of pollution and environmental degradation. These understandings encompassed thoughts about changes in the existing practice, but did not produce any debate as to what the modernizing developments should bring about, a debate not as an end it itself, but as a democratically minded process that could lead to social change and to a at least partially shared vision of the future.

Accordingly, Hajer sees the ideal reflexive ecological modernization as a democratic process with conscious choices relating to different alternative development scenarios. This choice should not merely be determined by instrumental rationality criteria, but also stimulates a debate on the norms and values that ought to underlie modernization. The form of reflexivity envisaged by Hajer in this connection is linked to Mary Douglas' perception of pollution as 'matter out of place'. This means that reflexive ecological modernization centres the discussion on the social order or structure, according to which we define what determines the pollution (Hajer, 1995, p281).

While a techno-corporative regime relies on an objective reality of expert explanations, which seek a universal language able to contribute to carrying through the most effective and efficient solution to an unambiguous problem, the reflexive ecological modernization takes the opposite path. It assumes that there is a public space, in which social realities and preferences determine which social practices are to be respected, and which ones must be changed. Within this space, the real challenge is to establish new institutional arrangements instead of relying on existing expert regimes.

One implication is a focus on interdisciplinarity as opposed to specialization. The scientific monopoly on the claim to truth is contested, and it is acknowledged that knowledge is conditional and not self-contained. This means, for instance, that the traditional view that science produces truth is no longer viable, whereas it must be recognized that science can, at most, put forward claims to the truth. Hajer refers to Beck's observation that the development in recent decades has brought about a neglect of critical capacities, and instead led to a delegation of some of the most significant decisions to expert committees and councils beyond democratic control (Hajer, 1995, p282).

With his ideal of a reflexive ecological modernization, Hajer demands the opposite, and calls for an institutional practice that makes it possible to contrast different forms of knowledge and 'rather than orientating ourselves on science as the universal discourse, one might choose to facilitate the institutionalization of a public language that would allow for productive inter-discursive debates. Here scenarios of societal modernization might become the point of integration' (Hajer, 1995, p282).

It is quite likely, Hajer thinks, that the public's understanding of key problems turns out to be much more mature than what is to the liking of both politicians and experts. However, they forget that – although examples can be found of people susceptible to apocalyptic narratives, to manipulation with statistics and visions of destruction – the image of the ignorant lay person and the all-knowing expert is no longer based on reality. The so-called experts have lost much authority over recent decades due to their flawed handling of environmental issues, for instance the denial of evident risks. Moreover, it is precisely the environmental question which has shown that, in many situations, expertise has been 'fabricated' by leaving out numerous other forms of relevant knowledge. In such situations, Hajer finds that a critical public may serve a clarifying function, as opposed to what is sometimes claimed by conservative politicians, who see the man-in-the-street as manipulated by shrewd purveyors of rhetoric.

Such a vision of an ideal reflexive ecological modernization will also require a comprehensive establishment of different forms of public space and debate capable of rendering visible the hidden assumptions, implicit commitments, and not least of creating and fostering insights into what Hajer calls the ecological dilemma, because a central aim of his book is to argue that environmental polity cannot be about solving the ecological crisis. It must be aimed at finding patterns of modernization that are, at best, less wasteful and free of undesired social side-effects. In addition, the reflexive debate should seek to lay out the options and costs, and in this manner end a mediocre natural-scientific environmentalist struggle, demanding instead a more explicit political exposition and reflection on what development society really wants (Hajer, 1995, p283).

Understandably, Hajer himself is not without concerns regarding such reflexive modernization. He refers to experiences of various public hearings in Germany and Holland, where for instance lack of commitment to reaching specific regulations and the use of professional information mediators has led to confusion, upsetting the environmental critique instead of bringing clarity. It is inferred that such confusion may indeed have been the goal. He also highlights how the generally growing environmental awareness has brought about a need to legitimize all sorts of decisions, and how public hearings have, on some occasions, turned out to be very useful to such legitimization, without producing actual environmental improvements. Finally, he stresses that some of the arrangements adduced in Europe as suitable to generate environmentally better and more democratic decisions have been in use in the USA for years, without necessarily achieving such improvements, indeed, having only increased the time and money costs (Hajer, 1995, pp284–85).

Nevertheless, he ascribes such cases to a misconceived design of hearings and reflexive institutional arrangements, and not to problems associated with public participation as such. Accordingly, he sees *reflexive institutional arrangements* as an alternative to institutional reflexivity, cf. Mol and others. He wants to establish such arrangements on the basis of an understanding of politics as a process in which discourse coalitions are created by a common definition of reality, whose success criteria are credibility, acceptability and trust. In addition, these preconditions must be met (Hajer, 1995, pp287–288):

1   Attention must be paid to the socio-cognitive basis for discourse coalitions, i.e. it must be assessed beforehand whether such coalitions can be forged, or whether unrelated circumstances rule this out in advance.
2   The arrangement cannot be based upon preconceived determination of the problems, but must indeed be aimed at piecing together the social or societal problems.
3   It must be clarified who defines the problems, who takes part, and what types of solutions may be considered.

He believes that the results of such reflexive arrangements will be (Hajer, 1995, pp291–292):

1   Nascent understanding of ecological modernization as a common political project for social change.
2   Dynamism being returned to the political process.
3   More balanced relations of power between companies, governments, NGOs and community groups.
4   Clarification of where social consensus is possible, and where it is *not*, hence requiring a choice to be made.

In this outline of both preconditions and expected results, it becomes clear that Hajer's idea of reflexive institutional arrangements is a kind of consensus-seeking conference on specific topics capable of gathering the social and the environmental dimension in the same discourse coalition, and thus achieving – in addition to transparency in the premises and consequences of decision-making – a decision that is socially embedded and shaped, as opposed to dominated by technical or economic criteria. This is what he elsewhere calls a 'socialization of ecology' (Hajer, 1996, p265). In the same part, he stresses that, viewed in this manner, it becomes clear that the debate on the ecological crisis is among the few spaces left in which we may reflect upon what modernity is. Apart from the environmental problems, we may discuss the issue of social justice, democracy, responsibility, the relationship between man and nature, the role of technology in society, what it means to be human, and so on.

Consequently, according to Hajer, ecology should not be technified, rationalized (as in Mol's emancipation) or 'overrule' the social, but instead be turned on its head to be seen as an element that does indeed influence social and societal conditions, which is precisely why it must be handled on the basis of social or societal needs. He admits that the predominant development trend consists of the former two (technification and rationalization), but sees it as the main task to create conditions paving the way for a socialization of ecology.

On the face of it, this standpoint may appear simply innocent, perhaps also self-evident. However, upon closer inspection, it should open one's eyes wide. Because the corollary of such thinking must be that it is society's conditions and needs that determine *how* an environmental problem is perceived, and *what* should and *can* be done about it, and *not* an abstract or indeterminate concept about some ecology. If an ecological analysis produces the assessment that the issue concerned is not satisfactory, it is also society's conditions and needs that have to determine in what manner the social practices must undergo change with a view to achieving a satisfactory outcome. It is also inherent to this line of argument that a satisfactory outcome *may* be a *change* in the ecology or ecosystem in question in a direction deemed to be desirable or acceptable to society. Thus, the order of priorities is clear and direct: society first.

Another task is to make this priority both explicit and deliberate. This certainly does not happen by itself, or follow from the given circumstances. On the contrary, it is Hajer's thesis that the predominant practice of rationalization and technification of ecology is also *de facto* ruled by specific needs and interests in society, but that this takes place discursively or within a 'framing' that does not reflect its social consequences and is not called by its proper name – that is, determined by vested interests and not by the processes of society.

It is definitely to Hajer's credit that his forthright insistence on the social context of ecology has not only pointed to the prioritization concerning environmental issues, but also shown that regardless of how environmental issues are perceived or interpreted, they always have social consequences that one may relate to, instead of 'only' acting in the name of ecology.

Paradoxically, despite this, the problems in his presentation occur precisely in the field of societal aspects. In the discursive analyses and mappings of actors in society and their forms of agitation, the structure and functioning of society 'is lost'. Hajer does not come much further than Beck, since they both see the need for incorporating alternatives, whether it be in the shape of expertise, interests or interpretation. Beck calls it 'subpolitics', Hajer uses the term 'reflexive institutional arrangements'. But why does the need for such arrangements arise? Why is the existing social practice on a collision course towards disaster? And why can society, despite massive endeavours, not steer clear of this course? What are the obstacles and what are the opportunities to incorporate the suggested arrangements in relation to existing practices and structures?

When Hajer holds up 'socialization of ecology' as a prospect for development and stresses the opportunities to discuss what modernity *could be* under this heading, I have to suggest that the starting point for such a discussion be the concept of modernity – that is, what is the content of the concepts of modernity that he has applied to arrive at such a discussion? At no point in his presentation of ecological modernization as discourse of cultural politics does he explain his concepts of the modern. He does not make clear how he understands modernity at present, or why he sees it is problematic.

In this manner, the questions that I raised at the beginning of the presentation in this Chapter 4, and also in Chapter 2, are left out of the analysis. First, how do the characteristics of modernity impinge upon the emergence of environmental problems? This question includes: what type of environmental problems, what are their characteristics, and how are they understood or interpreted? Second, how does modernity affect our forms of action, and our scope for action? Third, based upon such an understanding of modernization, what opportunities may be outlined for steering it in an ecological direction?

In fairness, Hajer is not totally silent on the issue of a concept of modernization, because he claims that he builds his analysis on Beck's theory of reflexive modernization. Perhaps the problem thus stems from Beck actually not having explained his concept of reflexive modernization, as discussed in Chapter 3. Hajer does state that his concept of reflexivity is decisively different from that of Beck. While Beck perceives 'reflexivity as the self-confrontation of society or unintentional self-endangerment and distinguishes this from reflection which refers to the knowledge one may have of these processes' (Hajer, 1995, p40), Hajer's own concept of reflexivity is related to the quality of discursive practices:

> *Drawing on the insights of discourse-theory (…) I see reflexivity in the first instance as a relational notion that should be seen as a quality of discursive practices in which actors engage. Such practices are reflexive if they allow for the monitoring and assessment of the effect of certain social and cognitive systems of classification and categorization on our perception of reality. Reflexivity can thus be a quality of a metaphor or story-line that in a given context changes the perception of future perspectives. [...] But reflexivity may also be a consequence of the introduction of dissident voices in established institutional routines which interrupts the routinized way of seeing a specific institutional realm. The reflexivity of actors is thus related to the extent to which they are able to mobilize and participate in practices that allow for the recognition of the limits to their own knowledge-base.*

> Hajer, 1995, p40

Included in the first and the second of the questions presented above must thus be: what can be understood by reflexivity, and in what manner is this linked to modernity itself?

The importance of determining this relation is abundantly clear from the quote in which Hajer sees reflexivity as a quality related to the *abilities* of the individual to see new perspectives or opportunities, or as a quality of a practice if it contains scope for nurturing new *perceptions* of the future. Here, he is attributing the reflexive elements to the actors as a property with which they may be equipped, or which they may be able to practise; in short, something they can *choose* to do, albeit based on mature insight.

I do not find such a view of the concept of reflexivity to be essentially different from Beck's concept, which is also determined according to categories of individual conduct, and not according to concepts of social structures, cf. Chapter 3 in the section on Beck's reflexivity.

If we compare such a concept with Hajer's critique of Mol's institutional reflexivity and his own vision of an alternative to this, namely reflexive institutional arrangements, which by definition have to entail an institutional form of action, it becomes clear that Hajer operates with several essentially different perceptions of what reflexive modernity is. Or more exactly, what reflexive modernity *can* be. Because what he ultimately associates with modernity is apparent in the above presentation of his view on ecological modernization – that is, that to him it is a question of *choosing* the *right form* of it. We shall examine this more closely in the next section.

Modernity and reflexivity according to Mol and Hajer

In the presentation of the theory of ecological modernization, we have become acquainted with three different uses of the concept of reflexivity in connection with modern society. Therefore, it is a well-founded assumption that the concept plays a special role, or occupies a central position in these theories.

Accordingly, both Mol and Hajer stress repeatedly that they are building theoretically upon Beck's and Giddens' concepts of reflexive modernity. However, while both Beck and Giddens see reflexivity as the aspect that creates the crisis of modern society, including environmental problems and risks, Mol and Hajer draw on their concepts with a diametrically opposite view, ascribing a decisive role to the reflexivity of modernity, or rather to the reflexivity *in* modernity, as an element contributing to *counter* the negative effects of modernity, particularly formulated in relation to the ecological crisis.

As mentioned, it is also my view that reflexivity should be seen as something beneficial, and not the opposite. But what motivates Mol and Hajer to change the meaning of reflexivity within the theory of ecological modernization? Is it because the concepts from the works of Beck and Giddens are unclear or contradictorily presented, as I have demonstrated above? Do Mol and Hajer deliberately attribute a different meaning to the concepts than what was originally intended? Or does it spring from the context in which the concepts are used being vaguely defined, and hence allowing for both the negative and the positive version of the meaning of reflexivity, depending on such definition?

In an attempt to shed light on these questions, I shall make the three uses explicit. This will serve to elaborate on the differences in approaches to ecological modernization theory, and to elucidate the chances of ecological modernization – in one form or another – enabling change away from the hitherto one-sided form of modernization.

The three uses of the reflexivity concept on the occasion of the presented theories of ecological modernization have already been described as, respectively, individual reflexivity, institutional reflexivity and reflexive institutional arrangements.

By using the term reflexivity as *individual reflexivity*, it is associated with individual action and reaction to a societal situation. Thus, it could also be characterized as individually *mediated* reflexivity. This is clearly the form that Hajer expresses in the above quote on his understanding of reflexivity. It is the individual who perceives an opportunity for reflexivity. This is also how both Wynne and Smart interpret Beck's and Giddens' concepts of reflexive modernity, cf. the critique in Chapter 3 of their 'rational-choice' approach and their failure to attribute any collective substance to the reflexivity of lay people.

If reflexivity is used as *institutional reflexivity*, it focuses on reflexive action as an institutional form of reaction in relation to external circumstances. This is what we meet in the works of Mol and Spaargaren, but also the authorship of Buttel may be seen as an example of this. Institutional reflexivity is when Mol talks of, for instance, 'reflexive (re)design of central institutions of modernity', when he states that 'reflexive modernity still rests on the central institutions of modernity', or when he writes about emancipation of *the* ecology from *the* economy. As mentioned, Mol builds his theory on Beck's and especially Giddens' concept of reflexive modernity (Mol, 1995, pp28–34). Accordingly, Giddens' concepts can be construed as both individual and institutional reflexivity. Mol also writes, as indicated above, that the concept of reflexive modernization seems to contain some connotations that are incompatible with institutional reflexivity (Mol, 1995, p25), and he thus insists on an interpretation of Giddens in this direction.

Finally, the use of reflexivity as *reflexive institutional arrangements* may be elaborated upon by direct reference to Hajer's formulation of such arrangements. They are a way of carrying through a true or ideal reflexive ecological modernization, as opposed to what Hajer sees as a techno-corporative ecological modernization. What is remarkable in this connection is that Hajer actually defines his understanding of reflexivity in a manner that has to be categorized as individual reflexivity in the above sense. However, at the same time, he finds an institutional reflexivity to be necessary to establish an ecological modernization that is not corporative and technocratic, but is capable of 'socializing' the ecological element, and also of stimulating the debate on norms and values.

This brings us to the core of ecological modernization theory's understanding of reflexivity, and of the use of this concept by the entire school of thought.

Reflexivity is something that we choose, it is an action form that springs from an *ecologically* rational choice and an *economically* rational choice.

Mol also sees reflexivity, with his vision of emancipating the ecology, as something the companies choose, because it is the wisest option, because it is ecologically *and* economically rational.

Equally according to Giddens and Beck, we see that the constant flow of information is something that results in reflexive conduct. However, since they give no other explanation as to why individuals react to this information flow, this form of conduct also has to be characterized as being of a voluntary nature, as it must thus be assumed that individuals *choose* to relate to this information.

Consequently, this theoretical tradition still needs to explain *why* this choice is taken and with a view to *what*.

It has thus been clarified once again that neither Mol nor Hajer have any explicit concept of modernization, which is why they cannot explain *what* motivates the described forms of action.

However, Chapter 3 has already pointed to the likely feasibility of identifying all three forms of reflexivity based on a concept of modernization which is different from ecological modernization. Therefore, I shall below determine these three forms of reflexive processes, using Habermas' modernization concept as the starting point.

Such an exercise will, *first*, elucidate the problems of the concepts of ecological modernization, including when we see them deployed in practice, as we will in the subsequent section. *Second*, I shall synthesize the definitions of reflexivity made thus far on the basis of the abstractions of the modernization concept in Chapter 4. And accordingly, *third*, prepare a presentation of such reflexive processes in their real form in Chapter 5.

The forms of reflexivity

A foundation in Habermas' concept of modernization reveals that the reflexivity concepts of the ecological modernization school mix together the action forms of the lifeworld and of systems. Put more succinctly, the theories of ecological modernization fail to make a distinction between these two forms of action, and hence allow for understanding the concept of reflexive modernity presented by Giddens and others as both an individual and an institutional form of action, though noticeably passing over the differences.

However, applying Habermas' concept of modernization allows us, first, to distinguish between these two forms of action, and second, to incorporate fundamental forms of modernization, respectively the continued rationalization of the lifeworld, continued capitalization concerning the economic system, and continued bureaucratization as regards the administrative system. This allows us to introduce the dynamism that is lacking in the understanding of the various reflexive forms of action or processes.

Accordingly, drawing on the concepts of the lifeworld and the system, I shall below distinguish between the two basic forms of reflexivity in the modernization process, using the terms, respectively, *reflexivity on the basis of the lifeworld* and *reflexivity with a systemic form of organization.* To this I shall add a third form of reflexivity, which arises when these basic forms are deployed in combination in one and the same process. I shall term this combined form a *reflexive arrangement.*

The modernization of society, in the Habermasian realm of concepts, is mediated by communication. Therefore, we may characterize reflexivity as a communicative form of action, distinguishing between the reflexivity that forms part of the rationalization of the lifeworld by means of communicatively accomplished mutual processes of understanding, and the reflexivity that forms part of communicative processes via systemic media. In the economic system, this is the medium of money – or, continued capitalization – and in the administrative system, this is the medium of power, that is, continued bureaucratization.

The dynamics behind these various reflexive processes are thus generated by, first, processes of understanding being enacted through linguistic communication, second, through media-steered processes that need to satisfy media imperatives – profit and legitimacy. In short, rationally motivated mutual understanding within the lifeworld, maximization of profit within the economic system, and maximization of legitimacy within the administration.

We may also characterize reflexivity within this framework as various learning processes involved in communicative forms of action. In this manner, the forms of action seek to achieve understanding or insight into a specific phenomenon, or into the origin and consequence of something. Moreover, such learning processes have to enable extrication from predeterminations laid down beforehand or passed down, though such given forms of understanding may also constitute part of the learning.

Reflexivity on the basis of the lifeworld may then be described as a process that aims to *reach understanding of something* – its origin and consequence – in the outer world, the social world or the inner world, in which this understanding is realized through a *combination* of communicative action, a normative foundation and cultural legacies.[11] The more reflexivity takes place against the background of a *rationalized* lifeworld, the more it will be based on communicative action rather than on normative and cultural legacies.

Although reflexivity in this form is construed as a communicative process with linguistically mediated action coordination – through the achievement of mutual understanding on the basis of the other components of the lifeworld – as an interactive process between two or more participants – reflexivity may well be exercised individually. In that case, the acting subject will incorporate the *experiences* or the results of previously conducted communicative action. Reflexivity on the basis of the lifeworld may thus be seen as a subjective as well as a social process. However, only when this subjective reflexivity targets or addresses all three world relations – that is, the outer, the social and the inner world, one may talk of a reflexivity that is involved in the continued rationalization of the lifeworld. And only this latter form of reflexivity is concerned with what is here described as individually exercised reflexivity on the basis of the lifeworld.

Against this background, *reflexivity with a systemic form of organization* must be characterized as a borderline case that concerns only the outer world, and in which the teleological and strategic forms of action, with their corresponding form of rationality, are decisive – that is, displace the forms of action oriented to reaching understanding. In this case, communication is media-steered, and the reflexive processes are involved in the pursuit of the imperatives of the steering medium concerned – just as their underlying and one-sided form of action, they are arranged with a view to *meeting a specific objective*. In the economic system, this is the maximization of profit, and in the administrative system, this is the maximization of legitimacy. This form of reflexivity thus cuts itself off from reflexivity on the basis of the lifeworld, focusing on technical and realizable knowledge in pursuit of the media-steered imperatives. In this sense, the reflexivity with a systemic form of organization 'colonizes' reflexivity on the basis of the lifeworld.

Both forms of reflexivity are essential to the modernization process, and take place precisely because of their differentiation one by one, independently of each other, although, in a wider sense, they may be construed as preconditions for each other. This is because continued growth in systemic complexity presupposes continued rationalization of the lifeworld, and vice versa, and because the more advanced modernization has become, the more the material reproduction of the lifeworld takes place through the system.

However, these different and apparently self-ruling reflexive processes may be brought together through an arrangement that makes the *linguistically communicative* and the *media-steered* reflexivity explicit through a variety of actors in one coherent process. That is, an arrangement that sets out to unleash reflexive processes concerning a given issue *both* on the basis of the lifeworld *and* with a systemic form of organization. Thus, this is not a reflexivity *either* on the basis of the lifeworld – that is, a process exclusively oriented to reaching understanding – *or* with a systemic form of organization – an exclusively purposive-oriented process. Instead, if both the understanding- and purposive-oriented aspects are made explicit, it may be characterized as a *specific* reflexive process. It is this specific reflexive process that I will call *a reflexive arrangement*. Its characteristic is an ability to transcend the *one-sidedness* of both the lifeworld and the systems.

Reflexivity on the basis of the lifeworld is thus involved in social integration on a modernized foundation – that is, precisely from the point in history when society must be understood as both lifeworld and system. Similarly, reflexivity with a systemic form of organization is part of systemic integration from this same point in time, cf. Habermas' distinction between *social* and *system* integration on pp93–94. Drawing on these concepts of integration, I shall therefore, for the sake of ease, also characterize reflexivity on the basis of the lifeworld as *socially mediated reflexivity*, keeping in mind that it may be exercised in a subjective as well as an interactive form. Along the same lines, I shall describe reflexivity with a systemic form of organization as *systemically mediated reflexivity*, which is, of course, exercised by individuals, but in pursuit of systemic objectives. The third form of reflexivity I shall still term only a *reflexive arrangement*, although it could also, in parallel with the conception of society as lifeworld and system at one and the same time, be called *society-mediated reflexivity*.

The two basic forms of reflexivity may be summed up as follows:
Reflexivity on the basis of the lifeworld (*socially mediated reflexivity*):

- Modern differentiation of the objective, the social and the subjective world enables a reflexive approach to the surrounding world.
- Reflexivity is possible in an individual form, if it encompasses the outer, the social and the inner world, as well as the experiences or results of previous communicative actions.
- Reflexivity contributes to continued rationalization of the lifeworld – that is, which forms of action determined by norms or cultural legacies are replaced by action oriented towards reaching understanding by means of communication.
- Reflexivity becomes a necessity as the action oriented to reaching understanding 'takes over'.
- Reflexivity in individual form = reflection, cf. the above on page 200.

Reflexivity with a systemic form of organization (*systemically mediated reflexivity*):

- Systemically mediated reflexivity is enabled by the modern differentiation of an independent economic system and an independent administrative system.
- Systemically mediated reflexivity contributes to a continuous increase in systemic complexity by means of capitalization within the economic system, and of bureaucratization within the administrative system.
- Systemically mediated reflexivity is required for the reproduction of the system.
- Systemically mediated reflexivity = institutional reflexivity = instrumental reflexivity.

Using these two basic forms, I am thus distinguishing fundamentally between *socially mediated* and *systemically mediated* reflexivity. The systemically mediated variant takes place within an institutionalized system, and may hence also be described as institutional reflexivity, in line with the above. On the face of it, this latter term may be preferable, since it more aptly fits the ability of an institution as such to act, whereas a system cannot be readily associated with an acting subject, but is rather something within which action takes place, or something that sets the framework for action.

Nevertheless, I shall insist on the term systemically mediated reflexivity, because it more directly contrasts this form with the reflexivity that starts from the lifeworld, though keeping in mind the nuances in the terms 'institutional' and 'systemic'.

Systemically mediated reflexivity affects the modernization process *directly*. This sets it apart from socially mediated reflexivity, which may, however, contribute to continued rationalization of the lifeworld, without which continued modernization of the system cannot, ultimately, occur. But systemically mediated reflexivity does not entail any break with *one-sided* modernization. This may instead happen by means of extraordinary mediation on the basis of socially mediated reflexivity.

Ecological modernization in the version of Mol uses reflexivity solely in the institutional sense, whereas Beck and Giddens refer to reflexivity in the individual sense. Hajer also conceives it in the individual sense, but finds that an institutional reflexivity is necessary to move beyond a techno-corporative regime.

Beck sees the existence of reflexivity as something creating problems, because the experts of the formal system focus on isolated objectives, and because lay people's critical reflection erodes the authority, and corresponding scope for action, of modern institutions. The theories of ecological modernization see reflexivity as a beneficial and necessary part of continued modernization. However, ecological modernization in Mol's version does not comprehend how institutional reflexivity causes limitations to the modernization process. He passes over the purposive imperatives of the modernization process. Hajer notes these limitations as an empirical fact, but wishes to change this trend by *choosing* the right form of reflexivity.

Reflexivity in the individual form, which is included in the definition of reflexivity on the basis of the lifeworld, is highly significant, because it stresses the individual's need for adaptation to the outer and to the social world, regardless of the freedom – attained under modernity – from cultural legacies and social norms. For example, reflexivity in the individual form is always attached to the lifeworld, but may well be related to activities aimed at securing the individual's reproduction through the system, even if it is not involved in reproduction of the system itself.

Conversely, reflexivity in the individual form is also manifested as the possibility and perhaps the necessity of criticism[12] of the outer and the social world, and conceivably of self-criticism, regardless of the subjective status attained. Whether we are dealing with criticism or adaptation, this is the socially mediated reflexivity in individual form which individuals must, according to Beck, exercise due to individualization in society forcing individuals to create their own biography, as well as to take on individual responsibility for action, even though such action is not determined by free choice, but is structured from the outside (Beck, 1994, pp15, 22).

Nonetheless, whether in the case of criticism of or adaptation to the outer world, reflexivity in individual form means the same as reflection. Beck fails in his attempt to distinguish between 'reflexivity' and 'reflection' (Beck, 1994, pp175–178), precisely because his concept of reflexivity really contains only individual reflexivity, as also stressed by the critique of Wynne and Smart referred to in Chapter 3 (page 126).

Due to the critical function of reflexivity, or its involvement in adaptation to the outer or social world, it may by oriented both towards reaching understanding and oriented to success.

Reflexivity within the economic system stems directly from the continued capitalization of productive enterprises, which are forced by market forces to constantly revolutionize their own material and economic foundations in order to preserve their market position. First a formal, then subsequently a real, subsumption of the productive process takes place, in line with the excursus covering this, presented in Chapter 3. This is the constant revolutionizing that occurs by means of a systemic form of reflexivity. The process is controlled by the steering medium of money and its attendant imperatives.

Reflexivity within the administrative system stems directly from continued bureaucratization – that is, judicialization of administrative action, which is forced upon the administration for it to preserve its legitimacy between the joint pressures of reproductive service delivery to the labour force and its crisis management vis-à-vis the economic system. Consequently, the reflexive processes of the administrative system are controlled by the steering medium of power and its attendant imperatives. Since the material production of the administration takes place through the economic system, its reflexive processes may well be oriented towards this reproduction – as it occurs through its crisis management – and thus be comparable to reflexivity within the economic system. This happens, for instance, when the state acts as an entrepreneur in connection with counter-recessionary and growth-boosting infrastructure policies.[13]

Accordingly, whether reflexivity takes place in the economic or the administrative system, it does not express a choice, but a necessity. It is characterized as purposive action, and it is always attached to the system. Thus, it always unfolds on the basis of the system's own rules and terms – that is, controlled by the steering media of money or power, and their imperatives. This clearly sets it apart from reflexivity in the individual form. Systemically mediated reflexivity is therefore different from reflection, or rather, it is more than mere reflection, since it is ultimately governed by the pursuit of certain objectives.

The forms of rationality associated with the various forms of reflexivity appear from the above. Only through the action orientation of reflexivity is it possible realize communicative rationality to its full extent. As seen above in Chapter 3, this implies proportional truth, normative rightness and subjective truthfulness within the three fields of objective thinking, moral-practical insight and aesthetic observation. Conversely, systemically mediated reflexivity, with its orientation to success, will be dominated by instrumental reason.

For that reason, systemically mediated rationality does not break with the one-sided modernization process. Nor does socially mediated reflexivity – which *may* have implications beyond instrumental reason – lead directly to a break with the one-sided modernization process, since it takes place on the basis of the lifeworld. Achieving such a break in specific instances requires *the socially mediated reflexivity's transcendence of instrumental reason to be mediated to the systemic modernization.*

This is where the *reflexive arrangement* enters the frame. The reflexive arrangement *may* imply a move beyond instrumental reason – that is, it may realize the communicative rationality to its full extent. However, since such an

Figure 4.1 *Three different forms of reflexivity or reflexive process, their motivation and action orientation*

Type of reflexivity or reflexive process	Motivation/reason	Action orientation
Socially mediated reflexivity	Criticism/adaptation	Oriented to reaching understanding/success
Systemically mediated reflexivity	Capitalization/ bureaucratization	Oriented to success
Reflexive arrangement	Criticism/change	Oriented to reaching understanding/success

arrangement is not a permanent part of the system, and furthermore is not involved in the lifeworld, such *transcendence of systemic instrumentality* must take place by means of *extraordinary mediation*. An extraordinary transcendence of instrumental reason may thus occur whether a reflexive arrangement targets the system or the lifeworld. It may also contribute to such a transcendence being mediated to the system where it concerns going beyond instrumental reason through individual reflexivity.

Figure 4.1 has been drawn up in support of the distinction between the two basic forms of reflexivity, and a reflexive process arranged on the basis thereof.

What first draws the attention is that the table combines the action forms of the lifeworld and the systems. This possibility arises by reflexivity in individual form taking place, on the face of it, on the basis of the lifeworld, but in fact being able to focus on the conditions of the system. Moreover, reflexive arrangements may be one-sidedly attached to the lifeworld or one-sidedly to the system. However, it is when a reflexive arrangement relates to both at the same time that momentous forces are unleashed. Though the starting point is the possibility of distinguishing between a systemically mediated reflexivity and the reflexive forms of the lifeworld, it is indeed the combination of these very forms of reflexivity that synthesizes the explosives for changing the one-sidedness of modernization.

In Chapter 5, we shall look at how extraordinary mediations between the various forms of reflexivity may take place in practice, and hence how to allow for the possibility of specific breaks with one-sided modernization.

The practice of ecological modernization

In the first half of this chapter, we looked at how widely differing meanings are attributed to ecological modernization, both concerning the dimensions covered by a theoretical approach, and in cases where more practical forms of deployment are involved. However, as wide-ranging as the meanings and applications of the concept appear to be, just as wide-ranging is the evident interest in both aspects. Indeed a series of external circumstances substantiate Buttel's claim that the explosive interest in ecological modernization is not matched by any clarity in its theoretical argumentation.

I have already depicted these external circumstances in Chapter 2. They concern a shift regarding environmental problems: in ontological, substantial and action terms. However, they also stem from the institutionalization of environmental issues in the public debate, in the political apparatus, and in terms of our views of values and overall guiding principles bringing new factors into play, impinging crucially upon the opportunities and limitations. For instance, I have drawn attention to the formation of what Eder calls an ecological masterframe, to which everyone can refer, instead of the earlier need to start the environmental discourse from each person's lifeworld. Another example of the decisive role of these new factors is the significance of opportunities for rationalization within the apparatus of (environmental) administration itself.

If the explosive growth in interest noticed by Buttel is understood in the light of ontological, substantial and action-related changes, it becomes clear that the interest can be explained by these overall changes alone.

Ontologically, the development is characterized by the environment, and the damage to it, being seen in relation to the culture as a whole. Substantially, the accumulation of environmental damage gives rise to qualitatively new environmental problems. And as for the action, we observe that the motivation is increasingly originating from inside the institutions – that is, on the basis of 'self-interest' and not legally compelled, which is what we also usually call reflexively motivated. In combination and in general, these three aspects represent a significant cross-section of the elements of the 'paradigm' of ecological modernization outlined previously

Moreover, in Chapter 2, we looked into how institutionalization of environmentalism in the public debate and in the political apparatus leads to a return of the modern ideology, in which the modern discourse absorbs the environment or ecology as a valid part of its own project – that is, ecology is no longer merely a counterdiscourse. In ethical terms, this is manifested by the environment being established as a public good, which may subsequently feature as relevant to the distribution issue. In terms of identity, this may be viewed in the context of growing individualization, another specific trait of modernity, leading *inter alia* to the creation of an ecological identification figure.

Moreover, by being institutionalized in the political apparatus, not only does the environment become an area of rationalization, it also delivers a new heading for the modernization process itself: it must be 'ecological'.

As a result of this trend, ecology also becomes involved in the counter-modern. Part of the critique of the modern is precisely that modern development has failed to take care of the environment, indeed leading to massive destruction of it. The criticism contains visions pointing to something postmodern as well as to something pre-modern, in addition to an anti-capitalist slant, the latter seen in the postmodern critique as well as in the socialist and neo-Marxist critique.

Therefore, ecological modernization remains a defence of the modern development process, and a claim that this can be arranged in a manner that preserves and protects the environment. In other words, that the existing practices in industry and administration can be modernized to spare the environment from harm. Early cases are Huber and Jänicke, though the other authors mentioned also exemplify this idea. This is in all likelihood why these writers use the term modernization predominantly in the sense of an innovation process, rather than as a specific rationalization process within the modern period.

Not until the widespread impact of the theories on a reflexive modernity, launched by Beck in 1986 and used by Giddens since 1990, does one sense that this group of authors on ecological modernization *attempt* to ascribe more explicit substance to the modernization concept – for example, Spaargaren and Mol in 1992, and later Hajer in his book from 1995. However, the above critique shows that they have not succeeded.

Conversely, the socialist critique is more split as regards the modern. Anti-capitalism is still throughout the 1980s overshadowing the stance towards modern elements. During the 1990s, the breakdown of the socialist alternative and the fall of the Berlin Wall largely turns the socialist critique into a defence of democratic rights. For instance, a healthy environment is included among the human rights.[14]

Philosophically, postmodernism may recede in prominence in the course of the 1990s, but it is certainly not dead at the practical level, where it becomes increasingly manifest – for example, aesthetically and within a new administrative culture that sets store by management. In architecture, we see clear trends towards aesthetics taking over at the expense of content, or the increasing dominance of form over function, something which must be characterized as a typical manifestation of a postmodern practice.[15] Similar trends can be observed in literature and sociology, in which the reappearance of positivism is expressed in the emphasis on leadership and power analyses, as well as in the accentuation of freedom of opinion as a virtue, and in the general levelling of differences in opinion.

On the emergence of ecology as a modern ideology in the 1980s and 1990s, Eder states that this takes place in competition with the major ideologies from the 19th century: liberalism, socialism and conservatism. Initially, throughout the 1960s and 1970s, the process takes shape in the three types of 'symbolic packaging', namely 'conservationism', 'political ecology' and 'deep ecology'. Each of these packages are much more dependent on what he calls 'the market place of public communication' than the packages associated with modern ideologies in the 19th century and first half of the 20th century, such as 'the proletariat', 'capitalism', 'communism' and 'human rights'. In their internal struggle for dominance in the communicative marketplace, they play a vital role in 'greening' modern society, but their 'joint' success also contributes to a blurring of their individual characteristics. This paves the way for the establishment of the new masterframe termed 'ecology' as everyone's discourse – that is, not just the discourse of certain actors or a counterdiscourse, as I called it earlier (Eder, 1996, p206).

Concerning the process, Eder writes:

> *'Ecology' has become a catchword that can be applied to every element in public discourse on the environment: to ethical questions, scientific*

theories, and to literary expressions of the relationship of man in nature.
The label 'ecological' can be attributed to these phenomena and this makes
sense, both from an internal and an external perspective. The increasing
dominance of the political ecology package thus leads to change in the
meaning of environmentalism, which is the precondition for transforming
environmentalism into a conflictual public discourse. The masterframe of
this conflictual public discourse is 'ecology' – a symbolic package which
contains all the elements necessary for constituting ecological discourse as
a major element in the legitimating ideology of advanced modern
societies.

Eder, 1996, p207

Thus, when Buttel makes the above distinction between ecological modernization as, on the one side, the dominant discourse of environmental politics, and, on the other, a series of sociological theories about modernization under the heading of ecology, I follow him with two reservations:

First, it may have to be ascertained that the dominant discourse has triumphed, before it can be put on a formula as ecological modernization. It is not, as he stresses himself, any particular clarity in the theoretical argumentation that gives rise to the intense interest in ecological modernization. Rather, it is a long and tough political struggle between various ideologies with the environment as the 'framing' or 'packaging', each of which endeavour to reshape society, resulting in the idea of integrating ecological 'needs' into modern society gaining a dominant position. This is also corroborated by the observation that it seems to be Beck's and Giddens' concepts of reflexive modernization that pave the way for more explicit attempts at formulating a theory of ecological modernization.

Accordingly, Buttel, Eder and Hajer all see ecological modernization primarily as a predominant discourse of environmental politics.

Second, the very sociological theories referred to by Buttel as well as Murphy, in the above, are spread across such a wide range of contents and emphases that each one of them could be given its own heading. For example, 'social change', 'macroeconomic restructuring', 'environmental and economic equality', 'cultural transformation', 'cleaner production', 'environmental refinement of consumption', and so on. Each of these theories has been drawn up without relying explicitly on an understanding of the modernization process. They may possibly still be grouped under a common heading or school of thought in environmental sociology, but this leads to such dispersion that a common conciseness seems to me rather unclear or useless. However, this attempt to patent a masterframe may in itself form part of the ideological struggle.

Furthermore, Buttel and others have interpreted the situation in the sense that the environment can be perceived as a differentiated (and hence independent) arena of decision-making. However, I cannot discern such an autonomy in the available theory on ecological modernization. Strictly speaking, it may also be considered a statement with a certain self-contradiction, as the ecological is indeed attached to the modernization process – that is, seen as part of it and not as freed from it. Therefore, I will interpret such a statement about the emancipation of ecology as an expression of the modernization process not being seen as a particular societal manifestation in modern times, but more pragmatically, as a process of innovation, or simply something more up-to-date in a more popular sense of the term.

What has here been observed or identified is how the environment is demarcated as a polity domain in its own right. However, this is hardly surprising, as the institutionalization of environmentalism in the public debate and the political apparatus calls for some measures, some facts on the ground. Obviously, 25 years of evolution in these areas leave their traces in terms of changes and emphases. Theoretically, the environmental field may here be conceived as a subsystem in the Habermasian sense. This serves to stress a certain separation or differentiation of environmental parameters, at the same time as the field is maintained within, or subordinated to, the economic system.

However, this does not rule out that practical elements of the pursued environmental policy as well as institutional role changes may express aspects of ecological emancipation. Indeed, it should be inherent to the institutionalization of environmentalism in the public debate and the political apparatus that it is associated with a certain degree of independent focusing.

Therefore, in the rest of this chapter, I shall look at a series of practical elements in environmental regulation which can be observed throughout the Western world, especially over the past ten years, searching within them for signs of the aforementioned characteristics. It is not decisive whether these elements are explicitly involved in the self-understanding of ecological modernization, which would anyway, given the wide spectrum outlined above, be of a more scholastic concern.

Hajer outlines six points which he sees as the core or substance of ecological modernization in practice (Hajer, 1995, pp24–30). His starting point in discourse theory provides him with a comprehensive overview, and in my view, his six points concerning the empirical level encompass the key developmental features in this field. They are highly appropriate to express the dominant trend in environmental polity over the past couple of decades, and cannot be seen as referring specifically to the practical implementation of ecological modernization. Thus, it is not the identification of these six points that gives rise to criticism. As will appear below, however, I shall question some of Hajer's explanations in some of the cases.

The six points identified are:

New means of environmental politics ('techniques of policy-making' in Hajer's terms). The new environmental policy instruments deployed in the gradual institutionalization may first and foremost be characterized in terms of: (a) a shift from reactive to proactive regulation, and in parallel to this: (b) efforts to deregulate. A proactive regulation involves remedial measures being replaced by preventative ones, and will also commonly imply the mainstreaming of environmental protection in policies and activities other than those directly concerning the environment and environmental measures. This amounts to a shift in the means as well as in the areas in which these are applied.

Deregulation measures convey an emphasis on voluntariness or self-interest instead of legally formulated impositions. They thus express a situation of change in the perception of *why* the environment should be taken into consideration, by *which* means this is to be achieved, and *who* this is meant to benefit. Deregulation tends to form part of more comprehensive strategies, or has primary objectives in which the environment only features in part. In general terms, it constitutes an attempt at building environmental concerns into other objectives – for example, strengthening of the market. Tradable pollution permits and green taxes serve as examples of this. However, using deregulation in pursuit of environmental goals, or rather arguments that deregulation measures of various types will bring environmental effects, in fact presupposes that environmentalism has been institutionalized in the public debate. In other words, that concern for the environment has become the discourse of everyone, and not just of certain people – that is, the environment or ecology has become a masterframe.

Other examples include the 'polluter pays principle', risk analyses, the cautionary principle and cost–benefit analyses. It is precisely the cautionary principle that is often built into specific regulations. These are frequently conditioned by the actual circumstances being impossible to grasp or calculate, requiring individual determinations or decisions taken in observance of the regulations to adhere to more strictly defined 'precautions'. Moreover, the use of such principles presupposes general acknowledgement that the environment 'demands' consideration or protection. This may also be expressed through prioritizing the environment above everything else to such a large degree that 'the likely outcome' does indeed become the outcome. The application of the precautionary principle requires it to be everyone's agenda, and moreover that this agenda has a high priority.

New role for science in environmental policy-making. There is scarcely any policy area as closely related to the realm of science as environmental policy. This stems logically from the role assigned to science from the outset in delivering proof of environmentally detrimental effects, typically by documenting the harm to humans and animals of particular substances. Accordingly, in the beginning, environmental policy sought to limit the use of such problematic toxins by issuing rules and standards. Subsequently, the scientific focus gradually changed from individual toxins and cases to following how the substances spread, accumulate, enter into synergy and so on. This also led to a more holistic analysis of ecosystems, of related effects and the combined systemic impact. In particular, this brought system ecology to the fore, and the spotlight was turned on the carrying capacity of ecosystems, strategic substances, 'critical load' and so on. In this manner, the role of science, not least of natural science, was changed from delivering proof of harm to delivering scientific insights into the carrying capacity of the environment.

The institutionalization of environmental politics has also entailed, as highlighted in Chapter 2, that the environmental endeavour and its efficiency becomes dependent on the rationalization efforts of society, and furthermore that these processes are subjected to economic and sociological analyses. The latter aspect has posed a major challenge to the status of natural science as environmental science *par excellence*, as new scientific perspectives are brought to bear on the environment and on environmental politics. Environmental economics emerges as a special discipline in economics, and in sociology, the issue of ethics and values takes centre stage revolving around the environment, as portrayed in Chapter 2. Moreover, these very themes are what prompts public participation in environmental policy decision-making processes. The following three characteristics express this trend in particular:

Pollution prevention pays. Perceiving pollution abatement as a cost was, understandably, associated with the initial wave of environmental policy in the shape of imposition, prohibition and standards: so-called legalistic environmental policy and its attendant 'end-of-line' solution strategy. Accordingly, the political demands raised in these first-generation environmental laws were accompanied by massive state support. Nevertheless, already at that early stage, the measures proved to have economic advantages for the firms involved in terms of reduction in raw material inputs, recycling opportunities and savings on waste disposal. In addition, the necessary equipment for environmental measures became an industry in itself. From the viewpoint of the national economy, export of this equipment was arguably beneficial, and pioneering environmental demands could lay the groundwork for the development of such an industry.

These experiences gradually linked up with environmentally determined rationalization measures, for example in the shape of cleaner technologies or low- and non-waste technologies. In microeconomic terms, the perspective changed from 'pollution abatement costs' to 'pollution prevention pays'. These experiences also made their mark on the macroeconomic level.

Nature as a public good. The idea that nature can or should be seen as a public good springs from two fundamentally different conditions. First, as depicted above, the experiences at the microeconomic level are also felt at the macroeconomic level. The rapidly accumulating extensive experiences of ecosystems make it clear that environmental harm prevention could also be cost prevention. Of course, this always presupposed that it was a generally accepted objective that ecosystems should not be polluted beyond a certain limit. For instance that lakes and streams should be kept free of industrial emissions of waste water and so on, that air pollution in cities should be contained or kept below a certain level, and be free of particular substances. In other words, the utilization of ecosystems for waste disposal was in the interest of the few, whereas the discourse that this had to be stopped was not just that of the few, but a generally acknowledged viewpoint. This was tantamount to seeing nature as a public good rather than as a sewage system to be used by each individual at will. Different strategies were deployed, such as ecological price-setting, recycling and technological innovations, aimed at preventing the transfer of costs through nature.

However, the concern for sustainability also implies a perception of nature as a public good, as it introduces nature in the equal distribution between generations. In this manner, it becomes *ethical* considerations that lead to the viewpoint that nature cannot simply be consumed by the few at their discretion.

Public participation. At the early stages, different forms of third-party involvement, for instance of environmental organizations in environmental regulations, is justified by the need for a stakeholder acting in the name of the environment.[16] Concurrently with the generalization of the environmental discourse, such scope for participation is expanded, in some cases to encompass the public at large. The fact that this occurs in the field of the environment in particular is not only because the environment belongs to all and is in everyone's interest, but also because regulations must increasingly be based upon values and ethics, which, precisely in the modern period, are not predetermined in the constitution of society, but are supplied through various discourses, through existing or actual 'framing', and through possible 'masterframes', in Eder's terminology. Ethical and value-related considerations must thus be supplied and discussed in the light of each case and the circumstances at hand, against the background of the existing 'framing'.

This trend marks a change from an antagonistic relationship between environmental organizations and the authorities towards a participatory approach, towards an opening of existing decision-making processes and a recognition of new actors in the political process. At the European level, this takes place, for instance, through the establishment of a system of environmental impact assessment (EIA), and by funding NGOs, instead of merely consulting them. Nationally, roundtable conferences and public hearings are held.

Shift in the burden of proof. The outlined trend towards a general environmental discourse and the idea of nature as a public good also affects the burden of proof in cases of doubt regarding the effects of various acts. When firms and assorted actors are expected to protect the environment, they are also expected to take responsibility for proving that their activities are not harmful, as opposed to others having to prove that they are. That is, in the general environmental discourse, the burden of proof is shifted from the injured party (e.g. represented by environmental organizations) to the injuring party (e.g. a corporation or a public entity).

These overall changes in the characteristics of environmental regulation express, on the one hand, an elementary evolution in how the environment is 'thought of', and on the other, that the general development of society has opened up new possibilities. In other words, environmental policies have not just been accepted, but their implementation contributes to changing society, and to changing the scope for its own practices.

Hajer attempts to explain the development outlined in the light of four different trends (Hajer, 1995, pp94–96).

First, in the course of the 1970s and early 1980s, the economic crisis throughout the Western capitalist world leaves environmentalism eclipsed by social and economic issues, which forces the environmental discourse to combine its think-ing on environment and economic reconstruction.

Second, a series of changes takes place within environmental movements. They increasingly have to seek specific results in order to preserve their broad popular backing. Moreover, they are forced to acknowledge the limitations of radical confrontation, particularly in light of the ever-wider acceptance of environmentalism in the population, a situation in which radical confrontation would prevent them from appearing as a power-broker in society.

Third, new types of environmental problems such as acid rain and depletion of the ozone layer were able to take on a symbolic or emblematic shape in favour of wider popular understanding of environmental issues:

> ... *there was a play on the symbolic, metaphorical meaning of key issues, yet this time they had to qualify on different criteria. Rather than illus-trating the perverted nature of the system at large to the radical core of the counter-culture, they now had to illustrate the vast threats that various industrial practices formed to society as a whole.*
>
> Hajer, 1995, p95

Fourth, a new alternative environmental discourse became available in the course of the 1980s. As university people and others had worked out alternative solutions, international organizations such as the Organisation for Economic Co-operation and Development (OECD),[17] United Nations Environment Programme (UNEP) and United Nations Economic Commission for Europe (UNECE) calculated models that combined environmental and economic concerns, both groups showing that the legalistic line hitherto pursued in the environmental regulations of governments had failed to produce satisfactory results. Against this background, they advocated new strategies based upon the *precautionary principle* and the *internalization* of environmental concerns in economic decision-making.

Hajer identifies three tracks along which this alternative discourse asserts itself politically towards the end of the 1970s and the beginning of the 1980s, thus laying the foundations for what he calls ecological modernization (Hajer, 1995, pp96–100). The *first track* is the publication of *The World Conservation Strategy: Living Resource Conservation for Sustainable Development*. The report was drawn up by the World Conservation Union (IUCN), Worldwide Fund for Nature (WWF) and UNEP, in collaboration with Food and Agriculture Organization (of the UN) (FAO) and United Nations Educational, Scientific and Cultural Organization (UNESCO), and advocated the protection of endangered species and ecosystems through sustainable development based on efficient resource utilization and considerate environmental planning.

The *second track* is the Environmental Committee of the OECD, which served as a think tank and conveyor of ideas arising in university circles. Like the OECD in general, the committee set much store by the relationship between economy and environment. At a meeting of the ministers of environment from OECD member countries in 1979, the official declaration suggested that the countries should incorporate environmental concerns at the early stages of decision-making processes, and focus on tools of economic and financial policy rather than on legal regulatory instruments.

Finally, the *third track* identified by Hajer is a series of UN commissions, such as the Brandt Commission (1980), Palme Commission (1982) and Brundtland Commission (1987), all of which address the issues of development, security and environment, of which the latter commission must be clearly seen in continuation or as a consequence of the two former. About the Brundtland Commission, Hajer writes that it 'explicitly aimed to get environmental issues out of the periphery of politics (as conservation issues) and sought to link them to the core – that is, economic – concerns. Likewise it aimed to resist the dichotomy between environment and development which had been the obstacle that split the North and South at the Stockholm Conference' (Hajer, 1995, p100).

Hajer clearly shows that the described course of events is associated with outstandingly massive *political* efforts to incorporate environmental regulations and concerns into an overall economic development strategy. It is also noticeable that practice in this case, as indeed in most situations, precedes the theory, and that the theoretical work in this regard is largely about explaining an observed trend in relation to accepted theorems and dogmas.

Moreover, the elements outlined substantiate, in my assessment, that these political efforts spring from just as massive material or structural needs for changes in environmental policy-making. Let me just highlight three conditions:

1   First-generation environmental regulations were obsolete from the outset, and rapidly outlived their usefulness. As a policy form, it must almost be characterized as pre-modern – that is, primarily based on prohibition and compulsion, as well as on fixed forms of understanding regarding what pollution is, what pollutes, and what to do about it.
2   Development nationally and internationally – with its economic crisis and the resultant accelerated pace of rationalization and technological innovations of industrial production processes, in addition to growing globalization – took most people by surprise, and created massive needs for cross-border and worldwide environmental collaboration; this could obviously not be based on the carrying capacity of local recipients of pollution (Elling, 1990, 1991).
3   The market became uncontrollable due to internationalization or globalization – that is, the market increasingly took over from state control. Consequently, environmental concerns had to be built into the market mechanisms, they could not be left under the aegis of entities based on central control.

Furthermore, it seems to me that the elements outlined to explain ecological modernization supplement and bear out the features outlined in Chapter 2 concerning the juxtaposition of environmentalism and the concept of modernity as well as the position of this relation in contemporary sociological thinking. However, Hajer's four points of explanation, including his three tracks where an alternative discourse asserts itself, almost exclusively encompass the economic aspects of modernity. Thus presented, it is clearly instrumental reason that drives the massive political efforts to draw attention to the environmental issue. Furthermore, just like the theoretical approaches to ecological modernization described above, it can be established that these four points also fail to offer theoretical elements that transcend such a perception of politics as driven by instrumental reason.

Accordingly, Hajer writes that ecological modernization must be seen first and foremost as an *efficiency*-oriented approach to environmentalism. This is precisely what turned it into the dominant discourse in the field of the environment, and made it so popular among governments. Despite the fact that the original visions within environmental movements were directed against these kind of notions of efficiency, originating – as they did – in the counterculture of the 1960s and its critique of technocratic institutional arrangements.

Hajer offers two explanations why this could nonetheless take place with the consent and active contribution of environmental movements.

One explanation is that environmental movements have a historical tradition of reflexivity – that is, of calling for debate on the direction of society's modernization. Environmental movements have not only espoused solutions to the problem of physical degradation, but have always combined this demand with a critique of the institutional conditions that cause the degradation, warning about the unacceptable effects of quick technocratic fixes (Hajer, 1995, p102).

The other explanation is that the environmental movement chose to pursue the line of ecological modernization for strategic reasons. In particular as a result of the disillusions after the antagonistic debate on nuclear power, the environmental movement opted for arguing in the same terms as governments in order to be perceived as 'the right kind of people, as realistic, responsible, and professional, avoiding being positioned as romanticist dreamers' (Hajer, 1995, p102). Some might see this as an expression of the movement's coming of age, says Hajer, though it is also evident that the new conditions for discursive action placed new constraints on what could be meaningfully uttered. He calls this situation the discursive paradox of the new environmental movement.

However, on this point it seems to me that Hajer's starting point in discourse theory makes him see this situation primarily as a question of discourse – that is, argumentation – about strategic stances. This leaves out material and structural factors. In their stead he places human calculation and general thoughtfulness, which is characterized as reflexivity.

In the same breath, when – as quoted above concerning the expectations of what is to come out of the reflexive arrangement – he writes that 'social inquiries could indicate where social consensus is likely to be possible, or where it cannot be achieved and choices will have to be made' (Hajer, 1995, p292), one has to raise the question of how such a decision is to be reached. If the reflexive process only has implications for the establishment of some degree of consensus, after which business merely carries on as usual, the value of the reflexive process must be considered dubious. Once again, in his focus on discursive processes, Hajer may be criticized for neglecting the significance of modernity's power structures and their legitimacy.

In 1991, along with a group of Nordic researchers, I published a book on the shift to ecological modernization in environmental politics.[18] Here, we analysed the development from the protection of nature to the protection of the environment and eco-policy, seen in relation to regional policy efforts in Norway, Sweden and Denmark. My contribution consisted of an analysis showing that *structural* factors brought the environmental policy based on norms and standards for the carrying capacity of pollution recipients into contradiction with long-term environmental objectives or goals within a series of other policy areas. This called for a restructuring, in which the policy had to be based upon a series of overall aims, and at the same time be coordinated with the efforts in other policy areas. Consequently, it was not merely the good ideas of thinkers from universities and officials from international organizations bringing the new perspectives into light, but simple material necessities that pressed for solutions.

Accordingly, in my assessment, the origins of what happened went beyond idealistic viewpoints among central decision-makers. It also stemmed from environmental regulations at that point having hit a wall, which it had helped erect itself, due to its blinkered point of departure. It was imperative to find new orientations and new ways of embedding this regulation, and in this panorama, the following possibilities had to be seriously considered:

> *Thus, in the course of the 1980s, it becomes increasingly clear that environmental policy cannot rely for its foundation on the establishment of emission standards based upon the local state of pollution. Instead, environmental policy must be founded upon more overall objectives and conditions, e.g. economizations, resource accounting, competitive advantages, national and international concerns, global effects, etc. Although the legislation for environmental protection has so far – if leaving its lenient enforcement out of account – brought the pollution from so-called point sources under control, this is not enough to secure a better state of the environment. New tools with new perspectives and mechanisms must be introduced. The 1980s also becomes a period in which the functionalistic planning ideal is challenged – in the environmental field, this is expressed through the dilution strategy – and in which new perceptions of the nature of planning and how to realize it are placed on the agenda.*
> Translation from original Danish, Elling, 1991, p20

This quote does not refer to the complex propagation of toxins and so on, although it also forms part of the analysis, as it indeed reinforces the arguments presented. Moreover, it is the very foundation of the existing, practised environmental regulation which, in the analysis concerned, works out as diametrically opposed to its own aims.[19]

I do not find Hajer's analyses and arguments to be sufficient to explain a shift in environmental policy-making that focuses on market mechanisms instead of central control. The discourses that he depicts do not encompass any material necessities and models of explanations. The shift appears solely as the result of reflection and discourse by groups and individuals. In this, the reflexive processes forced upon economic actors through the market are left out. Thus he neglects the systemic reflexivity which I have identified above. Therefore, I prefer to talk of the paradox of discourse analysis and of ecological modernization rather than of the discursive paradox within the new environmental movement, as Hajer calls it.

Internalization of environmental concerns in economic development strategy

The analysis of the modernization process in Chapter 3 demonstrated that it is not the mere possibility of technologies that brings them into play as solutions, thus creating problems and leading the development process to generate environmental damage. It is the capitalization and the application of technologies that cause the problems. However, the theory of ecological modernization ignores this, or shuts itself off from acknowledging this, when Mol for instance establishes that 'ecological modernization theory focuses primarily on the dimension of industrialism' (Mol, 1995, p41).

Another problem with the theories of ecological modernization is the paradox that they do not operate with an explicit concept of *modernization* as a societal process. In the case of both Mol and Hajer, the consequence is that their modernization concept appears to be vague, and only indicates that production becomes more modern or up-to-date – that is, the unmediated form of understanding of the expression 'modern'. In the case of Hajer, it implies that his concept of reflexivity becomes a question of choosing and thinking matters through, and not an institutional form of action. Conversely, Mol's concept of reflexivity does concern an institutional form of action, but it remains utopian, since he cannot explain how such form of action is to exceed the existing instrumentally determined barriers.

Against this background, I shall conclude, *first*, that ecological modernization, as a particular school of thought in environmental sociology, is in no manner entitled to claim a patent on identification with the shift in the focus of environmental polity and its means over the past couple of decades. Nor can it be characterized as able to supply a particularly adequate model of explanation for the occurred shift and its developmental features. It understands these almost 100 per cent within a traditional neoclassical economic paradigm. Thus, it does not permit the identification of elements with a different vision of the modern. Its sharpest statement is that it wishes to continue the modern project, and that this is understood as a modernization of capitalism by incorporating the environment as a scarce good. The closest we get to an alternative is Hajer's suggestion that modernity should be thought into a framework which he terms '*the socialisation of ecology'*. However, he refrains from analysing this framework in any detail, which must be seen as a perspective he suggests on the basis of a recognition that ecological modernization offers no other perspective on the modernization process than the instrumental *economic* reason.

Consequently, I shall conclude, *second*, that ecological modernization must be said to be a rather misleading term for this school of thought in environmental sociology, especially as it does not contain any explicit understanding of the modernization process capable of shedding light on how to make it ecological. A much more fitting denomination of the theories described and the practice identified would be *internalization of environmental concerns in economic development strategy*. By economic development strategy, I am referring to something parallel or comparable to, for instance, the Keynesian strategy towards recessionary phenomena in the capitalist economy or towards the problem of unemployment.

However, it has not been the aim of this chapter to *explain* the shift in environmental discourse. The aim has been to examine whether elements pointing beyond a one-sided modernization process can be identified, in practice, in the predominant discourse, namely ecological modernization. The conclusion must be no. Instead it has proved likely that ecological modernization expresses, also at the practical level, an efficiency strategy aimed at incorporating the environmental dimension into the modernization process *within* the boundaries of instrumental reason. Thus, the most characteristic feature is that modernization must take place through market mechanisms rather than a general and comprehensive planning process.

As briefly touched upon above, one instrument in the efficiency strategy of ecological modernization is the application of environmental assessment as a preventative tool aimed at incorporating environmental concerns into the actual decision-making processes. Therefore, this application will be subjected to closer analysis in the next chapter.

However, drawing on the analysis of ecological modernization, two further trends can be pointed out, both of significance to how reflexivity concepts – presented in the second section of the following chapter – will be applied in the same chapter's interpretation of environmental assessment.

Because the circumstances outlined above concerning the implementation of ecological modernization are, in reality, about the framework for systemic or institutional reflexivity. Hajer's discursive practices describe in which manner the various actors argue in the public discourse of environmental politics, and hence upon which interpretation of reality they wish to base their actions.[20] The discourses unfolding in the public debate thus set a series of bearings to be used by institutional actors to chart the course, if they are to navigate smoothly and effectively through these waters.[21]

Accordingly, the first trend is that the general environmental discourse creates or implies an attention to environmental issues and acts that may bring environmental effects of a kind difficult to evade. The systemically reflexive actors are forced to take this into account when taking decisions. This may undoubtedly bring about a beneficial development within *certain* limits.

The second trend that can be observed is that the radicalism of the public's reaction to environmental issues has waned in step with the spread of general alertness. The public debate does not question institutional arrangements or the existing order. Alternative forms of society or counter-images of the predominant scenario do not enter the debate on environmental problem areas.[22] This is comparable to circumstances at the empirical level, where it is also *instrumental reason* that defines the aforementioned limits.

These two highlighted trends point to the following conclusion. In the context of the development described, the limits of institutional reflexivity have been expanded to encompass the public's reaction in a very wide sense, whereas it used to be primarily the market's reaction that had to be considered. However, at the same time, the radicalism of the demands made by this public have waned. They may well involve constant innovation of practices, but rarely in a form that challenges the dominant order.

In other words, it can be observed that no actor is driven beyond the confines of purposive action, and additionally that public participation in the existing form does not counteract a one-sided modernization process. Consequently, other inducements are required to create a situation able to intensify pressures towards a modernization that is not one-sided. This is the subject of the next chapter.

Notes

1   Directive 85/337/EEC, Directive 97/11/EC, as well as various government orders on the Danish implementation thereof, the latest of which is the Consolidated Act of the Danish Ministry of the Environment and Energy, No 551 of 28 June 1999.
2   The two latter claims come from Buttel and Mol, and will be elaborated upon in the subsequent analysis of Mol's approach.
3   Murphy is here referred to without page number, and I have been unable to find these direct references to Mol in Hajer's work. On pp280–283, Hajer discusses the problems of what he compares to a techno-corporative regime of ecological modernization, instead of a truly democratic and reflexive ecological modernization. This is what I am referring to in the aforementioned critique presented by Hajer.
4   Murphy refers to Hajer's distinction between a techno-administrative ecological modernization and a truly reflexive ecological modernization. However, Hajer does not call it techno-administrative, but techno-corporative – see, for instance, p281. I am using the latter term.
5   Once again, contrary to what Murphy writes, Hajer is not referring directly to Mol on this issue.
6   Cf. the critique of Giddens and Beck in Chapter 3 concerning their application of reflexivity to individual action.
7   Cf. my presentation of Giddens' theory in Chapter 3, page 114 and also note 21 in Chapter 3. As we have also seen in Chapter 3, Habermas uses the term differentiation (*Ausdifferenzierung*) with a somewhat different meaning, using the concept in continuation of Kant, Hegel and Weber.
8   Indeed, such a furthering cannot be found in his own examination, cf. the quote from Mol on pp180–181.

9   That Mol is working within an instrumental view of the environment and its protec-
tion/conservation is also borne out by his acknowledgement of Schnaiberg's (1980)
distinction between a *scientific nature* (the foundation of subsistence) and an *intuited
nature* (the environment as experienced), while he stresses that ecological modernization is aimed at the former (Mol, 1995, pp52, 54). This focus on the scientific
nature is carried into his perception, which he shares with Spaargaren, of a third
dimension of nature, the inner nature, which is meant to imply the genetic elements
and so on.

10 For instance, Buttel writes (2000, p59): 'In addition to Hajer's constructionism
being in stark contrast with the objectivism of the core literature in ecological
modernization, Hajer's view is that ecological-modernizationist environmental-polit-
ical discourse may even serve to dilute the political impulse for environmental
reforms by obscuring the degree to which economic expansion, growth of consumption, and capital-intensive technological change compromise the ability of states to
ensure a quality environment.' See also Murphy, 2000, p2.

11 Habermas talks of reflexivity in this form as a cognitive activity of a different order:
as hypothesis-driven and argumentatively filtered learning processes in the field of
objective thinking, in the field of moral-practical insight, and in the field of aesthetic
observation, cf. point b) in the quote on page 93, ibid., pp81–82.

12 Here, I am employing the concept of criticism in the Habermasian sense, that is,
criticism is exercised when arguments are deployed, without those involved necessarily presuming fulfilment of the premises of a speech situation, which is free of
external and internal compulsion (TCA 1, p42).

13 Habermas is not particularly informative concerning this interplay between the
systemic steering media and the limitations they entail. However, both in this
function and in reproductive service delivery to the labour force, the state is caught
in a dilemma between political needs and fiscal constraints, which ultimately
narrows its scope for activities both fiscally and politically. Habermas puts it in the
following manner: 'The dilemma consists in the fact that the social welfare state is
supposed to head off immediately negative effects on the lifeworld of a capitalisti-
cally organized occupational system, as well as the dysfunctional side effects
thereupon of economic growth that is steered through capital accumulation, and it is
supposed to do so without encroaching upon the organizational form, the structure,
or the drive mechanism of economic production. Not the least among the reasons
why it may not impair the conditions of stability and the requirements of mobility of
capitalist growth is the following: adjustment to the pattern of distribution of social
compensations trigger reactions on the part of privileged groups unless they can be
covered by increases in the social product and thus do not affect the propertied
classes; when this is not the case, such measures cannot fulfill the function of
containing and mitigating class conflict.

'Thus, not only is the *extent* of social welfare expenditures subject to fiscal restrictions, the *kind* of social welfare performances, the *organized way* in which life is
provided for, has to fit into the structure of an interchange, via money and power,
between formally organized domains of action and their environments' (TCA 2,
pp347–348).

14 Cf. the Aarhus Convention (full title: 'Convention on Access to Information, Public
Participation, in Decision-Making and Access to Justice in Environmental Matters')
Article 1, which highlights its objective as: 'to contribute to the protection of the
right of every person of present and future generations to live in an environment
adequate to his or her health and well-being, […]'. This development is, of course,
the outcome of many circumstances, but may be seen to express an endeavour,

drawing on the concept of human rights, to secure environmental equality and justice among people, including an environment of a certain quality; see Koester, 2001, p144.

15   See, for instance, Schjerup Hansen and Bech-Danielsen, 2001.

16   In this regard, it must also be kept in mind that the economic interests, represented by consumers of the environment, were already widely present in decision-making processes, for instance through consultations and other opportunities to make objections.

17   See pxii for list of acronyms and abbreviations.

18   Berger et al, 1991, p5.

19   Cf. for instance the following quote: 'There are at least two general reasons why the form of regulation becomes inadequate, both environmentally and with regard to regional development:

•   Greater environmental awareness in the population makes the companies sensitive to criticism related to the environment, so that the entire local business community may be threatened by polluters (as seen from the local community).

•   Competition concerns: if the local firms are "allowed to pollute", they lag behind in national and international competition regarding technological development and so on, and hence the local community loses an economic asset anyway (as seen by the local community as well as by central institutions).

Translation of Elling, 1991, p23

20   Of course, this should not be understood as a static situation, but as an image of the *current* discourse. This discourse will change, at some stage giving shape to a new 'framing', in Eder's sense, depending on the course of events. However, although new 'masterframes' are to be expected in future, the ecological masterframe is likely to remain intact for some time ahead.

21   Specific circumstances alert them to how much money it could cost them to make mistakes, if they run a capitalist business, or how much legitimacy – and hence vigour and effectiveness – it could cost them, if they are, say, a public entity. One example is the Brent Spar affair, another is the case in Germany (April 2001) of nuclear waste storage. A third could be the use of genetically modified organisms, so-called GMOs in food production. Against the background of deep scepticism in the European population, the EU had to pass a moratorium on the spread of this kind of production. Other examples show how small-scale firms may also get into trouble if, for instance, they overstep certain boundaries of ethical conduct.

22   Such images quite simply do not exist, or they must be considered of the utmost particularity. Cf. the establishment in the introductory section of Chapter 3 of the absence of critique of the dominance of capitalism and the market.

Chapter 5

The Environmental Politics of Modernity

This chapter is about environmental assessment. In the preceding chapters, I have analysed the overall framework for this process: society in the modern era, when reflexivity becomes the possibility of each individual and the constitutive form of society, when the modernization process results in what has been called an ecological crisis, while the environmental polity is characterized as ecological modernization.

By means of these analyses, drawing on Habermas' theory of the modern, I have attempted to demonstrate that what is termed reflexive modernity by eminent sociologists of our times does not create environmental problems due to its reflexivity, as they claim, but quite the opposite, because this basic premise of the modern is not allowed to unfold to its actual full extent, but is foreshortened to encompass only the cognitive-instrumental perspective. This turns modernization into a *one-sided* process, which fails to take in the modern era's splitting of reason, in its full range, into its cognitive-instrumental, moral-practical and aesthetic-rational form. Reflexivity leads to purposive rationality, which does not contain the ethical and aesthetic rationales, but is indeed divorced from these.

However, the analyses also show that these rationales to their full extent can be found in modern society. The problem is indeed a repression of the ethical and aesthetic rationales, but on the other hand, it is precisely the environmental problematic that is shining a light on their existence. It thus becomes apparent that only an integral modernization may bring about conditions in society in which environmentalism can become part of the modernization process, and not continue to be a problematic that needs to be supplied with 'solutions', after attempting to meet some other and more significant objective.

Now, I shall not claim, on the basis of the above analysis, that environmental assessment as an environmental policy tool has been brought into play in order to create an integral modernization. Because in that case, the problem posed would be simple, perhaps even redundant, and at the very least wrongly presented. In that case, it would almost be tantamount to asking why the objective has not been fulfilled.

No, I wish to argue that this is indeed *not* the case. Environmental assessment has entered the environmental polity of states because the efforts so far have proved inadequate, and the environmental problematic has pushed the existence of rationales other than the purposive one into the light. The problem is how to understand and treat these in a world dominated by one kind of rationality, namely the instrumental one.

Therefore, I shall claim that environmental assessment in environmental polity fits the patterns of practising precisely such a purposive rationality, and has primarily been deployed as part of the predominant discourse of ecological modernization as portrayed in Chapter 4.

The presentation below will demonstrate how environmental assessment may be seen both as *the states'* tool to involve citizens in decision-making processes concerning the environment and, conversely, as the *citizens'* tool against the states, but also that none of these perspectives will decisively affect the existing situation, in which a one-sided rationality dominates. Therefore, the starting point will be all the aforementioned defining features of the modern: the forms of reflexivity, the tripartite rationality complex, capitalization and modernization, colonization and cultural impoverishment, the modern form of understanding, lifeworld and system and so on, all of which is brought to bear on a characterization of environmental assessment as the key environmental policy tool of modernity. Against the background of these concepts, I shall interpret the tool of environmental assessment from two sides, perhaps more properly termed two 'extremes' and alternatives to each other:

On the one side, an environmental assessment practised from the perspective of purposive rationality, seeing the tool as a pragmatic way to avoid dealing with those two subjugated aspects of rationality, whose existence is invariably manifested, but which are nevertheless handled by being subordinated or subdued by purposive rationality.

On the other side, an environmental assessment practised with a view to realizing an integral modernization, in which all the rationality forms of modernity are allowed to unfold.

These two sides may be seen as, respectively, a continuation of the existing practice and an attempt at formulating an alternative strategy breaking with this self-same practice. That is, (a) business as usual, and (b) *what* does it take, as a minimum, to break this situation and give rationality a chance to unfold to its full extent in the process.

In these two interpretations, I shall characterize environmental assessment as, respectively, *an ecological modernization* and a *reflexive arrangement*. The sole conclusion of the chapter is the one that lies in the presentation of these two interpretations. Accordingly, the presentation is not meant to lead to an empirical analysis of environmental assessments, for example, concerning how they are practised, who takes part, which rationales they rely upon, and so on. On the contrary, the entire theoretical and analytical presentation so far springs from my empirical analysis of environmental assessment practices at the so-called strategic level (within a Danish *amt* – that is, a subnational region, and within the central administration), as set out in more detail in Chapter 1. Here below, the presentation will thus return to the real level, which may be characterized as the level of societal practice in its generality.

In the interpretation of *environmental assessment as an ecological modernization*,[1] the task is to show how this form of understanding has informed the establishment of the European environmental assessment system from the outset, and furthermore until today. The presentation will be clearly in summary form and concentrate on various key authors' definitions and views of environmental assessment. Conversely, the alternative interpretation of *environmental assessment as a reflexive arrangement* will be more extensive. It will encompass a discussion of the rationality concept at the level of practice. Subsequently, it will contain a presentation of the actors' forms of reflexivity in connection with environmental assessment at the level I have called societal practice in its generality. Thereafter, the reflexive process is portrayed as the very assessment of how the environment is affected, separate from a political decision-making process, whose content is also outlined. The interpretation is finalized with a presentation of the *effects* of such a practice. This completes not only the chapter, but the entire book.

I shall also characterize the one-sided purposive-rational environmental assessment as *technical-scientific* in order to stress that, under this form, the environmental assessment is based on the technical and scientific rationales, and that these thus control the *knowledge* supplied to the process as well as the result at which it is aimed. The other form, I shall call *political-democratic* to emphasize that this form is a *political* process whose contents build upon argumentations or discourses drawing on all available rationales, and whose results cannot, therefore, be governed by a particular discourse or form of knowledge, but must be attained democratically. The result under this form must thus be reached through communication, and drawing on communicative rationality. Consequently, I will also describe this interpretation as a model of *communicative reflection*.

There is a twofold intention behind the title of this chapter, 'The Environmental Politics of Modernity'. First, I understand environmental assessment interpreted as ecological modernization as a key tool in, precisely, *the* practice of environmental politics that continues one-sided modernization within the boundaries of modernity. Admittedly, this 'continuation' takes place on a modernized basis, in which the ecological question and the wider population are directly involved, but it does indeed happen in continuation of the instrumental form of modernity dominant thus far, without challenging its fundamental premises.

Second, I understand environmental assessment interpreted as reflexive arrangement as more than simply environmental assessment, involving also *the* precise form of environmental politics that may bring about scope for transcending one-sided modernization. It presents the basic elements of such a transcendence or emancipative practice within environmental politics under a non-instrumental modernity. This is a practice that I shall also characterize as communicative reflection.

Environmental assessment as ecological modernization

Environmental assessment as a prominent tool in the EU countries' environmental policy became a reality with the publication of Directive 85/337/EEC[2] on 27 June 1985, with mandatory implementation in member countries within the following three years. It is thus established precisely at the time when European countries are readjusting their environmental policies from primarily applying legalistic means to drawing on more marked-based devices. However, it is not so much the timing that makes it a typical tool in the readjustment to what has been termed ecological modernization, as it is the actual justification for the passing and substance of this directive.

In the preamble to the directive, the primary reasons stated for enacting it is that 'the best environmental policy consists in preventing the creation of pollution or nuisances at source', and that 'disparities between the laws in force in the various Member States with regard to the assessment of the environmental effects of public and private projects may create unfavorable competitive conditions and thereby directly affect the functioning of the common market'. Thus, the justification for carrying out environmental assessments is *prevention* and *favourable competitive conditions*, which may indeed be referred to as the cornerstones of the environmental political discourse taking shape at this exact point in time.

Looking at the elements of substance prescribed by the directive as the minimum to be carried out in an environmental assessment, the picture is sharp. The demands encompass the totality of characteristics of ecological modernization as the new environmental political discourse. This expresses that *new means of environmental politics* are replacing the traditional compulsion and prohibition. The regulation is proactive – that is, it is built upon prevention. The *role for science* in environmental assessment is not to prove the damage, but indeed, to the extent possible, to help *predict* a possible effect on the environment where a policy, a plan, a programme or a project is to be realized in a specifically determined fashion. Moreover, the directive states that *pollution prevention pays*, that the aim of predicting a particular impact on the environment at the stage of realization is to prevent it, or to the greatest extent possible ameliorate it, if it is unwanted, and to promote it, if it is wanted. *Public participation* in an environmental assessment is a basic principle, which expresses the directive's attempt to pursue new paths distinct from the centralistic control of the past, by means of acknowledging perspectives other than those of administration and expertise. Moreover, the directive reflects a recognition of nature and/or the environment as a *public good* which *everyone* may have an interest in using and protecting. Finally, the directive entails a *shift in the burden of proof* from the injured to the injuring party, since it is, in keeping with the formal requirements, incumbent upon the developer to produce the necessary information and to carry out the environmental assessment as such.[3]

In formal terms, this brings the directive fully in line with the new environmental political discourse prevailing at the time (1985).

In reality, at that point in time, there was indeed an evident need for modernizing environmental regulations. Along with the changes in the ontological as well as in the substantial and action-related field, a situation had arisen in which a series of conditions and activities acknowledged to exercise a major influence on the environment were left out of the regulatory framework. Moreover, the growing accentuation of value-based issues in environmental regulation left the expert control looking almost pre-modern, given the growing need for involving citizens whose situation and conditions were dictated by the regulations, and whose views and priorities were necessary to carry them out.

Some specific circumstances of this scenario will be mentioned briefly. The environmental protection laws enacted towards the end of the 1960s and early 1970s in Denmark as well as in most Western European countries were mainly based upon a series of prohibitions and impositions, including an authorization system for particularly polluting activities, primarily within industrial manufacturing.[4] In addition, most of these countries would apply more overall regulation in the shape of nature protection legislation and physical planning. Consequently, altogether, what was embarked upon in 1985 was an endeavour to regulate conditions of significance as a whole, on a specific as well as on a general basis.

A so-called Chapter 5 approval in accordance with the Danish legislation for environmental protection was primarily concerned with problems of a local character, being used to authorize the operating conditions of clearly delimited and technically comprehensible processes. Therefore, it was possible to lay down technical criteria for environmental demands and rules concerning what was allowed and not allowed in the various situations. Accordingly, approvals of this type were pure expert decisions (Elling, 1995, p56).

Landscape, cultural heritage and other visual concerns were not included in such specific authorizations, but usually addressed by general regulations in the field of physical planning, nature protection and conservation. In many countries, such general regulations comprised public participation in the shape of hearings. Thus, it was not only a case of two different starting points, but also of two different forms of decision-making.

Although the established technical protection of nature was far from managing to control the point sources, the development gradually led the more complex spread of environmentally harmful substances – for example, through air, water and soil, as well as the propagation through the consumption and disposal of goods – to play a more crucial role for the state of the environment regionally and globally, though often locally as well. However, many activities and factors causing this complex spread fell outside the regulations, whether it be specific or general. In Denmark, this was the case of agricultural production and public works, such as construction works for transport. Furthermore, the development led ever-more to those construction works that were to be approved, in conformity with the technically dominated environmental protection legislation, taking on physical dimensions and characters that strongly affected the landscape and visual conditions, cultural heritage and so on, *without* the possibility of including these aspects in the requirements for authorization.

This gave rise to an evident need for regulations other than technical approvals, covering new activity areas and being based upon decision-making forms involving other people than technical experts, that is first and foremost citizens affected by the problems and regulations.

The environmental assessment system passed by means of Directive 85/337/EEC was, in many ways, capable of satisfying these needs, although it was far from the only initiative taken at the level of the European Community or in individual countries with a view to meeting the needs for modernization of environmental regulations within the EC, as described in Chapter 4 concerning the practice of ecological modernization. However, the directive was particularly appropriate for incorporating new areas into environmental regulations, including an expansion of the concept of the environment to include the man-made environment, and not merely biological/chemical/technical environmental factors, and to involve citizens in decision-making processes.

The EIA as a regulatory system and process is usually defined precisely in relation to these latter aspects. The National Environmental Policy Act (NEPA), the first US environmental law from 1969, which originally introduced environmental impact assessment as a tool, emphasizes in its definition of the EIA process the interdisciplinary use of both natural and social sciences:

> *A systematic, interdisciplinary approach which will insure the integrated use of the natural and social sciences and environmental design arts in planning and decision-making which may have an impact on man's environment*
>
> NEPA, 1969, Section 102, p2

In his definition, Wathern also stresses a broad concept of the environment as well as an integrated approach, encompassing not only specific projects, but also, in a wider sense, planning, policies and programmes of various kinds:

> *EIA can be described as a process for identifying the likely consequences for the biogeophysical environment and for man's health and welfare of implementing particular activities and for conveying this information, at a stage when it can materially affect their decision, to those responsible for sanctioning the proposals. [...]*
>
> *Thus EIA is a process having the ultimate objective of providing decision makers with an indication of the likely consequences of their actions. [...] The definition above is equally applicable to this expanded view of decision making in the planning of development proposals. [...] EIA is no longer seen as an 'add-on' process. Indeed, the greatest contribution of EIA to environmental management may well be in reducing adverse impacts before proposals come through to the authorization phase.*
>
> *Although generally considered a tool of project management, EIA is equally applicable at other levels of planning. Little experience, however,*

yet exists of the use of EIA for assessing legislation, programmes, policies and plans.

Wathern, 1988, p6

Lee focuses on the projection of environmental effects, public participation and incorporating the environmental assessment into the decision-making process. He defines environmental assessment as:

> *A process designed to ensure that potentially significant environmental impacts are satisfactorily assessed and taken into account in the planning, design, authorization and implementation of all relevant types of action. Essential ingredients in the EIA process are:*
> * *Preparation of a study of the potentially significant environmental impacts of the proposed action (hereafter the EIA study).*
> * *Consultation and public participation following the publication of the EIA study.*
> * *Incorporation of the findings of the EIA study, and of the comments made upon it, into the decision making process of authorizing and implementing that action*
>
> Lee, 1989, p3

Later authors bear out this view of the principles of EIA. Wood for instance:

> *Environmental impact assessment (EIA) refers to the evaluation of the effects likely to arise from a major project (or other action) significantly affecting the natural and man-made environment. Consultation and participation are integral to this evaluation.*
>
> Wood, 1995, p1

Since Wood's definitions build upon other scholars, and at the same time so directly and accurately express the above, his definitions and references to other authors are reproduced here. His views stand out as an authoritative expression on which there is widespread consensus among researchers in the field:

> *EIA is a systematic and integrative process, first developed in the US as a result of the National Environmental Policy Act of 1969 (NEPA), for considering possible impacts prior to a decision being taken on whether or not a proposal should be given approval to proceed. NEPA require, inter alia, the publication of an environmental impact statement (EIS) describing in detail the environmental impacts likely to arise from an action.*
>
> *The EIA process should supply decision-makers with an indication of the likely consequences of their actions. Properly used, EIA should lead to informed decisions about potentially significant actions, and to positive benefits to both proponents and to the population at large. As the UK Department of the Environment (1988b, para. 7) put it, formal EIA:*

is essentially a technique for drawing together, in a systematic way, expert qualitative assessment of a project's environmental effects, and presenting the results in a way which enables the importance of the predicted effects, and the scope for modifying or mitigating them, to be properly evaluated by the relevant decision-making body before a decision is given. Environmental assessment techniques can help both developers and public authorities with environmental responsibilities to identify likely effects at an early stage, and thus to improve the quality of both project planning and decision-making.

In principle, EIA should lead to the abandonment of environmentally unacceptable actions and to the mitigation to the point of acceptability of the environmental effects of proposals which are approved. EIA is thus an anticipatory, participatory environmental management tool, of which the EIA report is only one part. The objectives of the Californian EIA system make this very clear (Bass and Herson, 1993b, p1):

1   *To disclose to decision-makers and the public the significant environmental effects of proposed activities.*
2   *To identify ways to avoid or reduce environmental damage.*
3   *To prevent environmental damage by requiring implementation of feasible alternatives or mitigation measures.*
4   *To disclose to the public reasons for agency approvals of projects with significant environmental effects.*
5   *To foster interagency coordination.*
6   *To enhance public participation.*

Appropriately employed, EIA is a key integrative element in environmental protection policy, but only one element in that policy (Lawrence, 1994).

EIA is not just a procedure, or for that matter just a science. Its nature is dichotomous, rather like the duality of matter. As Kennedy (1988b, p257) has put it, EIA is both science and art, hard and soft:

EIA as 'science' or planning tool has to do with the methodologies and techniques for identifying, predicting, and evaluating the environmental impacts associated with particular development actions.

EIA as art of procedure for decision-making has to do with those mechanisms for ensuring an environmental analysis of such actions and influencing the decision-making process.

Caldwell (1989c, p9) has summarized the significance of EIA as follows:

1   *Beyond preparation of technical reports, EIA is a means to a larger end – the protection and improvement of the environmental quality of life.*
2   *It is a procedure to discover and evaluate the effects of activities (chiefly human) on the environment – natural and social. It is not a*

single specific analytical method or technique, but uses many approaches as appropriate to a problem.

3   *It is not a science, but uses many sciences (and engineering) in an integrated inter-disciplinary manner, evaluating relationships as they occur in the real world.*

4   *It should not be treated as an appendage, or add-on, to a project, but regarded as an integral part of project planning. Its costs should be calculated as a part of adequate planning and not regarded as something extra.*

5   *EIA does not make decisions, but its findings should be considered in policy- and decision-making and should be reflected in final choices. Thus it should be part of the decision-making processes.*

6   *The findings of EIA should focus on the important or critical issues, explaining why they are important and estimating probabilities in language that affords a basis for policy decisions.*

It should be emphasised that EIA is not a procedure for preventing actions with significant environmental impacts from being implemented. Rather the intention is that actions are authorised in the full knowledge of their environmental consequences. EIA takes place in a political context: it is therefore inevitable that economic, social or political factors will outweigh environmental factors in many instances. This is why the mitigation of environmental impacts is so central to EIA: decisions on proposals in which the environmental effects have palpably been ameliorated are much easier to make and justify than those in which mitigation has not been achieved.

Wood, 1995, pp1–3

Also Sheate, who tends to see the process from an environmental organizational viewpoint, defines the process within this form of understanding:

EIA is a process by which the likely significant effects of a proposal on the environment are identified, assessed and then taken into account by the consenting authority in the decision-making process. It provides the opportunity to take environmental considerations into account at the earliest opportunity before the decisions are made about whether to proceed with a proposed development or action. EIA enables proposals to be modified in the light of potential impacts identified in order to eliminate or else mitigate them.

Four key principles should be recognised from the start. The first is that EIA is inherently procedural; EIA establishes a systematic procedure for incorporating environmental considerations into decision making. The second is that it is informational; the procedures created by EIA enable information about the environment to be provided to the decision making authority and the public in a early defined way. The third principle is that EIA is preventive; it should happen at the earliest opportunity in the

> *decision-making process and before a consent decision is made. The fourth*
> *principle is that EIA is iterative; the information it provides feeds back*
> *into the EIA process and the design process of the activity concerned.*
>
> Sheate, 1994, pp22–23

These extensive references of various definitions and perceptions of environmental assessment have been included, because – notwithstanding different emphases on parts or elements of the process – they show general agreement in principle on the definitions. At the same time, they reproduce miscellaneous information on environmental assessment as an instrument and process in the landscape of environmental politics.

However, upon closer analysis, they may also give a more exact impression of this instrument as, indeed, instrumental. Notice for instance:

- That Lee writes: 'consultation and public participation *following* the publication of the EIA study' (my italics) – that is, that consultation and public participation must take place *after* publication of the assessment of environmental effects.
- That Wood writes that 'properly used', EIA may lead to '*informed* decisions', and that 'actions are authorised in the *full knowledge* of their environmental consequences' (my italics) – that is, that decisions may be taken on a fully informed basis.
- That the UK Department stresses that 'Environmental assessment techniques can help both *developers* and *public authorities* with environmental responsibilities to identify likely effects' (my italics) – that is, that it is first and foremost the one who tables the proposal and the authorities who must be informed, while nothing is said about the public.
- That Bass and Herson write that the aim of the environmental assessment is to 'disclose to *decision makers* and *the public* the significant environmental effects' and 'disclose to *the public* reasons for agency approvals of projects' (my italics)– that is, to make it evident to decision-makers and the public which effects occur, and to inform the public about the reasons for a decision taken, mentioning only as the sixth and last principle that the aim is to enhance public participation.
- That Caldwell emphasizes that EIA 'is not a science, but uses *many sciences* (and engineering) in an integrated *inter-disciplinary* manner' (my italics) – that is, that environmental assessment is built upon science, while no other forms of knowledge are mentioned.
- That Sheate writes that EIA is 'informational' as the second principle out of four, which means that 'the procedures created by EIA enable information about the environment *to be provided to the decision making authority and the public* in an early defined way' (my italics) – that is, that the informative principle implies that decision-makers and the public are the ones to be informed in a clearly defined manner, without one word about the public's opportunities to supply information to the process or take part in the assessment.

These definitions and characteristics, with their inherent sets of priorities, may be summed up in the following manner:

*   EIA is a process capable of achieving *full information* on the likely environmental effect of implementing a proposal or an activity.
*   This information can be attained by means of scientific, interdisciplinary methods, and is essentially composed of *scientific knowledge*.
*   The population is first and foremost to be *informed and orientated* about the effects and decision-making process, even though it may be stated that *public participation* is also to be enhanced through EIA.
*   Proposals whose expected environmental effects at the time of decision-making have been clearly ameliorated by means of EIA are easier to *justify* than proposals whose effects have not.

Against this background, I will characterize *environmental assessment as an ecological modernization* as a process whose *self-understanding* is a typically modern form of understanding, in the Habermasian sense. It is seemingly open in the definition of the problem and regarding the objective of shedding light on it, seemingly open in the utilization of knowledge, and seemingly open as regards citizens' co-determination. However, this is indeed only *seemingly*. Because in reality, the complex of problems to be assessed has been systematically delimited, the process is oriented to success, the form of knowledge is exclusively scientific, and the attendant form of rationality is solely cognitive-instrumental. Finally, the public's function in the process is not to join in the decision-making, but primarily to be *available for information*, and thus deliver legitimacy to the decisions taken.

Thus, environmental assessment as an ecological modernization may be characterized as a typically modern systemic decision-making process, whose contents reach deep into the lifeworld and which derives its legitimacy from this, but whose instrumental form keeps it bound up with systemic imperatives, for instance, by virtue of the communication between the actors in the process taking place on systemic terms, being constrained accordingly. In this manner, two primary systemic functions/needs are fulfilled. First, it grants the decision legitimacy through its seeming involvement of the people affected by the decision, and second, it meets the systemic need for implementation of the activity concerned. The former need is related to the state system, the apparatus of power. The second need is attached to the economic system, the capitalist economy.[5]

Naturally, this characterization is only valid from the perspective applied here, seeing environmental assessment as an example of ecological modernization. As we have seen above, what characterizes this approach is that it does not start from concepts regarding the modernization process itself, but is confined to internalizing environmental concerns into the economic development strategy. Consequently, the perspective will be expanded below.

Environmental assessment as reflexive arrangement

The core of this section will be the forms of reflexivity defined in Chapter 4 – that is, on the basis of the lifeworld and with a systemic form of organization, respectively. The looking-glass through which they will be examined here is environmental assessment as reflexive arrangement.

Therefore, after discussing the concept of rationality in connection with environmental assessment, these forms of reflexivity will be analysed more closely in the specific form that they take on in an environmental assessment process, seen from the viewpoint of individual actors in this process. Subsequently, the *motivation* of the actual reflexive process will be addressed, and it will be briefly outlined which *dividing lines and cracks* in 'the real world' – and not merely in 'the system' or in 'the lifeworld' – may influence the contents and effects of the process upon the final political decision.

As a prelude to the analysis of the reflexive processes, I shall briefly repeat the concepts regarding one-sided modernization from Chapter 3. Habermas defines the modernization process as a rationalization of the lifeworld *and* as growing systemic complexity, in which the latter depends on the former, at the same time as these two realms differentiate themselves in relation to each other. Moreover, this definition includes:

- that the modern period sees a systemic influence upon the lifeworld via certain media, the so-called colonization of the lifeworld;
- that the lifeworld is, in addition, subjected to a cultural impoverishment due to the differentiation of the expert cultures of science, morality and arts;
- that these expert cultures are professionalized – that is, the potentials of reason that they develop are only returned to the lifeworld to a limited extent.

The consequence is a *one-sided modernization of society*. The structural causes of this are:

- that the media-steered and differentiated systems, the economy and administration, are dominated by a particular form of action, strategic action, with its attendant cognitive-instrumental rationality, and moreover
- That such forms of action, with the corresponding dominance of cognitive-instrumental rationality, penetrate into, or affect, ever-more areas of the lifeworld's action coordination.

Modernization with rationalization of the lifeworld and a parallel increase in systemic complexity thus become synonymous with greater systemic pressure upon the lifeworld's forms of social integration. The system integration increasingly dominates over social integration. Cognitive-instrumental rationality dominates over moral-practical and aesthetic-expressive rationality. All this is thrown into relief in the cultural impoverishment of the lifeworld.

However, a contraposition to this one-sided modernization can be found in communicative everyday practice, in which the wholeness of reason has been preserved in the mutual linguistic forms of understanding. Consequently, there is a development potential in the lifeworld's remaining elements of communicative rationality. The central question will thus be: can this potential be utilized in the various reflexive processes involved in an environmental assessment?

On the face of it, it may be tempting to directly compare an environmental assessment with a rationalization process. This would enable an interpretation of environmental assessment as a process setting free potential of reason. In other words, rather than simply adhering to, say, authorized standards and norms for environmental protection, instead of simply complying with rules, obligations and habits, the process turns into a 'test' of what the environment and the citizens affected in the case concerned could bear and accept, on some point perhaps even benefit from; a course of events in which a result is attained without predetermined positions of power, norms and perceptions being decisive for the outcome. This would allow rationality to unfold. In isolated terms, this is presumably exactly what an environmental assessment is seeking to achieve in connection with the decision of whether to carry out development projects: assessing if the effects on the environment likely to be caused by the implementation of a given activity are acceptable, or to what degree.

However, such a comparison commits the elementary mistake of confusing the systemic conditions with the possibilities of the lifeworld. Indeed, an environmental assessment has not been developed on the basis of the lifeworld, which is why it will, in the first instance, be a systemic process and an expression of increasing systemic complexity rather than rationalization. Such systemic complexity is tantamount to greater latitude for instrumental reason at the expense of, or instead of, practising the wholeness of reason in the shape of the communicative rationality of the lifeworld.

However, a glance at the aforementioned definitions of environmental assessment show that they all, in their self-understanding, adhere closely to this confusion of systemic conditions with the possibilities of the lifeworld. An essential explanation of this may be that these definitions are not underpinned by any distinction between system and lifeworld. Therefore, I shall claim that the common perceptions of environmental assessment as a concept and tool for incorporating environmental concerns into decision-making processes *implicitly* end up constricting the rationality concept to encompass only instrumental rationality.

Accordingly, they end up unconsciously applying a foreshortened rationality concept based upon questions such as: 'How do we reach an *efficient* decision?' or 'How do we establish *efficient* regulations?' rather than questions such as 'How do we reach a decision *informed by reason*?' or 'How do we establish regulations *informed by reason*?' The applied concept of rationality thus refers to *efficiency* instead of a specifically determined perception of *quality*. It refers to the meeting of objectives instead of a value-based foundation for the assessment of an environmental effect. In short, the concepts applied operate with a one-sided form of rationality by exclusively involving *instrumental reason*.[6]

A discussion of rationality

If environmental assessment is carried out as a reflexive arrangement, the intention will be to generate reflexivity. The various reflexive processes of the environmental assessment will be aimed at creating knowledge and insights that may facilitate a decision, which is thus expected to contain a higher degree of reason than if no assessment had been conducted. The concept of reason that is drawn upon, and the manner in which it is elicited, thus become decisive.

Kørnøv and Thissen – starting from current decision-making theories which they believe ought to feature much more prominently in the theoretical research on environmental assessment than is currently the case – have criticized the common perception of rationality in environmental assessment. It is, they claim, based on the misconception that decisions are taken on a rational basis concerning knowledge and the behaviour of decision-makers.[7]

Their argumentation for this viewpoint brings them to distinguish between an *individual* and a *collective* level of decision-making. At the individual level, rationality is limited by the fact that individuals do not act rationally, but are subject to a series of constraints in terms of cognition and resources, as well as to behavioural differences and obstacles. For example, there are limits to what individuals can take in cognitively in a decision-making situation, which is, in addition, governed by personal preferences, expectations, habits and traditions.

At the collective level too, empirical research in decision-making shows that a host of idealized assumptions of rational conduct are not borne out in reality. Kørnøv and Thissen see the alternatives to rational-behaviour models in models based upon decision-making networks of independent actors, where compromises are accomplished on the basis of available means and solutions rather than scientific proofs, in which facts cannot be disentangled from values, as there is no such thing as objective knowledge, and in which knowledge[8] may generate ideas, but is primarily deployed as strategic ammunition rather than as instrumental determinants.

They focus on the trend away from decision-making models based on rationalism, highlighting new ways of supporting the decision-making processes, including participation and interactivity, normative debates and process design.

Not only is the involvement of experts, stakeholders and the public in a decision-making process able to increase the wealth of available information and enhance the acceptance of the decision-making outcome, it may also entail a more democratic process. For example, the public's participation will first and foremost contribute to the democratic process, the authors find.

However, the participants' perception of what the problem is, what the possible solutions might be, and what is desirable is 'framed' by their worldviews and underlying norms. The so-called argumentative trend in policy analysis[9] stresses that the objective of argumentative discourse, learning and debate is to reach a higher degree of mutual understanding among those with diverging opinions who take part in a decision-making process, and to create a 'frame-reflective discourse',[10] in which the frames are adjusted and a new common foundation for action is created.

Process design may also favour the development of environmental assessment. Which design for the decision-making process is recommendable depends on the available input. The extremities are great disparities and great likenesses in values and interests on one axis, and a high degree of knowledge versus lack of knowledge on the other axis. This may lead to situations in which traditional rationalistic problem-solving is recommendable, and to situations in which the argumentative approach is the most useful.

Such a theoretical and empirical development must, in the opinion of Kørnøv and Thissen, gain decisive influence on both practice and research in the field of environmental assessment.

First and foremost, they find that the traditional view of the role of environmental assessment – that is, to advocate in favour of the environment, is being challenged by a new practice, whose ambition is to deliver an integrated assessment that includes decision-making guidance. That is, support for the integration of technical knowledge as well as for the articulation of interests and citizen participation. Environmental assessment in such a function is closely related to that of the policy analyst. In the traditional function, the environmental assessment serves as a piece of advocacy. In an integrated practice, it needs to remain neutral vis-à-vis the interests involved and to pass on the viewpoints of stakeholders. The success criteria (by which they mean the criteria for rationality) is, in the former case, the extent to which environmental concerns are taken into account, whereas in the latter case, it is process efficiency, the satisfaction of stakeholders with the result, openness and balanced knowledge information, learning processes and so forth, regardless of the decision contents. The two authors do not come out directly in favour of or against these positions, but find it important that the practice of environmental assessment remains aware of the dilemma that arises in the choice between them.[11]

Another consequence which they highlight is that a conscious choice should take place between the various courses of action in order to apply the most promising one in view of the established objectives. This implies, for instance, replying to questions such as: should the procedure concentrate on substance or process? Should the process be open and interactive, or should it be closed? If interactive, what is the primary objective of this interaction? Enhancing the contents? More democracy? Ensuring the commitment of important stakeholders?

In view of the cognitive limitations of decision-makers, the two authors also find that the focus should be limited to a number of key subjects in the assessment, rather than an attempt to expand the level of detail, contents and alternatives. Concentrating on the capacity, interests and timetables of decision-makers rather than a more advanced scientific approach will enhance decision-making efficiency.

As a last point, I wish to draw attention to their recommendation that the methods used include some to analyse actor configurations, interests and perceptions. In a decision-making situation, this will provide insights fostering the identification of creative and viable solutions.

In synthesis, Kørnøv and Thissen think that current theories concerning decision-making should feature much more prominently in theoretical research in the field of environmental assessment than is presently the case, because this could help make the exercise more efficient (Kørnøv and Thissen, 2000, p199).

In her PhD thesis, Kørnøv has elaborated on these viewpoints, suggesting a distinction between *procedural* and *substantive* rationality. By the former, she implies 'whether a decision-making behaviour follows a procedure that analytically assesses the consequences of alternative solutions, hence leading to the desired result'. This is the dominant perception of rationality in research concerning environmental assessment, she asserts (Kørnøv, 2000, p2). It is equivalent to what she and Thissen, as referred to above, consider a traditional concept of rationality within an advocating view of environmental assessment. By substantive rationality she understands 'whether a decision can be described as good in view of the established objectives'.

It thus becomes patently clear that the rationality concept applied both by Kørnøv/Thissen and by Kørnøv on her own is one of exclusively purposive rationality. It is not conceived from the value-based foundation upon which the environmental assessment is to be conducted, but from the degree to which the assessment affects the decision-making process. Their starting point in decision-making theory enables them to challenge a series of implicit assumptions in the research on environmental assessment, hence forcing them to become explicit. This can only be welcomed, since there is undeniably a series of muddled points in this field.

Conceptually though, the two authors keep the debate within a one-sided and foreshortened rationality concept, which substitutes efficiency for quality, on the pretext of this being something substantially novel. However, the crucial question concerning their notion of 'substantive rationality' must be: according to which rationale have the objectives concerned been established?

It is to Kørnøv's and Thissen's credit that, drawing on decision-making theory, they have drawn attention to rationality problems in environmental assessment, in addition to raising the question of the function of the strategic environmental assessment, in particular in relation to the decision-making process. Regarding both issues, there is a great deal of confusion and implicit assumptions, both in research and in practical planning. Accordingly, it is a debate that is much needed in order to overcome the impasse in which the development of particularly the strategic environmental assessment is mired;[12] among other reasons due to the question of how to integrate the strategic assessment into the planning process, or *whether* it should be integrated, and not least how this will impinge upon the actual planning process and its objectives.[13]

However, Kørnøv's and Thissen's proposal does not contribute to clarifying the problems that they raise. Their suggested rationality concepts stay within the confines of purposive rationality, in addition to repeating the mistake of confusing rationality with efficiency. Besides, their characterization of a widespread perception of rationalistic thinking within the research on environmental assessment may be more to the point concerning decision-making theory than in the case of strategic environmental assessment. Similarly, the suggestion of adjusting strategic environmental assessment to a new role aimed at good decision-making – on the basis of *balanced* appraisals of consequences, including economic and social ones and so on, and support for learning and negotiating processes between stakeholders and politicians – must be said to avoid the core question in the research on environmental assessment by reducing this exercise to support and guidance in decision-making.[14] I shall elaborate on this critique here below.

Their article is interesting as it highlights a series of limitations in assessments and decision-making which it ascribes to the individual – that is, the participant persons, and not to the framework within which they operate. The individuals taking part are thus constrained by their cognitive capacity, as well as by a host of preconceived opinions, such as preferences, expectations, norms and values, in addition to behavioural factors governing their views of the problems involved. The authors thus draw attention to psychological factors as well as to social and cultural circumstances as constraining each individual.[15] Conversely, the overall social structures, under which the individuals function and which restrain them in various ways, are totally absent in their analysis.[16] Everything is seen through the prism of the individual's freedom to choose, and limitations therein are attributed to the individual's own distorted picture of reality and limited cognitive capacity.

Perhaps this is why their proposal for measures in response to these factors is primarily of an organizational nature, simultaneously intensifying the requirements for cognitive capacity among participants, even though they try, by other means, to curb such demands. Nonetheless, crucially from my point of view, these factors do not bring them to revisit their concepts about the process, its objectives as well as its answers to the actual problems with which society is confronted in the environmental field in these times.

They thus mix up various courses of events and concepts, contributing to disorientation regarding the end goals, both in the research on environmental assessment and in the practical planning. In particular, they mix up the environmental assessment and the decision-making process by turning the planners into politicians and reducing the political decision-makers to the tools of technocrats. In other words, they foster the understanding that political decision-making is always based upon a rationale, which is what should be presented to decision-makers, who are thus relieved of setting political priorities and taking on political responsibility. Such courses of action will not further the protection of the environment, let alone the awareness of the need for this among citizens and politicians. It will, in other words, fail to produce the necessary political priorities of environmental considerations on the basis of society's structural functions and social processes, leading instead to the continued belief that everything can be balanced in a manner that will benefit all interests. One aim of this book is precisely to contribute to creating another kind of awareness among the principal actors.

At the risk of being accused of rationalism, I shall therefore claim that environmental assessment is *not* a decision-making process, but a *reflexive process*. This is crucial to determining whether and how the political, the planning and the assessing elements *should* be viewed in the process. Because I intend to argue that all these elements should form part of the process, and simultaneously claim that this need not lead to the problematic mix-up criticized above.

The elements will be addressed one by one. First, I shall describe the assessing element of the process. Then the planning element. And finally, I shall highlight the character and significance of political elements concerning the decision to be taken by politicians in a given case.

By emphasizing environmental assessment as a reflexive process, I wish to underline that such a process in modern society does indeed stand in contrast to habits, traditions, experiences and so on. It is a modern action-guiding process built upon analysis and argumentation rather than on custom. This contradicts what Kørnøv and Thissen see as limitations. The significant (i.e. systematic) constraints that may be brought to bear on a decision-maker on the basis of a reflexive process is not the amount of information that he or she can take in cognitively, but the narrowing of possibilities dictated by *systemic* imperatives.

Accordingly, instrumental rationality is not an individual question, but one of society. It is the outcome of one-sided rationalization. Therefore, the essential limitation does not stem from individuals' limited cognitive capacity, but from the fact that reflexive processes are confined to addressing only the cognitive aspect – that is, the rationality concept is reduced to the cognitive-instrumental dimension, thus omitting precisely that which concerns norms and values, as well as aesthetic and expressive preferences.

Kørnøv and Thissen address these aspects by moving them from the individual to the collective level of decision-making, simultaneously reducing the rationality concept to cognitive-instrumental rationality.

Conversely, an environmental assessment perceived as a reflexive process requires norms, values, aesthetic and expressive preferences and so on to be dealt with at all three levels: the personal, the cultural and the societal. A mediation must take place between the forms of reflexivity, and this may indeed happen by means of the environmental assessment as a reflexive arrangement, which allows for an extraordinary mediation from the lifeworld to the system, of socially mediated reflexivity to institutional reflexivity. In this manner, the reflexive arrangement ends up constituting the level of society.

Here below, at the level of abstraction – or, for that matter, concretization – that I have called 'practice in its generality', I shall rehearse the forms of reflexivity in an environmental assessment, thus demonstrating where the systemic limitations enter into the process, and how this affects it overall; in other words, why it is so crucial that the overall process be composed of both socially and systemically mediated reflexivity.

In this manner, I have levelled yet another point of criticism at Kørnøv and Thissen, who make the cavalier assumption that decision-makers are *free* to choose action, but constrained by their cognitive capacity and so on, apart from the fact that they depend on each other to reach consensus on the resolution of a proposal. However, it is indeed a determining factor that decision-makers *cannot* simply choose freely, and that environmental assessment may contribute to *expanding* the framework within which a decision is to be taken.

This brings us back to the political element.

When previously arguing that environmental assessment has a political character, and particularly so at the strategic level,[17] I am not hinting that those who take part in this exercise should take over politicians' role as decision-makers, but rather the opposite. My aim is to make it clear that there is a political element in the assessment itself, as much as there is a scientific one. The assessment in itself is a political process that leads to exposing the interests and values of citizens, albeit based upon a scientific and technical foundation. The assessment is not science. And it should not be. Neither should it be technocracy. This would be just as likely to lead to technical and economic 'necessities' overriding any scientific *and* democratic foundation.

Consequently, one may argue, as Kørnøv and Thissen do, that public participation is something that contributes primarily to the democratic character of the process. It is of course correct that it may contribute towards democratization. But if *this* effect were the only one intended, it could quite possibly be attained in other and more effectual ways.[18]

Much more crucially, the participation of citizens allows for the involvement of elements from the lifeworld in the assessment. This enables cultural norms and values, experiences and traditions, preferences and expectations to be expressed and brought into the reflexive process. What matters is that this can take place *without* the planners or other participants having to carry out a 'translation'. The elements of the lifeworld are not brought forth in a disconnected, fractured or split form, but in the form of citizens' specific life context, their communicative everyday practice. Accordingly, by involving the lifeworld – that is, the citizens – in the process, the wholeness of reason can be incorporated. This enables a transcending of instrumental reason to occur.

However, by its very nature, citizen participation evidently underscores the political character of the assessment. The result of the reflexive process is a series of assessments of the effects on the environment, and various attitudes to these effects, including possible alternatives. In short, it is a political document that does not tell politicians what to think, opine and decide, but on the contrary, something they should relate to politically, and draw upon to set political priorities and make a political choice. Therefore, Kørnøv and Thissen are wide of the mark in their description of the process as a rational one that moves along in the belief that producing better and valid scientific information on the question to be decided will lead to a more rational decision.

The actors' forms of reflexivity

In theoretical terms, we may compare an *environmental assessment as a reflexive arrangement* with a systemic process. Although the media of money and power steer the action coordination, there is also an attempt at anchoring the assessment in the lifeworld through a process of public hearing. The foundation in the lifeworld thus becomes an *ad hoc institutionalization*.

Such an ad hoc institutionalization shows something unique about a decision-making process against the backdrop of an environmental assessment as a reflexive arrangement. A decision-maker, the developer, wishes to carry out an instrumental or strategic action based on money as the medium of coordination. However, in order to obtain permission for this from the administrative authorities, he, the developer, must enter into a series of reflexive processes, which are based on a linguistic form of action and criteria for rationality that are substantially different from the action form constituting the starting point.

Here below, I shall analyse the reflexive processes to be performed by the various actors in an environmental assessment as a reflexive arrangement. What *are* the specific contents of each, and in what do their differences consist? The analysis is also intended to answer whether a reflexive arrangement can be established in a form that allows it to go beyond both individual reflexivity (i.e. to become more than reflection) and institutional reflexivity (i.e. not be confined to stay within the boundaries of instrumental rationality). As we have seen in Chapter 4, socially mediated reflexivity, when it takes on the form of criticism, may transcend the success-oriented form of action – that is, take on forms that are beyond purposive rationality. However, it remains within a form of social mediation and rooted in the lifeworld. The reflexive arrangement through which one aims at moving beyond instrumental rationality must thus be capable of containing both the socially and the systemically mediated reflexivity at one and the same time. They must be *coupled together by means of an extraordinary arrangement.*

The analysis must demonstrate that an environmental assessment as a reflexive arrangement contains such an extraordinary chance to couple together the socially and the systemically mediated reflexivity. Accordingly, the analysis undertakes to show the minimum conditions for a transcendence of instrumental reason to take place. Put differently, it must be established that it is not only the cognitive-instrumental rationality that is involved in the assessment, but additionally both the moral-practical and the aesthetic-expressive. In short, all three forms of rationality which were differentiated into the expert cultures of science, morality and the arts with the breakthrough of modernity.

The analysis will take place at a level I have called practice in its generality, and starting from the reflexive forms that were defined in Chapter 4. Thus, the spotlight will be on practices overall, leaving out *specific* conditions and forms of action.

Moreover, environmental assessment is perceived as a reflexive arrangement undertaken in line with the rules and provisions currently in force.[19] It is seen as a process aimed at estimating the likely effects on the environment in case of implementation of a proposal for a development activity tabled by a developer, and which needs to be granted various permissions to go ahead by the competent authorities on the basis of, among other materials, this assessment. According to the provisions, the public must be given an opportunity to take part in the actual assessment of effects on both the man-made and the natural environment. Furthermore, all significant effects, that is, positive as well as negative in accordance with a specific view of significance, must be included. Finally, if they let the activity go ahead, the authorities are obliged to state how the assessed effects on the environment have been taken into account, and perhaps mitigated in the permission given, as well as to publish this permission and its conditions.

Thus, the starting point is that three different basic actors take part in the process: the *developer*, the public *administration* and the *citizens*. The public is identified as those citizens who wish to participate in the assessment concerned. This means the public has been specified in terms of citizens, putting a name to what Habermas describes as 'technologies of communication [...] make possible the formation of public spheres, that is, they see to it that even concentrated networks of communication are connected up to the cultural tradition and, *in the last instance*, remain dependent on the actions of responsible actors' (TCA 2, p185).

Moreover, the term developer implies the person, organization or institution proposing or wishing to carry out a certain activity. This may be a project, a programme, a plan or a policy, which – in keeping with the provisions in force – demands the realization of an environmental assessment, whether the developer belongs to the economic system or the administration.

Here below, the various forms of reflexivity and their specific contents are presented in the order in which they will normally appear in the course of an environmental assessment.

It is the *developer* who initiates the process.

The very first thought on the developer's mind is to venture into the activity in the first place. For this, he has a *motive*, which will be determined by the usefulness to his own interests or, in the case of an official authority, to its tasks. This could either be the streamlining of an existing activity, or an entirely new one, which the developer reckons will bring certain benefits, for example, profit. It may also – if the developer is an official authority, be an activity aimed at a particular supply, for example, transport works or energy, including raising the efficiency of existing activities.

In these initial considerations as to whether the activity should be launched, the developer carries out the first reflexive process. We presuppose it results in his decision to carry the case forward.

Before the developer can table his proposal, he will have to draw it up in detail to make it suitable for submission to the competent authorities. In this process, he has to take into account that his proposal must go through an environmental assessment with public participation and so on, since we are here assuming that his idea is of a nature that makes this obligatory.[20] Thus, at this stage, not only must the developer reflect upon the most appropriate manner of carrying out his proposal as such in relation to its objective, but also upon what the other actors in the decision-making process may possibly think about it. The next reflexive process to which the developer is subjected will thus force him to pose the following questions:

- What is, *ceteris paribus*, the most adequate way of designing the proposal in relation to its objective?
- What will the authorities demand from the proposal's design and function, including what regards its influence on the surroundings?

- How will the citizens view the proposal, and what demands might they possibly place upon it?
- How will the citizens' reaction to the proposal possibly influence the decision of the authorities?

When the developer knows the full or partial answers to these questions, he must undergo a third reflexive process. He must incorporate these answers into his final considerations about the existing chances of carrying out the proposal.

Does the developer exercise *socially* or *systemically mediated reflexivity* in the course of these reflexive situations?

The doubt may be minor if the developer is an official authority, say, the Ministry of Transport. But what if the developer is a private individual or firm? Well, according to my definition of the various forms of reflexivity, the criterion to determine this is whether it is a voluntary situation, or whether there is a necessity present that brings about the reflexive process. A necessary reflexive act may, for instance, arise from an adjustment imposed by the market, or from a demand for legitimizing a certain political power. Thus, the criterion is whether the reflexivity concerned can be said to be steered by the medium of money or of power, hence be characterized as systemic, and hence take place on the terms of systemic imperatives.

Regardless of whether the developer is an individual, a major business corporation or a public administrative entity, on this basis, the outlined series of a developer's reflexive processes must be characterized as *institutional* reflexivity. It is clearly oriented to success, it is governed by the pursuit of a particular purpose, and the steering medium is money or power. The reflexive processes aim to ensure the greatest possible efficiency in the implementation as well as in the functioning of the activity concerned.

Initially, we have passed over the developer's possibility of involving the expert cultures, or some of them, in these reflexive processes. Indeed, perhaps it should not only be seen as a possibility, but as typical of him to draw on these expertises in order to reach what is most convenient for him. In many cases, he may even leave it entirely in the hands of an expert to carry out the reflexive processes on his behalf. Will that change anything about the above characterization of the process? Will the incorporation of expert cultures change the characteristics of the developer's reflexive processes? For instance in the case in which an expert culture does indeed constitute the highest form of insight into an area?

One of the authorities' demands assumed to be faced by the developer is the execution of an environmental assessment. That is, an analysis of the likely environmental consequences of a given implementation of the activity, which must be presented to the public and competent authorities, giving both of them a chance to weigh in. To this end, the developer is likely to hire an expert in the field concerned.

However, given the developer's starting point, the task of the expert is not merely to achieve full insight and understanding of those effects, but to see them in relation to the purposive aspect of the action. Nor is it the developer's mission to protect the environment to the greatest extent possible. Because if it were, in most cases he would be best advised to refrain from the action, although there are, of course, areas in which an action will lead to mitigation of harm on the environment, and possibly also affect it in a favourable direction. The developer's primary objective is implementation of the envisaged activity. The authorities' demand of him will be that he do so with the least possible negative impact on the environment. An analysis of how a given activity affects the environment may bring the authorities to refuse approval, because the effects are considered unacceptable. *What matters is that the limits in this regard are fluid, and hence cannot be mapped out beforehand.*

At this point, it really shows that the expert cultures in modernity have evolved differently as a result of one-sided modernization. The development of instrumental sciences and the techniques based thereon make it possible, technologically speaking, to immediately implement almost any conceivable activity. Conversely, the underdevelopment of the ethical and aesthetic expert cultures will imply that, to the extent that ethical and aesthetic questions are raised as part of the assessment of environmental effects, these usually *cannot* be answered *immediately*. The replies must be developed in relation to the concrete action, or they must be specifically tested on a given public and/or arranged hearing process. In other words, such questions will rarely have been developed systemically. They have to be consigned to testing at the one place where there are elements of a culture capable of processing them specifically in relation to a whole, that is, in the lifeworld. They must be developed or communicatively tested, with a corresponding communicative rationality.

In addition, there is public attention being paid to the area, or what can be termed an already formed or existing public opinion (cf. TCA 2, pp318–319). This may be, for example, a series of generally acknowledged truths concerning the environment, such as 'rare species of wild animals and plants must be protected!' It may also be a 'masterframe' about sustainable development. At present, such a masterframe is in place. It alone could make for a brilliant picture of the extent to which the ethical discourse has been developed – that is, very little or only in a highly abstract manner.

Consequently, it will often be within the expert's list of tasks to inform the developer of the public opinion to be expected in a given area, for example, moral or aesthetic. The information could be, for instance, *whether* a public opinion exists on this point, or it may be information about how public opinion is likely to play out, or to what degree any expression of public opinion can be foreseen about a specifically defined environmental issue. Obviously, the developer will use such information most effectively in pursuit of his objective behind the realization of the activity. The developer's primary concern is, for example, not the aesthetic issue in its own right, but the extent to which it may further or hamper his project. Accordingly, he uses this information purposively, and he measures the rationality of his actions against this objective.

Regardless of whether the moral or aesthetic expert cultures in the field concerned have been developed or not, the situation in which the developer involves the expert cultures in his projection could be described as one *abstraction* (at a time) being incorporated into one *one-sidedness*. That is, one expert culture at a time is involved in an already purposive context, the developer's specific proposal. Thus, it does not change the characteristics of the developer's reflexive processes that he incorporates or draws upon expert cultures. They remain institutionally reflexive.

Let us now look at the environmental assessment from the viewpoint of the *administration*!

The authorities responsible for processing and possibly approving the developer's project have the legislation as their foundation. In a modern bureaucratized society, it is the law that substantiates the administration's decisions, and not some universal ethics of society.

In addition to the general administrative law, they draw on specific legislation pertaining to the activity area in question, for example, building law and public works law, environmental legislation (laws on planning, protection of the environment, protection of nature, water supply and so on), and finally the legislation prescribing the realization of an environmental assessment.[21] These are the laws that institutionalize power as the steering medium of the authorities. Consequently, there can be no doubt that the reflexivity exercised by the authorities in relation to this legislation is of an *institutional* character.

The reflexive processes exercised by the competent authorities in relation to the legal foundation are clearly oriented to success, and aim to maximize the *legitimacy* of a subsequent approval.

Furthermore, the whole point of an environmental assessment is that the combined picture of effects must substantiate the approval or rejection. It naturally follows that an estimate – that is, a judgement based on an educated guess – has to be made in a host of areas. Partly where the legislation is unspecific (e.g. only stating that groundwater cannot be polluted), partly where areas are only covered by law in terms of categories (e.g. that visual effects and cultural heritage must form part of the assessment), that is, where the significance of an effect hinges on a specific estimate (is, for instance, an annual emission into the air of 300 tonnes of CO_2 a significant or insignificant effect?). Finally, an estimate must be made in scenarios that require a balancing of effects.

In their estimates, do the authorities also exercise an institutional/systemic reflexivity? On the face of it, the answer must be yes! However, at least three factors beyond the legislation must be included in these reflexive processes. *First*, the authorities may also draw upon the expert cultures. *Second*, the authorities have to relate to public opinion on these matters. And *third*, they will have to relate specifically to the consultations with citizens, which they are obliged to carry out, and which are to give citizens direct opportunities to take part in the assessment of environmental effects. Let us look closely at each factor.

The authorities' use of expert cultures is comparable to the situation of the developer. Under modernity, these cultures have evolved very differently, favouring the scientific-technical culture at the expense of ethical and aesthetic cultures. Accordingly, it is easy for the authorities to obtain technical-scientific advice or to use the knowledge available in the field, whereas morality and aesthetics are very weakly developed, and generally do not contain instructions for action that are directly applicable.

In a way, all three expert cultures have been professionalized, that is, the gap to the public at large is wide and growing, being – as they are – divorced from the stream of tradition that is continually formed in the hermeneutic everyday practice. Therefore, problems may also arise for the authorities in the technical field, if they cannot obtain knowledge and advice that is generally trusted by the population, although in such scenarios there will usually still be useful expertise at hand. This expertise will, of course, be contradicted by other expertise, but at least the administration will have an expert-based platform, which could be corrected later. In this manner, the administration can expect a certain legitimacy in the field concerned, regardless of possible disagreement among the experts.

Conversely, the problem is manifest within the moral and aesthetic dimension. To the same extent that these areas are underdeveloped, the distance to the public at large is wide. When such dimensions form part of the assessment, the administration must foresee legitimacy problems, hence impelling it to arrange specific tests of moral and aesthetic judgement among citizens. Thus, the situation may serve to exemplify that, as regards environmental regulations, the authorities need to involve citizens in decision-making processes and specific resolutions.

Therefore, we may expect the administration to want to involve the reflexivity of citizens in these areas. Accordingly, the further course of events pertains to the analysis below concerning consultation with citizens.

As for the administration's manifest use of the expert cultures – that is, the utilization of immediately available knowledge within these cultures – this scenario may be characterized as *one abstraction (at a time) being drawn into one one-sidedness*. In other words, expert cultures are involved one by one in a pre-determined purposive context – that is, the administration's authorization of the developer's proposal. Accordingly, this does not change the manifest characteristic of the administration's reflexive processes, which remain institutionally reflexive.

The administration's incorporation of public opinion in the reflexive processes is the second significant area in which a factor other than current legislation may be decisive for the administration's reflexive processes. This is a factor outside the bureaucratic systemic context in which the administration is operating. Public opinion belongs to the lifeworld. Above, I indicated, as examples of public opinion, that wild plants and animals should be protected, and that sustainable development is desirable. However, another example could be wind energy, in which public opinion is split between those who advocate renewable energy and those who oppose windmills due to their visible effects on the landscape or attendant noise problems. In short, this is an example of public opinion not being unambiguous, but rather being composed of some highly marked, even conflicting viewpoints.

Keeping these examples in mind, the public opinion – particularly in those areas of assessment in which the authorities are compelled to make an estimate –

plays a decisive role for the legitimacy that a resolution may attain. If the opinion is unambiguous and widespread, for instance in the shape of a masterframe, it may exercise critical influence on the authorities' assessment, even if public opinion will still have to be balanced against the developer's right to a so-called fair process, including, for instance, an offer of alternatives that are technically, financially and environmentally reasonable. When public opinion is split, it may often be a case of either weak or strong environmental arguments. Such a classification is analogous to the one-sided modernization with its strong technical culture dominating the weak values within ethics and aesthetics. However, this division is not clear-cut, as it is not uncommon to have strong public opinions in which moral considerations are at the forefront – for example, the views on genetic manipulation, or when animal welfare is involved in environmental issues.

Depending on the situation at hand, public opinion may thus open a crack in the administration's institutional reflexivity, and hence allow for transcending instrumental reason. What catches the attention here is that what forces open this crack originates from the lifeworld.

Consulting with citizens is, of course, not confined to those areas in which the administration – due to the wording of the law and indeed the very scope for legislating – has to resort to making an estimate. Only that the administration will, on the face of it, have greater incentives to do so in these areas. The general or direct incorporation of citizens through hearings and various forms of participation opens up the next crack in the administration's institutional reflexivity, because it confronts it with viewpoints and arguments that rest on a different aspect of rationality than the instrumental one.

However, apart from the special situations highlighted above, may it nevertheless be claimed that the administration has a need for involving citizens? I believe the answer is yes, and I shall substantiate this on the basis of the Habermasian coupling of the system and lifeworld concepts, and his definition of the system's necessary institutionalization of the lifeworld.

As we have seen, the modernization process is largely the manifestation of a rationalization of the lifeworld, which entails a growing degree of communicative action coordination, and a simultaneous increase in systemic complexity, which expresses a greater degree of media-steered action coordination. The systemic connection is created without linguistic communication – that is, without norms and values – through the media of money and power. For example, coordination between the economy and the administration may take place directly or exclusively through these media. However, this is only feasible because both systems have been institutionalized in the lifeworld, which sets the framework for society's social integration and cohesion. The steering medium of the administration, power, has been institutionalized in the lifeworld by means of law. In a host of areas, legislative regulations are of a nature that requires an estimate to be made, particularly regarding the interpretation and enforcement of the law.

Moreover, in the field of the environment, legislative provisions are of a nature that make this estimate by the administration necessary far beyond the application of law, relating indeed to the very substance of the decision. Whenever such an estimate of a substantial nature must be made in an area seen by the population – that is, from the perspective of the lifeworld – as a 'public good', the administration may suffer a legitimacy problem. This may, for instance, stem from this public good being reduced at the expense of the general public, but to the benefit of vested interests, for example, private business interests. Or it may be a situation in which a part of this public good (the environment) will give way to another public good (e.g. traffic works), each of which has different users. Such a legitimacy problem can only be 'resolved' by means of what I have termed an *ad hoc institutionalization* in the lifeworld. This refers to affected citizens being heard *prior* to the administration's resolution, giving them a chance to take part in the decision. The use of power is thus 'tested' in relation to existing viewpoints on the situation at hand. For this to work, citizens must feel that they are taken into account and hence exercise real influence on the decision.

Accordingly, it should not be considered a coincidence that environmental regulation is the first area in which citizens are offered this opportunity. This is the expression of a necessity that arises the moment when the environment achieves real status as a public good in the general popular awareness. The historical situation prior to this development, when the environment was seen as a giant sewer to be used by anyone at will, throws this into sharp relief.

Examined in this manner, the administration's incorporation of citizens in reflexive processes starts to make sense, not only to deal with each case, but also in view of the administration's long-term interests. Citizen participation expands the logic of power, making it encompass more than just nonverbal communication. The mutual understanding communicatively achieved, or the mere possibility of this, is incorporated as part of the foundation of power. However, this also breaks with the sovereignty of instrumental reason by allowing space for the aspects of communicative rationality.

Finally, we may look at the course of events from the viewpoint of *citizens*. The reflexive processes that *citizens* may exercise on the occasion of an environmental assessment are of an entirely different nature from those of the developer and the administration, because their starting point is situated in the lifeworld. The citizens' reflexive processes regarding a developer's proposal for a given activity are thus not conditioned by the imperatives of steering media – that is, neither by power nor by money. Therefore, the citizens exercise a social and/or individual reflexivity when taking part in an environmental assessment.

What inputs do citizens receive to their reflexivity? First, they have the developer's proposal. Then they have the draft environmental assessment, and finally the legislation in the area concerned. This is information they may get from the competent authorities, or possibly from the developer. There may also be a public opinion of relevance to the area. Finally, the citizens have the option of consulting with the expert cultures.

Since the citizens are neither tied to nor dependent upon economic efficiency or political legitimacy, they have a chance to take a performative approach to this information – that is, they can act communicatively in response to it. This requires them to relate to the four validity claims that may be voiced regarding the information presented: (a) its *intelligibility*, (b) its *truthfulness*, (c) its *rightness*, for example, concerning the order of priorities, and finally, (d) its *trustworthiness*. This brings all three rationality aspects into the discourse on the proposal concerned – that is, cognitive-instrumental, moral-practical and aesthetic-expressive rationality. The citizens' possibilities to relate in this way originate precisely from what Habermas describes as the communicative everyday practice of the lifeworld.

The citizens (individuals, groups, private organizations and so on, though for the sake of simplicity, here just *the citizens*) may assume such a relation acting communicatively vis-à-vis: (1) the administration/the developer, and (2) other (groups of) citizens. In both cases, the crux of the matter is to reach mutual understanding of the action proposed. Admittedly, the administration has initially applied a cognitive-instrumental rationality criterion, but the performative outlook of citizens forces it to relate to the other rationales raised in connection with the proposal. At the same time, any relation of type 2 may be entered into on purely performative terms. The more widespread this communicative action between citizens becomes, the more the authorities will be under pressure to enter into a dialogue with the citizenry on the citizens' terms, in other words, the more the full extent of the rationality complex will substantiate an approval or rejection of the proposal, rather than just instrumental reason.

Likewise, regarding incorporation of the expert cultures, the distinct starting point of citizens opens up new possibilities. Whereas the developer as well as the administration allowed for one abstraction (at a time) to be drawn into one one-sidedness, the citizens will be able to incorporate one abstraction (at a time) into an *entirety* – that is, into the wholeness of communicative everyday practice – which we may also characterize as the element of a wholeness of reason that is hidden inside the mutual understanding of the lifeworld. Put differently, the various insights from the expert cultures are drawn upon in a holistic understanding, thus assuming the character of a widening of this holistic understanding, and not as a fortification of the already established one-sidedness.

Without going into further detail in the analysis of the various actors in an environmental assessment process, it is possible to conclude that the scope for transcending instrumental reason can only come from citizens, since they are the only group of actors whose reflexive actions are not conditioned by systemic and hence instrumental imperatives. In an empirical reality, such a transcendence obviously depends on the case at hand. It depends on the citizens gaining an opportunity to take a stance on their own terms, and not just on those of the developer or the authorities, and on citizens being given a genuine chance to influence the decision in areas that may entail such a transcendence.

Concerning the various actors present in principle, we may now summarize their logical forms of action and reflexivity, their operational imperatives and support from the expert cultures.

The developer:
> Systemic action coordination through the medium of money.
> Purposive or instrumental form of action – that is, strategic action that contemplates other actors in the pursuit of particular intentions.
> Use of the expert cultures science/technique, morality and arts as a cognitive-instrumental form of action.
> Profit as a systemic imperative.
> Institutional reflexivity as a form of reflexivity.

The administration:
> Systemic action coordination through the medium of power
> Purposive or instrumental form of action.
> Use of the expert cultures science/technique, morality and arts as a cognitive-instrumental form of action.
> Control and legitimacy as a systemic imperative.
> Institutional reflexivity as a form of reflexivity.
> Establishment of a reflexive arrangement as relief mechanism.

The citizens:
> Condensed linguistic action coordination through the media of the public, which link up with the lifeworld – that is, social action coordination.
> Communicative action.
> Use of the expert cultures science/technique, morality and arts as a communicative form of action.
> Socially mediated reflexivity as a form of reflexivity.

Against the background of this analysis of the forms of reflexivity in the course of an environmental assessment, we may thus far draw two conclusions:

First, that the reflexive processes of both the developer and the administration are of an institutional type, and each have to occur logically within the action framework of their respective systems, including their form of rationality, whether instrumental or purposive. It is only the reflexivity of citizen actors that has not been tied beforehand by external conditions, and may draw upon rationality in all its aspects – that is, as cognitive-instrumental, moral-practical and aesthetic-expressive.

Second, that the one-sided modernization or instrumental concept of reason cannot be transcended on the basis of the expert cultures, since each of them has been differentiated and rendered one-sided. They operate separately on a one-sided, an abstracted and a differentiated foundation. Both the developer and the administration use the expert cultures in a specific form of reflexivity that cannot allow for such a transcendence. As the tool of citizens, the expert cultures may be involved in communicative everyday practice, but only if they can break down their respective abstractions, and thus insert themselves into a specific context. Only in that case do these direct forms of reflexivity offer the possibility of moving beyond instrumental reason.

In synthesis, we may conclude that neither the developer nor the administration face any immediate incentive to supersede instrumental reason. Nor do the expert cultures seem to bring about such a move. The inducement to this *must* come from the outside. Transcendence of instrumental reason must necessarily be based upon the communicative everyday practice of citizens, whose content does not indeed have to be 'translated' by the planners – that is, converted into expert language or instrumentalized – but must be mediated *within* the reflexive arrangement.

The reflexive process – assessment

In a way, it is logical that the actual assessment of the environmental impact of a given proposal is an explicitly modern and reflexive process not based on custom, because the proposals to be environmentally assessed are virtually always singular cases. An *assessment* to the best of abilities is to take place in the case at hand, which is without precedent. When it is carried through as a reflexive process with all stakeholders, it has to take on a dialogical form. All parties concerned must provide inputs to the dialogue, and all have to reflect on these inputs. Although such inputs obviously have to be prepared, this dialogue between those involved is the actual assessment. This clearly sets it apart from a traditional hearing or public exposure, in which the assessment[22] of the parties is submitted to other parties for their orientation, and possible objection. It is a communicative process with three (types of) participants, in principle on an equal footing and with an unpredictable course of events, except for the focus on environmental concerns.

Although the process cannot be mapped out beforehand, it must have an orientation. If the communicative rationality is to unfold in all its aspects – cognitively, normatively and aesthetic-expressively – the reflexive process must be oriented towards *mutual understanding*. Furthermore, the incorporation of the communicative everyday practice makes it relevant to distinguish between assessment and decision – that is, between reflexive process and decision-making process. Only in this manner may the reflexive process be geared towards mutual understanding, while also laying the *groundwork* for a *subsequent* decision-making process whose outcome has not been predetermined by particular conditions and interests. And only in this manner can the reflexive process be kept safe from *domination* by specific scientific-technical forms of understanding, and from specific economic or administrative interests.

Thus, the reflexive process must be kept free in three different senses:[23] (a) from control by any party, though the process may well be facilitated by a plan of events, list of participants' duties and rights and so on, as set out further below, (b) from orientation towards a particular result – that is, its content must be geared towards a consensus – and (c) from any kind of hindrance to participation – that is, it must be open in all regards, obviously in keeping with the legislation in force, only that this cannot constrain the degrees of freedom presupposed here.

The reflexive process being open in all regards thus implies: openness in the formulation of environmental problems in connection with the proposal, openness to the participation of all interested parties, and openness as to what may come out of the process. However, it also means that all three forms of reflexivity, associated with each of the fundamental actors, must be allowed to unfold in the course of the reflexive process. Furthermore, there must be room for pursuing specific reflexive courses on the expert cultures' own terms, regardless of their use by particular actors. For both the actors and the expert cultures, this entails that, by joining in the overall reflexive process, they may be forced to go beyond the aforementioned specific forms of reflexivity. However, this should indeed be seen not only as a possibility, but as the actual goal of the dialogical reflexive process, which is meant to spur or provoke such transgressions. The fundamental idea is precisely that participant actors should endeavour to reach mutual understanding concerning the most significant environmental problems, to what degree these are acceptable and how to achieve this acceptability most appropriately, or whether they are unacceptable altogether.

Nonetheless, it may be stated that the demand for letting all forms of reflexivity unfold for consensus orientation and openness contains a contradiction. As we have seen, it is to be expected that both the developer and the administration reflect purposively; whereas the citizens can be foreseen to reflect with an orientation towards reaching understanding. This gives rise to the possibility that what are also termed teleological argumentation and deontological argumentation, as regards the normative statement of the dialogue, become mutually exclusive. Thus, the reflexive process may be doomed from the outset. Not only because the problem may preclude a consensus, but also because it eliminates, in fact, the chance of even conducting *reflexive* processes in a *dialogue* between the actors.

The problem may be illustrated on the basis of the points of departure expected from each form of reflexivity.

The developer starts from a *given objective*: he espouses the realization of his proposal in a relationship between means and end. He will also use arguments concerning the consequences of implementing his project – for example, of a technical nature – concerning the economic effects, moral values and interests in the proposal, such as benefits to the environment. He will deploy teleological arguments *for* the realization of the proposal.

The administration must look into the likely environmental consequences of the proposal, and do so in the light of the *means* to realize the objective pursued by the developer.[24] Accordingly, the administration will argue in favour of the least possible harm and the highest possible benefits – that is, the administration will champion environmental values as a means of realizing the objective. Such arguments will also be teleological.

Conversely, the citizens will *not consider the proposal in the means-to-an-end dimension*, but will question both its objective and the means for its realization, including the consequences thereof. Accordingly, as far as citizens are concerned, the environmental values being affected feature as an end, and not as a means. The citizens' argumentation will be geared towards enhancing environmental values, and take a critical approach to any weakening of these. Their argumentation will thus seek out possible improvements in the environment, unfettered by the developer's objective behind the proposal. As a result, the citizens argue in a manner that subordinates the developer's proposal to environmental values, and not vice versa. This means that their arguments are deontological.

Accordingly, for the chance of a consensus to be present beforehand, it must be possible to argue with teleological *or* with deontological primacy. If primacy is given to teleological argumentation, the process will be reduced to instrumental thinking, and hence in actual fact give the developer or the administration the option of controlling the contents and aim of the process in line with the given relation between means and end. Conversely, deontological primacy will enable emancipation from such a relation between means and end, setting free the diversity of communicative rationality.

Deontological primacy is not tantamount to preventing the developer and the administration from tabling teleological arguments. But it does mean that these cannot *a priori* set the terms or preconditions for the dialogue. Nor is it desirable to veto such arguments from the developer or administration, because they need to be presented before they can be responded to.

In addition, if teleological arguments are not stated at this stage, they could be deployed and become decisive in the subsequent decision-making process, alleging that – although the assessment showed that a series of environmental considerations would be desirable – in view of the actual objective, these nevertheless need to be passed over to some degree.

Deontological primacy thus only refers to instrumental reason not being in control from the outset. One example[25] serves to illustrate how, respectively, a deontological and a teleological approach to environmental assessment have widely differing implications for the *optimization of environmental concerns*.

A *deontological* approach implies a starting point in a possible world of alternatives for action, in which means and ends are chosen freely in order to avoid constraining the scope for rationality beforehand, searching for the alternative that may optimize concern for the environment, subsequently adapting the means to realize this alternative to the greatest extent possible. In this situation, environmental factors or conditions will feature as values to be protected and promoted – that is, as possible ends. Accordingly, this approach *sets the objectives*, or seeks out the objectives in relation to what may be perceived as *optimization of environmental concerns*.

A *teleological* approach implies a starting point in a pre-determined objective, pursuing alternatives that, in their realization of this objective, are able to pay optimal attention to the environment. Consequently, it remains within a means-to-an-end perspective, to which its rationality is confined. In this case, environmental factors and conditions will feature as means to be optimized with a view to achieving a given objective. Accordingly, such a teleological approach *pursues the objective*, seeking to optimize environmental concerns *on the condition* that the given objective is attained.

Therefore, the task of the reflexive assessment of the environmental impact must be to optimize concern for the environment in a form that sets/seeks out the objective, not just stating what this objective consists of, but also how it may be fulfilled in the situation at hand. In this manner, the environmental assessment aims to set reason free in connection with the projected action to the greatest extent possible, thus letting the environmental optimization encompass cognitive-instrumental facts, normative values and interests, aesthetic and visual conditions, as well as self-expressive factors. Moreover, it must be possible to view these aspects in a universal as well as in a cultural dimension, as will appear from the following. Thus, it must be clear, for instance, in which manner humanity as such has a stake in the conditions concerned, and where the interest in protection is of a cultural – that is, local, nature.

Naturally, such a deontological primacy is not brought about merely by stating its desirability, but must, in the real world, be advanced through various means. By way of introduction, a series of preconditions for the process were brought to attention, and various specific points of these can be reinforced.

As a first point, it may be stressed that the orientation of the process towards mutual understanding, towards a consensus on environmental concerns and priorities, is tantamount to a situation in which *argumentation* plays a decisive role. When this takes place openly before the public, it imposes demands upon the arguments advanced. One statement will be tested by the other participants or by people from the outside who merely belong to the observing public. To describe such a situation, Habermas has presented the so-called *discourse ethics* about a non-coercive dialogue (Habermas, 1990, pp43–115). The discourse ethics is about the reason that may unfold between human beings in a dialogue that deploys reasoned arguments, and in which a consensus may be attained around one 'best argument', which in this manner also acquires validity. It is the assertion of discourse ethics that both cognitive and normative statements can be tested in a dialogue, resulting in validity in the shape of a rational consensus.[26] A dialogue between free and equal participants moves towards a consensus, which is achieved by means of the forceless force of the best argument, and not by the use of power (Habermas, 1990, p198).

If these conditions for participation and argumentation in the reflexive dialogue are met, the Habermasian discourse ethics holds that a situation can be attained in which the best argument, rather than external circumstances, prevails.

A second point to be elaborated upon here is that the reflexive process *shall not* lead to a specific *outcome*, for example, in the shape of a *balanced solution*. Accordingly, the premises for the reflexive process contemplate no inducement to instrumental action and thinking. The conduct normally associated with public planning is that the civil servants – against the background of available knowledge, repeated inquiries and possible public hearings – produce a balanced solution, in which the advantages and disadvantages of various alternatives have been reconciled concerning a given action to be decided upon politically. One example could be the aforementioned teleological optimization of environmental concerns in an environmental assessment practised as ecological modernization.

The shortcomings of such a course of action are evident from the viewpoint of someone wishing to prevent a one-sided modernization process. It encourages instrumental thinking from the outset, monopolizes knowledge within the administration, and obscures the conflicts to citizens. Both citizens and political decision-makers are barred from knowledge and insights that could contribute to another decision. The citizens especially are prevented from joining actively in the planning process and adding precisely those experiences and insights that induce rationalities other than those of the administration to determine the outcome.

Conversely, in an environmental assessment conceived as a reflexive arrangement, the reflexive process *is not aimed at producing a solution* to environmental problems associated with the implementation of a specific project, or for instance a planning activity. It is meant to shed light on the likely environmental advantages and disadvantages to the best of abilities through the participants' dialogue about this. Assertions about, say, a beneficial environmental effect, or about limits to the harmful effects, will be tested for validity. Statements concerning moral or ethical issues related to the environment will be tested for rightness, and for whether they are universal[27] or belong to the realm of local culture. Moreover, the reflexive process may lead to disagreement and conflict over the use of the environment for the activity at hand, over what is the bone of contention, and over who is in conflict – that is, what sectors of the population, branches of the administration or economic stakeholders, and so on. The process is thus to meant to approach the truth as much as possible, a truth that is determined by the various participants' cognitive, moral and expressive habitus. In this manner, a decisive element of the reflexive process becomes to *bring conflicts to the surface* concerning environmental values, as opposed to a procedure in which these are balanced against each other, and hence obscured to the public.

The 'outcome' of the process is its course of events. This can be made available by reporting on it, which thus also becomes the *information on the environmental assessment*.[28] Such information must encompass:

- a summary of the entire process;
- assertions advanced and how they have been dealt with in the dialogue;
- possible conflicts concerning the assessment of environmental values and interests at stake;
- who is involved in these conflicts;
- and additionally, if the reflexive process has made it to this point, a report on how to optimize possible goals for environmental concerns, how to fulfil these and by which means.

This report subsequently serves to substantiate the political decision-making process, in which a solution is to be drawn up and decided (as described further below).

Finally, a so-called *facilitation* may contribute to keeping the process within an orientation towards mutual understanding. Such facilitations may adhere to certain rules, as long as these do not contradict the aforementioned preconditions and premises. The rules may contemplate both rights and duties of participants.[29]

In addition to purely practical matters, such as timetable, deadlines,[30] and the requirement to take minutes of all meetings and events, available for inspection and correction by participants prior to publication, such rules may set out a series of rights and duties of participants. For instance, the authorities must have an obligation to prepare meetings and debates about a proposal, and to take minutes at these events. Likewise, the citizens could have the *right* to arrange meetings, debates and so on, *and* both the developer and the authorities have a *duty* to take part in them. Another major task of planners in the process could be to prepare the minutes of meetings and debates, have these verified by the participants, and subsequently publish and circulate them to all interested parties. Finally, one may envisage a set of rules for the argumentation associated with the reflexive process, for example, fleshing out the Habermasian discourse ethics, for which the afore-mentioned aspects already represent some first embryonic steps. Such rules contain the formal pragmatic requisites to the discourse, namely that: (a) every-one is allowed to take part in equal measure, (b) everyone is allowed to make validity claims, (c) everyone is allowed to raise problems and criticize, (d) nobody has the prerogative to decide or interrupt the discourse, the so-called symmetry and accessibility conditions, (e) time pressure cannot exert an influence, (f) coercion to act cannot occur, (g) pressure from reality cannot occur, and (h) external and internal empirical coercion cannot occur, the so-called suspensions (Habermas, 1990, pp65–66; Bordum, 2001, p257).

It makes no sense, and is not the intention at this stage in the presentation, to delve further into an analysis and justification of the use of discourse ethics in the situation described. Nevertheless, I wish to stress that Anders Bordum has already presented a series of explications of the foundation of discourse ethics in the theory of science, which I find highly useful in an effort to lay the practical groundwork for carrying out environmental assessments through reflexive dialogues. In particular, I wish to draw attention to his presentation of the *formal-pragmatic demands on discourse participants*[31] and his explication of the *methodology and normativity of discourse ethics*,[32] which he also calls a list of the methodological priorities of central concept pairs in discourse ethics (Bordum, 2001, pp258, 263).

I am convinced that a glance at these explications is enough to get an idea that this contains material capable of pointing towards useful sets of rules. If one believes, as I do, that the citizens' statements in a process of public consultation should not have to be 'translated' by planners, because such statements reflect the context in the communicative everyday practice, and hence elements of commu-nicative rationality, then for instance the order of priorities concerning rationality (knowledge above opinion, view and belief) may be perceived as somewhat of a provocation. However, just as environmental issues often lead us to rely on intuition towards matter-of-fact problems, and on views regarding ethical or aesthetic issues, there will indeed also be situations in which knowledge may legit-imately contradict opinions and views. This merely highlights that planners need to see it as their task to listen to citizens and enter into a dialogue with them.

Moreover, I wish to stress the significance of having access to written guidance, enabling the use of a principle of universalization and a principle of estimation in such a process as the one described here. The *principle of universal-ization* concerning the justification of moral norms makes it possible to place the generally human above the local or the individual. This possibility must be seen as crucial. When environmental values are to be exploited, it is sometimes necessary to be able to do so. However, just as evidently, this may require the people affected to take part in an assessment of whether such a situation is present – that is, in which the universal must take precedence over the individual.

As for the *principle of estimation* about the application of norms, the aforementioned considerations about the administration's necessary exercise of an estimate may equally underscore its importance. This is a case of a principle that can be explicitly applied in connection with the citizens' involvement in the process of making such an estimate, which includes, *inter alia*, demands for willingness to abandon an individual perspective for the benefit of a collective one, which places knowledge above opinion, view and belief.

In both situations, it is crucial that citizens be involved, because they need to have a *genuine chance to exert influence*, as *they* are ultimately responsible, and not just because they have to contribute to legitimizing the dispositions of an *administration*.

In synthesis, concerning the use of discourse ethics, I am *not* claiming that consensus can be achieved, regardless of guidance and explications. The crux of the matter is that consensus-seeking is the starting point and the orientation – that is, the attempt is made. Because only by trying may one influence the content and the outcome in a favourable direction.

Thus far, the actors in an environmental assessment have been portrayed on the basis of the categories of system and lifeworld. Consequently, in the presentation to this point, the citizens emerge as a unanimous voice, while the system only differs between the administration and the private economic sector. Accordingly, the emphasis is placed on the main contradiction between system and lifeworld. The aim has been to identify how to establish the conditions for the lifeworld's action motives feeding into systemic actions, thus imposing rationales other than systemic instrumentality and efficiency. However, this assumed unanimity is obviously not present in the real world, in which systematic fault lines and systemic realizations give rise to disagreement among citizens and to diverging interests within the system, respectively, in the administration and the capitalist economy.

We thus have to dissolve the abstraction of an assumed unity within each of the three categories of actors. The distinction thus far between system and lifeworld has proved tremendously fruitful as regards clarifying the modernization process and the key concept within this process, or just within the modern, namely reflexivity. It has also been shown useful to determine the nature of environmental problems, and how, on the basis of the modern, political reactions to the problems can be created.

As for the determination of possible forms of action, and hence cracks in relation to the hitherto assumed unity within each of the three actor categories, further differentiation on the basis of the system will have a *material* background. Similarly, a differentiation on the basis of the lifeworld concept will relate to the *symbolic and linguistic* comprehension of the world, hence encompassing the dividing lines that are mediated from this, as opposed to containing immediate and functional material substance.

Of course, there is a material world behind these symbols and linguistic structures, namely the cultural mediation of the concepts. Moreover, the material background for differentiation within the economic system will interfere in, or be part of the material background for, the lifeworld, namely the reproductive processes of the labour force.

Finally, the cracks and dividing lines may be determined by the character of the environmental problems, and how these create problems for or affect people's *practical* day-to-day life. This involves the material structures behind the reproduction of the lifeworld.

We thus see that at the moment when – endeavouring to deepen the differentiation – we wish to involve both symbolic structures and their material background, the gap between system and lifeworld will be bridged, and the phenomena that may be attached to both of them can appear as pivotal points more in touch with reality.

The modernization process, which has been a category throughout the presentation, may thus serve as the starting point for specifying the scope for cracks – that is, disruptive conduct – within the groups of actors, which was already depicted in Chapter 1, but may now be presented systematically.

As a consequence of the modernization process, we have seen a series of phenomena manifest in the same historical period as the institutionalization of environmentalism in the public debate, the political apparatus, the accentuation of modernity's value problematic, and the attempts at transcending the modern (cf. Chapter 2 and part of Chapter 3).

First, internationalization and globalization of economies has led to a series of cultural contradictions which, in the field of the environment, express themselves in a *clash between universal moral requirements and the demands and needs of local cultures*. This phenomenon has also been called Western cultural imperialism – for instance when Greenpeace has campaigned against seal hunting in Greenland – though as we have seen, the contradictions lie far deeper than that. Second, a much greater degree of *self-interest in acting institutionally and personally* has seen the light, which may be considered reflexively motivated, rather than being judicially imposed. One example is the voluntary initiatives by corporations in dealing with environmental problems. Third, we have seen businesses resort to a kind of direct *defence of the modern*, for instance through marketing in environmental high-tech or through the publication of 'ethical accounts'. This has sought to demonstrate explicitly that environmental considerations can go hand in hand with advanced industrial production, in a self-controlled manner, that is. Fourth, at the personal level, we have seen a sweeping *individualization*, which has rolled back the class cultures of the old days, and set individuals free to pursue their own action orientation, also as regards environmental issues. And fifth, the emergence of our surrounding environment *as a public good* has entailed a transformation of the state apparatus that both protects and uses this good, and also of the outlook of citizens, who are ascribed a moral responsibility in both types of activity. As a by-product of the creation of this public good, a sixth phenomenon has entered the stage, in which the environment has become a *political distribution issue* featuring on a par with, and partly in contradiction to, the distribution of economic goods. Finally, as the seventh trend, there is the *ideological status of ecology* next to the ideologies of liberalism and socialism, neither of which have managed to take in the ideological aspects of ecology, but left it to autonomous formation of, for instance, identity figures in a world in which the old distinctions are crumbling, and in which the sense of it all is lost in the unknown.

In relation to the three categories of actors, these phenomena have widely differing repercussions.

The *competent authorities* are faced with a host of new initiatives involving ethical and moral aspects, for example, genetic and biotechnology projects. The emergence of the environment as a public good imposes upon the authorities the role as user and protector of this good. Moreover, the authorities are under pressure to carry out economic rationalizations in the field of the environment, just as in all other areas of their competence, which pushes them towards efficiency rather than giving priority to more value-related orientations. In other words, the competent authorities are increasingly faced with multiple and frequently contradictory demands. This does not serve to diminish their need for legitimacy among citizens, but it does make it significantly harder to achieve such legitimacy. The authorities' performance in the role as developer only reinforces these dilemmas quite severely. Altogether, the aforementioned phenomena serve to intensify the competent authorities' dependence on legitimizing their decisions among citizens.

The private *developer* will, in this situation, experience the opening of the market. Both in terms of greater accessibility and a more diverse market. However, to the same degree, he will become much more sensitive to the reactions of the market. The chances of realizing financial benefits through activities with environmental ramifications will increase. It is possible to carry out marketing with a high environmentally conscious profile. But to the same extent that such possibilities become available, the developer will experience his sensitivity to this market. Tiny missteps or others throwing suspicion on him may cost in terms of reputation, market share, falling share price and so on. The market will be both informed and capable of reacting with breakneck speed by virtue of the same mechanisms that open up its possibilities: fast, easily spread and well-informed communications in all directions. In certain respects, a developer's scope, in specific cases, for meeting his actual objective, and simultaneously complying with environmental demands, may well have been widened. However, at the same time, in many situations he is faced with more diverse and often contradictory demands, and his sensitivity to citizens' reactions will have increased.

The citizens will not become united, but split by the phenomena charted here. The general individualization will be experienced both as freedom to opine and to act, but also as being set free from communities and shared values. The chances of pursuing self-interest through reflexively motivated argumentation will doubtless encourage some to take part in environmental assessments, but will also make their acts unpredictable. The environment as a public good, in the context of a political distribution struggle, will bring the conflict between economy and environment, which has long featured at a more collective or societal level, down to the individual level, paralysing the opinions and actions of individuals. Figures of identification will play a prominent role. All in all, the citizens will not find it easier to gather around shared views and actions, but will actually be subject to conditions that introduce dividing lines.

Accordingly, the actors' scope for action in a reflexive process will be heavily marked by the occurrence of the depicted phenomena that arise from the far-reaching changes brought about by the modernization process over the past decades. The authorities have become more dependent on achieving legitimacy among citizens. The developer has acquired more latitude, but also greater sensitivity to the reactions of citizens. The citizens are subjected to intensifying individualization and a parallel lack of common bearings. One by one, they experience a split between pursuing an individual economic interest and collective demands concerning the environment.

In the reflexive process, what may unite the citizens will gain in influence. The same can be said about what may divide the citizens.

This is why the aspect termed 'framing' by Eder takes on such importance. It is something capable of uniting, providing a perspective, creating hope and confidence in a future. Whatever can draw together different outlooks and assessments, create links between values and views, highlight the universal above the specific, or rather the universal in the specific, is bound to have overwhelming significance.

If the disagreement or split between citizens is vast, it reflects a political reality. It makes it essential to map out theses discrepancies and their foundation in each case. This serves to lay the groundwork for a reasoned compromise in the subsequent decision-making process. If the disagreement or split between citizens is less pronounced, it is easier to report on it in the environmental assessment. Moreover, it will be possible to build the ensuing decision upon a solution that will not be difficult to produce.

The political process – decision

The crucial condition for the reflexive process is that it is not started, implemented or finalized with a view to arriving at a solution. It is meant to result in a report on its own course, the reflexive dialogue. The construction of a solution must occur in a political process following *after* and clearly *detached* from the reflexive process. Accordingly, the political process is not one that decides upon a proposal, but one that *draws up* a solution. It is a process oriented to producing a result, a solution, as opposed to orientation to reaching understanding of the reflexive process.

Consequently, the course of an environmental assessment will be divided into two processes which occur in series, yet are sharply divided in time and contents. The first is based upon the exercise of reflexive communicative reason in a dialogical form. The subsequent one is based on a formal political power with a view to arriving at a compromise. Therefore, the participants in the latter are exclusively the politically elected representatives. They alone are to take the decision. They have also taken part in the reflexive process, and are thus informed about the actual assessment of environmental effects, in addition to the *report* on the process at their disposal. However, in the political process, their task is different altogether. They have to construct or draw up a solution on the basis of the assessment of the environmental impact of the proposal at hand, and obviously the other inputs available in the case concerned. However, their work on this construction and decision takes place under the full scrutiny of public attention.

At their disposal, the politicians also have the civil servants, administrators and planners, who have joined in the reflexive process too, alongside, and as representatives of, the politicians.

The political decision-makers are not bound by the report issued on the environmental assessment, but solely by their own convictions. However, when publishing the solution at which they arrive, they have to explain how the environmental impact stated in the report has shaped their decision. For instance, they must give reasons why they accept one environmental effect rather than another, why they choose to overlook an assumed effect, how they balance the values at play against each other, and what is their environmental objective behind the decision.

Just as in other political decisions, the politicians will depend on the legitimacy ascribed to their disposition within the population. This is their only and decisive tie. This is why it is so important that all aspects which have surfaced in the course of the reflexive process have been made visible to the participants and to the public, because this implies that all compromises and balancing acts concerning environmental effects that may have been necessary in the construction of a solution will become fully visible to *decision-makers* as well as to *the public*. The legitimacy of a given solution that may be arrived at by decision-makers will thus be measurable against the effects assessed in the report and the various views expressed by different population groups in the reflexive process. Accordingly, the report will serve as a guide in their search for legitimate solutions.

The aim of separating into a reflexive process, built on communicative reason, and a political decision-making process, built on a power-based compromise, is to ensure that politicians are fully aware of all information available on environmental effects, uncertainties, margins of error, points of contention and so on when they are to forge a compromise. Furthermore, the public or the citizens are also fully informed. Therefore, the politicians may take a well-founded approach to a solution, and they may act politically in relation to views, values and priorities manifested within the affected population.[33]

This does not lead this interpretation of environmental assessment as a reflexive arrangement to ignore the realities of power. Indeed, it seeks to have power exercised by those who have been elected to do so. Conversely, if this interpretation is carried out, it will be harder to continue the hidden exercise of power by the administration vis-à-vis decision-makers, population and developers, and vice versa.

Effects

An environmental assessment as a reflexive arrangement cannot have a predictable outcome, at least not to the same degree as an environmental assessment as ecological modernization. What makes the difference is the sharp separation between reflexive process and decision-making process, between the part of the assessment oriented to understanding and the part oriented towards success.

Of course, the political process, the actual decision-making process, produces an outcome. However, the extent to which the reflexive process impinges on the substance of this decision depends upon a series of political or social conditions, which make it hard or outright impossible to foretell any kind of result. However, it *is* indeed the point of an environmental assessment in this form to make the outcome less controllable, at least by the developer and the administration. The result must be 'set free'; it shall not be possible for specific interests or actor to control it. Freedom from the specific interests of the developer or administration is thus one effect that may spring from this form of environmental assessment.

But of course, any decision will have a specific content in each case. It will influence the actual realization of each project, or of each activity, more or less specifically, and hence also its specific impact on the environment. Moreover, this impact may be divided into immediate or short-term effects and long-term effects. They may be straightforward and measurable, or they may be complex and intangible. They may be direct or indirect. And finally, they may be of a completely unpredictable or incalculable nature, popping up where nobody had expected it, or it may not even be observed and identified. All this will depend on the activity at hand, the specific decision and its actual realization.

However, regardless of this, the implementation of environmental assessment in the form depicted as a reflexive arrangement may have repercussions for all these effects. If there is a break with the instrumental dominance of the developer and/or administration, and if the communicative everyday practice of citizens is given genuine scope for influencing the process, the preconditions may be in place for a qualitatively different substance in the effects, regardless of their manifestation.

First and foremost, the specific decision will not merely reflect systemic efficiency, but be just as sculpted by communicative rationality, by all aspects of rationality. It will be *society* that frames the environmental outcome of the environmental assessment, that generates the criteria for what is environmentally reasonable and what must be considered not to be so. The criteria of society will determine the outcome, not only those of the economic or the administrative system, and not only those of the lifeworld.

In this manner, the environmental concept to its full extent can be said to be involved in the decision, encompassing the technical-scientific elements and the man-made environment, including the visual, cultural-historical and ethical sides of the environmental problematic.

However, society's criterion for this wide-ranging concept of the environment also implies that the environment as such is *not* seen as the goal of society or as defining the meaningfulness in society. Because as we have seen, making the environment the goal of society does not lead to anything other than preservation of tradition or a return to something original, or to leaving all meaning to the actual form. That is, either a backwards search in history or a reduction of reality to form. None of these paths can take us closer or contribute to a better state of the environment.

Instead, practising the environmental assessment as a reflexive arrangement may help keep the development of society within the modern, in which environmental concerns are understood as part of the rationality of this modernity. Furthermore, this modern rationality is conceived in a wider sense than what can spring from the modern economic system, precisely because the environment has been emancipated from such a particular type of rationality. Nor can it be considered an ecological modernization, whose self-understanding is the emancipation of a distinct *ecological* rationality, though showing in practice to be nothing more than the internalization of ecology in economic development strategy.

In other words, the hope is not to make it possible to place ecology on top as the goal of society, nor to integrate it into economic efficiency, but to reach the point where environmental concerns are contained within the rationality of the modern, to its full extent; where concern for the environment is internalized in reason. This is what we set our sights on when practising environmental assessment as a reflexive arrangement rather than as an ecological modernization.

Meanwhile, in a wider perspective, it must be insisted that modernization in this sense is not only the realization of the full range of reason in the development process of *the system*, keeping in mind that it is private producers in the economic system or the administrations of the state power who initiate development projects or activities. Modernization must be the modernization of the *whole* society, which must therefore entail that the conquests of the differentiated expert cultures – setting free potential of reason – are made available to citizens too, and not reserved for systemic use. As Habermas puts it, there must be feedback in the shape of cultural transmission across its full breadth.

It does not lessen the significance of such a restitution of reason that citizens are assigned the role at the core of environmental assessment as a reflexive arrangement. However, one may also take the perspective that modern environmental politics makes no sense if it is not based upon the participation and adherence of citizens. After all, it is all about the citizens' environment, and it is the citizens' conduct, whether as private individuals in the lifeworld or as agents in the economic system or the administration, that is to be emancipated in the name of reason in order to improve the state of the environment. Such emancipation undoubtedly entails a deprivation of freedom in the sense that not everything is allowed or desirable, and that not all degrees of freedom can be satisfied if one also wishes to be free of the scourge of environmental problems.

In other words, if citizens are to play a reasoned or responsible role, they have to possess information capable of guiding their conduct at all levels. In a modern society, such information cannot simply flow to citizens through the stream particular to the communicative everyday practice. It has to come from all nooks and crannies of the activities and specializations of the modern. Communication must criss-cross society, everywhere, between all parts, and along all paths. And it must be free and accessible to everyone.

Therefore, I also see environmental assessment practised as a reflexive arrangement as an opportunity to provide citizens with information, to let citizens share in the insights and experiences of the expert systems concerning specific and special conditions which the citizens are well-equipped to take in, since it affects them. Such an information flow through reflexive arrangements may contribute not only to a sense of responsibility among citizens, but also to preventing risks, both their production in the system and their effects in the lifeworld. Moreover, it will help keep the abuse of power in check.

Since I have attributed the environmental problems to the one-sidedness of modernization, and thus associated their solution with an end to this one-sided process, which I believe can be broken, at least partially, by practising environmental assessment as a reflexive arrangement, I also have to acknowledge that the lifeworld cannot be held free of responsibility. Although the cultural impoverishment is a result of the expert systems' continuous differentiation of aspects from the lifeworld, it cannot be fought one-sidedly as the system's responsibility. A development and enrichment has to be added by means of participation. The motivation and desire to take part must remain up to citizens themselves. It must be their own responsibility to contribute and make a difference. If they lack insights, they should not just demand them, but also seek them.

Although we may often claim, rightfully, that the system has failed (abuse of power, production of risks and so on), conversely, it serves no purpose to ignore that we, in modern society, are living off the system. The system's rationality enables modern life. Given that Habermas, in particular, has stressed that the system's formation impoverishes the lifeworld, and that its pursuit of efficiency colonizes the lifeworld, it must be in order to draw attention to the reverse, namely that the lifeworld is needed for the development of the system. The constant emphasis that it is the lifeworld that is being rationalized stems from the fact that this is where the starting point for everything lies. When norms and customs are endlessly rolled back, bringing understanding and insights to the fore, it is knowledge that is substituted. It is knowledge that determines the outcome, instead of habits and blind faith. If the system is to evolve on the basis of the lifeworld, and vice versa, it plainly implies that the two worlds must communicate with each other in order to prevent a continued detachment which would lead to the failure of both.

If the rationality forms of the lifeworld *must* be brought into the system to prevent it from breaking down, the implication in relation to this book concerning the environmental problematic is that knowledge cannot be one thing in the lifeworld and another in the system. Knowledge must be assigned the same value whether it is seen from one side or the other. And of course, it must play the same role whether it appears in one place or the other.

I have thus signalled a belief that *knowledge* is useful. That knowledge *can* move mountains. That knowledge can lead to action, and that knowledge can lead to refrain from action. But also that communication in all directions across society can prevent knowledge monopolies, both in the sense of the *distribution of knowledge* and in the sense of what *type of knowledge* is attributed value.

When power is ascribed its own rationality, and hence turned into the decisive factor in society, we overlook that it must ultimately be based upon knowledge, information and insight. Therefore, power should not be separated from the concrete forms of life and modes of thinking, but actually be acknowledged as a part thereof. Ultimately, it is untenable to split our actions in modern society into two or several different or independent worlds, each with their respective intentions. In the end, they must be viewed as a kind of whole.

Under this form, planning does not pertain to the experts, but to the administration's dialogue with the population. Politics is no longer for the few and select, it becomes communication criss-crossing all over society.

Notes

1   In this context, I have chosen to keep the term *ecological modernization*, despite the conclusion of the analysis in Chapter 4 that this is a misnomer for what could much more appropriately be called 'the internalization of environmental concerns in economic development strategy'. This choice is primarily because, notwithstanding its misleading wording and unjustified claim of ownership, the term ecological modernization has become a 'frame' within the theory of environmental sociology. Thus, I am preserving the term in the presentation below in order to send a clear signal about the trends in sociology that I am discussing. I am adhering to what could be called the current practice to avoid confusing the reader unnecessarily in relation to presentations encountered elsewhere.

2   In 1997, Directive 85/337/EEC is supplemented by Directive 97/11/EC, introducing new provisions for scoping, new contents in the Annexes 1 and 2, as well as a new Annex 3 concerning screening. These are the official names in English for the Europe-wide *legal documents* (including the outdated acronyms EEC and EC), even though, since 1993, the official name for the *political* dimension of the cooperation is the European Union (EU).

3   Exceptionally among the EU countries, Denmark has special provisions on this point. Though the developer is still obliged to produce the necessary information, after that, it is the competent authorities who, on this basis, carry out the environmental impact assessment as such, in keeping with the Danish Government Order concerning the Planning Act No. 763 (*Bekendtgørelse om Lov om Planlægning Nr. 763*) of 11 September 2002, Article 7. This does not contravene Article 5 of the Directive, which stresses the developer's duty to place the necessary information at the authorities' disposal. If the conditions informed turn out not to be valid, it is incumbent upon the developer to bring them into line with the permission granted. This responsibility must also be assumed by the developer in Denmark, since the authorities have carried out the assessment on the basis of his information.

    Concerning the more detailed demands of the directive concerning the contents of an environmental impact assessment, see the directive itself, including Annex 1-3 (europa.eu.int/comm/environment/ eia/full-legal-text/85337.htm & europa.eu.int/comm/environment/eia/full-legal-text/9711.htm), in addition to Elling, 1994, pp12–13. Concerning the Danish implementation of the directive and the interaction with the remaining body of environmental regulation, see the same article, pp11–17, as well as Elling, 1995.

4   For instance, none of agricultural production was covered by this regulation, as will be mentioned below.

5   If the state acts as a developer, these needs will be linked to the same system.

6   See, for instance, Wathern, 1988, pp25–28, and Wood, 1995, pp9–11.

7   Kørnøv and Thissen, 2000, pp191–200, Kørnøv, 2000, pp2–3.

8   They only write 'knowledge', but clearly mean scientific knowledge.

9   The reference to this approach is Fischer and Forester, 1993.

10   This term comes from Schön and Rein, 1994.

11   However, we recognize in both these forms the neomodernistic approach to the decision-making process: focusing on form rather than content, cf. Chapter 2.

12   A current example of this, containing a number of problematic perceptions of rationality, values and decision-making processes is the so-called ANSEA project. See Jiliberto, March 2002, pp61–70.

13   Concerning this problematic, see Elling, 2000a.

14   Somewhat teasingly, as an additional critique, I wish to put the following questions to Thissen and Kørnøv, to which I cannot find the answers based on their approach:
     Where lies the cause that the knowledge produced in the rational process of an environmental assessment (in the traditional sense) is not realized? How does one gain insights into conditions that can only be demarcated through a dialogue with the population, when it is first and foremost the planners who are to achieve learning, and subsequently bring forth their rationale to the politicians? How can it be determined what is good and evil (that is, good and bad) for the environment, if we cannot let this depend on what is true and false? (which we cannot, since we cannot map out the consequences by means of scientific prediction!). The question can thus be rephrased: how do we determine what are good norms and values? This is relevant since they stress that facts and values cannot be separated (Table 2, p195).

15   The conditions addressed may be seen as the lifeworld leaving its cultural and normative mark on individuals. However, this is the mark of the non-rationalized lifeworld. What they overlook in this context are the processes of mutual understanding of the rationalized lifeworld, which would indeed be able to counteract the limitations and constraints highlighted here by Kørnøv and Thissen.

16   This may thus be perceived as the systemic influence on the action forms.

17   See Elling, 1997a, p171.

18   In addition, the unfortunate experiences of 'public participation' in the US may be kept in mind, as referred to by Hajer (1995, p284). Regarding these experiences in the US, see also Sorensen and West, 1992, pp86–97.

19   This aims to make the process more 'realistic'. Moreover, it will be possible to show that an interpretation of *environmental assessment as a reflexive arrangement* may be carried out in practice within or in accordance with the current formal requirements for environmental assessments. A concrete concept of strategic environmental assessment capable of conveying the meaning of environmental assessment used in this section has been presented in Elling, 1997a, p162 and Elling, 1997b, pp42–144. A procedure and a concrete course of events for an environmental assessment at the project level have been presented in Elling, 1994. A procedure and a concrete course of events for an environmental assessment at the planning level have been presented in Elling, 1998, pp13–65, and Elling, 2000a, pp234–239. Finally, a procedure and a

concrete course of events for strategic environmental assessment concerning legislative bills (policies) have been presented in Elling, 1997a, pp162–168.

The current *formal* requirements for environmental impact assessment are, as mentioned, Directive 85/337/EEC and the additional Directive 97/11/EC, which are implemented in Denmark by the Ministry of Environment, cf. Danish Government Order concerning Planning Act No. 763 [*Bekendtgørelse om Lov om Planlægning Nr. 763*] of 11 September 2002, the Government Order on Supplementary Rules Pursuant to the Planning Act No. 428 [*Bekendtgørelse om supplerende regler i medfør af lov om planlægning (samlebekendtgørelse) nr. 428*] of 2 June 1999, and Government Order on Modifications in the Government Order on Supplementary Rules Pursuant to the Planning Act No.605 [*Bekendtgørelse om ændring af bekendtgørelse om supplerende regler i medfør af lov om planlægning nr. 605*] from 15 July 2002. See also the ministry's 'Guidelines for the environmental impact of certain public and private works EIA' [*Vejledning om visse offentlige og private anlægs indvirkning på miljøet VVM*] October 2001, and 'Guidelines for environmental assessment of legislative bills and other government proposals' [*Vejledning om miljøkonsekvensvurdering af lovforslag og andre regeringsforslag*], December 2001.

20   I am thus neglecting the detail that the developer may choose, by means of various considerations, to shape his project in such a manner that a screening will be likely to lead to *exemption* from an environmental impact assessment, in accordance with the Government Order on Supplementary Rules Pursuant to the Planning Act No. 428 [*Bekendtgørelse om supplerende regler i medfør af lov om planlægning (samlebekendtgørelse) nr. 428*] of 2 June 1999, Article 3, Section 2.

21   In Denmark, this is the Planning Act concerning EIA. As regards strategic environmental assessment, it is the government circular of the Prime Minister's Office entitled 'Observations on legislative bills and other government proposals, Circular No. 159' [*Bemærkninger til lovforslag og andre regeringsforslag, Cirkulære nr. 159*] of 16 September 1998.

22   As the EIA directives have been implemented differently across Europe, in the case of Denmark, this means the administration's proposal, and in the other EU countries, the developer's proposal.

23   Securing these degrees of freedom is tantamount to institutionalizing the reflexive process. The need for institutionalization springs from the fact that a so-called ideal speech situation cannot be unconsciously pre-conceived, since the dialogue will be conducted as a mix between forms of reflexivity. It does not take place in the lifeworld, and it is not lifeworld-determined, on the face of it, but must be 'converted' into discourse – that is, to orientation towards a rational consensus in a dialogue free of coercion. How to go about this in practice is the subject here below.

24   Notice that Directive 85/337/EEC, Directive 97/11/EC and Directive 2001/42/EC do not at any stage mention the *aim* of the proposal at hand as relevant to the assessment of its environmental impact.

25   The example has been inspired by A. Bordum, who shows the difference between a deontological and a teleological approach to the optimization concept within an economic framework of understanding, Bordum, 2001, pp313–314.

26   The discourse ethics may be divided into three principles:

1   The principle of discourse ethics (D): 'Just those action norms are valid to which all possibly affected persons could agree as participants in rational discourse' (Habermas, 1996, p107).

2   The universalization principle (U): 'For a norm to be valid, the consequences and side effects that its *general* observance can be expected to have for the satisfaction of the particular interests of *each* person affected must be such that *all* affected can accept them freely' (Habermas, 1990, p120; 1996, p566 n15).

3   The democratic principle, or principle of legitimation (L): 'Only those statutes may claim legitimacy that can meet with the assent (*Zustimmung*) of all citizens in a discursive process of legislation that in turn has been legally constituted' (Habermas, 1996, p110).

27   On the basis of Habermas, we may distinguish between moral statements of a universal nature, which can be tested through the principle of universalization, cf. note 131 of Habernas, 1996, and moral statements that cannot be universalized, which he calls ethics. The latter thus belong, given their non-universality, to the local culture (Habermas, 1996, p153).

28   Cf. Directive 85/337/EEC and Directive 97/11/EC Article 5, which lay down the conditions for information on the finalized environmental impact assessment. Furthermore, Article 5 of Directive 2001/42/EC makes a demand for a report on the assessment of environmental effects of a plan or programme.

29   As a whole and individually, Directive 85/337/EEC, Directive 97/11/EC and Directive 2001/42/EC lay down precisely such rules for how to carry out an environmental assessment. They cover the duties of the competent authorities and the developer, as well as the rights of citizens and the developer.

30   In connection with EIA cases, all EU countries have established a framework for the duration of the public hearing. In Denmark, it is 8 weeks, which may often seem too brief, if the process is to unfold on the citizens' terms as well. However, this has been somewhat compensated for by the Danish authorities' duty to convene a so-called preliminary hearing, also of at least 8 weeks, in which ideas and proposals are invited for the upcoming planning process.

31   **Formal-pragmatic demands on discourse participants**
A fundamentally rational approach requires the participants to:
- Communicate, attempting to coordinate action.
- Express themselves sincerely (avoiding manipulation).
- Be sane, and able to commit themselves seriously to a consensus.
- Be oriented to reaching understanding.
- Be rationally orientated towards the validity claims.
- Justify criticism, contributions and changes of subject.
- Argue post-conventionally, in principle and reflexively.
- Be willing to abandon the individual perspective (hypothetically).
- Be willing to justify deontologically (moral viewpoint).
- Accept the forceless force of the better argument.
- Acknowledge justified validity as beyond context.
- Accept symmetry requirements (reciprocity, respect, equality).
- Know and relate to the consequences of assertions.
- Be willing to learn from the best argument.

32   **Methodology and normativity of discourse ethics**
List of methodological priorities concerning central concept pairs in discourse ethics

Relation and subject	**Priorities of discourse ethics**
Logically:	Freedom of contradiction above contradiction
Performatively-pragmatically:	Performative freedom of contradiction above performative contradiction
Form of justification:	Dialogue above monologue
Force of assertion:	Justification above non-justification
Rationality:	Deontological diversity above teleological givens
Cognitive computability:	Binary logic above axiology
Validity of consensus:	Rational consensus above rational compromise
Political approach to action coordination:	Consensual means above non-consensual means

Political approach to   Legitimacy above illegitimacy
decision-making processes:
Basic orientation: Consensus orientation above conflict-seeking
                               behaviour
Rationality: Knowledge above opinion, view and belief
Demands for openness: Tolerance above intolerance
Political perspective on   Legitimacy perspective above decision-making
decision-making processes: perspective
Consensual strength: Dialogue-internal above dialogue-external
Form of argumentation: Post-conventional above conventional
Cognitive justification: Reflexive justification above non-reflexive
                               justification
Form of justification: Universal above particular
Attitude to dialogue: Articulated speech above silence, open above closed

33 This also conforms to Wynne's analyses referred to in Chapter 3 concerning the
    relationship between citizens and authorities, which serve to substantiate the idea
    that fully informed citizens will respond rationally to environmental questions.

Bibliography

Aagaard Nielsen, K., F. Greve, F. Hansson and K. Rasborg (eds) (1999) *Riscko, politik og miljø t det moderne samfund – En antologi om en aktuel kontrover* [Risk, Politics and Environment in Modern Society – An Anthology about a Current Controversy], Forlaget Sociologi, Frederiksberg

Andersen, H. and L. B. Kaspersen (eds) (1996) *Klassisk og Moderne Samfundsteori* [Classic and Modern theories of Society], Hans Reitzels Forlag, Copenhagen

Anderson, T. and D. R. Leal (1991) *Free Market Environmentalism*, Pacific Research Institute for Public Policy, San Francisco

Austin, J. L. (1992) *How to Do Things With Words*, Oxford University Press, Oxford

Baglioni, G. and C. Crouch (eds) (1990) *European Industrial Relations – The Challenge of Flexibility*, Sage Publications, London

Baudelaire, C. (1964) *The Painter of Modern Life and Other Essays*, translated and edited by J. Mayne, Phaidon, London

Bauman, Z. (1991) *Modernity and Ambivalence*, Polity Press, Cambridge

Beck, U. (1986) *Risikogesellschaft: Auf dem Weg in eine andere Moderne*, Suhrkamp Verlag, Frankfurt am Main

Beck, U. (1992) *Risk Society – Towards a New Modernity*, Sage Publications, London

Beck, U. (1994) 'The Reinvention of politics: Towards a theory of reflexive modernisation', in Beck, U., A. Giddens and S. Lash, *Reflexive Modernisation*, Polity Press, Cambridge

Beck, U. (1996) 'Risk society and the provident state', in Lash, S., B. Szerszynski and B. Wynne (eds), *Risk, Environment and Modernity – Towards a New Ecology*, Sage Publications, London, pp27–43

Beck, U. (1997) 'Subpolitics. Ecology and the disintegration of institutional power', *Organization and Environment*, vol 10, no 1, March 1997, pp52–65

Beck, U., A. Giddens and S. Lash (1994) *Reflexive Modernisation*, Polity Press, Cambridge

Benhabib, S. (1992) *Situating the Self – Gender Community and Postmodernism in Contemporary Ethics*, Polity Press, Cambridge

Bennett, J. and W. Block (eds) (1991) *Reconciling Economics and the Environment*, Australian Institute for Public Policy, Perth

Berger, J. (1988) 'Modernitätsbegriffe und Modernitätskritik in der Soziologie', *Soziale Welt*, vol 2, pp224–236

Berger, S., I. Carlman, B. Elling, K.G. Høyer and T. Selstad (1991) *Regionalpolitikkens økologiske grundlag i Norden* [The Ecological Basis for Regional Policy in the Nordic Countries], NordREFO 1991. vol 5, Academic Press, Copenhagen

Berman, M. (1982) *All That Is Solid Melts Into Air – The Experience of Modernity*, Simon and Schuster, New York

Bohrer, K-H. (ed.) (1983) *Mythos und Moderne*, Suhrkamp, Frankfurt am Main

Bordum, A. (2001) *Diskursetik og den positiv selvreference* [Discourse Ethics and Positive Self-reference], Samfundslitteratur, Frederiksberg C

Bourdieu, P. and L. J. D.Wacquant (1992) *An Invitation to Reflexive Sociology*, University of Chicago Press, Illinois/Polity Press, Cambridge

Buttel, F. H. (2000) 'Ecological modernisation as a social theory', in *Geoforum*, vol 31, no 1, February, pp57–65

Carson, R. (1987) *Silent Spring*, Houghton Mifflin Co., Boston, MA

Christensen, E. (1990) *Nye værdier i politik og samfund: paradigmeskift og kulturbrydninger* [New Values in Politics. Paradigm Shifts and Cultural Upheavals], Hovedland, Copenhagen.

Christoff, P. (1996) 'Ecological modernisation, ecological modernities', *Environmental Policies*, vol 5, no 3, pp476–500

Commoner, B. (1972) *The Closing Circle – Confronting the Environmental Crisis*, Jonathan Cape, London

Crook, S. (1991) *Modern Radicalism and its Aftermath – Foundationalism and Anti-Foundationalism in Radical Social Theory*, Routledge, London

Dryzek, J. (1992) 'Ecology and discursive democracy: Beyond liberal capitalism and the administrative state', *Capitalism, Nature, Socialism*, vol 3, no 2, pp18–42

Dryzek, J. (1993) 'Policy analysis and planning: From science to argument', in Fischer, F. and J. Forester (eds), *The Argumentative Turn in Policy Analysis and Planning*, Duke University Press, Durham and London, pp213–232

Dryzek, J. (1995) 'Towards an ecological modernity: A book review', in *Policy Sciences*, vol 28, pp231–242

Dryzek, J. (1997) *The Politics of the Earth: Environmental Discourse*, Cambridge University Press, Cambridge

Eder, K. (1996) 'The Institutionalisation of environmentalism: Ecological discourse and the second transformation of the public sphere', in Lash, S.; B. Szerszynski and B. Wynne, *Risk, Environment and Modernity – Towards a New Ecology*, Sage Publications, London, pp203–223

Elling, B. (1990) 'Tænk lokalt – handl globalt!' [Think local – act global], Internationaliseringen og det regionale miljø' [Internationalization and regional development] (1990) *Internationalisering och regional utveckling*, NordREFO, vol 2, University Press, Copenhagen, pp235–246

Elling, B. (1991) 'Sammenspillet mellem regionalpolitik og miljøpolitik i Danmark' [Interaction between Regional Policy and Environmental Policy in Denmark], in Berger, S., I. Carlman, B. Elling, K. G. Høyer and T. Selstad (1991) *Regionalpolitikkens økologiske grundlag i Norden*, NordREFO, vol 5, Academic Press, Copenhagen

Elling, B. (1994) 'Miljøet og VVM-direktivet' [The environment and the EIA-directive], in *Samfundsøkonomen*, April, vol 3, pp11–17

Elling, B. (1995) 'VVM i Praksis' [EIA in practice], *Byplan* no 2, pp54–62

Elling, B. (1997a) 'Strategic environmental assessment of national policies: The Danish experience of a full concept assessment', *Project Appraisal*, vol 12, no 3, pp161–172

Elling, B. (1997b) 'Strategisk miljøvurdering' [Strategic Environmental Assessment], J. Holm, B. Kjærgård and K. Pedersen, *Miljøregulering – tværfaglige studier* [Environmental Regulation-Interdisciplinary Studies], Roskilde University Press, Copenhagen, pp140–159

Elling, B. (1998) *Strategisk miljøvurdering i regionplanlægningen* [Strategic Environmental Assessment in Regional Planning], TemaNord519, Nordic Council of Ministers, Copenhagen

Elling, B. (1999a) *Miljøvurdering i regionplanlægningen – Evaluering af Nordjyllandsprojektet* [Environmental Assessment in Regional Planning – Review of the

North Jutland Project], published by Miljø og Energiministeriet, Landsplanafdelingen, August 1999

Elling, B. (1999b) 'Kan man kommunikere sig til bedre miljøbeslutninger?' [Can Communication Result in Better Environmental Decisions?], *Miljønyt*, No 38, Miljøstyrelsen, Miljø- og Energiministeriet, Copenhagen

Elling, B. (2000a) 'Integration of strategic environmental assessment into regional spatial planning', *Impact Assessment and Project Appraisal*, vol 18, no 3, September, pp233–243

Elling, B. (2000b) *Erfaringer med miljøvurdering af lovforslag* [Experiences from Environmental Assessment of Bills], published by Miljø og Energiministeriet, Landsplanafdelingen, [Ministry for Environment and Energy, Department for Spatial Planning], July

Elling, B. (2005) 'SEA of Bills and other Governmental Proposals in Denmark', in Sadler, B. (ed.) *Strategic Environmental Assessment at the Policy Level*, Ministry of the Environment, Czech Republic, UNECE, and VROM, Prague, Geneva and The Hague, pp46–54

Elling, B. and J. Nielsen (1996) *Miljøvurdering af regionplaner* [Environmental Assessment of Regional Plans] TemaNord: vol 602, Nordic Council of Ministers, Copenhagen

Elling, B. and J. Nielsen (1997) *'Miljøvurdering af lovforslag – Studie i strategisk miljøvurdering og 2 eksempler'* [Strategic Environmental Assessment of Bills. Two Examples], published by Miljø og Energiministeriet, Landsplanafdelingen [The Ministry for Environment and Energy, Department for Spatial Planning], Copenhagen

Elling, B. and J. Nielsen (1998) *Strategic Environmental Assessment of Policies in Denmark*, Issued by the European Commission, Directorate-General, Environment, Nuclear Safety and Civil Protection, Brussels

Erickson, K. (1976) *Everything in its Path: The Destruction of a Community in the Buffalo Creek Mining Disaster*, Simon and Schuster, New York

Ersbøll, N. and J. Bostrup (1998) *Danmark og EU i Europa* [Denmark and EU in Europe], Gyldendal, Copenhagen

Fischer, F. and J. Forester (eds) (1993) *The Argumentative Turn in Policy Analysis and Planning*, Duke University Press, Durham and London

Flyvbjerg, B. (1991) *Rationalitet og magt* [Rationality and Power], Bind 1+2, Akademisk Forlag, Copenhagen

Frank, M. (1988) *Die Grenzen der Verständigung – Ein Geistersprüch zwischen Lyotard und Habermas* [The Boundaries of Communication – a Conversation between Lyotard and Habernas], Suhrkamp Verlag, Frankfurt am Main

Friedmann, J. (1987) *Planning in the Public Domain – From Knowledge to Action*, Princeton University Press, Princeton, New Jersey

Frisby, D. (1985) *Fragments of Modernity*, Polity Press, Cambridge

Giddens, A. (1990) *The Consequences of Modernity*, Stanford University Press, Stanford

Giddens, A. (1991) *Modernity and Self-Identity – Self and Society in the Late Modern Age*, Polity Press, Cambridge

Giddens, A. (1994a) *Beyond Left and Right: The Future of Radical Politics*, Polity Press, Cambridge

Giddens, A. (1994b) 'Living in a post-traditional society', in U. Beck, A. Giddens and S. Lash, *Reflexive Modernization*, Polity Press, Cambridge

Giddens, A. (1998) *The Third Way*, Polity Press, Cambridge

Glebe-Møller, J. (1996) *Jürgen Habermas – En protestantisk filosof* [Jürgen Habermas – A Protestant Philosopher], Gyldendal, Copenhagen

Habermas, J. (1976) *Zur Rekonstruktion des Historischen Materialismus*, Suhrkamp Verlag, Frankfurt am Main

Habermas, J. (1979) *Communication and the Evolution of Society*, Beacon Press, Boston

Habermas, J. (1981a) *Theorie des kommunikativen Handelns*, vols 1 and 2, Suhrkamp, Frankfurt am Main

Habermas, J. (1981b) *Kleine Politische Schriften* vols I–IV, Suhrkamp Verlag, Frankfurt am Main

Habermas, J. (1981c) 'Modernity Versus Postmodernity', *New German Critique, Special Issue on Modernism*, no 22, Winter, pp3–14

Habermas, J. (1981d) *Teorier om samfund og sprog* [Theories on Society and Language], Gyldendal, Copenhagen

Habermas, J. (1982) 'A reply to my critics', in J. B. Thompson and D. Held (eds) *Habermas – Critical Debates*, Macmillan Press, London, pp219–283

Habermas, J. (1984) *The Theory of Communicative Action*, vol 1, *Reason and the Rationalisation of Society*, Translated by T. McCarthy, Polity Press, Cambridge

Habermas, J. (1985) *Der philosophische Diskurs der Moderne*, Suhrkamp, Frankfurt am Main

Habermas, J. (1987a) *The Philosophical Discourse of Modernity*, Polity Press, Cambridge

Habermas, J. (1987b) *The Theory of Communicative Action*, vol 2, *Lifeworld and System: A Critique of Functionalist Reason*, Translated by T. McCarthy, Polity Press, Cambridge

Habermas, J. (1988) *Nachmetaphysisches Denken – Philosophische Aufsätze*, Suhrkamp, Frankfurt am Main

Habermas, J. (1990) *Moral Consciousness and Communicative Action*, MIT Press, Cambridge, Massachusetts

Habermas, J. (1993) *Justification and Application*, Polity Press, Cambridge

Habermas, J. (1992) *Faktizität und Geltung*, Suhrkamp, Frankfurt am Main

Habermas, J. (1996) *Between Facts and Norms – Contributions to a Discourse Theory of Law and Democracy*, Polity Press, Cambridge

Habermas, J. (2001) *Politisk filosofi – Udvalgte tekster* [Political Philosophy – Selected Texts], Gyldendal, Copenhagen

Hajer, M. (1995) *The Politics of Environmental Discourse – Ecological Modernization and the Policy Process*, Oxford University Press, Oxford

Hajer, M. (1996) 'Ecological modernization as cultural politics', in S. Lash, B. Szerszynski and B. Wynne, *Risk, Environment and Modernity – Towards a New Ecology*, Sage Publications, London, pp246–268

Hauge, H. (1998) *Den danske kirke nationalt betragtet* [The Danish Church Viewed Nationally], Forlaget Anis, Copenhagen

Honneth, A., T. McCarthy, C. Offe and A. Wellmer (eds) (1992) *Philosophical Interventions in the Unfinished Project of the Enlightenment*, MIT Press, Cambridge, Massachusetts

Horkheimer, M. and T. W. Adorno (2002) *Dialectic of Enlightenment: Philosophical Fragments*, Stanford University Press, Stanford

Huber, J. (1982) *Die Verlorene Unschuld der Ökologie – Neue Technologien und Superindustrielle Entwicklung*, Fischer Verlag, Frankfurt am Main

Huber, J. (1984) *Die Zwei Gesichter der Arbeit – Ungenutzte Möglichkeiten der Dualwirtschaft*, Fischer Verlag, Frankfurt am Main

Huber, J. (1985) *Die Regenbogengesellschaft – Ökologie und Sozialpolitik*, Fischer Verlag, Frankfurt am Main

Jänicke, M. (1985) 'Preventive environmental policy as ecological modernisation and structural policy', Discussion Paper IIUG dp 85-2, Internationales Institut für Umwelt und Gesellschaft, Wissenschaftszentrum Berlin für Sozialforschung (WZB), Berlin

Jänicke, M., H. Mönch, T. Ranneberg and U. Simonis (1988) 'Economic structure and environmental impact: empirical evidence on thirty-one countries in east and west', Working Paper FS II 88-402. Internationales Institut für Umwelt und Gesellschaft, Wissenschaftszentrum Berlin für Sozialforschung (WZB), Berlin

Jänicke, M., H. Mönch, T. Ranneberg and U. Simonis (1989) 'Economic structure and environmental impacts: east west comparisons', *The Environmentalist*, vol 9, no 3, pp171–183

Jiliberto, R. (2002) 'Decisional environmental values as the object of analysis for strategic environmental assessment', *Impact Assessment and Project Appraisal*, vol 20, no 1, pp61–70

Jupp, A. (1989) The provision of major accident hazard information to the public, unpublished M.Sc. thesis, Manchester University, Manchester

Keane, J. (1991) *The Media and Democracy*, Polity Press, Cambridge

Kolb, D. (1986) *The Critique of Pure Modernity – Hegel, Heidegger and After*, Chicago University Press, Chicago

Koester, V. (2001) 'Borgernes rettigheder på miljøområdet' [Citizen's Rights in Environmental Matters], in E. M. Basse (ed.) (2001) *Miljøretten* [Environmental Law], vol I, Almindelige emner, Jurist- og Økonomforbundets Forlag, Copenhagen

Kuhn, Th. S. (1996) *The Structure of Scientific Revolutions* (3rd ed), University of Chicago Press, Chicago

Kørnøv, L. (2000) *Strategisk miljøvurdering i en ufuldkommen verden* [Strategic Environmental Assessment in an Imperfect World], Ph.D. thesis, Institut for Samfundsudvikling og Planlægning, Aalborg Universitet, Aalborg

Kørnøv, L. and W. Thissen (2000) 'Rationality in decision- and policy making: implications for Strategic Environmental Assessment', *Impact Assessment and Project Appraisal*, vol 18, no 3, September, pp191–200

Lash, S. (1994) 'Reflexivity and its doubles: Structure, aesthetics, community, in U. Beck, A. Giddens and S. Lash (eds) Reflexive Modernism, Polity Press, Cambridge

Lash, S., B. Szerszynski and B. Wynne (eds) (1996) *Risk, Environment and Modernity: Towards a New Ecology*, Sage Publications, London

Lee, N. (1989) *Environmental Impact Assessment: A Training Guide*, Occasional Paper No 18 (2nd ed.) EIA Centre, Department of Planning and Landscape, University of Manchester, Manchester

Liedman, S-E. (2000) *I skyggen af fremtiden – Modernitetens idehistorie* [In the Shadow of the Future: The Modern History of Ideas] Gads Forlag, Copenhagen

Luhmann, N. (1984) *Soziale Systeme*, Suhrkamp, Frankfurt

Luhmann, N. (1987) 'Machtkreislauf und recht in demokratien' *Sociologische Aufklärung*, band 4, Vestdeutscher Verlag, Opladen, pp142–151

Luhmann, N. (1993) *Risk: A Sociological Theory*, Walter de Gruyter, Berlin/New York

Lyotard, J.-F. (1979) *La Condition postmoderne: Rapport sur le savoir*, Minuit, Paris

Lyotard, J.-F. (1984) *The Postmodern Condition*, Manchester University Press, Manchester

MacIntyre, A. (1981) *After Virtue – A Study in Moral Theory*, University of Notre Dame Press, Notre Dame

March, J. G. and J. P. Olsen (1989) *Rediscovering Institutions*, The Free Press, New York

Marx, K. (1994) '*Results of the Direct Production Process*', in *Marx Engels Collected Works (MECW)*, Vol 34, Lawrence and Wishart, London

Marx, K. (1996) 'Capital, Vol. I', in *Marx Engels Collected Works (MECW)*, vol 35, Lawrence and Wishart, London

Marx, K. (1998) 'Capital, Vol. III', in *Marx Engels Collected Works (MECW)*, vol 37, Lawrence and Wishart, London

Matthews, R. A. (1996) *Fordism, Flexibility, and Regional Productivity Growth*, Garland Publishing, New York/London

Milbank, J. (1993) 'Out of the greenhouse', *New Blackfriars*, vol 74, pp4–14

Miller, D. (1992) 'Deliberative democracy and social choice', *Political Studies*, vol 40 (Special Issue), pp54–67

Mol, A. (1995) *The Refinement of Production: Ecological Modernisation Theory and the Chemical Industry,* Van Arkel, Utrecht

Murphy, J. (2000) 'Ecological modernisation', *Geoforum,* vol 31, no 1, February, pp1–8

Næss, A. (1991) *Økologi, samfunn og livsstil* [Ecology, society and lifestyle], University Press, Oslo

NEPA (1969) *National Environmental Policy Act, Code of Federal Regulations (CFR),* title 40, NEPA, Washington DC, pp1501–1508

Nielsen, T. H. (1988) *Samfund og Magt – Om samfundstyper og mennesketyper* [Society and Power: Types of Society and People], Akademisk Forlag, Copenhagen

Nørager, T. (1985) *System og livsverden – Habermas' konstruktion af det moderne* [Systems and Lifeworld – Habermas' Construction of the Modern]. Forlaget Anis, Copenhagen

Outhwaite, W. (1994) *Habermas – A Critical Introduction,* Polity Press, Cambridge

Overbeek, H. (2002) Neoliberalism and the regulation of global labor mobility, *Annals of the American Academy of Political and Social Science,* vol 581, pp74–90

Pepper, D. (1993) *Ecosocialisme – From Deep Ecology to Social Justice,* Routledge, London

Piaget, J. (1973) *Die Entwicklung des Erkennens,* Bant 3, Ernst Klett, Stuttgart

Polanyi, K. (1957) *The Great Transformation,* Beacon Press, Boston

Popper, K. (1968) *Conjectures and Refutations – The Growth of Scientific Knowledge,* Harper Torchbooks, New York

Ransome, P. (1999) *Sociology and the Future of Work: Contemporary Discourses and Debates,* Ashgate, Aldershot

Sabel, C. F. and J. Zeitlin (eds) (1997) *World of Possibilities: Flexibility and Mass Production in Western Industrialization,* Cambridge University Press, Cambridge

Schirmacher, W. (1984) 'The end of metaphysics – What does this mean?', *Social Science Information,* vol 23, no 3, pp603–609

Schjerup Hansen, J. and C. Bech-Danielsen (eds) (2001) *Modernismens genkomst* [The Return of Modernism], Arkitektens Forlag/Statens Byggeforskningsinstitut, Copenhagen

Schnaiberg, A. (1980) *The Environment – From Surplus to Scarcity,* Oxford University Press, Oxford/New York

Schnädelbach, H. (1984) *Philosophy in Germany 1831–1933,* Cambridge University Press, Cambridge

Schön, D. and M. Rein (1994) *Frame Reflection – Towards the Resolution of Intractable Policy Controversies,* Basic Books, New York

Searle, J. R. (1970) *Speech Acts: An Essay in The Philosophy of Language,* Cambridge University Press, Cambridge

Sheate, W. (1994) *Making and Impact,* Cameron May, London

Simonis, U. (1989a) *Industrial Restructuring for Sustainable Development: Three Points of Departure,* Working Paper FS II 89-401, Internationales Institut für Umvelt und Gesellschaft, Wissenschaftszentrum Berlin für Sozialforschung (WZB), Berlin

Simonis, U. (1989b) 'Ecological modernization of industrial society: Three strategic elements', *International Social Science Journal,* vol 121, pp347–361

Smart, B. (1999) *Facing Modernity – Ambivalence, Reflexivity and Morality,* Sage Publications, London

Sorensen, J. and N. West (1992) *A Guide to Impact Assessment in Coastal Environments,* Coastal Resources Center, The University of Rhode Island, Kingston, Rhode Island

Spaargaren, G. (1997) *The Ecological Modernization of Production and Consumption,* Thesis, Landbouw Universitet Wageningen, Wageningen

Spaargaren, G. and A. Mol (1992) 'Sociology, environment and modernity – ecological modernisation as a threory of social change', *Society and Natural Resources,* vol 5, pp323–344

Spear, J. (1984) *Dreams of an English Eden – Ruskin and His Tradition in Social Criticism*, Columbia University Press, New York

Szerszynski, B. (1996) 'On knowing what to do: Environmentalism and the modern problematic', in S. Lash, B. Szerszynski and B. Wynne, *Risk, Environment and Modernity – Towards a New Ecology*, Sage Publications, London, pp104–137

Tenbruck, F. H. (1975) 'Das Werk Max Webers', *Kölner Zeitschrift für Soziologie und Sozialpsychologie*, vol 27, Band 4, p663–702

Tonboe, J. (1993) *Rummets sociologi* [The Sociology of Space], Akademisk Forlag, Copenhagen

Waltzer, M. (1983) *Spheres of Justice – A Defence of Pluralism and Equality*, Martin Robertson, Oxford

Wathern, P. (ed.) (1988) *Environmental Impact Assessment – Theory and Practice*, Unwin Hyman, London

von Wright, G. H. (1993) *Myten om framsteget* [The Myth of Progress], Albert Bonniers Förlag AB, Stockholm

Wood, C. (1995) *Environmental Impact Assessment – A Comparative Review*, Longman, Harlow

Woolgar, S. (1988) *Science – The Very Idea*, Tavistock, London

Wynne, B. (1996) 'May the sheep safely graze? A reflexive view of the expert-lay knowledge divide', in S. Lash, B. Szerszynski and B. Wynne (eds), *Risk, Environment and Modernity: Towards a New Ecology*, Sage Publications, London, pp44–83

Index

Handbook of Environmental Protection and Enforcement
Principles and Practice
By Andrew Farmer

'This Handbook provides an excellent, practical overview of one of the most important aspects of any environmental regulatory system, namely the processes and practice of enforcement. It is highly recommended to anyone interested in the day to day enforcement of environmental regulation. The use of interesting case studies and comparative analysis of different regimes makes it both accessible and authoritative. Most of all, it is a book to be used in the real world and not just left on the book shelf'

Stuart Bell, Professor of Environmental Law, Nottingham Law School

The Handbook of Environmental Protection and Enforcement is an authoritative, one-of-a-kind guide to Environmental Enforcement Authorities (EEAs) / Environmental Protection Agencies (EPAs), how they work and the complexities, requirements and costs of environmental enforcement and regulation.

Hardback £49.95 • 978-1-84407-309-2

Risk Governance
Coping with Uncertainty in a Complex World
By Ortwin Renn

This book, for the first time, brings together and updates the groundbreaking work of renowned risk theorist and researcher Ortwin Renn, integrating the major disciplinary concepts of risk in the social, engineering and natural sciences. Renn provides comprehensive coverage of all the key areas of risk – assessment, evaluation, perception, management and communication – in a new framework of 'risk governance'. The focus of the book is on systemic risks, such as genetically modified organisms, with a high degree of complexity, uncertainty and ambiguity, and which have major repercussions on financial, economic and social impact areas.

Hardback £85.00 • 978-1-84407-291-0
Paperback £24.95 • 978-1-84407-292-7

Uncertainty and Risk
Multidisciplinary Perspectives
Edited by Gabriele Bammer and Michael Smithson

Uncertainty and Risk provides the most comprehensive and thorough examination to date of 'uncertainty' in risk theory and management and develops an integrated view of uncertainty. The book covers a wide range of disciplinary perspectives, practice and problems including environmental risk, emergency planning, law, terrorism and law enforcement, communicable disease and public health, and provides fresh jumping-off points for risk researchers and academics studying uncertainty and risk management. This volume is the most wide-ranging and thorough examination of the uncertainty that governs all aspects of our lives.

Hardback £65.00 • 978-1-84407-474-7

For more details and a full listing of Earthscan titles visit:

www. earthscan .co.uk

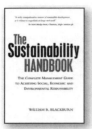